CONVIVIUMPRESS

Albert Vanhoye

«A Different Priest»
The Letter to the Hebrews

Translated by Leo Arnold SJ

CONVIVIUMPRESS
GREGORIAN & BIBLICAL PRESS

SERIES RHETORICA SEMITICA

2011

A Different Priest
The Letter to the Hebrews

http://www.conviviumpress.com
sales@conviviumpress.com
ventas@conviviumpress.com
convivium@conviviumpress.com

7661 NW 68th St, Suite 108,
Miami, Florida 33166. USA.
Phone: +1 (786) 8669718
Fax: +1 (305) 8875463

Edited *by* Rafael Luciani
Translated *by* Leo Arnold SJ
Designed *by* Eduardo Chumaceiro d'E
Series: *Rhetorica semitica*

ISBN: 978-1-934996-20-1

Printed in Colombia
Impreso en Colombia
D'VINNI, S.A.

Convivium Press
Miami, 2011

PUBLISHED IN COLLABORATION WITH THE SOCIETY FOR THE STUDY OF BIBLICAL AND SEMITIC RHETORIC (RBS)

THE TRANSLATION OF THIS VOLUME WAS MADE POSSIBLE WITH THE COLLABORATION OF THE SACRO MILITARE ORDINE COSTANTINIANO DI SAN GIORGIO (WWW.CONSTANTINIANORDER.ORG), BASED IN ITALY.

SOCIETY FOR THE STUDY OF BIBLICAL AND SEMITIC RHETORIC (RBS)

Several learned societies exist whose objective is the study of rhetoric. The «Society for the Study of Biblical and Semitic Rhetoric» (RBS) is the only one

- that is devoted exclusively to the study of Semitic literature, in particular the Bible, but also others texts, for example of Muslim origin;
- that consequently is dedicated to listing and describing the particular laws of a rhetoric that have governed the composition of texts which are of no less importance than those of the Greek and Latin world, of which modern Western civilization is the heir.

It must not be forgotten that this same Western civilization is also heir to the Judeo-Christian tradition, which has its origin in the Bible, that is to say, in the Semitic world.

More broadly, the texts that we study are the foundational texts of the three great monotheistic religions: Judaism, Christianity and Islam. Such academic study, the primary condition for better mutual knowledge, can contribute to a rapprochement between those who belong to these diverse traditions.

Founded in Rome, where its headquarters are situated, the «Society for the Study of Biblical and Semitic Rhetoric» (RBS) is a not-for-profit organization, under Italian law, that promotes and sustains research and publications

- especially in the Biblical field, both the New and Old Testaments;
- but also of other Semitic texts, in particular those of Islam.

The essential objective of the RBS is to promote research projects, exchanges between Universities and publications in the area of Biblical and Semitic Rhetoric, thanks especially to the collection of necessary funds for financing these diverse projects.

The «Society for the Study of Biblical and Semitic Rhetoric» first and foremost welcomes and brings together Scholars and University Professors who, in different Universities and Institutes, both in Italy and abroad, work in the area of Biblical and Semitic Rhetoric. It is open also to those who are interested in research and are intent on supporting it. For more information on the RBS, see:

www.retoricabiblicaesemitica.org

RHETORICA SEMITICA

Series directed by Roland Meynet s.j.

Many people think that classical rhetoric, inherited from the Greeks via the Romans, is universal—this is what seems to govern modern culture, which the West has spread through the whole world. But the time has come to abandon this ethnocentrism— classical rhetoric is no longer alone in the world. We cannot judge everything according to the small village where we were born and which we have never left, whether that little «village» is Paris, Rome, Berlin, or even New York.

The Hebrew Bible, whose texts were mostly written in Hebrew, but also in Aramaic, uses a very different rhetoric from Greco-Roman rhetoric, so we need to acknowledge that there is another rhetoric, which we refer to as «Hebrew Rhetoric».

Other biblical texts from the Old and New Testaments, which were translated into or written directly in Greek broadly follow the same rules; we can therefore rightly talk not just about Hebrew rhetoric but more broadly about «Biblical Rhetoric».

Furthermore, these same laws were later recognized to be at work in Akkadian, Ugaritic and other texts which were earlier than the Hebrew Bible, and then in Arabic texts from the Muslim tradition and the Qur'an, later than the biblical literature. This rhetoric, then, is not only biblical, and we might even say that all these texts, which come from the same cultural sphere, belong within the same rhetorical style which we refer to as «Semitic Rhetoric».

Contrary to the inevitable impression of western readers, these texts from the Semitic tradition, whether the Prophets, the Gospels, or the Qur'an, are carefully composed, providing that they are analyzed according to the rhetorical laws which govern them. We know that the text's form and arrangement is the main gate which gives access to its meaning; although its composition does not directly and automatically provide the meaning. However, when formal analysis leads to a thoughtful division of the text, defining its context more objectively, emphasizing the way it is organized at its different structural levels, then the conditions which allow the work of interpretation come together on less subjective and fragmentary bases.

Contents

Foreword

Rhetorical analysis is a particularly well-adapted method in the case of the interpretation of the Letter to the Hebrews, because that «letter» is in reality a speech, a magnificent homily, made to be delivered to a Christian assembly in apostolic times. In all probability it was in fact delivered, even in several places, because certain details in his text show that its author was an itinerant preacher. But it was also sent in writing to one or several distant communities. On that occasion some epistolary sentences (13,22-25) were added to it after its solemn conclusion (13.20-21). It is thanks to that circumstance that it was preserved for us. It also caused it to be called an epistle or letter. But is it enough to send a homily by post for it to be transformed into a letter? Quite clearly not. Its literary genre remains the same. From its exordium (1,1-4) until its conclusion (13,20-21) the Letter to the Hebrews has the literary genre of oral discourse and not that of the written letter. There is hardly any recent commentator who does not recognize that fact. Consequently, it is not only useful but indispensable to submit this text to rhetorical analysis if one wishes to interpret it correctly.

To proceed any other way leads to dead-ends. To give an example straight away, the famous passages on «unforgivable sins» (6,4-8; 10,26-31) give rise to inextricable doctrinal difficulties, unless one recognizes in them an oratorical device which has to be analysed as such in order to give it its correct meaning. Only rhetorical analysis makes it possible to follow correctly the development of the thought in its overall movement and in the detail of its expression. It alone can get the zeal of the preacher fully appreciated as well as his skill in drawing his listeners towards the heights of the faith and Christian life.

In one sense the text of the Letter to the Hebrews lends itself well to rhetorical analysis, in another it makes it difficult. It lends itself well to it because the author regularly uses certain compositional procedures easy enough to identify, such as inclusion and symmetrical arrangements. But a full analysis is difficult because the author clearly has a complex, Judaeo-Hellenistic education and so plays on several planes at the same time. To varying extents he associates procedures of biblical rhetoric with those of Greek rhetoric which, in general, are clearly different[1]. This association takes different forms. Sometimes it is just a matter of simple juxtaposition and sometimes a more or less complex amalgam.

1 The relationship between the Letter to the Hebrews and Greek rhetoric has been studied especially in the two books: ÜBELACKER W.G., *Der Hebräerbrief als Appell*, and GARUTI P., *Alle origini dell'omiletica cristiana. La Lettera agli Ebrei.*

Thus it is that one of the most important procedures in Greek rhetoric, the *prothesis*, is used by the author of Hebrews in a way that is not Greek but biblical. The *prothesis*, in Latin *propositio*, consists in announcing the subject one is about to treat. In the interests of clarity we shall usually call it «announcement of the subject». When the announcement contains several themes which will be developed later one after the other, classical rhetoric requires that they be developed in the order in which they were announced. According to Quintilian's rhetoric, which offers us the quintessence of Graeco-Latin rhetoric, not to follow in the development the order adopted in the *propositio* is a very serious fault: «Turpissimum vero non eodem ordine exsequi, quo quidque proposueris» (*Orat. Inst.*, book 4, end of chapter 5). The author of Hebrews, as we shall discover, never conforms to this prescription but, on the contrary, he always first of all develops the theme that he announced at the end. Why? Because biblical rhetoric urges him in that direction with its very strong tendency in favour of chiastic constructions (A B C D C B A) in which to the last element in a series there corresponds immediately the first element of the next series.

Another example of disagreement: classical rhetoric recommends avoiding verbal repetitions, especially when ending a paragraph. The end of a paragraph must certainly correspond with its beginning but it is suitable, they say, not to express oneself in identical terms in it because that would manifest a lack of mental ability or laziness and would be likely to bore the hearers. Clever variation, on the contrary, arouses admiration and renews interest. Biblical rhetoric knows nothing of this concern and calls much more for the regular use of verbal repetitions to mark out clearly the limits of literary units, great or small. This is what is called the process of *inclusion*; it consists of repeating at the end of each passage a more or less long expression that was used at the beginning of the same passage; on recognizing that expression, the listeners understand that the passage is finished. The author of Hebrews shows himself particularly faithful to this biblical way of writing. On this point, as on others, his turn of mind is more Semitic than Hellenistic.

To appreciate fully the details of the text, it helps to have first taken an overall view of its composition, because each detail is determined by its function in the whole document. We shall therefore start with a quick reading which will be interested only in indications of structure and the main divisions of the text.

I would not like to end this brief introduction without expressing here all my gratitude to the persons who have helped me to compose this book; in the first place to so many exegetes whose publications have enlightened me on many points; then to my students who encouraged my research; to my community who constantly supported me; to so many colleagues and brethren who gave me hearty support; in particular to Father Roland Meynet, who brought about this publication and contributed to it in many ways, and to my secretary, Mrs. Maria Grazia Franzese, for her dedication and competence without which my work would not have gone forward. To all these persons, and to many others, I express my heartfelt gratitude.

TRANSLITERATION

The transliteration system for Hebrew and Greek is the one used in the periodical *Biblica.*

Chapter 1

General outline of the composition

Despite its traditional title, the Letter to the Hebrews does not start like a letter but like a homily with a solemn sentence that presents an overall view of Christian revelation. Having been prepared by the Word of God in the Old Testament, the coming of the Son of God, his work of purifying and his heavenly glorification constitute the decisive divine intervention in our history:

> 1 On many occasions and in many ways in the past
> God has spoken to the Fathers in the prophets
> 2 in the last period, which is this one
> he has spoken to us in a Son,
> whom he has established as heir to everything,
> he through whom he had made the ages,
> 3 and who, resplendent with his glory and the expression of his being,
> and bearing the universe by the word of his power,
> after having achieved purification of sins,
> sat at the right of the Majesty in the heights,
> 4 having become that much superior to the angels
> as the name he received as an inheritance is very different from them (1.1-4).

1

Announcement of the subject of the first part of the homily (1,4)

When ending his exordium, every self-respecting orator must normally indicate the subject he intends to treat. In general, that subject offers a certain degree of novelty. Position within the text and degree of novelty are two criteria that make it possible to identify the announcement of a subject.

At the end of his exordium, what does our preacher insist upon? On the «name» that the Son, that is to say Christ, has received as an inheritance on completing his work of purification of sins. In the Greek text the word *onoma*, «name», is the last word in the sentence; that position makes it stand out, as does the alliteration with the previous word (keklēr-*onomē*-ken / *onoma*). The preacher is therefore announcing that he will speak about the «name» of Christ, that is to say —because such is the underlying idea in the Semitic mentality— that he will define the personal position of Christ and his relational capacities. To this effect just one title cannot be sufficient. A whole series of explanations, even two series are needed for it, as we shall see. It is mistaken to look for *one* title in the context which would on its own be Christ's name.

The sentence explains the way in which the preacher will go about better defining the name of Christ: he will use a comparison with «the angels». This mention of the angels is another element of novelty which makes it possible to discern the announcement of the subject. Commentators have always recognized that, in the next verses (1,5-14), the author is effectively going on to a comparison between Christ and the angels. They conclude that the subject being dealt with is that of «Christ's superiority over angels». Is that right? Strictly speaking, no. The comparison with the angels is not the main theme of what follows, but only a means used to highlight the main theme better, which is, as we have seen, the «name» of Christ. The commentators who here restrict the subject to the idea of superiority over the angels later find themselves embarrassed when they have to explain chapter 2 where the author remarks that the name of Christ brings with it an aspect of abasement below the angels (2,9). When, however, it is understood that the main theme is the «name» of Christ (that is to say, we repeat, his personal position and his relational capacities) the explanation of chapter 2 is made without the slightest difficulty.

2
Structure of the first part of the homily (1,5-2,18)

It is easy to verify that, from 1,5 to 2,18, the preacher is in fact defining the personal position of Christ and his relational capacities. He does so in two paragraphs because the position of Christ must be defined from two complementary points of view: firstly in relation to God and then in relation to mankind. The two paragraphs are quite distinct: a brief exhortation separates them (2,1-4). Their boundaries are marked by two inclusions. The formula in 1,5:

> To whom among the angels did he ever in fact say...?

finds its echo in 1,13:

> To which of the angels did he ever say...?

And the formula in 2,5:

> For it was not to the angels...

finds its echo in 2,16:

> For it certainly is not of the angels...

After the end of this second inclusion the angels disappear from the scene. Their name comes back only in the last part of the homily, in 12,22 and 13,2, incidentally.

The first paragraph (1,5-14) reminds us that, with regard to God, Christ is the «Son» (1,5), «God» with God (1,8.9), Creator of the universe and «Lord» (1,10), called, in his Easter glorification, to sit at God's right hand (1,13). In all this, obviously, his position is much higher than that of the angels.

After the exhortation, which immediately draws some conclusions concerning Christian living from the doctrine expounded, the other paragraph (2,5-16) deals with the human aspect of the name of Christ. As regards human beings, Christ is one of them; he is called «Jesus» (2,9); he has human beings as «brothers» (2,11-12), because he has shared their condition of «flesh and blood» (2,14) and has passed through suffering and death (2,9,10,14,18). In him the call of man to dominate the universe is realized (2,5-9), a call which, before coronation «with glory and honour», involves a period of abasement below the angels (2,7-9). Because it corresponds to a position of superiority obtained by accepting abasement, the «name» of Christ really is «very different from that of the angels» (1,4). Among its various aspects not the least important is that he is the «cause of the salvation» of mankind and became so by passing «through suffering» (2,10). Christ did not choose solidarity with angels but with men by becoming a member of the «posterity of Abraham» (2,16).

3
Announcement of the subject of the second part of the homily (2,17-18)

After the inclusion in 2,16, the second paragraph of the exposé is somewhat drawn out. The tone indeed remains the same in the two following verses (2,17.18), whereas a very distinct change occurs in 3,1. For the first time the preacher then addresses his listeners, and with great solemnity:

> Thus therefore, holy brethren, who share in a heavenly vocation, consider the apostle and high priest of our profession of faith, Jesus … (3,1).

In all the rest of the homily such a solemn formula will never be found. The preacher will be content to use the simple title «brothers» (3,12; 10,19) or a more affectionate term, «beloved» (6,9).

The solemnity of 3,1 indicates that the preacher is there beginning to treat the particular theme in his homily, which is the priesthood of Christ, the «apostle and high priest of our profession of faith» (3,1). The preceding part, about the «name» of Christ, was only an introduction. Its rhetorical function corresponds to what classical rhetoric called «*narratio*»[1], recalling facts on which orator and listeners are agreed and which constitute the starting point for the announcement of the thesis and for its demonstration. In our case, the glorification of Christ (1,5-14) and his passion (2,5-16), fundamental events of Christian faith recognized as such by all the faithful, have been dealt with. The preacher was refined enough not to recall them like a schoolmaster, but to present them in an original way, by means of a comparison between the position of Christ and that of the angels.

His thesis is that these events have made Christ a high priest. This will be the subject of the second and third parts of his discourse (3,1-5,10 and 7,1-10,18).

Where is the announcement of this subject of which the development, as we have just seen, starts in 3,1? It comes immediately before, in 2,17-18. This passage occupies a very particular position, well suited to its function of announcing the subject, since it is placed after the inclusion in 2,16 which marks the end of the first part (1,5-2,16), and before the words addressed to the listeners in 3,1, which mark the beginning of the next part. In that very special place the preacher introduces the great novelty he wants to speak about, the priestly aspect of the mystery of Christ:

> So then, he had to become in everything similar to his brethren,
> in order to become a merciful high priest
> and worthy of trust for relations with God,
> with a view to blotting out the sins of the people.
> In fact, by reason of having suffered himself by being tried
> he can come to the help of those who are tried (2,17-18).

The theme announced is completely new; no other writing in the New Testament ascribes the title of high priest to Christ. Particular position and novelty of theme lead one to recognize in these verses the announcement of the subject the author is preparing to treat. This perception is also confirmed by the next

1 See ÜBELACKER W.G., *Der Hebräerbrief als Appell*, 185-193.

sentence, the solemn beginning of the second part, which calls upon the hearers to consider the priestly dignity of Christ (3,1).

Some commentators, impressed with the novelty of the theme, think that it arrives abruptly and unexpectedly. In fact it was carefully prepared by all the preceding part. It appears as its conclusion, which in fact it is. Actually, once it is realized that the first part of the homily has as its subject the «name» of Christ and that it defines that name with a twofold relationship, Son of God (1,5-14) and brother of mankind (2,5-16), it becomes clear that the author has thereby highlighted the position of Christ as mediator between God and mankind or, in other words, as the «high priest». Finally, if a unique title for resuming the various aspects of the «name» of Christ had to be chosen, the title of «high priest» would suit best or, more exactly, «perfect high priest». «Made perfect» thanks to his passion (2,10; 5,8-9), the glorified Christ henceforth is in an ideal position to exercize priestly mediation. What follows in the homily will be applied to showing this.

4 *Structure of the second part of the homily (3,1-5,10)*

In 2,17 the title of «high priest» comes then as conclusion to the first part of the homily and announces the subject which the author wishes to treat. The following chapters depend on this announcement. They expound a priestly Christology and its consequences for Christian living[2].

But it should be noted, on the other hand, that this title is accompanied by two adjectives which specify it: «merciful and trustworthy». As can easily be understood, it is a question of two indispensable qualities in exercizing priestly mediation.

The high priest must be «merciful» to have good relations with unfortunate mankind. He must be «trustworthy», so as to provide them with an authentic relationship with God. These two qualifying terms announce a first exposé of priestly Christology, divided, in a corresponding way, into two sections which will show that Christ possesses those two qualities (3,1-5,10).

2 See ÜBELACKER W.G., *Der Hebräerbrief*, 193-195.

4.1. FIRST SECTION (3,1-4,14)

The order of the development is the reverse of the one in the announcement which, as we have said, is contrary to the rules of Graeco-Latin rhetoric, but in conformity with the usages of biblical rhetoric. In the first sentence of the section that follows (3,1-2), it is not the first of the two qualifying terms that the author takes up («merciful»: 2,17), but the second: «trustworthy».

> Consider the apostle and high priest
> of our profession of faith, Jesus
> who is trustworthy for the one who constituted him,
> like Moses in all his house (3,1-2).

None of the many terms which, in 2,17-18, have a connection with mercy appear in this passage or in all the succeeding development. We have to wait until 4,15-16 to see them appear again and will then find them in large numbers.

To obtain a parallelism of themes with the title they have chosen for the previous part («Superiority of Christ over the angels») many commentators, starting with Thomas Aquinas, here adopt as title «Superiority of Christ over Moses». But the announcement of the subject in 2,17-18 does not speak either of superiority or of Moses; it presents Christ as «merciful and trustworthy high priest». Nor does the first sentence of the next part speak of superiority either. It takes up «trustworthy high priest [...]» (3,1-2). To develop this theme it introduces the figure of Moses and expresses a relation between Christ and Moses, not of superiority, but of resemblance: «Jesus is trustworthy [...] *like* Moses» (3,1-2). A relationship of superiority is, however, stated, but only secondarily and to bring out the idea of credibility. Verses 5-6 explicitly come back to this theme. The parallelism of the titles is therefore doubly unfaithful to the text: the precise subject of the first part (1,5-2,18) is not, as we have seen, «the superiority of Christ over the angels», and the precise theme of the first verses of the second part (3,1-6) is not «the superiority of Christ over Moses» either. The false symmetry obtained by adopting these two titles, both equally inexact, sets exegesis off in the wrong direction.

Exegetes are not unanimous on the literary genre of these verses (3,1-6). Do they belong to the genre of doctrinal exposé or to that of exhortation?—To that of exhortation, some reply, for they start with an imperative: «consider» (3,1). To that of doctrinal exposition, others answer, because that exhortation is only a call for attention; it is really a call to listen to the doctrinal explanations that follow. It is this second opinion that deserves to prevail, as is shown in a similar case in 7,4 where the presence of the imperative «contemplate» does not lead any exegete to place the passage that follows among the exhortations.

In 3,1-6 the author briefly sets out an important point of doctrine which could be called the «trustworthiness» of the priesthood of Christ The vocabulary is that of the two texts that serve as the basis of the argumentation: Num 12,7 («trustworthy», «house», «Moses», «servant»), and Nathan's oracle to David (1Chr 17,12-14, «house», «construction», «son», «to make trustworthy»).

As regards the exhortation, prepared at the end of verse 6, it only really starts in 3,7-8 with the quotation from Ps 94 (95): «harden not your heart», on which the preacher then comments in the same tone. He uses the expressions from the psalm «heart», «harden», etc., and adds the theme of «lack of faith» (3,12.19) and of «faith» (4,2.3) to them so as to establish more clearly the connection between the exhortation and the brief doctrinal exposé preceding it (3,1-6). The latter has shown that Christ is a trustworthy «high priest».From this it follows that we are urgently exhorted not to be «lacking in faith» when we hear his voice. The warning about lack of faith is drawn up in three paragraphs. The boundaries of the first are marked out by an inclusion that speaks of «lack of faith» (3,12.19); the boundaries of the last by an inclusion speaking «of indocility» (4,6-11). Then comes praise for the Word of God (4,12-13), stressing the fact that it vigorously exercizes the powers of a judge.

4.2. TRANSITION (4,14-16)

Between this praise for the divine Word and the beginning of the following exposé dealing with the second qualifying term of the priesthood of Christ, a short paragraph provides a transition (4,14-16). A precise analysis of these few sentences shows that they contain firstly the conclusion (4,14) of the preceding section and then the introduction (4,15-16) to the following section[3]. Joining up these two elements that are clearly different from each other is achieved by repeating a link-formula which explains the point they have in common: «we have a high priest» (4,14.15).

3 It is rare for commentators to make this precise analysis. W.G. ÜBELACKER rightly refuses to see in Heb 4,14-16 a *propositio* or the announcement of a subject, but he, too, considers these verses as referring to one and the same theme, that of the glorified high priest, *Der Hebräerbrief als Appell*, 196.

Verse 14, an excellent conclusion, resumes both the doctrine explained in 3,1-6 and the exhortation developed from 3,7 up to 4,11. The doctrine is that we have «an excellent high priest who has gone through the heavens, Jesus, the Son of God»; the exhortation that derives from this is that we must «hold firm to the confession of faith». The connection between 4,14 and 3,1-6 is not just one of idea; it is also verbal, in conformity with the usages of biblical rhetoric. A very marked inclusion actually refers back from 4,14 to 3,1. Let us compare the two verses:

> So then, holy brethren, who share in a
> HEAVENLY calling, consider the apostle and the HIGH PRIEST of our PROFESSION OF FAITH, JESUS (3,1).
> Therefore, having an excellent HIGH PRIEST, who has gone through the
> HEAVENS, JESUS, the Son of God, let us hold firm to the PROFESSION OF FAITH (4,14).

It is easy to see that in these two passages three terms are repeated identically («high priest», «Jesus», «confession of faith») and that a close connection links «heavens» and «heavenly». On the other hand, let us note that the title of «Son of God» in 4,14 refers back to the expression «Christ, as Son», at the end of the doctrinal exposé (3,6). This supplementary contact makes the conclusion even more perfect.

The next verses (4,15-16) move on to the other aspect of Christ's priesthood, not now the sovereign authority of the glorified Christ, but the capacity of Christ to show compassion, having been put to the test. After 4,14 which refers back to 3,1, the two sentences in 4,15-16 have a close connection with two earlier verses (2,17-18). We thus have a chiastic arrangement, B A A' B', frequent in biblical rhetoric, B and B' representing 2,17-18 and 4,15-16, A and A' 3,1 and 4,14.

The sentences in 4,15-16 represent everything which, in the announcement of the subject (2,17-18), refers to priestly mercy:

> Indeed, we do not have a *high priest unable* to show com*passion* towards our weaknesses, but a high priest *likewise put to the test in everything*, except *sin*.
> So let us with confidence approach the throne of grace, to receive *mercy* and to find grace for help in time of need (4,15-16).

The words we have placed in italics —there are a number of them, as can be seen— are all taken over from the text at 2,17-18. One absence is to be noted: the epithet «trustworthy» in 2,17 does not occur in 4,15-16. There is nothing surprising about that because it was the main theme in the previous section (3,1-4,14).

4.3. DOCTRINAL PRESENTATION (5,1-10)

After the exhortative sentence in 4,16 the tone changes. From 5,1 to 5,10 we find once again a doctrinal presentation which matches the one in 3,1-6. It is built on a parallelism. The first sentences list the traits that characterize «every high priest» (5,1-4). The following sentences show their realization in the case of Christ (5,5-10). Just one relation of resemblance is affirmed: «Thus Christ also...» (5,5). The point of view is that of the solidarity of the high priest with human weakness. In 5,1 and 5,10 the word «high priest» forms an inclusion.

Thus ends the the second section (4,15-5,10) of the first exposé of Christological priesthood (3,1-5,10). The latter has shown that Christ possesses in full the two qualities that are indispensable for exercizing mediation: Christ is a high priest «trustworthy in relations with God» and full of «mercy» towards his brothers and sisters in mankind.

In closing, let us note that the construction of this second part (3,1-5,10) is parallel to that of the first part (1,5-2,18). Two doctrinal exposés (3,1-6 and 5,1-10) in it enclose an exhortation (3,7-4,16). But the proportions are inverse: the exposés are short, the exhortation is long, while in the first part the exhortation was short (2,1-4) and the exposés relatively long (1,5-14 and 2,5-18). More importantly, a similarity of themes corresponds to the symmetry of the layout. In each case, the first doctrinal exposé concerns the glorious aspect of the mystery of Christ, his glorification as Son of God (1,5 and 3,6), whereas the second exposé concerns the sorrowful aspect of solidarity with human misery (2,8-16 and 5,7-8). This similarity of themes confirms that the author conceived the first part, about traditional Christology, as a preparation for the second, about priestly Christology.

5
Announcement of the subject of the third part of the homily (5,9-10)

As he ends his second part (3,1-5,10), the preacher announces the subject of the next part. The conclusion (5,9-10) draws attention in fact by its breadth. With a triple affirmation it defines the outcome of Christ's passion:

made perfect.
he became, for all who obey him, the cause of eternal salvation,
proclaimed by God high priest according to the order of Melchisedek (5,9-10).

Each of these points obviously needs explanation, although none are entirely new. The first two have been rapidly mentioned in the course of the first part, but not as established facts, simply as in keeping with theological «fittingness»: «It was fitting» for God, in order to lead a multitude of sons to glory, «to *make perfect* through suffering the chief who would lead them to *glory*» (2,10). The third point was mentioned in 5,6, where the author quoted the priestly oracle in Ps 109(110): «You are a priest forever according to the order of Melchisedek». Being the scriptural basis of priestly Christology, this oracle calls for an in-depth commentary. Shrewd listeners can then understand that the preacher has just announced the subject of his third part. Their guess is immediately confirmed, for, in the next sentence, the preacher explicitly declares his intention by saying:

On this subject we have much to say... (5,11)

The less shrewd listeners are thereby informed: the sentence in 5,9-10 is announcing the part of the homily starting in 5,11 and that part will be a long one. In fact, with its 132 verses (2,170 words), it is the longest of all. On its own, it is much longer than the two previous parts put together (77 verses; 1,300 words) and than the next two parts (89 verses; 1,536 words).

In fact, this third part contains no less than five sections. The announcement makes provision for three sections of doctrinal exposé. The author has thought it useful to place exhortative sections before and after them, the first (5,11-6,20) to call for greater attention on the part of his listeners, for the subject is important and difficult, the second (10,19-39) to provide the link between the doctrine expounded and Christian living.

6

Structure of the third part of the homily (5,11-10,39)

6.1. PREAMBLE (5,11-6,20)

In 5,11 a change of tone and vocabulary are observable. Instead of immediately developing one of the points in the theme announced (5,9-10), the preacher begins by reproaching his audience. He accuses them of spiritual nonchalance. The word «nonchalant» is used twice here to form an inclusion from 5,11 to 6,12; it is found nowhere else in the New Testament. The need for progress in Christian life is strongly inculcated in this passage (5,11-6,3). Then comes a severe warning against the danger of falling (6,4-8). However, some encouraging words (6,9-12) mitigate the severity of the warning. And considerations on God's promises (6,13-20) then give rise to hope. This is the end of the preamble. Immediately afterwards, in 7,1, the tone changes once again, in the opposite direction: the preacher resumes the tone of the exposé.

The final verse (6,20) offers a significant detail: it repeats the announcement of the subject made in 5,9-10, not entirely, however, but only its last point and changing the order of the expression so as to get a chiastic arrangement. The sentence in 5,10 said that Christ was proclaimed «high priest according to the order of Melchisedek» by God; the one in 6,20 declares that Jesus has become «according to the order of Melchisedek high priest» which draws attention to the «order» to which the priesthood of Christ belongs.

The author went to a lot of trouble to place this repetition of the announcement of the subject at the end of his preamble. In fact, his sentence, which begins in 6,17, makes many twists and turns: a final proposition (6,18) is prolonged by a qualifying relative one (6,19) to which is attached a relative clause of localization (6,20). It is clear that the author at all costs wanted to recall at the end of this exhortative preamble one of the points in the announcement of the subject to indicate to his audience that he intended to develop that point immediately afterwards, leaving the two others until later.

6.2. FIRST SECTION (7,1-28)

The beginning (7,1) of the section following confirms this intention. The name of Melchisedek is repeated in it, which gives a link-word transition. This name introduces an exposé on priesthood according to the order of Melchisedek.

Commentators are unanimous in recognizing the boundaries of this section. They coincide with those of the chapter (7,1-28). The literary signs of composition are so many and so converging that the unity of the section is perceived even before making a precise analysis of it.

The literary genre is clearly different from that of the preceding exhortation (5,11-6,20). It is one of exposé. From the first person plural (6,18: «we might be»; 6,19: «we have»; 6,20: «for us») a transition is made to the third person (7,1: «this Melchisedek..».). The imperative in 7,4 («*Contemplate* how great is the one..». is only an appeal for attention: the tone remains henceforth one of exposé.

The author comments methodically, one by one, on the two Old Testament passages mentioning Melchisedek; first, in the short account in Gen 14,17-20, then, in Heb 7,11-28, the oracle in Ps 109(110),4. The vocabulary is therefore first that of Gen 14,17-20 («Melchisedek, king of Salem, etc».), but it is also based on certain omissions in that text («without father, without mother, etc».). Moreover, certain significant additions are to be noted («the Son of God»: 7,3; «the sons of Levi»: 7,5); they open up the perspective. Then, as from 7,11, expressions from Ps 109(110) appear several times; the vocabulary is that of priestly institution: «priesthood», «order of Aaron», «order of Melchisedek», «priest», «oath-taking».

The boundaries of the paragraphs are marked by inclusions. For the first one (7,1-10), the final sentence takes up, in inverse order, two important terms in the initial sentence: «Melchisedek» and «met». For the second (7,11-28), the inclusion comes between the first noun in 7,11 (*teleiōsis*: «action of making perfect») and the last word in 7,28 (*teteleiōmenon* «made perfect»); this inclusion is strengthened by the double reappearance in 7,28 of the theme of the «Law», mentioned in 7,11. The inclusion system even extends to the minor subdivisions. The first of these (7,1-3) has the word «priest» at its beginning and end. The second (7,4-10) has the name of «Abraham» and the mention of the «tithes» in its first and penultimate sentence (7,4.9). For the third (7,11-19), the inclusion is made thanks to some related words that speak of «perfection» and the «Law» (7,11.19). For the fourth, it comes about with «oath-taking» (7,20-28). Lastly, the small subdivision in 7,26-28 has «high priest» at the beginning (7,26) and at the end (7,28). Along with the small initial subdivision (7,1-3) of which the beginning (7,1) and end (7,3) contain the word «priest», it thereby constitutes a kind of general inclusion taking in the whole of the section.

Such a way of composition may seem surprising. To be sure, it is completely foreign to Greek rhetoric. But it corresponds to biblical literary tradition. Similar inclusion systems are to be found in the Book of Wisdom (for instance, Wis 1,16-2,24; 2,1-21; 2,1-5; 2,6-11; 2,12-16; 2,17-20).

6.3. SECOND SECTION (8,1-9,28)

While confirming other indications, the inclusion system shows quite clearly that the sentence in 7,28 concludes the section begun in 7,1. The last words in that sentence, «made perfect», attracts attention because, being in a statement, it forms an antithesis with the negative assertion in 7,19: «the Law has made nothing perfect» and with the doubt expressed in 7,11. Let us note in this connection that when dealing with the last of the three points announced in 5,9-10, priesthood according to the order of Melchisedek, the author did not lose sight of the question of «perfection» mentioned in the first point (5,9). In his perspective, priesthood and perfection are closely linked. To be a priest in the true sense means that one has to have been «made perfect». The institutions of the Old Testament were unable to lead to perfection.

At the end of chapter 7 the author comes back precisely to the first point of the announcement, because here, and here only, he uses the verb «to make perfect» affirmatively and applying it to Christ, exactly as in 5,9. Given its position at the end of the sentence and the section, this resumption of the «making perfect» from 5,9 is understood as a signal like the one in 6,20, that is to say, like the reminder of one of the points in the announcement of the subject (5,9). It indicates that the section dealing with that point will start immediately afterwards.

In the next sentence the author actually confirms this indication (8,1). Referring to the expression in 7,28, which defines the ideal high priest as «a Son made perfect», he declares: «The main point in what we are saying is: we have *a high priest* like that . . ».. It is difficult to express oneself more clearly. Coming at the head of the proposition, the qualifying term «like that» refers back to the explanation given in the previous sentence (7,28) and, more particularly, to the last word in it: «made perfect». It is strange that certain commentators have not realized this and have linked the expression «a high priest like this» only with what follows, thus depriving the section of its connection with the preceding context. The literary facts show clearly that, in the mind of the author, the section starting in 8,1 will deal with the first theme announced in 5,9: Christ's priestly «perfection». The term «main point» shows the importance that the author ascribes to it. That importance was already there in 5.9, for, being put in first position, the participle «made perfect» naturally commanded all the rest of the sentence.

In the whole of the homily, the section beginning with 8,1 is in the middle of everything, being preceded by 129 verses (2,134 words) and followed by 128 verses (1,986 words). With its 41 verses (787 words), it is also the longest of all the sections. Our analysis of the internal structure of the text will show that, from that point of view also, this section occupies a central position: it is situated in the middle of the third part (5,11-10,39), which itself is the central part of the homily; it is preceded and followed by five sections.

By placing the point he considers «main» in the centre of his address, the author once again departs from the rules of classical rhetoric. The latter required that the principal subjects be placed at the beginning and end of the demonstration and that subjects of minor importance be left in the middle[4]. The reason for this arrangement was of a psychological order and corresponded to the purpose sought in legal or political eloquence: to win over the audience's agreement with a decision. To this end it really is important to create a favourable impression at the outset and to confirm it decisively at the end. Christian preaching, however, first had another purpose when addressing an assembly of the faithful. It was concerned above all to nourish their faith by getting them to know the gift of God, the mystery of Christ, better. This first aim is certainly completed with a call to receive the message of faith properly and to adopt a conduct in conformity with its dynamism. But the teaching dimension of the faith remains fundamental. That is what makes the originality of Christian preaching as distinct from legal or political eloquence. For that reason it is unadvisable to wish to apply the categories of classical rhetoric as they stand to Christian preaching and, in particular, to the Letter to the Hebrews.

The statement in 8,1, «we have a high priest like that», as we have seen, continues with a further description of this high priest, first in traditional terms, inspired by Ps 109(110),1 (Christ sitting at the right hand of God), then in new terms: «minister of the sanctuary and of the true tent which the Lord planted, not man» (8.2). Being placed as an introduction to the whole section, these new expressions constitute a reformulation of the announcement of the subject. The action that «made Christ perfect» made him perfect in the sense that it made him the «minister of the sanctuary and of the true tent». The analysis of the section shows that this really is the subject that the preacher is developing in it.

4 See GARUTI P., *Alle origini*, 195.

The commentators are not unanimous on the extent of this section. Some fix its last limit in 10,18[5], others place it in 9,28[6]. The diversity of opinions is not surprising because, on this point, the composition of the text lends itself to discussion. If, between chapter 7 and the following chapters the distinction is clear, the same cannot be said about chapters 8 to 10. Two main arguments for extending the section starting with 8,1 to 10,18 are put forward: on the one hand, the sacrificial vocabulary («to offer», «sacrifice», «blood»), which was introduced at the end of chapter 7 (7,27), is still present up to 10,18; on the other hand, the oracle about the «new covenant», quoted in 8,8-12 (Jer 31,31-34), is taken up in part in 10,16-17[7].

These facts deserve consideration but they are not decisive, because they take no account of the rhetorical function of the introductory sentence (8,1-2). The latter takes as coordinates for the liturgical action of Christ the «*sanctuary* and the true *tent* which the Lord planted, not man» (8,2). Now these coordinates hold our attention throughout chapters 8 and 9, but are not there in 10,1-18. The opposition expressed in 8,2 between the tent planted by the Lord and a tent planted by a man introduces an exposé divided into two antithetic paragraphs the first of which (8,3-9,10) describes and criticizes ancient worship, characterized by «the tent» which «Moses» constructed (8,5), «a holy place which was of this world» (9,1), whereas the second paragraph (9,11-28) describes and places value on Christ's oblation, characterized by its connection with «the greater and more perfect tent» (9.11) and by Christ's entry «once and for all into the sanctuary» (9,12). The author makes it clear, a little further on, that it was not a matter of a «sanctuary made by hand of man» but of «heaven itself» (9,24).

The word «tent» in 8,2 is repeated no less than seven times in chapters 8 and 9 (8,5; 9,2.3.6.8.11.21); in vain does one look for it in chapter 10. The same goes for the word «sanctuary» in 8,2; it is found four times in chapter 9 (9,8.12.24.25) and never in 10,1-18. Add to this the fact that on two occasions (9,8 and 9,11-12), a connection is expressed between «tent» and «sanctuary», a negative one in the case of «the first tent» (9,8), a positive one in the case of Christ's liturgy: «by the greater tent [...] he entered into the sanctuary» (9,11-12). Lastly, it is remarkable

5 This is the opinion of O. MICHEL, H. BRAUN, H. ATTRIDGE, and E. GRÄSSER, just to cite some of the more important commentators.

6 This is the position of C. SPICQ, P. ANDRIESSEN - A. LENGLET, G.W. BUCHANAN, N. CASALINI, and P. ELLINGWORTH.

7 See ATTRIDGE H., *The Epistle to the Hebrews*, 18.

that the action of «entering» into the holy place or «into the sanctuary», mentioned four times in chapter 9 (9,6.12.24.25), is never mentioned in chapter 10. The same goes for the action of «offering oneself» (9,14.25), characteristic of the liturgy of Christ; it is not mentioned any more in chapter 10. These indications show that the initial sentence in chapter 8 introduces a section that does not go beyond the end of chapter 9. Confirmation of this is provided by the fact that between the last sentence of chapter 9 and the beginning of the next chapter a very clear break is seen. 9,28 speaks of the second coming of Christ; 10,1 returns abruptly to the old Law.

The inner composition of the second central section (8,1-9,28) serves to support these early observations, for it follows a concentric plan *a b a'* A' B A, which forms a complete whole and rejects the addition of any additional units. From this point of view a notable difference between concentric symmetries and parallel symmetries of the type A B A' B' is in fact observed. In the case of the latter, there is nothing to prevent adding another series of elements or even several others; AB A'B' A" B", etc. But when the symmetry is concentric the last element corresponds to the first and necessarily marks the end of the plan. Any addition would look like an excrescence.

We have already remarked that the central section is divided into two long paragraphs (8,3-9,10 and 9,11-28), the opposition between which corresponds to the introductory formula: the first concerns a tent «that a man planted»; the second «the true tent that the Lord planted» (8.2). The distinction between these two paragraphs is made more obvious by the absence, in the first, (8,3-9,10), of any mention of the name of Christ, while in the second (9,11-28) that name is repeated four times (9,11.14.24.28).

Another significant observation: in the middle of both these paragraphs a passage speaks of «covenant». In the middle of the first (8,7-13), we have the oracle of Jeremiah on the «new covenant» (Heb 8,8-12; Jer 31,31-34); in the middle of the second (9,15-23), mention is made of the way in which the covenant on Sinai was established (Exod 24,4-8). From these two insertions there clearly emerges an arrangement of the text in six subdivisions. The initial (8,3-6), central (9,1-10 and 9,11-14) and final subdivisions (9,24-28) are characterized by the vocabulary of the offering in worship («to offer»: 8,3.3.4; 9,7.9; 9,14; 9,25.28); the central subdivisions (8,7-13 and 9,15-23), by the vocabulary of the covenant («covenant»: 8,6.8.9.10; 9,15.16.17.20).

The paragraph concerning the worship in former times (8,3-9,10) attaches the formula «to offer gifts and sacrifices» (8,3; 9,9) to that worship; the paragraph of accomplishment (9,11-28) confronts it with the formula «to offer oneself» (9,14.25), which is specific to the liturgy of Christ.

An inclusion marks the boundaries of the first paragraph (8,3-9,10): the expression in 8,3: «to offer gifts and sacrifices» finds an echo, in chiastic form, in the one in 9,9: «gifts and sacrifices are offered». Subdivisions are marked by minor inclusions. The first of these relates the «minister of the worship (*leitourgos*)» in 8,2 to the «liturgy» in 8,6. The second inclusion is created by the repetition of the expression «the first (covenant)» in 8,7 and 8,13. The third, by the repetition of the word «rites» in 9,1 and 9,10.

As regards the second paragraph (9,11-28), it has the name of «Christ» to mark the beginning and end of the first (9,11.14) and last (9,24.28) of its subdivisions.

The six subdivisions are arranged in concentric symmetry. In the case of those concerning worship the links are antithetic, complementary, rather, in the case of those speaking of the covenant. The first subdivision defines the level to which the former worship was confined: an earthly and figurative level (8,3-6), whereas the last subdivision (9,24-28) proclaims that Christ has reached the heavenly level, the one of perfect reality. In the central subdivisions, 9,1-10 and 9,11-14, opposition is expressed between «the first tent» (9,2.6.8) which served the former worship and «the greater and more perfect tent» (9,11), through which Christ «has entered into the sanctuary» (9,12). Added to this is the opposition between the «gifts and sacrifices» offered by the old priesthood, «rites of flesh» external to the person and manifold (9,9-10), and the offering of Christ, which is personal, spiritual and unique (9,14).

The links connecting the two subdivisions devoted to the theme of the covenant (8,7-13 and 9,15-23) are more complex. Both, in fact, speak about the new as well as the old covenant. But the first takes a critical perspective: it uses the oracle about the new covenant to show that the first covenant was not «irreproachable» (8,7.13). The other subdivision, contrariwise, adopts a positive attitude: it presents the covenant rite performed by Moses on Sinai as a prefiguration of the death of Christ, who established the new covenant (9,15-18).

Many indications therefore show that the section starting at 8,1 arrives at its conclusion with the last sentence in 9,28. Even without having noticed these clues, the attentive reader realizes that that sentence is final for it expresses the eschatological aspect of Christ's offering. Let us note that a structure like that constitutes a system of relations at once complex and well-ordered. The exegete is called upon to study first the connection of linear succession that links each subdivision to the preceding subdivision; then the particular connection between the first subdivision (8,3-6) and the third (9,1-10), which mutually complete each other, and even between the fourth (9,11-14) and the (9,24-28); lastly, the relations of opposition between the two paragraphs. The general layout is the following:

Succession:	a -	b -	a'	-	A' -	B -	A
Complementarity:	a		a'		A'		A
Antithesis:	a						A
		b				B	
			a'	-	A'		

Each of these six subdivisions is in relation to all the others; the relation is direct with three of them, indirect with the two others. The a' subdivision (9,1-10), for example, is in a succession relation with b (8,7-13), a relation of precedence and antithesis with A' (9,11-14), of complementarity with a (8,3-5); through the mediation of b (8,7-13) or A' (9,11-14), it is in relation to B (9,15-23) and through the mediation of A' (9,11-14) to A (9,24-28).

Anyone who has not discerned the unity of the section and its structure remains in confusion in the face of the multiplicity of possible relations and imagines that the author is improvising, expressing himself in a disorderly way. But when one has recognized the structure, the skein is unravelled without the slightest difficulty.

6.4. THIRD SECTION (10,1-18)

At the end of this «capital» section (8,1-9,28), the audience expect some indication about what will follow. The preacher does not fail to satisfy this expectation: the last word of the last verse is significant. It is the word «salvation», which recalls the only point in the announcement which has not yet been developed: after his passion Christ «became the cause of eternal *salvation* for all who obey him» (5,9). With the two other points having been dealt with, it was predictable that the preacher would devote a third and last section of doctrinal exposé to that last point.

The clue here is not so evident as in the two preceding cases, for the word «salvation» is not taken up at the beginning of the section, whereas the «Melchisedek» of 6,20 had been taken up immediately in 7,1 and the «made perfect», last word in 7,28, had found its echo in the expression «a high priest like that» in 8,1. In the text of the third section (10,1-18), the vocabulary of «salvation» does not appear. Hence it is possible to cast doubt on the rhetorical function of the word «salvation» placed at the end of 9,28. But what leads one to recognize it is that this indication is part of a whole. The word «salvation» actually occupies a position exactly parallel to the two partial resumptions of the announcement made in 5,9-10. The latter (6,20 and 7,28) came at the end of the last sentence of a section and were immediately followed by the corresponding development. The word «salvation» in 9,28 attracts attention more especially as it has not reappeared since the sentence in 5,9-10. It has an undeniable relation with that sentence which the author, in 5,11, clearly presented as the announcement of his subject. There is therefore reason for understanding it as an allusion to 5,9 and as indicating the theme of the section beginning immediately afterwards.

Indeed, without using the word salvation itself again, the author, in 10,1-18, develops the idea when dealing with the problem of what Luke calls «salvation through the forgiveness of sins» (Luke 1,77). The frequent repetition of the word «sins» (nine times in 18 verses) is an obvious indication of it, just like the formulas «reminder of sins» (10,3), «take away sins» (10,4), «remove sins» (10,11), «to offer for sins» (10,12), «to remember sins no more» (10,17), «remission of these» (10,18), and «sin offering» (10.18). A complementary indication: the «sacrifice» and «offering» vocabulary is also very frequent; in fact it is thanks to a sacrificial offering that «salvation through the forgiveness of sins» can be hoped for. «Sacrifice» is used five times; «to offer» is also used five times, as is «offering». A contrast is expressed between the inability of the old Law in regard to the remission of sins (10,1-3) and the perfect efficacy of Christ's offering for that same purpose (10,15-18). On three occasions the author denounces the inability of the Law and its worship. The latter could neither remove sins nor lead to perfection (10,1.4.11). Christ's offering, on the contrary, was fully effective: «we have been sanctified by the offering of the body of Jesus Christ once and for all» (10,10); «with one offering he made perfect those who receive sanctification» (10,14). In the new covenant, salvation is really received, for that covenant brings not only remission of sins (10,17-18), but, furthermore, sanctification (10,10) and perfection (10,14), which give access to the presence of God.

An antithetic inclusion marks the limits of the section: with the statement in 10,1: «they offer perpetually» the declaration in 10,18: «there is no more any offering» comes as a contrast. Some minor inclusions mark out the subdivisions: «every year» in 10,1 and 10,3; «offering» in 10,5 and 10,10; «while offering» and «offering» in 10,11-14.

The relations between the four subdivisions conform to a concentric plan. The last subdivision (10,15-18) is in opposition with the first (10,1-3). The latter actually notes the indefinite repetition of sacrifices and the annual recollection of sins. The last one, on the contrary, announces the overlooking of sins and the cessation of sacrifices. The intermediary subdivisions are parallel with each other, for each one expresses an antithesis, the second (10,4-10) between the old sacrifices and Christ's personal offering; the third (10,11-14) between the continual agitation of the priests of old and the supreme tranquillity of Christ at the right hand of God.

The third exposé section (10,1-18) therefore has its own appearance and effectively deals with the subject indicated: Christ «has become the cause of eternal salvation» (5,9). With that said, it must be admitted that the previous section (8,1-9,28) had already given much space to that subject. The very composition of that section reveals this, for it is unexpectedly long. Its subject, expressed in its introduction (8,2) is the sacrificial activity whereby Christ was «made perfect» (5,9; 7,28). That theme, as we have seen, is developed in two long antithetic paragraphs (8,3-9,10 and 9,11-28) which contrast ancient worship with Christ's personal offering. These two paragraphs both speak of liturgy, tent and sacrifice, as the introductory sentence (8,1-2) earlier hinted at. But, moreover, both touch on another theme, of which this sentence says nothing, the theme of covenant. In the middle of the first paragraph (8,3-9,10), the considerations on worship are interrupted at 8,7 to make room for the oracle about the new covenant (8,8-12 = Jer 31,31-34), which has absolutely no interest either in worship or sanctuary. In the middle of the second paragraph (9,11-28), considerations on Christ's personal offering are interrupted in 9,15 to make room for the theme of the new covenant presented under its aspect as testament (9,15-17) and placed in connection with the Sinai covenant. That double insertion is very significant.

It shows that the author refused to ascribe only a vertical dimension to Christ's oblation, a dimension of movement towards God, and that, on the contrary, he insisted on giving it a horizontal dimension, one of human solidarity, at the same time. The sacrifice of Christ did not result in breaking the links of nature uniting him with his brothers and sisters; rather, it reinforced them and made him their saviour. It follows that the theme of salvation appears right from the first sentence of the positive paragraph (9,11-12). The author is not content there with saying that «Christ [...] by the tent [...] and by his blood entered into the sanctuary», he immediately adds that he thus «found an eternal liberation». The following sentence makes it clear that this liberation is destined for us: «the blood of Christ [...] will purify our conscience from dead works» (9,14). The rest of the text contains still other remarks that have a similar meaning (9,15.24.28).

This way of thinking is new in connection with the Old Testament, in which the vertical dimension of priesthood monopolized attention. At that time it was all about being a priest «for God» (see Exod 28,1.4; 29,1). While reversing the perspective, the author of Hebrews declared at the outset that «every high priest [...] is established *in favour of mankind* for relations with God» (5,1). He is careful to unite the two dimensions closely, the vertical and the horizontal ones. That is why, in the central section (8,1-9,28) he anticipated the theme of the following section (10,1-18). This particular point leads certain commentators to refuse to distinguish these two sections. Nevertheless they are distinct. It is only in the 10,1-18 section that the sanctification of the faithful (10,10) and the gift of perfection (10,14) are stated as accomplished facts. In the central section the purification of consciences is expressed in the future tense (9,14) and the redemption of sins is presented as an aim in sight (9,15).

6.5. CONCLUDING EXHORTATION (10,19-39)

The last sentence in 10,18 marks the end of the long exposé that started in 7,1. But that sentence, without any breadth to it, is not presented as the conclusion to the *whole* part. The author, in fact, does not intend to end with a doctrinal statement but with an exhortation. He goes on to say: «Having *therefore*, brethren, full confidence [...] *let us approach...*» (10,19).

The first paragraph of this exhortation (10,19-25) performs an extremely important function in the homily, for it establishes a close connection between priestly Christology and Christian living. Here the author clearly shows that he does not see the doctrinal explanation he has just made as an abstract theory only suitable for satisfying the intellectual needs of theologians. He sees it much more as a source of new vital spirituality. His long sentence contains two parts. The first (10,19-21) describes the situation resulting, as regards Christians, from the sacrifice and priesthood of Christ, a special situation of free access to the presence of God. The second part (10,22-25) urgently calls upon the faithful to accept their privileges actively by approaching God by means of a life of faith (10,22), hope (10,23) and charity (10,24). All the following exhortations are thereby firmly attached to the priestly doctrine which has been expounded. They draw their dynamism from it. Even the earlier exhortations are seen in a new light.

The first subdivision (10,19-25) ends with an allusion to the «Day» of judgment (10,25). The author thus introduces a very severe warning against obstinacy in sin (10,26-31). An inclusion on the words «terrible» (10,27.31) and «judgment», «to judge» (10,27.30) sets the limits to this admonition. Then comes a paragraph of encouragement (10,32-35), based on recalling past generosity. This passage from warning to encouragement corresponds exactly to the oratorical trend observed in the previous exhortation (6,4-8 and 6,9-12).

An inclusion is observable between the end of this paragraph (10,35) and the beginning of the exhortation (10,19). The author said at the beginning: «Having therefore, brethren, *full assurance* for entrance into the sanctuary…» (10,19). In 10,35 he recommends: «Do not therefore reject your *full* assurance…».

The exhortation tone is maintained, however, beyond this inclusion, up to the end of the chapter (10,39). Only at the beginning of the next chapter (11,1) does one observe a very definite change: the author moves to the exposé genre by giving a definition of faith.

7
Announcement of the fourth part of the homily (10,36-39)

At the end of the exhortation section (10,19-39) which concludes the third part of the homily (5,11-10,39), one usually expects some indications about the subject of the next part. The last verses of the section (10,36-39) offer these indications. They come, let us note, in a particular position which corresponds to a function of announcing the subject. They are in effect situated after the inclusion that goes from 10,19 to 10,35 («complete assurance») and before the change of literary genre made in 11,1. This position is like the one of the announcement of the subject of the second part, an announcement coming in 2,17-18, that is to say after the inclusion in 2,5.16 and before the change of tone to be noted in 3,1.

In 10,36-39 two themes are present: that of necessary «endurance» (10,36) and that of «faith» (10,38-39). The word «endurance» is stressed by its position; in Greek it is the first word of the sentence:

> Of *endurance*, indeed, you have need,
> so that having done the will of God,
> you may obtain the promise (10,36).

The theme of faith is next underlined, thanks to a repetition:

> Now my just man, it is by *faith* that he will live
> and if he falls away my soul takes no pleasure in him.
> We, however, are not people who fall away for our perdition,
> but of *faith* for the safeguarding of the soul (10,38-39).

These two themes are not completely new. The author has spoken of endurance in 10,32 and of faith in 10,22. The fourth part is therefore firmly connected with the final exhortation of the third part, and, through that, to the priestly Christology presented in the third part. But there is a certain aspect of novelty all the same. In 10,32 there was a reminder of the past: the author recalled the endurance shown by the faithful at the time of their conversion, while in 10,32 he affirms the present need of that strength of soul. As for the faith, the author will find a new way of speaking of it.

8

Structure of the fourth part of the homily (11,1-12,13)

In conformity with the announcement of the subject, the Fourth Part of the homily consists of two sections which speak of endurance and faith.

8.1. FIRST SECTION (11,1-40)

Another repetition of the word «faith» provides the transition between the last sentence of the previous development (10,39) and the first of the new part 11,1). While waiting for the definition of faith, the listeners find that, here again, the preacher starts with the theme that comes last in the announcement. Though mentioned first (10,36), endurance will be the subject only of the second section (12,1-13).

Having defined faith, the preacher describes the way in which he will deal with that theme. The announcement made in 10,38-39 in fact leaves room for possible hesitation. Is the author going to speak about our faith (10,39) or about the faith of the just person (10,38)? And in the latter case, will he expound the doctrine of justification by faith? The sentence in 11,2 answers these questions; it shows that the author will praise the faith of the «ancestors»: «It is that whereby our ancestors received approval» (11,2). By «ancestors» he means the just people of the Old Testament.

The extent of the section is quite evident: the praise of the ancestors goes to the end of the chapter (11,40). The constant repetition of the word «faith» (24 occurrences) characterizes this development. The word comes back again in 12,2, but it is then in an exhortation sentence begun in 12,1. Although the author, in chapter 11, obviously intended to encourage his hearers to live by faith he never takes on the tone of exhortation in it; no direct appeal, no imperative, everything is spoken in a narrative tone, in the indicative and in the third person.

An inclusion marks the boundaries of the section. When saying: «And all those, having *received approval* thanks to *faith*» (11,39), the author is referring back to the sentence at the beginning, where he says: «*Faith* [...] *through it* the ancestors *received approval*» (11,1-2). It might be objected that the word «faith», so often repeated, is no longer suitable for use in an inclusion. But actually the author stopped repeating it in the last paragraph of his eulogy and there changed his expression; at the beginning of this last paragraph, instead of saying, as before, «by faith» (*pistei*), he said «through faith» (*dia pisteōs*; 11,33) before a long list of triumphs of faith (11,33-35) and of its trials (11,35-38). In 11,39, a concluding sentence, the formula «through faith» is resumed and serves as a double inclusion: it marks the end of the last paragraph (11,32-40) and, on the other hand, linked with «to receive approval», at the same time it marks the end of the whole section (11,1-40).

The author divided up his development into four paragraphs, following the order of the biblical account: first, the definition of faith and three early examples, Abel, Enoch and Noah; a particular use of the word «faith» in 11,7 marks the end of that series. Then comes Abraham (11,8-19), followed by his first descendants (11,20-22). Thirdly, Moses appears —an inclusion is noticeable between 11,23 («they saw», «they did not fear», «of the king») and 11,27 («not having feared», «of the king», «seeing»)— then the Exodus Passover, crossing the Red Sea and the capture of Jericho (11,28-31); lastly, clearly separated from the previous ones by a rhetorical question, the last paragraph offers, as we have seen, an overall picture (11,32-38) and ends with the concluding sentence (11,39-40).

8.2. SECOND SECTION (12,1-13)

In 12,1 the author assumes the exhortation tone, expressed in the first person: «So then, we, too, [...] let us run with perseverance the race that is set before us...». He soon goes into the second person: «Think about him who endured...» (12,3), to return later on to the first: «We have had our earthly fathers as educators...» (12,9). All the rest of the homily will maintain that tonality. It follows that it is not easy to perceive divisions in it. More than one commentator considers the whole chapter as one and the same literary unit.

In reality, the announcement of the subject made in 10,36-39 provides a criterion for division. The author then presented two themes: necessary endurance (10,36) and the faith of the just person (10,38-39). He first dealt with this second point (11,1-40). One can see in advance that he will then deal with the first one. In fact, the word «endurance», which had not reappeared since the sentence in 10,36, comes again at the beginning of the section (12,1) and it is followed by the verb of the same family, «to endure», in 12,2.3.7. This vocabulary is relayed by the one about educational correction (*paideia* and related words), which occurs persistently as from 12,5. The link between these two vocabularies is explicit in 12,7: «It is for your education that you endure». After this verse, «endurance» gives way completely to «education», which is found in one form or another in every sentence up to 12,11. Then a «that is why» introduces the conclusion of the section (12,12-13), which is at the same time that of the part. The vocabulary then changes completely. An inclusion confirms this demarcation: the verb «let us run» in 12,1 finds an echo in «racetracks» in 12,13; the Greek words translated thus are used in this sense in Hebrews only.

9 *Announcement of the fifth part of the homily (12,13)*

The announcement of the fifth part of the homily comes, as is normal, at the end of the fourth. Is there anything new in the concluding sentence of the latter (12,12-13)? If we look at it closely we see that it contains two propositions and that the second brings in a new element. The first proposition (12,12) corresponds perfectly with the theme of the section which is strength of soul amid tribulation. Taking his inspiration from a text in Isaiah, which encourages the exiled Israelites to await with strength of soul the intervention of God (Isa 35,3), the preacher calls upon the faithful to «lift your drooping hands and strengthen your weak knees» (12,12). After this call, the second proposition opens up another perspective, not the one of endurance in expectation, but the one of uprightness in acting: «make straight paths for your feet» (12,13). This expression does not take its inspiration from Isa 35,3, nor from any similar context. It comes from a very different context, that of Proverbs (4,26), where it is applied to the correct orientation of conduct:

> Make straight paths for your feet
> and straighten out your ways;
> do not swerve to the right or to the left,
> turn your foot away from the way of evil (Prov 4,26-27).

This sentence therefore moves us on from the theme of Christian endurance, which is that of Heb 12,1-12, to the one of Christian activity, which will be that of the following part. In the New Testament, endurance has links with the virtue of hope (see 1Thess 1,3; Rom 5,4; Matt 10,22; 24,13; 2Tim 2,12), activity with the virtue of charity (see Heb 6,10; 1John 3,18).

Expressed in metaphorical terms («making paths straight») the announcement of the subject may seem too vague. That is why the author is careful to explain it at the beginning of his development, saying:

> Pursue peace with everyone and sanctification ... (12,14).

The «straight paths» are those that lead to «peace with everyone» and to «sanctification», in other words: to good relations with one's neighbour and with God.

This is not the first time that the author sets out his subject at the start of his development: in 3,1-2, to the epithet «trustworthy» expressed in the announcement (2,17), he added the comparison with Moses; in 8,1-2, he explained the «made perfect» in the announcement (5,9; 7,28) by saying that Christ is «minister of the sanctuary and of the true tent»; in 11,2 he specified the way in which he would deal with the theme of faith, announced in 10,38-39.

At first sight the relation between the themes in 12,14 («peace with you and sanctification») and the expression of the announcement of the subject in the preceding verse («straight paths») may seen too distant but if one refers to the biblical context of the two expressions, one perceives that the relation is close. The formula in 12,14 actually comes from Ps 33(34) and, more precisely, from a wisdom passage in that psalm which bears great similarities with the verses from Prov 4,26-29 used in Heb 12,13. Like Prov 4,26-29, the psalm exhorts people to behave well and places the search for peace in relation with the flight from evil: «Let him keep away from evil (see Prov 4,27) and do good; let him seek peace and pursue it» (Ps 33[34],15). From this it can be seen that, for someone who knows the Bible, the sentence in Heb 12,14 appears as a reformulation of the announcement made in 12,13.

How far does this fifth part extend? For those who are attentive to the indications of literary structure the answer to that question does not cause any great difficulty; this fifth part is the last, it extends to the solemn conclusion to the homily, easily recognizable in 13,20-21:

And may the God of PEACE,
who brought back from the dead
the great shepherd of the sheep
in the blood of eternal covenant,
Our LORD Jesus,
make you complete in everything good
so that you may do his will,
doing in us what is pleasing in his sight
through Jesus Christ,
to whom be the glory for ever and ever.
Amen.

It is certainly not by chance that two important words in this final sentence, «peace» and «lord», form an inclusion with the first sentence of the part (12,14), which recommends pursuing «*peace* and sanctification, without which no one will see the *Lord*». Two minor inclusions mark the limits of two long paragraphs: the word «grace» in 12,15 and 12,28 and the word «leaders» in 13,7 and 13,17, as well as «conduct» (13,7) and «to conduct ourselves» (13,18). These inclusions isolate a short intermediary paragraph (13,1-6). It will be noticed that this arrangement corresponds exactly with the one in the first part of the homily (1,5-2,18), in which two long paragraphs marked out by inclusions (1,5 and 1,13; 2,5 and 2,16) enclosed a small paragraph (2,1-4) of a different genre. In the last part, however, such a change of genre is not to be seen, for that part belongs entirely to the exhortation genre. It is by an asyndeton and a change of rhythm that the beginning of the small paragraph (13,1) is marked: the long periods in the preceding paragraph (12,14-17.18-21.22-24.25-27.28-29) are followed, without any transition, by a short proposition, of only three words in Greek (four in English: «May brotherly love continue!»).

From one end of the part to the other, the theme remains that of conduct to be followed, but a certain distinction can be perceived between the first paragraph and the other two, in accordance with the initial distinction between «peace with all» and «sanctification». Of course, these aspects are developed in reverse order. The content of the first paragraph (12,14-29) corresponds to the aspect of «sanctification»: it warns against all profanation (12,16), compares two religious experiences (12,18-24), exhorts to docility towards the voice of the Almighty (12,25-27) and recalls that «our God is a consuming fire» (12,29).

On the other hand, the other two paragraphs are especially attentive to relations between human persons, along the lines of «peace with all»; «brotherly love» (13,1), «hospitality» (13,2), solidarity (13,3), conjugal fidelity (13,4), absence of greed (13,5) are the orientations given in the short paragraph (13,1-6). As for the last long paragraph (13,7-18), framed within two references to «leaders» of the community (13,7.17), it is concerned with making provision for church cohesion, through fidelity to the faith of the first leaders (13,17) and through generous docility towards the present leaders (13,7-9). But that cohesion also involves an element of break with the earthly city, in the footsteps of Jesus who died «outside the gate» (13,12). The reminder of the passion of Christ provides the preacher with the opportunity to allude for the last time to his priestly Christology (13,10-13).

In his final solemn closing sentence (13,20-21), which we have quoted above, he resumes his teaching in new terms: instead of speaking of «eminent priest» (10,21) or of «eminent high priest» (4,14), he applies the title of «eminent shepherd» to Christ, whose paschal mystery he mentions by placing it in relation to the theme of «the everlasting covenant» (13,20). An invocation of grace is then expressed in terms recalling the exhortations made in the course of the homily. A short doxology and an «Amen» brings the whole work to a close.

11 *Dispatch note (13,22-25)*

After the conclusion of the homily (13,20-21), all the manuscripts contain some supplementary verses (13,22-25) of a completely different kind. They are in fact some epistolary sentences, written in a familiar style. The first of these verses on its own is significant from the outset:

> I beseech you, brethren, to accept the exhortation speech and indeed I have sent it to you with a few words (13,22).

This sentence reveals an epistolary context, one of separation in space between sender and addressee. That is never the case in the homily. Besides, a distinction is clearly expressed between these lines and the «exhortation speech», the homily, that is to say.

The lines that follow pass on news about Timothy's release and express the intention to visit, as well as greetings to be given and to be received. Everything ends with an invocation of grace, similar to those found at the end of the letters of the apostle Paul.

These last verses obviously belong to the epistolary genre therefore. They are a dispatch note, added to the text of the homily when it was sent to one distant community or another. In everything that precedes, one verse offers the same characteristics; it is 13,19, a short sentence inserted between the end of the paragraph at 13,7-18, marked by an inclusion, and the solemn conclusion to the homily (13,20-21). Only these verses (13,19.22-25) correspond to an epistolary context. All the rest belongs to the genre of oral speech, delivered by a preacher in the presence of a Christian assembly. No clue allows us to establish that the homily was composed to be sent in writing to a community, as is the case of the Letter of Paul to the Romans. Were this so, the beginning of the text would be of the epistolary genre, just like the beginning of the Letter to the Romans. The reality is quite different: the Letter to the Hebrews begins as a sermon, without any epistolary element at all.

II.1. THE QUESTION OF HEB 13,1-6

More and more exegetes recognize that the Letter to the Hebrews is a sermon to which an epistolary ending has been added. But unanimity does not reign concerning the extent of that ending. Not having studied the sermon's literary structure methodically and not having analysed the epistolary sentences with precision, many ascribe to the dispatch note an extent it does not have. They make this note start at 13,1 because they notice at that point an abrupt change of rhythm, which they think is a change of literary genre. So they put the end of the homily at 12,29 and the beginning of the letter at 13,1.

The change of rhythm is undeniable. We have already pointed it out. After some flowing periods there comes a sentence of three words. But is there, for that matter, a passage to a different genre, that of the letter? Nothing is less evident. In a speech, in fact, it is normal that there should be changes of rhythm; monotony must be avoided. In the Letter to the Hebrews, for instance, a change of rhythm is noticeable at 12,7. There, too, a sentence of three words, without any co-ordination, follows some long, well-connected periods. Elsewhere, rhetorical questions follow each other closely (3,16-18), interrupting the flow of the speech.

An attentive examination of 13,1-6 shows that this little literary unit is in no way heterogeneous to the homily as a whole[8]. It does not contain the slightest epistolary element and, far from being careless, as has sometimes been maintained, it has a very careful composition; we shall show this in detail later on. Let us say immediately that three subdivisions (13,1-3.4.5-6) are distinguished within it, each of which begins with a double exhortation, followed by some words to motivate people. The central subdivision (13,4) has only these two elements whereas the two others have a supplementary element. The result is that the overall arrangement is harmonious: two longer subdivisions frame a smaller one. This arrangement reflects that of all the last part of the homily in which two longer paragraphs (12,14-29 and 13,7-18) frame a shorter one (13,1-6). The same is also true for the first part (1,5-14; 2,1-4; 2,5-16). The details of the style reveal a talent equal to that in the preceding chapters and the same skill in the use of parallelisms.

The absence of any connection between the exhortations in 13,1-6 and the conclusion to chapter 12 is only apparent. When, after having said: «Let us pay to God a worship acceptable to him» (12,28), the preacher unexpectedly continues with an exhortation to «brotherly love» (13,1), he is suggesting to his listeners that they bring worship paid to God into connection with the life of charity. Without brotherly love there is no genuine worship. For those who might not have understood him he was to spell it out a little further on: «Do not forget beneficence and solidarity, for such *sacrifices are pleasing to God*» (13,16).

Furthermore, these verses offer many similarities of theme with other passages in the homily: attitudes of charity (13,1-3; see 6,10; 10,24; 12,14), solidarity with captives (13,3; see 10,34; 11,36), the judgment of God (13,4; see 6,2; 9,27; 10,27.30-31), detachment from riches (13,5; see 10,34); confidence in divine assistance (13,6; see 2,18; 4,16). In short, there is no serious reason for questioning these verses' (13,1-6) belonging to the homily begun in 1,1, then continued until 13,18 without any admixture of epistolary elements.

On the other hand, the sentence in 13,1 is not suitable for constituting the start of a major section of the homily. Its form is too short and its content too limited. The theme it expresses does not denote that of the whole of the following text. This latter will not actually be a long exhortation to brotherly love. Heb 13,1 is only the beginning of a small paragraph (13,1-6) coming between two

8 I showed this in an article: «La question littéraire de Hébreux XIII.1-6».

other more important ones. The abrupt change of rhythm and theme observable between 12,29 and 13,1 fulfils a double role: on the one hand it clearly marks out the passage from one paragraph (12,14-29) to the other (13,1-6); on the other, it draws attention to the paradoxical relationship linking the two themes expressed one after the other: between worship (12,28) and the life of charity (13,1-6), there must no longer be any separation, but rather identification.

We have thus finished the examination of the composition of the Letter to the Hebrews, which is a homily accompanied by a short dispatch note. The homily was put together with the greatest care. The author divided it into five great parts. He announces the subject of each one before starting it. The plan obtained is as follows:

Exordium: God has spoken to us in his Son (1,1-4)

Announcement of the subject of the First Part: 1,4b

Part One: The «name» of Christ: general Christology (1,5-2,18)

Christ is Son of God (1,5-14) and brother of mankind (2,5-16)

This double relationship makes him a mediator between God and mankind, a high priest

Announcement of the subject of Part Two: 2,17

Part Two: Christ is trustworthy and merciful high priest: priestly Christology, general characteristics (3,1-5,10)

1st section: Christ is trustworthy high priest (3,1-6); appeal for faith (3,7-4,14)

2nd section: Appeal for confidence (4,15-16), for Christ is compassionate high priest; he has suffered and offered (5,1-10)

Announcement of the subject of Part Three: 5,9-10

Part Three: Christ is the perfect high priest: priestly Christology, specific characteristics (5,11-10,39)

Preamble: Appeal for attention and generosity (5,11-6,20)

1st section: Christ is a high priest of a special kind (7,1-28)

2nd section: Christ offered a sacrifice of a new kind (8,1-9,28)

3rd section: Christ's offering was fully effective (10,1-18)

Epilogue: Appeal for union with Christ, our high priest (10,19-39)

Announcement of the subject of Part Four: 10,36-39

Part Four: Union with Christ high priest through faith and endurance (11,1-12,13)

1st section: Eulogy of the faith of ancestors (11,1-40)

Achievements and trials of faith in the Old Testament

2nd section: Call to imitate Christ in his passion and practising endurance in trials (12,1-13)

Announcement of the subject of Part Five: 12,13

Part Five: Call for upright conduct in the search for holiness and peace (12,14-13,18)

Search for holiness (12,14-29) and Christian solidarity (13,1-18)

Final invocation and doxology: Invocation for divine assistance through the mediation of Jesus Christ (13,20-21a), doxology (13,21b)

Dispatch note (13,19.22-25): Exhortation, news, greetings.

This plan offers more than one remarkable feature. It is closely linked to biblical rhetoric, for it is built in a concentric way. By their length and the number of their sections, four parts are arranged symmetrically around the third part, which is central. The first and the last parts are short and the announcement of their subject is simple, without any distinction of different aspects: the «Name» inherited by Christ (1,4), on the one hand, the «straight paths» for the conduct of Christians (12,13), on the other. These two parts have an identical layout: two more extensive paragraphs (1,5-14 and 2,5-18; 12,14-29 and 13,7-18) are on either side of a much shorter paragraph in them (2,1-4; 13,1-6).

The second and the last part but one are clearly longer. The announcement of their subject distinguishes two aspects of their theme: the «merciful and trustworthy high priest» (2,17), on the one hand, «endurance» and «faith» (10,36.38-39), on the other. In conformity with these announcements, each of these two parts is divided into two sections; the order of development there is the reverse of that in the announcement: first, «trustworthy high priest» (3,1-6) and then «merciful high priest» (4,15-5,10); first, the «faith» of the ancestors (11,1-40) and then «the endurance» of the Christians (12,1-13). The links between these two parts are particularly close because they are both composed of a long section (33 verses; 40 verses) followed by a short section (12 verses; 13 verses) and the subjects of these sections correspond: faith in the first sections and, the attitude in the face of suffering in the second sections.

With its 132 verses, the central part is the longest of all. It is almost five times longer than the first part and three times longer than the second. It is alone in containing five sections (two sections of exhortation and three of doctrinal exposition). Even without making a precise study of the composition of the homily, one can easily see that the three sections of doctrinal exposition constitute, in the middle of the homily, a block that is clearly marked out by the exhortation sections framing them. This homogeneous block of 87 verses is preceded by 101 verses and followed by 110 verses, two groups which, on the contrary, offer a very diversified structure, in which exhortation passages alternate with doctrinal exposés.

It is clear that the author wanted above all to pass on a substantial lesson in priestly Christology to his listeners. But he passes this teaching on in a pastoral and not professorial way. He takes care first to nourish their faith; he is also careful to call upon them to live generously in accordance with the gift of God received in faith.

Chapter 2

Exordium (1,1-4)

An itinerant preacher has arrived. He takes part in the meeting of the Christian community which consists of prayers, reading of some biblical texts, a homily and, probably, the celebration of «the Lord's supper» (see 1Cor 11,20). The itinerant preacher is invited to deliver the homily.

A. *COMPOSITION*

+ 1,1	On many occasions and in many ways in the past,			
–	God	*spoke*	to the Fathers	in the prophets;
+ 2	in this last period,			
–	he has	*spoken*	to us	in a Son,
:	*whom* he has established as HEIR			of all things,
:	he *through whom* he had made the ages,			

: 3	and *who*, being splendour of his glory and expression of his being
:	and bearing the universe by the word of his power,
=	having achieved purification of sins,
-	sat at the right hand of the Majesty in the heights,
= 4	having become as superior to the angels
-	as the name he has INHERITED is more different from them.

This exordium is a masterpiece. Grammatically, it consists of just one Greek sentence. Its English translation is not altogether faithful; the first verb which, in Greek, is a participle meaning «having spoken», is there rendered with an indicative «spoke», to lighten the sentence.

While being very harmonious, the style is yet more Hebrew than Greek, for it is strongly marked by parallelism, so that one can divide this text into six distichs which form two groups of three (1ab, 2ab, 2cd; 3ab, 3cd, 4ab).

In the first group of three, «God» is the subject of all the verbs («having spoken», «spoke», «established», «had made»).

In the second group of three distichs, the «Son», represented by the relative «who», is the subject of all the verbs («being», «bearing», «having achieved», «sat», «having become», «inherited»).

The two groups are cleverly joined by means of the succession of three relative clauses which are all related to the «Son» but in differentiated ways; in the two first, which belong to the first group, the relative—and therefore the «Son»—

is not the subject; it is the direct object, «whom», then it is used to express the means, «through whom»; in the third clause, on the other hand, corresponding to the second group, the relative «who» is the subject.

Hence it follows that by taking different points of view one can divide this exordium in two different ways: the first, as we have said, based on the subject of the verbs distinguishes two groups of three distichs (1-2 and 3-4); the second, based on the series of the three relatives qualifying the «Son» (2c-4), distinguishes a set of two distichs ending with the word «Son» (1-2b), and a set of four which takes up the rest of the sentence (2c-4).

The succession of the three relative clauses —the two first (2c.2d) being short; the third (3-4), very spread out, produces a powerful rhetorical thrust which ends with the proclamation of the «Name» (4b), the last word in the Greek sentence. That ends by saying: «he has inherited a NAME»; the Greek words produce an alliteration, «*keklēr-onomē-ken*, onoma», which contributes to emphasizing the importance of the «Name».

In the first distich (1ab) there is no parallelism, strictly speaking, but only a binary arrangement of two complementary members:

> On many occasions and in various ways in the past, God,
> having spoken to the Fathers in the prophets,

It is the same in the second distich (2ab):

> in this last period,
> has spoken to us in a Son,

But between these two distichs there is parallelism: 2a corresponds to 1a; 2b corresponds to 1b. In 2a, the parallelism with 1a is incomplete; in meaning, the expression «in this last period» corresponds in a merely antithetic fashion to «formerly»; but, being much longer than that word, it corresponds, as regards rhythm, to the whole of the stich 1a. In 2b, on the other hand, correspondence in content is perfect: after the action, which is the same («having spoken», «has spoken»), the addressees («to the Fathers», «to us») and the intermediaries («in the prophets», «in a Son») are named.

In the third distich (2cd) the parallelism is one of complementarity, between two of God's actions which are both in relation to the Son and the universe; the most recent action is given first (he has established him «heir of all things»); the thought then goes back to the initial action (through him «he had made the ages»). To the complementarity is added a note of antithesis between the initial aspect (2d) and the final one (2c).

In the fourth distich (3ab) we first notice a complementary parallelism, inside the first stich, between the two expressions that define the Son's essence in relation to God («splendour of his glory» and «expression of his being»). We then observe another complementary parallelism between the two stichs: the first, as we have said, expresses the relationship of the Son with God; the second, his relationship with the world («bearing the universe by the word of his power»). This second stich, furthermore, is in a relation of complementarity with the second stich of the preceding distich (2b); both put the Son in relation to the world, one (2d) in the act of creation in the past, the other (3b) in the present act of providing support for the world. As these two stichs come on both sides of the definition of the Son's being, it follows that that definition occupies a central position. This is not surprising, for it in fact constitutes a high point in the New Testament revelation.

Once again a complementary parallelism characterizes the fifth distich (3cd). This expresses the two aspects of the paschal mystery of Christ: his victory over evil («having achieved the purification of sins») and his glorification («he sat at the right hand of the Majesty in the heights»).

The sixth and last distich (4a) develops the theme of glorification. From the grammatical and stylistic point of view it is more complex than the previous ones, because it contains a comparative clause of proportionality («*as* superior [...] *as* quite different»), which is very rare in the Bible[1].

Between the last distich and the two first ones a certain relation of similarity is observable: the two first distichs suggest, without expressing it explicitly, a comparison between the «Son» and «the prophets» which leads to recognizing the Son's superiority as mediator of the Word of God; the last distich explicitly compares the Son to the angels, to state very clearly the superiority of the Son.

1 In the Septuagint only three similar cases are met with: Tob 2,10s; Sir 3,18; 4 Macc 15,5; in the New Testament, only one other case: Heb 10,25.

B. *BIBLICAL CONTEXT*

The text of the exordium does not contain any quotation from the Old Testament, but it is replete with allusions to the Old Testament. The first distich resumes the whole history of the Word of God in the Old Testament. It is more closely in relation to texts in Jeremiah in which God says and repeats: «Since their *Fathers* came out of the land of Egypt until today I have not ceased to send them *all my servants the prophets*, every day, unremittingly» (Jer 7,25; see 25,4; 26,5; 35,15; 44,4). To interpret correctly the parallelism established in the sentence between the first mediators of the Word of God and the last —«the prophets» and «the Son»— we have to remember Jeremiah's expression which gives the prophets the status of «servants». The suggested parallelism is therefore between «servants» and a «Son».

The expression «in the last [period] of days» (Heb 1,2a) comes from the Septuagint, which has brought out the «eschatological» bearing of several Old Testament texts. In Greek the expression contains the adjective *eschaton*, «last»; see Num 24,14: oracle of Balaam on the sceptre to arise from Israel; Ezek 38,6: struggle against Gog; Mic 4,1: extraordinary grandeur of Zion; Dan 2,28.45: the definitive kingdom; Dan 10,14: the events of the end. By adding «these» the author states that the coming of the «Son» has marked the beginning of eschatological times (see Heb 9,26; 1Cor 10,11).

The word «Son» (Heb 1,2b) is an early allusion to the oracle of the prophet Nathan (2Sam 7,4-17; 1Chr 17,3-15), in which God announced that a son of David would at the same time be a son for himself (2Sam 7,14; 1Chr 17,13). This subject is taken up in Ps 2,7. Immediately after the exordium, the author quotes Ps 2,7 and the oracle of Nathan.

The word «heir» (Heb 1,2c) continues the allusion to the son of David—Son of God, because Ps 2,8 ascribes «the nations as inheritance» and «as domain the ends of the earth» to him. The theme of heir and inheritance makes its first appearance in the Bible in Gen 15,4,7, promises made by God to Abraham.

The allusion to creation (Heb 1,2d) takes up the Greek verb in Gen 1,1 (*epoiēsen*: «he made»), but makes a change in the direct object: «the ages», instead of «heaven and earth».

In the Bible, the word «splendour» (Heb 1,3a) is only found here and in Wis 7,26, where it is applied to Wisdom, «splendour of eternal light».

The expression «purification of sins» (Heb 1,3c) is very rare in the Old Testament; it is met with only in Job 7,21; but equivalent expressions are used in

Leviticus concerning the great Atonement (Lev 16,30) and in Ezekiel for a promise made by God (Ezek 36,25.33).

The main statement: «he sat at the right hand of the Majesty» (Heb 1,3d) is an evident allusion to the oracle in Ps 109(110),1 where God invites the king of «Zion» (verse 2) to sit on his right. This oracle will be quoted in Heb 1,13 and recalled in Heb 8,1; 10,12 and 12,2. It prepares for the application to Christ of the second oracle contained in verse 4 of the same psalm (Heb 5,6.10; 6,20; 7,11-28), an oracle of fundamental importance for the subject which the author is getting ready to deal with, for it constitutes the scriptural basis of the doctrine of the priesthood of Christ.

C. *INTERPRETATION*

The preacher begins his homily with an overall reminder of God's plan. The first words —in Greek two adverbs linked by a conjunction— give an impression of abundance and recall God's generosity. This beginning is in conformity with the usage of Greek rhetoric. Greek orators readily started their speeches with the word «many»[2]. But biblical rhetoric at the same time shows itself with a parallelism between «on many occasions» and «in diverse ways». The notion of multiplicity can be ambivalent. To the many opinions of orators who had preceded him, the Greek orator opposed his own opinion, which was superior to theirs. Later on our preacher will express similar opposition between the ineffective multiplicity of the priests and sacrifices of the Old Testament and the efficacious unicity of the priesthood and sacrifice of Christ (Heb 7,23-24; 10,11-12). He does not express that opposition here, his sentence points out only a succession: God had spoken earlier, he has spoken again. But a nuance of superiority comes through in the parallelism between the solemn «in this last period» and the simple «earlier», as well as between the «Son» and «the prophets». The rest of the sentence shows to what extent the «Son» is superior to the prophets.

God's interventions in human history are presented as interventions in words. That perspective corresponds well with biblical revelation. The God of the Bible is a God who speaks to mankind, who enters into communion with them and who has frequent contact with them. This fact is astonishing. When one thinks of the greatness, the power and the holiness of God and one consid-

2 For example Isocrates' Areopagiticus speech and Demosthenes' Philippics. In the New Testament similar beginnings are found in Luke's writings: speech by a lawyer in Acts 24,2, response by Paul the apostle in Acts 24,10; see also the prologue to his gospel, Luke 1,1.

ers on the other hand the pettiness, weakness and moral misery of human beings, one can only be surprised at seeing God putting himself into personal contact with them. The surprise increases even more when it is seen that God's plan is to set up a stable relationship, a covenant, with those fragile creatures and to bring them into close communion with him. By saying that «God spoke» to the Fathers then «to us», the author is preparing the subject of the covenant.

Being a plan for personal relationships, God's design is not achieved by means of a speech impersonally addressed to the whole of humanity, but by means of words addressed to chosen people, at precise times, through mediators of the Word. The author cannot enter into details. He restricts himself to a distinction between two periods, characterized by two different categories of addressees and two kinds of mediators. The first period belongs to the past; it is the period of the Fathers and the prophets. It begins with Moses, a prophet without equal (see Deut 34,10; Hos 12,14), and extends over all the subsequent centuries until the time of Malachi. «The Fathers» are therefore the Israelite generations of those times.

The author uses an unusual expression for the mediation of the prophets, as later for that of the Son: God has «spoken *in* the prophets»[3]. This expression suggests the active presence of God himself in his messengers and thus makes the relationship between God and the hearers of the prophets closer.

The second period in which God spoke is qualified, without a shadow of hesitation, as eschatological and at the same time present. The author's calm assurance is impressive. It shows full awareness of the decisive and definitive importance of the coming of the «Son». A new era has begun and is the last. The word «Son» is not preceded by the definitive article. This absence does not mean that it is a question of a son among others. The context shows that it wants to draw attention to the idea of sonship and to arouse a desire for clarifications. In fact, those clarifications are given immediately. They fill up all the rest of the sentence.

The first clarification given does not direct minds towards the idea of exclusively divine sonship, for it speaks of an accomplishment in history. The Son is someone whom God «*has established as heir of all things*» (Heb 1,2c). The theme of the universal inheritance is in full agreement with the notion of eschatological period. According to Psalm 2, the universal inheritance was promised by

3 It is normally said that God has spoken «through» the prophets (Hebrew *b^e^yad*, Greek *dia*). «In» is found in 1Sam 28,6; 2S 23,2.

God to the king whom he consecrated «on Zion, his holy mountain» (6), that is to say a son and successor of David. God tells him: «Ask and I shall give you the nations as inheritance; as domain, the ends of the earth» (8). This son of David is at the same time Son of God; God himself tells him so: «You are my son; I, today, begot you» (7). We shall come across this text again later on in Heb 1,5, and then examine it more closely. The oracle in Ps 2 does not say «heir *of everything*». This last word is connected to Ps 8 which describes the calling of the «son of man» to rule over «all». This psalm will be quoted and applied to Christ in Heb 2,6-10. It opens up the perspective by moving from the son of David to the son of Adam.

A second clarification carries the hearers of the homily from point omega of the inheritance to point alpha of the creation of the world. The «Son» is the one «*through whom*» God «*made the ages*», literally «eons» (Heb 1,2d). To speak about creation, the author uses a mysterious term of which the primary sense is temporal, designating a time to which there are no foreseeable limits; here, as in other texts, the word designates at the same time all the realities contained in that time. The plural recalls the immensity and complexity of creation. The «Son» is the mediator of creation (see John 1,3; 1Cor 8,6; Col 1,16); he is not therefore just simply a son and successor to David adopted by God. He existed long before David, even before the creation of the world (see John 1,1-2; 17,5.24). The way in which the author conceives this mediation will be clarified later on, in Heb 1,10.

From the role of the Son in the creation of the world, the author rises up to a contemplation of the very being of the Son, whom he defines through his relation to God. The Son is «*splendour of his glory and expression of his* being (literally: imprint of his substance)». As regards the first expression, the author apparently gets the idea from the description of Wisdom in the Book of Wisdom. The latter is called «very pure emanation of the *glory* of the Almighty, [...] *splendour* of eternal light» (Wis 7,25-26). Rather than «emanation», the author chose «splendour», which is less material; rather than «light», he chose «glory», a more divine term. Then, instead of saying «image of his bounty», like Wis 7,26, he said «imprint of his substance». The «image» takes shape at a distance and may not be faithful; the «imprint» is obtained and reproduces all the traits exactly in relief by direct contact. «Bounty» is a virtue among so many others, the «substance», a philosophical term, designates the whole being in its deepest reality. The author has thus expressed the closest possible relationship uniting the Son to God.

He then goes down to the relationship of the Son with the world, not now at the moment of creation as in 1,2d, but throughout the existence of the universe. Of Wisdom it is written that she «extends from one end of the world to the other with strength and she governs the universe with goodness» (Wis 8,1). Of the Son the author says even more: he is the one «who bears the universe» and that, not with an extreme effort, like Atlas the hero in Greek mythology, but simply by the power of his word. This power is evidently divine. It corresponds to the creative power of the word of God: «He speaks, this is; he commands, this exists» (Ps 33,9; see Gen 1,3.6.9 etc.).

In 1,3c the sentence no longer uses the present as in the previous distich (1,3ab), but expresses itself in the past to recall events of capital importance: the work of the Son and his glorification in the sight of God. The author does not make it clear that, to achieve that work, the Son took on a nature of flesh and blood. He will say so later on in 2,14. He likewise omits any allusion to the humiliating and painful aspects of the Easter mystery. He does not say that the Son suffered and died for our sins. He stays in the positive register, which is proper in an exordium, and says that the Son «carried out a purification of sins». This general formula, unique in the whole Bible[4], discreetly prepares the theme of worship and sacrifice, for the vocabulary of purity is used very much in ritual laws; they are found particularly at the conclusion to the liturgy of Kippur (Lev 16,30) which the author will place in parallel with the sacrifice of Christ (Heb 9,7-12.25), as well as in an important oracle in Ezekiel (Ezek 36,25) to which the author will allude when speaking of ablutions «of pure water» (Heb 10,22).

The glorification of the Son is expressed as installation at the right hand of God: «he sat at the right hand of the Majesty in the heights» (1,3d). An allusion to Ps 109(110),1 often applied to Christ in the New Testament is easily recognizable. The detail «in the heights» excludes any earthly interpretation of the utterance in the psalm. It is not on an earthly throne that the Son went to sit, but in heaven. In his reply to the high priest at the time of his trial before the Sanhedrin, Jesus announces a heavenly fulfilment of the oracle («on the clouds of heaven»: Matt 26,64), which calls forth the accusation of blasphemy (Matt 26,65). The glorification of the Son is on God's level.

4 With «my sin» in the singular, it is found once in the Greek translation of Job 7,21: «Why *have you not caused* oblivion of my iniquity and *purification of my sin*?».

The last distich (1,4ab) insists on this point by stating that the glorified Son has «become superior to the angels». The word «become» lets it be understood that, when he «carried out the purification of sins» the Son was paradoxically in a position of inferiority in comparison to the angels. But that is not said. It will be said further on, in 2,9. The exordium cannot explain everything. Besides, it is not necessary for the listeners to the homily. They know very well what the preacher wants to talk about.

The new superiority of the Son over the angels is made manifest by the ascription to him of a «Name». This word, as we have already noted, is made to stand out noticeably by its final place in the Greek sentence and because it is announced at the beginning of the clause by an emphatic qualification: «very different». It could be translated: «more excellent», a possible meaning for the Greek comparative *diaphorōteron*, but it is good to keep the idea of difference, for the author is going to show that the Name of the glorified Son has an aspect of difference to it. A connotation of excellence is by no means excluded, quite the contrary, it is suggested. From the point of view of rhetoric, «very different» has the advantage of arousing the curiosity of the listeners. They are waiting for explanations of this very different Name. They can understand that by ending his exordium in this way the author has just announced the subject of the first part of his homily (Heb 1,5-2,18). This will explain which Name the Son has received as inheritance. The name defines the person's dignity as well as his relational capacities. The first part will define the dignity obtained by the Son after the cleansing from sin and will show what relational capacities he has acquired.

Part One

The «Name» of Christ: general Christology (1,5-2,18)

Chapter 3

The divine Name of Christ (1,5-14)

In its first paragraph (Heb 1,5-14), the first part of the sermon expounds a first aspect of the «Name» inherited by Christ at the end of his paschal mystery, the really divine aspect and hence «very different» from the position of the angels with respect to superiority.

A. *COMPOSITION*

This paragraph is composed of three subdivisions. The first (Heb 1,5-6) and the last (Heb 1,13-14) are short; they frame the central subdivision (Heb 1,7-12), much longer. Each subdivision expresses a contrast between the Son and the angels, based on the words of the Old Testament.

First contrast

1,5 TO WHOM, indeed, did he EVER SAY among THE ANGELS;
«You are my **SON**,
I this day *have begotten you*?» (Ps 2,7)
And again:
«*I shall be a father for him*
And he will be for me a **SON**?» (2Sam 7,14; 1Chr 17,13)
1,6 Yet, when he introduced the First-born
into the inhabited world, he says:
«And let all THE ANGELS of God worship him!» (Deut 32,43).

Second contrast

1,7 And concerning THE ANGELS he says:
«He who makes of HIS ANGELS ***SPIRITS***
And of his ***SERVANTS*** a flame of fire». (Ps 103,4)
1,8 But addressing the Son:
«Your throne, O God, [is] for ever and ever!»
And: «The sceptre of righteousness [is] sceptre of your kingdom.
1,9 You loved Justice and hated Iniquity,
That is why on you God, your God, has bestowed anointing
With an oil of gladness rather than on your companions». (Ps 44,7-8)
1,10 And: «You, at the beginning, Lord, you founded the earth
And work of your hands are the heavens.

1,11 They will perish, but you, you remain
And all like a garment will be worn out
1,12 And like a cloak you will roll them up
Like a garment also they will be changed
But you are the same and your years will never end».
(Ps 101,26-28).

Third contrast

1,13 But TO WHICH of THE ANGELS did he EVER SAY:
«Sit at my right
Until I have placed your enemies
as footstool of your feet»? (Ps 109,1)
1,14 Are they not all ***SPIRIT-SERVANTS***,
sent to serve for the sake of those who are to inherit salvation?

Between the beginning of the first contrast (1,5a) and the beginning of the third (1,13a), one notices a close synonymous parallelism, embellished with some stylistic variations, especially in the order of words: «to whom/to which», «ever/ever», «said [aorist]/said [perfect]», «of the angels/of the angels».

This parallelism fulfils the function of a general inclusion: while waiting for the rhetorical question in 1,13a, similar to the one at the beginning (1,5a), the listeners can understand that the speaker is thus introducing the last element in his demonstration.

An inclusion marks the boundaries of the first contrast (1,5-6) with the word «angels». Another inclusion, with the words «spirits» and «servants», brings together the second and third contrasts (1,7-12 and 1,7-14); for «servants» the Greek terms are slightly different: a noun in 1,7c, the corresponding adjective in 1,14a.

In 1,5 the two quotations about the Son are arranged so as to form an inclusion by means of the word «son» (1,5b and 1,5e) and an arrangement in chiastic form (Son—to beget: father—Son).

In 1,5 and 1,13 the texts quoted concern the Son, but are introduced by a rhetorical question about the angels: the suggested answer is obviously negative: God has never said anything like that to an angel.

The general arrangement is as follows:

Question about the angels (1,5a)
quotations about the Son (1,5b-c)
glorification of the Son (1,6a)
quotation about the angels (1,6b)

Quotation about the angels (1,7a-c)
long quotations about the Son (1,8a-12c)

Question about the angels (1,13-a)
quotation about the Son (1,13b-d)
question about the angels with return to the quotation in 1,7b-c (1,14a)
transition by mentioning the heirs of salvation (1,14b).

Most of the texts quoted show parallelisms of various kinds:

1. *Synonymous parallelism, similar arrangement:*

Son of mine you are,
I begot you this day (1,5de).

He who makes spirits of his angels
And a flame of fire of his servants (1,7bc).

The sceptre of righteousness
sceptre of your kingdom (1,8c).

And all like a garment will grow old
Like a garment also they will be changed (1,11b.12b).

2. *Antithetic parallelism, similar arrangement:*

You loved Justice
and you hated Iniquity (1,9a)

They will perish,
but you, you remain (1,11a)

3. *Complementary parallelism, similar arrangement:*

I shall be a father for him
And he will be a son for me (1,5de).

4. *Complementary parallelism, chiastic arrangement:*

You founded the earth
And works of your hands are the heavens (1,10ab).

5. System in concentric symmetry:

(A) They will perish
(B) but you remain
(C) And all like a garment will grow old
(D) And you will roll them all up like a cloak
(C') Like a garment they also will be changed
(B') But you are the same
(A') and your years will never end (1,11a-12c).

The correspondence is antithetic between (A) and (A'), synonymous between (B) and (B') and between (C) and (C'). A regular alternation between the 3rd persons plural and the 2nd persons singular: they (3rd)—you (2nd)—all (3rd)—you (2nd)—they (3rd)—you (2nd)—the years (3rd). The central element (D) is the most important because it is the only one to express an action by the Son on the heavens and earth: «you will roll them up»; the verb there is in the second person; it has an object in the 3rd. The heavens and the earth are absent from the final element (A'); they are replaced there by a reference to the Son: «your years» (literally: «the years of you»); the third person there is subject, the second is object.

To obtain this symmetry the author adds an expression to the text of the psalm: he repeats «like a garment» at the beginning of (C').

B. *BIBLICAL CONTEXT AND INTERPRETATION*

In this paragraph, one can separate interpretation and biblical context, for the author is content to quote texts without commenting on them. He obviously reads them in the new historical context resulting from the coming of Christ, the context of the paschal mystery which he has just recalled at the end of his exordium (1,3).

Let us first notice a rhetorical peculiarity of the text: to introduce his Scripture quotations, the author never says: «it is written», which the other New Testament authors do; he uses the verb «to say» which gives more direct contact with the texts and harmonizes better with oral preaching[1]. The subject of the verb is hardly ever expressed; it has to be supplied from the text quoted.

1. First contrast (1,5-6)

The rhetorical question in verse 5 is directly attached by an «indeed» to the statement in the preceding verse. The response it elicits must therefore prove that the Son has indeed inherited a name «very different» from that of the angels (see 1,4). With this question the preacher arouses the co-operation of his listeners. To be able to answer it they must be capable of identifying the two texts quoted, that is to say, of discerning which writings they are drawn from, who the person is that utters them, the person to whom they are applied and, moreover, they have to verify that such declarations were never addressed to any angel. All this supposes that the listeners have a good knowledge of the biblical foundations of Christian catechesis.

To tell the truth, the two texts quoted are not difficult to identify. The first (1,5bc) comes from a royal psalm, Ps 2, understood at the time in a Messianic sense and applied to Jesus by the Christian community (see Acts 4,25-28; 13,33); the second comes from the divine oracle transmitted by Nathan to king David (2Sam 7,5-17; 1Chr 17,3-15), an oracle which is at the source of the whole Messianic current. Both for Ps 2 as for the oracle of Nathan, the biblical context states clearly that the person speaking is God himself, the «Lord» (Ps 2,7; 2Sam 7,4-5.8; 1Chr 17,3-4.7). The problem is more complex in the case of the person to whom these oracles apply. Nathan's oracle promised David a «royal» house (2Sam, 11.16), that is to say a dynasty that would continue to reign after him. Ps 2 contains the word «Messiah» in Hebrew, «Christ» in Greek (Ps 2,2) but originally that word was taken in the sense of an anointing received by the king at the time of his consecration (see Ps2,6). These texts were however open to a Messianic interpretation, for they spoke of a son of David whose royal throne would be strengthened for ever (2Sam 7,13). The expectation of an ideal king, a Messiah-king, arose

1 The expression «it is wrìtten» is found once in Heb 10,7, but it is within a text being quoted (Ps 39,9).

gradually. This comes home to us when we compare the first redaction of the oracle (2Sam 7) with the one given very much later in the First Book of Chronicles. In 2Sam 7,14 the oracle foresees that the son and successor of David will perhaps commit faults; the passage is omitted in the text at 1Chr 17,13; the ideal king, the Messiah-king, will not commit any fault. Moreover, whereas in 2Sam 7,16 the conclusion to the oracle promises stability to the house of David and his kingship, which normally means a dynastic succession, in 1Chr 17,14 it is to the son of David that God promises stability, saying: «I shall maintain *him* for ever in *my* house and in *my* kingdom for ever and his throne shall be strengthened for ever». In Luke's gospel, the story of the Annunciation states the coming fulfilment of this promise. A speech by Paul in the Acts of the Apostles applies the oracle in Ps 2,7 to the risen Jesus (Acts 13,33).

The listeners to our text (Heb 1,5) could therefore immediately recognize the origin of the texts quoted (Ps 2,7 and 1Chr 17,13), and understand by whom they were uttered—by God himself— and to whom they were applied—to the risen Christ. They could also give the preacher the answer he was waiting for: «Never did God speak like that to an angel»; in fact, the Bible does not record any similar oracle addressed to an angel. In the Bible it does happen that the angels are called «sons of God» in the plural (Job 1,6; 2,1), but in that expression the word «sons» has not got its full meaning; as often in Hebrew, it simply expresses belonging to a certain category, here the category of heavenly beings. It should be noted in this connection that the preacher's question does not concern this category as a whole. It is more precise. It asks whether, among the angels, there can be found *one* to whom God has spoken personally to recognize him as his son, begotten by him. The answer is in the negative: not one can be found. There is therefore a contrast between the name of the Son and that of the angels; the relation of the Son to God is much more intimate than that of the angels.

This negative response is not expressed, which agrees with the law of the genre; a rhetorical question suggests an answer but the speaker does not formulate it, leaving that to the listeners. The speaker, however, must confirm the answer he has suggested. This is what our preacher does in verse 6, which is not interrogative now but affirmative and explains a relation of complete subordination of the angels with regard to the Son at the time of the Son's introduction to «the inhabited world». A new title is ascribed to the Son, that of «First-born», an allusion to Ps 88(89), which takes up Nathan's oracle. The psalmist there paraphrases the announcement of the divine sonship promised to the son of David;

the promise in the oracle «I shall be a father for him and he will be a son for me» (Heb 1,5; 1Chr 17,13) in the psalm becomes:

> He will call upon me: You are my Father,
> My God and the one who cares for my salvation!
> And I shall establish him as First-born,
> The Most High over the kings of the earth (Ps 88,28-29).

Divine sonship is thus presented from the point of view of its sharing in God's power.

In relation to Nathan's oracle, the psalm has originality in that it applies the promise of divine sonship to David himself and not to «his sons» (Ps 88,31). The perspective is similar to the one in Ezekiel in which God promises his sheep that David will be their shepherd (Ezek 34,23-24). The Messianic interpretation of these texts can hardly be more natural and, for Christians, it became Christological: the new David was the risen Christ. That is the meaning adopted by our preacher.

In speaking of the introduction of the First-born into the inhabited world, he is not in fact referring to the incarnation but to the resurrection and glorification of Christ. In fact he explains a little further on that by «inhabited world» he means the eschatological world (Heb 2,5), that is to say the new creation inaugurated by the resurrection of Christ. The Greek term he uses is not *kosmos*, as in Heb 10,5, but *oikoumenē*, a term open to an eschatological interpretation. A psalm actually says: «the Lord has begun to rule, he has set up the *oikoumenē*, which will not be shaken» (Ps 95,10 see 92,1).

When the Son is glorified as «First-born», «the Most High over the kings of the earth», the angels receive the order to prostrate themselves before him or even to adore him, for the Greek verb used often has that meaning. The preacher here quotes a sentence from the canticle of Moses (Deut 32) in its Greek translation, a sentence that does not feature in our editions of the Hebrew Bible but was found in a Hebrew fragment at Qumran:

> «And let the angels of God prostrate themselves before him» (Deut 32,43 Septuagint).

In the text at Heb 1,6, the pronoun «him» («before him») refers to the «First-born». It is an innovative interpretation which is not without a certain audacity, for the context of the canticle did not suggest a distinction between two persons; it is before God that the angels of God must prostrate themselves. The wording chosen, however, made the distinction possible and our author does not hesitate to make it. Applying to Christ a text that refers to God, he calmly shows his faith in the divinity of Christ. This faith, expressed as early as the exordium (see Heb 1,3a), will be reaffirmed in the verses following (1,8-10). What provides the author with the opportunity to claim adoration by the angels, of which the canticle of Moses speaks, for the risen Christ is the aspect of eschatological judgment which is expressed in the context (Deut 32,40-43). In it God announces his decisive intervention: «I shall take judgment into my hands» (Deut 32,41). Christians know that judgment has been entrusted to Christ by God (see Acts 10,42; 17,31; John 5,22.27; 2Tim 4,1). In consequence, Christ has the right to the adoration of the angels. The contrast between the position of Christ and that of the angels is thus expressed extremely forcefully.

2. Second contrast (1,7-12)

In the second contrast, the superiority of the Son to the angels is not shown only by the content of statements concerning them. It also appears structurally in the difference in length of the texts quoted: only two lines for the angels, twelve for the Son.

The noun for the angels serves as a link-word to provide the transition from the end of the first contrast (1,6) and the beginning of the second, where it is repeated twice (1,7ab). Here the contrast bears upon stability and authority. The angels are dependent and malleable beings, while the Son possesses supreme authority and immutability.

To define the nature of the angels, the preacher uses a distich from a psalm of creation which sings the glory of the Creator and his power over all creatures. This distich (Ps 103,4) can be understood in different ways because the terms used have several possible meanings and the grammatical construction is ambivalent. In Greek as in Hebrew one and the same word means «messenger» or «angel» and another word «breath» or «spirit». It can therefore be understood that God uses winds as messengers or that he makes spirits of his angels. The difference seems enormous, but it is fitting to note that the ancient mentality did not make the clear distinctions that were imposed later on. What we call meteorological phenomena were considered manifestations of angelic powers. It is clear that our author takes the Greek word *aggelos* in the sense of «angel»; in that he is following the Jewish tradition which saw in this text a statement about the way in which God used his angels, giving them various forms in keeping with the circumstances. The short commentary on the distich a little further on (Heb 1,14: «they are servant-spirits sent to serve») shows that the author has been especially attentive to the parallelism between «angels» and «servants» Angels do not have a place of authority but of service. The Son, quite to the contrary, has a position of sovereign authority.

To define this position, the preacher uses several verses from two psalms in the Septuagint translation: Ps 44,7-8 and Ps 101,26-28. Ps 44 is not Messianic. It is a royal epithalamium, a poem written for the king's wedding. But it lends itself to a Messianic reading because it idealizes the king, presenting him as «the most beautiful of the sons of men [...] blessed by God for ever» (Ps 44,3). The Targum of the psalter has such a reading, for it inserts the title of «Messiah-King» into this verse 3.

The first verse quoted in Heb 1,8 contains another title and is therefore suitable for defining an aspect of the Name of Christ. This title is «God»:

> Your throne, O God, [is] for ever and ever (Ps 44,7a).

This title corresponds entirely with the statement that is made: God alone possesses eternal power. Seated at the right hand of the divine Majesty in the heights (Heb 1,3), the Son is God with God.

Some translators and commentators hesitate to accept this interpretation. They think it unlikely that a royal psalm should ascribe the title of «God» to the king for, according to them, such an ascription is incompatible with biblical monotheism. They point out that the sentence, being elliptical, can be translated otherwise:

> Your Throne [is] God for ever and ever.

They opt for this translation, but the latter is untenable, for it presents God as a seat on which the king is sitting! No text in the Bible proposes this aberration. Besides, it is easy to answer objections raised against ascribing the title of «God» to the king. This title, in fact, is not reserved in the Bible for the only God; it is found applied to human beings in it (see Ps 81,6; Exod 4,16; 7,1). Its use in Ps 44 is hyperbolic, like the statement into which it is inserted: the king's throne is declared eternal, it is not really, but the style of the royal court required these exaggerations.

Applied to the risen Christ, the statement loses its hyperbolic character and becomes the expression of genuine reality, for the reign of Christ is not situated on the earthly level but on the fully divine one; it is no longer limited to the short span of a human life; Christ has victoriously overcome the obstacle of death and his renewed humanity henceforth shares in the divine eternity.

The rest of the quotation fills in some details about Christ's kingly power. In saying: «The sceptre of righteousness is sceptre of your kingdom» the preacher is not simply saying that Christ's kingly power is *a* just power, among others; he is stating that it is *the* just power, which suggests that it is the divine power, for the only perfectly just power is that of God. The Greek psalter says and repeats that God judges «with uprightness (*en euthytēti*)» (Ps 9,9; 66,5; 95,10; 97,9).

The next verse (1,9) recalls in veiled language the passion of Christ and, more clearly, his glorification. It does not speak of suffering and that omission here suits our author who wants to keep that feature for the second doctrinal paragraph (2,5-18). The psalm speaks of love of justice and hatred of iniquity. The nuance expressed by the Greek translation is that of something that happened in the past (aorist) which showed that love and hatred[2].

To Christ's generous action God replied by bestowing an anointing on him. The expression in the psalm is original: «he has anointed you with an oil of gladness». Some understand this as preparation for a feast: one perfumed oneself to go to a feast. But the verb chosen (Hebr. *māšah*; Greek *chriein*) is the one for the royal consecration (1Sam 10,1; 15,17; 2Sam 12,7; Ps 89,21). The note of gladness accompanying it means that the consecration of the king brings out the joy of the king himself and that of all his people. The Messianic, then the Christological, reading of the psalm finds strong support in the verbs chosen, for the word «Messiah» comes from the Hebrew verb and the word «Christ» from the Greek verb. The name of Christ appears explicitly at the beginning of the second part, in Heb 3,6; it often comes back; in all it comes twelve times in the sermon.

2 The form of the two verbs in Hebrew permits of several interpretations because they are verbs expressing feelings. In such a case the Hebrew perfect may express a state that lasts in an indeterminate present (many modern translators opt for this possibility and say: «You love justice…») or refer to past actions. The Septuagint chose this second solution, probably because it fits in better with the rest of the text which speaks of a very definite action of God: «your God gave you the anointing».

The divine anointing gives the glorified Son superiority over his «companions». In the original context of the psalm, the word is understood to refer to the other princes. Ps 89 speaks of a superiority of David over «the kings of the earth» (Ps 89,28). The context of the sermon leads to a heavenly interpretation and so to an application of the word «companions» to the angels. In the context, the expression in the psalm comes in relation to the last statement in the exordium, which affirms the superiority of the Son to the angels (1,4).

The next quotation expresses another aspect of the Name of the Son, for it bestows on him the title of «Lord» and explains the meaning of that title. What is surprising is that the author here applies the text of a psalm that speaks of God to the Son—that is to say in reality to the risen Christ. In Hebrew the first word of this psalm is the proper name of God, *Yhwh*, and this name is then repeated no less than seven times (Ps 102,2.13.16.17.20.22.23). The situation is very different in the Greek translation, for that replaces the sacred name with the title of *Kyrios*, «Lord». The result is that a Christological reading is possible. In fact, Jesus has been established «Christ and Lord» by God in his paschal glorification (Acts 2,28) and Christians have understood that the title of Lord is to be understood in the fullest sense, the properly divine sense. The Christological hymn in the Letter to the Philippians proclaims that Jesus Christ has a right, as Lord, to the homage that the only God keeps for himself (Phil 2,10-11; see Isa 46,22-23). In Ps 101,26-28, the author therefore sees a definition of the Lordship of the risen Christ. This is that much easier for him because a verse in the same psalm uses the Greek verb employed for saying «to raise up». Instead of translating: «You, having arisen, will have pity on Zion» (Ps 101,14), one can translate: «You, having been raised, will have pity on Zion».

The text is clearly divided into two parts. The first (Heb 1,10; Ps 101,26) recalls the creation of the world; the second (Heb 1,11-12; Ps 10,27-28) announces its disappearance. We have seen above that the arrangement of the text indicates this division. The two parts have the highlighting of the pronoun «you» in common; it is the very first word in the quotation (« *You*, at the beginning, Lord…») and it comes again in the second verse (in Greek «your hands» is given as «the hands of *you*»). A close relationship is thus expressed between the «Lord» and creatures. In other contexts this relationship is understood as an assurance of stability: «Yhwh reigns, he fixed the universe, unshakeable» (Ps 96,10; see 93,1). It comes as a surprise here to find the reverse perspective: the second part of the text announces the disappearance of heaven and earth and expresses a strong contrast between them and the Creator: «They shall perish, *but you*, you remain» (1,11). The pronoun «you» is thus once again given great prominence. It is given it again at the end: to the change that heaven and earth will undergo («like a garment they will be changed») are opposed the immutability and eternity of the Lord («*but you*, you are the same and your years will not come to an end»). The central verse of this concentric unit completes the picture by showing that the destiny of heaven and earth will be fixed by the Lord: «like a cloak you will roll them up».

It was certainly that eschatological statement that led the author to apply this passage of the psalm to Christ. The resurrection of Christ, as we have already said, was in fact understood as an intervention by God who made Christ the eschatological judge. Here the author, on this matter, takes up the first two statements that he made about the Son, the universal heir and mediator of creation (Heb 1,2bc). This time he puts them in their chronological order, speaking first about creation and then about the final transformation. Yet he does not confine himself to repeating what he said; he says more. In Heb 1,2c he presented the Son as the mediator of creation, «through whom» God made the ages». Here (1,10), he reveals in what sense this mediation must be understood. It is not a question of second rank, but of full participation in God's creative activity: the Son has been Creator with the Creator, as he is God with God. Nowhere in all the New Testament does one find such a strong statement of the role of the Son in the creation of the universe. Not even the prologue to the fourth gospel expresses itself with such clarity; it simply says that everything came into existence «through» the Word (John 1,3: in Greek *dia*); the same is true of the Christological hymn in the Letter to the Colossians (Col 1,16).

On the eschatological aspect of the position of the Son the sentence in verse 12a, too, presents a more forceful statement than the one in verse 2b. A transition is made from the position of universal heir (Heb 1,2b) to that of absolute master of heaven and earth who will put an end to the first creation and will make room for eschatological realities, that new «oikumene» (see 1,6; 2,5) into which his resurrection brought him. Nothing like this could of course be said about the angels.

3. Third contrast (1,13-14)

Introduced by an oratorical question parallel to the one in the first contrast (1,5a), the third contrast requires the same kind of co-operation from the hearers: they must recognize the provenance of the text quoted, identify who speaks in it and to whom it is addressed and, moreover, verify that nothing of that kind was ever said to an angel.

The text quoted is easily recognizable for it is a verse in a psalm very often used in early catechesis which applies it to the risen Jesus (Ps 109[110],1; see Matt 22,44 and parallels, 26,64 and parallels; Acts 2,34-35; Rom 8,34; 1Cor 15,25). The beginning of this verse shows who is speaking; «*Yhwh* said» (in Greek: «the *Lord* said») and to whom the speech is addressed: «to my Lord».

As in the case of Ps 2, quoted after the first rhetorical question (Heb 1,5bc), the quotation is drawn from a royal enthronement psalm which lent itself to a Messianic interpretation. The invitation to sit at God's right hand meant that the power of the king was a sharing in the power of God. The First Book of Chronicles says that Solomon was «chosen to sit on the throne of the kingship of Yhwh over Israel» (1Chr 28,5) or even that he «sat on the throne of Yhwh to rule in the place of David his father» (1Chr 29,23). Furthermore, it has been pointed out that in Jerusalem the royal palace was built to the right of the Temple so that one could say that the king sat at the right hand of God.

Earthly Messianism did not go beyond such representations but things were quite different when the words in the psalm are applied to the risen Christ. The latter in fact is no longer on the earthly level. He has gone to heaven to sit at the right hand of God. At the very beginning of his exordium the preacher reminded his listeners of this (Heb 1,3); he was to say it again in the middle of his sermon (Heb 8,1). Hence it follows that, in this new context, the oracle manifests all its transcendent potential and reveals the infinite superiority of the Son over the angels. None of the latter, in fact, have ever been invited to sit on God's heavenly throne. That is the answer suggested by the rhetorical question. It is confirmed by the examination of the texts. The listeners must know it: when angels are represented in the Bible as in the presence of God, they are not sitting but standing (see 1Kgs 22,19; Isa 6,1).

To conclude the contrast, the preacher this time does not quote any new text as he did for the first contrast (see Heb 1,6); he refers back to a text already quoted (Ps 103,4; Heb 1,7) by means of a new oratorical question which has its answer in this text:

> Are not they all spirit-servants
> sent to serve for the sake of those who are to inherit salvation? (1,14).

The question adds some further elements to the text being referred to: it fills out the notion of service (*diakonia*), contained in the other name given to the angels by the text being quoted (*leitourgous*, «servants»). Finally it explains who are the recipients of this service: «those who are to inherit salvation», that is to say the human persons called by God. This remark prepares the next paragraph, for that paragraph will concern those persons. The listeners know what the preacher means by the word «salvation». He is going to remind them of it further on: salvation is liberation from evil and all its consequences and, moreover, free access to the presence of God.

Thus ends this paragraph (Heb 1,5-14) which, by citing Scripture, has magnificently expressed the divine aspect of the Name of the risen Christ and thereby demonstrated his infinite superiority over the angels. Christ is the Son of God, the First-born, Creator of heaven and earth, eschatological Judge, Lord enthroned with God. None of that can be said of any angel.

Chapter 4

First exhortation (2,1-4)

Being prepared by the last words of the first paragraph, which spoke of «those who were to inherit salvation» (Heb 1,14), the second paragraph takes on a note of exhortation, but in the first person plural («we»: 2,1.3), whereby the preacher modestly places himself in the same category as his listeners.

The link with the preceding context is provided in several ways: 1) an initial «that is why» presents the exhortation as a logical consequence of the doctrine that has just been expounded; 2) the theme of «salvation», introduced by the last word in Heb 1,14, is taken up with emphasis («such a salvation») in Heb 2,3; 3) the title of «Lord» given to the «Son», that is to say to the risen Christ in Heb 1,10 and recalled in Heb 1,13 by the quotation from Ps 109(110),1 addressed to «my Lord», that title is taken up in Heb 2,3; 4) the comparison between Christ and the angels is continued in an *a fortiori* reasoning, based implicitly on the superiority of the «Lord» over the «angels».

A. *COMPOSITION*

2,1 That is why
– we must *adhere* much more
+ to the **message heard**
= so as not to GO ASTRAY.

2,2 + For **if** the **word announced** BY ANGELS went into force
– and **if** every ***transgression and disobedience*** received just retribution,
2,3 = HOW SHALL WE OURSELVES ESCAPE
– having ***neglected*** suchlike **salvation**,
+ which, **announced** in the beginning BY THE LORD,
+ was, by those who **had heard**, put into effect for us
2,4 also with the support of God's testimony
with signs and prodigies
and miracles of all kinds
and distributions of holy spirit
according to his will.

This short paragraph, written in a masterly fashion, lends itself to minute analyses[1]. It is composed of two sentences. The first (2,1) soberly expresses the need to adhere to the message. The second, five times longer, (2,2-4), shows this need with *a fortiori* reasoning given in the form of a rhetorical question that enlists the co-operation of the listeners. From the rhetorical point of view this second sentence is animated by a powerful inspiration, especially in its second part where the importance of «salvation» is stressed with three supports («the Lord», «those who had heard» and «God») the last of which is amplified into four members.

After the transitional «that is why», the first sentence (2,1) contains three elements: the necessary adhesion, the message heard, the danger to be avoided. These elements are taken up again in different ways in the second sentence.

In an antithetic way as regards adhesion, by opposing «transgression and disobedience» (2,2b) to it as well as negligence, with regard to salvation (2,3b).

The «message heard» is put into relation with «the word announced through angels» (2,2a), then with «salvation» (2,3b), which was also «announced» (2,3c) and «heard» (2,3d); the end of the sentence completes the perspective by adding the idea of witness and that of the means taken to witness (2,4).

The danger to be avoided is evoked first by the allusion to the «force» of the word (2,2a), then defined more clearly by the mention of «just retribution» that punishes faults (2,2b), and finally included in the terrifying idea that it would be hard to «escape» from it (2,3a).

In verse 2 a parallel symmetry of arrangement is to be noted between the two conditional clauses (subject, predicate, subject, predicate). But the relations of meaning are antithetic for the first members: to «the word announced by angels» there is opposed «every transgression and disobedience»; they are synonymous for the second members: «entered into force» is taken up and given precision by the mention of a «just retribution».

The two conditionals form the protasis of the period: they are followed by the apodosis which consists of a long rhetorical question («how shall we ourselves escape…?». The latter takes up the elements of the protasis in a concentric order. To the idea of «just retribution», punishment, that is to say (2,2b), there immediately corresponds the concern «to escape» from it (2,3a), which turns out not to be easy. This beginning of the rhetorical question is the strong

1 See AUFFRET P., «Note sur la structure littéraire d'Hb II.1-4».

point of the period, meant to impress the listeners terribly: how will they be able to escape?!

Next comes the mention of the fault committed: «to have neglected» (2,3b) is parallel to «every transgression and disobedience» (2,2b). The fault is not identical, for it is not related to any «word» that commands but with a «salvation» which is offered. One does not transgress an offer of salvation, one neglects it and by neglecting it one condemns oneself to not being saved.

Between «salvation» and the «word», the preacher establishes a parallelism, for he says that «salvation» has been «announced» as the «word» had been announced. But the parallelism brings out the difference there is between old Law and the situation in the New Covenant. On the one hand there are commandments to be observed and on the other there is salvation to be obtained.

The superiority of the new situation comes, besides, from the difference between the mediators: the Law was announced «by angels», salvation was announced at the beginning «by the Lord», of whom it was said that he is Creator and judge of the universe (1,10-12), whereas the angels are only servants (1,14).

A final parallelism provides the occasion to manifest another element of superiority: on both sides there has been an «entering into force» (2,2a; 2,3b), but in the case of «salvation» announced by the Lord, the entering into force is supported with an overwhelming testimony from God.

The detail of this testimony is described with lyricism: verse 4 is composed of five members, three of which are *isokōla*, i. e. of equal length (eight syllables), and they rhyme together, their last syllable being *-sin*; the two other members are of six syllables. Together they are arranged as follows:

10 - 8 - 8 - 10 - 8, which is harmonious:

synepimartyrountos tou Theou
*sēmeiois te kai tera**sin***
*kai poikilais dyname**sin***
kai pneumatos hagiou merismois
*kata tēn autou thelē**sin**.*

This ending has a triumphal ring, which greatly reduces the impression of fear provoked by the beginning of the proposition («how shall we ourselves escape…?»). It thus prepares the next exposé, which speaks of God's positive design.

B. *BIBLICAL CONTEXT*

This short exhortation does not contain any biblical quotation. By speaking of the «word announced by the angels», it alludes to the revelation on Sinai, but as such it comes in Jewish traditions and not in the Old Testament. The Hebrew Bible actually makes no mention of angels doing anything on Sinai. The Septuagint adds something new by speaking of the presence of angels coming therefrom: «The Lord has come from Sinai [...] on his right angels are with him» (Deut 33,2). Later on, angels will be ascribed the role of spokespersons of God for the promulgation of the commandments[2]. According to a rabbinic text, «two myriad of the best angels came down with God on Mount Sinai to give the Law to the people of Israel»[3].

This tradition is found again in two passages of the New Testament (Acts 7,53; Gal 3,19).

When he speaks of faults committed against the word and of the punishment of those faults, the preacher completely agrees with the Old Testament but he uses a different vocabulary: the Pentateuch in Greek never actually uses the word «transgression» (*parabasis*, found only four times in the Old Testament), nor the word «disobedience» (*parakoē*, completely absent), nor «retribution» (*misthapodosia*, completely absent). In the New Testament, «transgression» and «disobedience» are found in the Pauline Letters, while «retribution» is met with only in Hebrews (2,2; 10,35; 11,26); this word does not appear elsewhere in the whole of the Greek Bible, nor in the Greek authors in antiquity. This detail and many others show the author's originality.

In the main clause, the idea of «salvation» takes up a very frequent theme in the Bible, both in the Old and New Testament, but the verb «to neglect», extremely rare, is never joined to it. A passage from the first gospel may, however, provide a link-up: the people invited to the feast, «having neglected [the invitation], went away» (Matt 22,5).

The expression «signs and wonders» is often met with in the Old Testament, in particular in Deuteronomy to recall the miracles of the departure from Egypt[4]. It comes again in the New Testament, especially in the Acts of the Apostles, either to recall the miracles of Jesus (Acts 2,22), or to mention the miracles that accompanied the preaching of the Christian faith (Acts 2,43; 4,30; 5,12; 6,8; etc.).

2 See *Jubilees* 1,27; 2,1,26-27; JOSEPHUS, *Jewish Antiquities* 15,5,3; PHILO, *De somnis* I, 141-143.

3 *Pesiqtha Rabbathi*, 21 (103b), cited by STRACK-BILLERBECK, *Kommentar zum* N.T., III, 556.

4 See Deut 4,34; 6,22, etc.; Jer 32,20-21Ps 135,9; Neh 9,10.

In Acts 14,3 it is said, about the apostolate of Paul and Barnabas, that «the Lord bore witness to the word of his grace by granting signs and wonders to be done through them».

The apostle Paul himself speaks several times of the «signs and wonders» that confirmed his own preaching (see 15,19; 2Cor 12,12). To designate the miracles of Jesus the fourth gospel usually employs the word «signs» without adding «and wonders» (John 2,11.23; 3,2; etc.); this is also what the close of Mark does to announce the miracles that «will accompany the believers» (Mark 16,17-18).

The expression «distribution of holy spirit» is unique in the whole Bible. Without speaking of «distribution» the Old Testament announces that God «will give» his Spirit (Ezek 36,27) or will «pour» it out (Joel 3,1.2). The New Testament proclaims the realization of that promise (Acts 2,16-17.33). The Septuagint translation gets near the idea of distribution by saying that God will pour out «some of» his spirit (Joel 3,1.2). The apostle Paul, for his part, expresses this idea in other terms, when he explains that the gifts of the Holy Spirit are distributed in diverse ways (1Cor 12,4.7-11).

From all this it can be seen that the exhortation in Heb 2,1-4 is deeply rooted in the Old Testament and in the apostolic preaching, while expressing itself in an original way.

C. *INTERPRETATION*

The insertion of this short exhortation in the middle of the doctrinal exposé clearly shows the author's intention and the nature of his speech. The author's intention is pastoral; his speech belongs to the category of Christian preaching. Saying that the author's intention is pastoral does not mean that, for him, doctrinal exposés have only a secondary importance and that only exhortations really count. Christian preaching is in fact chiefly proclamation of God's work accomplished in the passion and resurrection of Jesus. The doctrinal aspect therefore comes first. It is what exhortation draws all its strength from. It is an urgent call to accept God's work effectively by being converted to faith in Christ and to a life based on faith. It follows that Christian preaching does not really correspond to any kind of ancient rhetoric. It is a new genre.

There is nothing aggressive about this exhortation. The preacher actually does not use the second person plural, but the first; he therefore addresses the exhortation to himself as well as his audience, thus showing a fraternal spirit. Later, he will take on a more direct tone (see 3,1.7-13). That progression is rhetorically astute.

The initial «That is why» ties the exhortation to everything said in the previous paragraph (1,5-14). It is because Christ is Son of God and Lord that we have to hold fast very seriously to the message heard (2,1). That message in fact comes from him (2,3). It therefore merits the greatest attention. It must not only be listened to but held fast to by conforming one's life to it. This is all the more necessary because the Lord has the power to fix the destiny of heaven and earth (1,10-12) and will therefore be our judge.

To designate the danger to which one would be exposed if one did not hold fast to the message heard, the preacher uses a verb which is not found elsewhere in the New Testament and only twice in the Old Testament (Prov 3,21; Isa 44,4). This verb means «to flow aside» A nautical sense has been ascribed to it «to drift», but that meaning is never attested to. It is therefore better to translate it as «to go astray», which designates at once the fault and its negative consequences (2,1).

The next sentence expresses these two aspects more distinctly, first in relation to «the word announced by the angels», i. e, the revelation of the Law on Sinai (2,2), then to the «salvation» announced «by the Lord» (2,3). In the first case the fault is called «transgression», for it is a question of the Law, and «disobedience» (in Greek «refusal to listen»), for it is a matter of a spoken word. The negative consequence is called «just retribution» (2,2). The Old Testament testifies abundantly that «every transgression and disobedience received just retribution» (2,2). Even when God therein proclaims himself «God of tenderness and mercy [...] who bears with fault, transgression and sin», he adds that he «leaves nothing unpunished» (Exod 34,6.7). The fate reserved for Jerusalem, a sinful city, and its Temple in 587 B. C. is the most impressive illustration of this (see 2Kgs 24,18-25,21).

In the case of Christians the negative consequence of the fault is straightaway mentioned but in an indirect and imprecise way, like something from which one wants «to escape». Far from lessening the danger being run, the lack of precision makes it all the more fearful, for the thrust of the sentence makes it understood that the fault of Christians would be more serious than the transgressions of old and would therefore be punished more severely. That fault would consist in «neglecting» the salvation offered. Its gravity is in proportion to the quality of that salvation, which the preacher expresses first with an emphatic adjective «*so great* a salvation», then with long explanations which show its full importance (2,3b-4). «Neglecting so great a salvation» obviously means consigning oneself to perdition.

The preacher still does not say that it is a question of «eternal salvation» (5,9); in an early exhortation, it is good not to say everything explicitly. The importance of salvation is manifested by the authority of those who announced and confirmed it: in the first place «the Lord», then «those who heard», finally «God» himself. Where is the «beginning» of the announcement of salvation to be placed? One might think of the public ministry of Jesus, «beginning of the good news of Jesus Christ, Son of God» (Mark 1,1). But the title «the Lord» suggests placing it rather after the resurrection of Jesus, for it was then that God «made him Lord and Christ» (Acts 2,36) and that «rising first from among the dead, he must announce the light to the people and to the pagan nations» (Acts 26,23). Given the fact that this exhortation rests upon the earlier context which proclaims the glory of the risen Christ (1,5-14), the second interpretation seems the most probable. Other passages in the sermon speak in the same sense (see 3,6-7; 12,25-26).

Still remaining in the realm of speaking and listening, rather than that of facts and seeing, the preacher recalls «salvation» was, «by those who had heard, put into effect for us». This formula is very vague. It does not say what person or what persons the evangelizers «had heard». It could be said that it was Jesus, but the expression does not say so. It fits also in the case where, between Jesus and those who put the message into effect for the listeners to the sermon, other intermediaries would have intervened. It may be pointed out here that, as regards the reception of the message, the preacher is on the same footing as his audience. He too received it from «those who had heard» and not from Jesus himself. He was not therefore one of the Twelve nor, probably, a Jew from Palestine.

The announcement of salvation was confirmed by the testimony of God himself, a testimony that was expressed by impressive deeds, more eloquent than just words. The expression «signs and wonders» places these divine interventions in the line of the great events in the Old Testament, starting with the «signs and wonders» which preceded, accompanied and followed the departure from Egypt. The «distributions of holy spirit» are a specific characteristic of the New Testament. When the latter speaks of holy spirit it is often difficult to make out whether the Holy Spirit is considered as a person or not. Here one can hesitate between two interpretations: distributions made by the Holy Spirit or distributions in which some holy spirit is distributed. The second interpretation is preferred, on the one hand by the absence of the article and, on the other, by the final remark that says that distributions are made according to the will of God.

From this point of view the perspective is different from that of the first letter to the Corinthians where Paul declares, concerning the various charisms: «all this is achieved by one and the same Spirit, distributing to each one in particular as he wishes» (1Cor 12,11). In this passage the Spirit clearly appears as a person because he acts «as he wishes». In our text, however, it is God who does the distributing «according to his will»; the preacher therefore does not speak of the person of the Holy Spirit but of a force that comes from God. On other occasions he has spoken of the Holy Spirit as a person, while using the article (Heb 3,7; 9,8; 10,15).

He does not say in what the «distributions of holy spirit» consists. To have some idea, we have to have recourse to other New Testament writings, especially 1Cor 12,4.7-11. These «distributions», at all events, constitute a very positive element, more positive, from one point of view, that the «signs and wonders», for the latter are external whereas the «distributions *of holy spirit*» are internal gifts given to believers.

The exhortation thus ends on a very persuasive note, after expressing itself, from 2,1b to 2,3b, on a dissuasive note. The hearers are forcefully encouraged to accept fully the «salvation» offered them by the risen Lord.

Chapter 5

The human Name of Christ (2,5-18)

In its third and last paragraph (Heb 2,5-18), the first part of the sermon expounds the human aspect of the «Name» inherited by Christ resulting from his paschal mystery, an aspect which is «very different» from the position of the angels (1,4). Paradoxically, the difference brings with it a relation of inferiority and at the same time one of superiority.

A. *COMPOSITION*

The limits of this paragraph are clear from two changes of tone. In Heb 2,5 the preacher passes from the exhortation tone, adopted in the preceding paragraph (2,1-4), to the doctrinal exposé tone. In 3,1, he goes in reverse, addressing his hearers directly, for the first time in his sermon. Thus the paragraph extends from Heb 2,5 to Heb 2,18.

An inclusion is noticeable between 2,5 and 2,16:

INDEED, it is	NOT to	ANGELS that he subjected the universe... (2,5)
INDEED, it is certainly	NOT	ANGELS that he took charge of...(2,16).

Coming after the inclusion and before the change of tone, verses 17-18 occupy the right position for an announcement of a subject. In fact, they introduce a new theme, that of the priesthood of Christ, which will be the theme of the next chapters.

Within these limits two parts are distinguished, the first of which (2,5-9) consists of quoting and commenting on a passage from Ps 8, while the second (2,10-18) offers a doctrinal reflection.

Introduction of the theme

5 Indeed, it was not to angels that he subjected the world to come, of which we speak.

Argument from Scripture

6 Someone has testified saying:
«What is man, for you remember him
or a son of man, for you care for him?
7 You made him a little less than the angels,
With glory and honour you crowned him.
8a You subjected all things beneath his feet».

Commentary

8b Indeed, in this act of subjecting **all** things to him,
He left **nothing** that might be unsubjected to him.
Now, we do not yet perceive
that to him **all** things have been subjected,
9 but he who a *little was made lower with respect to the angels*,
we see him, Jesus, for having suffered death,
with glory and honour crowned,
so that, by God's grace, it is to the good of all that he tasted death.

Doctrinal exposé

10 IT WAS FITTING, indeed,
for him for whom all beings
and through whom all beings [exist],
leading many ***SONS*** to glory,
to make perfect through SUFFERING the pioneer of their salvation.
11 Indeed, he who sanctifies and those who are sanctified
are all of one origin.

Scriptural proofs

11b For that reason, he is not ashamed to call them ***BROTHERS***, saying:
12 I will announce your name to my ***BROTHERS***,
In the midst of an assembly, I will sing to you;
13 and again:
I shall be full of trust in him,
and again:
Here I am, I and the CHILDREN whom God has given me.

Doctrinal exposé

14 So then, since the CHILDREN have blood and flesh in common,
he too, likewise, shared the same things,
so that through death he might reduce to nought
him who held the power over death,
that is to say, the devil,
15 and that he might deliver all those
who, through fear of death
throughout their life
were held in slavery.
16 Indeed, it is certainly not of angels that he takes charge,
but it is of descendants of Abraham that he takes charge.

Conclusion

17 Thus HE HAD
in all things to be made like unto his ***BRETHREN***,
in order to become merciful high priest
and trustworthy in regard to relations with God,
with a view to blotting out the sins of the people.
18 Indeed, by the fact that he himself SUFFERED, having been tested,
he is in a position to bring help to those who are being tested.

Being in the negative, the *introductory sentence* (2,5: «Indeed, it is not to angels that he subjected the world to come of which we speak») cleverly raises a question in the minds of the listeners: «To whom did God subject the universe to come?» It thus prepares them for the explanations that follow.

The argument from Scripture is composed of five stichs (2,6b-8a):

6 Someone has testified saying:
«What is man, for you remember him
or a son of man, for you care for him?
7 You made him a little less than the angels,
With glory and honour you crowned him.
8a You subjected all things beneath his feet».

The two first are rhetorical questions, actually, one question expressed twice in synonymous parallelism (2,6bc); it bears on the mystery of mankind. The two following stichs reply to the question with an antithetic parallelism, abasement-coronation (2,7ab). In the psalm, there comes next a synonymous parallelism which develops the second member of the antithesis:

You established him over the work of your hands
You subjected all things under his feet (Ps 8,7).

The preacher has omitted the first of these two stichs. The effect of this omission is that we now have a set of three stichs. The central stich (2,7b) affirms the glory of mankind. It is in a relation of antithesis with the preceding stich (2,7a), and in a relation of synonymy with the following stich which confirms it (2,8a).

The commentary is immediately interested in the third stich (2,8a), of which it takes up the expression «to subject all the things», filling it out by adding the article.

8 Indeed, in that act of subjecting all the things,
He left **nothing** that might remain unsubjected to him.
Now, we do not yet see
that to him **all** the things have been subjected,
9 but he who *was somewhat brought low with regard to the angels,*
we see him, Jesus, for having SUFFERED death,
with glory and honour crowned,
so that, by grace of God, it may be for the good of all that he has tasted death.

It then expresses an antithesis between two negative assertions, the first of which (2,8c) says that «nothing» was excluded, whereas the second (2,8d) notes that «everything» has not yet been achieved.

The preacher then states, in contrast, the realization of the two previous stichs (2,7ab) in the person of «Jesus», named here for the first time in the sermon, in a context of abasement and death, then coronation (2,9abc).

A last proposition, final or consecutive (2,9d), completes the perspective on an essential point: «by grace of God», the death of Jesus was «for the good of all». This proposition announces the subject of the next doctrinal exposé.

This *doctrinal exposé* (2,10-18) does not have a very evident structure:

10 IT WAS FITTING, indeed,
for him for whom all beings
and through whom all beings [exist],
leading many ***SONS*** to glory,
to make perfect through SUFFERING the pioneer of their salvation.
11 Indeed, he who sanctifies and those who are sanctified
are all of one origin.

- - - - - - - - - - - - - - - - - - - -

11b For that reason, he is not ashamed to call them ***BROTHERS***, saying:
12 I will announce your name to my ***BROTHERS***,
in the midst of an assembly, I will sing to you;
13 and again:
  I shall be full of trust in him,
and again:
  Here I am, I and the CHILDREN whom God has given me.

- - - - - - - - - - - - - - - - - - - -

14 So then, since the CHILDREN have blood and flesh in common,
he too, likewise, shared the same things,
so that through death he might reduce to nought
him who held the power over death,
that is to say, the devil,
15 and that he might deliver all those
who, through fear of death
  throughout their life
  were held in slavery.
16 Indeed, it is certainly not of angels that he takes charge,
but it is of descendants of Abraham that he takes charge.

- - - - - - - - - - - - - - - - - - - -

17 Thus HE HAD
in all things to be made like unto his ***BRETHREN***,
in order to become merciful high priest
and trustworthy in regard to relations with God,
with a view to blotting out the sins of the people.
18 Indeed, by the fact that he himself SUFFERED, having been tested,
he is in a position to bring help to those who are being tested.

Between the beginning and the end, one verbal connection is made (2,10e) «he has suffered» (2,18a). Yet the connections between ideas are plentiful: between «It was fitting» (2,10a) and «he had to» (2,17a); between the «sons» of God (2,10d) and the «brethren» of Christ (2,17a); between «salvation» (2,10e) and «blotting out sin» (2,17d); lastly, for those who have noticed that, in the Pentateuch in Greek, the very frequent verb «make perfect» serves exclusively to designate the consecration of the high priest, the «make perfect» in 2,10e prepares for the «become high priest» in 2,17b.

Four subdivisions can be distinguished. The first (2,10-11a) does not contain any quotation from Scripture. The second (2,11b-13b) has three quotations. The third (2,14a-16b) takes up the tone of the exposé without quoting Scripture; its final limit is marked by the sentence in 2,16 which makes an inclusion with 2,5. The fourth (2,17a-18b) fulfils the double function of conclusion of the paragraph (2,5-18) and of announcement of the subject (*propositio*) of the next part.

The parallelisms are many and very varied. In verse 10 the expressions «for whom all the beings and through whom all the beings» constitute a very well supported complementary parallelism. Then, in Greek, there is a synonymous chiasm between «unto glory leading» and «the pioneer of their salvation», for «salvation» corresponds to «glory» and the «pioneer» is the one who «leads». Moreover, an antithetic chiasm is observable in the expression «to make perfect through suffering the pioneer of their salvation»; suffering is a paradoxical means to obtain salvation and in the two Greek words translated as «pioneer» (*archēgos*) and «make perfect» (*teleiōsai*), there is the antithesis between beginning and end, the «pioneer» being «the man of the beginning (*archē*)» and «make perfect» meaning «bring to a successful conclusion» (*telos*).

Verse 11a also offers a very marked complementary parallelism between «the sanctifier» and the «sanctified», followed by an antithesis between «all» and «one».

In verse 12, the quotation presents a synonymous parallelism in a reversed arrangement: the beginning of the first stich («I will announce your name») finds its echo at the end of the second («I will sing to you»); the end of the first stich («to my brethren») is filled out at the beginning of the second («in the midst of an assembly»).

The two quotations in verse 13 are related by the parallelism of the same initial emphatic pronoun: «I...», «I, here I am...».

The beginning of verse 14 presents a quite obvious synonymous parallelism (2,14ab): «the children»/«he also»; «have in common»/«shared»; «blood and flesh»/«the same things». The rest of the sentence (2,14cd) contains an antithetic parallelism in reverse order: the «by death» at the beginning is opposed to the «of death» at the end; the «brought to naught» is opposed to ««he who held the power».

Another relation is noted between «brought to naught» and «might deliver»; there it is a question of two aspects of a complementary parallelism between two aspects of the same action: bringing the oppressor to naught, i. e. freeing the oppressed.

Verse 15 has an antithetic parallelism in inverse order: «he might deliver», at the beginning, is opposed to «slavery» at the end; in the middle, «fear of death» and «throughout the whole of life» form a contrast.

10 IT WAS FITTING, indeed,
for him for whom all beings
and through whom all beings [exist],
leading many ***SONS*** to glory,
to make perfect through SUFFERING the pioneer of their salvation.
11 Indeed, he who sanctifies and those who are sanctified
are all of one origin.

11b For that reason, he is not ashamed to call them ***BROTHERS***, saying:
12 I will announce your name to my ***BROTHERS***,
in the midst of an assembly, I will sing to you;
13 and again:
I shall be full of trust in him,
and again:
Here I am, I and the CHILDREN whom God has given me.

---

14 So then, since the CHILDREN have blood and flesh in common,
he too, likewise, shared the same things,
so that through death he might reduce to nought
him who held the power over death,
that is to say, the devil,
15 and that he might deliver all those
who, through fear of death
throughout their life
were held in slavery.
16 Indeed, it is certainly not of angels that he takes charge,
but it is of descendants of Abraham that he takes charge.

---

17 Thus HE HAD
in all things to be made like unto his ***BRETHREN***,
in order to become merciful high priest
and trustworthy in regard to relations with God,
with a view to blotting out the sins of the people.
18 Indeed, by the fact that he himself SUFFERED, having been tested,
he is in a position to bring help to those who are being tested.

In verse 16, the repetition of the verb «to take charge of» is superfluous as regards the meaning; it accentuates the parallelism between the two propositions. This parallelism is antithetic; what is denied of the angels is affirmed of the descendants of Abraham.

Only verse 17 has a very prosaic look to it. At the most one can see in it a not very evident complementary parallelism between the relation with «the brethren» and «the relations with God».

Verse 18, on the contrary, contains a marked parallelism between «having been tested» and «those who are tested». The «has suffered» at the beginning is presented as basis for the ability to «bring help» expressed at the end (in Greek, «to bring help» is the last word in the sentence).

Biblical parallelism therefore strongly marks the composition of this paragraph.

B. *BIBLICAL CONTEXT*

The argument from Scripture in verses 6 to 9 is based on Ps 8, which is of the Wisdom type. The psalmist admires the greatness of God who manifests himself in creation and, in particular, in the creation of mankind. The preacher quotes the Septuagint translation, which expresses a relation between mankind and angels: «You have made him a little lower than the angels». The Hebrew text would not suit him in this particular because there is no mention of angels in it. The word *'ĕlōhîm*, which can have three meanings, is found in it: God, a god, the gods: «God» does not suit the sentence because it cannot be said of Yhwh: «You brought him low as regards God», which would give the impression that Yhwh is not God. When *'ĕlōhîm* is not a plural of majesty designating the one true God, it is normally taken as a simple plural designating gods, i. e. celestial beings. The Septuagint has therefore in this case rendered this word as «angels», as in Ps 96,7 or 137,1.

After verse 7 (2,8a in Hebrews: «You subjected all things beneath his feet»), the psalm explains the meaning of «all things» by saying:

> sheep and cattle, all together,
> beasts, even the wild ones,
> birds of the air and fish in the sea,
> moving through the paths of the waters (Ps 8,8-9).

The preacher takes great care to omit these details because what he wants to propose is another reading of the psalm in the context of «the world to come» (Heb 2,5), that is to say, of the new creation inaugurated by the resurrection of Christ (see Heb 9,11). The new creation must be the perfect realization of God's plan for man and that plan is expressed in the psalm in the words: «You subjected all things beneath his feet», which corresponds to the picture in Genesis in which God says to the human couple: «Fill the earth and subject it» (Gen 1,28; see 9,2).

Ps 8 speaks of mankind in general and not of the Messiah, the descendant of David. But it can be considered as the basis of Messianism because it proclaims mankind's calling to universal domination and that it is through the Messiah that that calling was to be carried out (see Ps 2,8; 1Chr 17,14).

A few verses after the long quotation from Ps 8, other quotations come in Heb 2,12-13 to prove that, according to the Scriptures, Christ «was not ashamed to call *brethren* the people he leads to salvation» (Heb 2,11).

The first text quoted fits in perfectly with this demonstration. It is a verse from Ps 21 in which the persecuted just person announces what he will do when he is freed by God. He will show his gratitude by announcing God's name to his «brethren» in the course of a liturgical thanksgiving which a fraternal «assembly» will attend.

Ps 21 is not Messianic in the strict sense, but Jesus on the cross applied it to himself by calling out the first verse: «My God, my God, why hast thou forsaken me?» (Matt 27,60; Mark 15,34). Jesus, in fact, took upon himself the lot of the persecuted just person. It follows from this that verse 23 of the psalm is a prophecy that foretells the fraternal attitude of the risen Christ towards those whom he leads to salvation. Far from breaking the links with his human brothers and sisters, his glorification has strengthened them, for it is based on the passion, the utmost testimony of solidarity.

The preacher then adds two quotations which do not contain the word «brothers» (Heb 2,13). The first does not even express any connection with mankind, but only trust in God. It is through its connection with the second that it enters into contact with the theme of solidarity with mankind. If it stayed on its own the first quotation would give the impression that Christ is a lonely conqueror. One would think it came from the canticle of David (2Sam 22,3), in which that person actually appears as a lonely conqueror: the personal pronoun *I* recurs in Greek in it more than eighty times in fifty verses. But the same declaration is also found in Isa 8,17 and is followed in it by another sentence which changes the perspective because to the «I» it adds some «children» entrusted by God. So instead of being in solitariness the conqueror is in solidarity.

In the context of Hebrews, the two quotations in verse 13 are, like the one in verse 12, predictions of the position that Christ was to obtain after his passion, a position that was achieved in his glorification. The risen Christ is henceforth established in a relationship of special trust in God, but this trust is not that of a solitary conqueror, because the passion has strengthened to the utmost the ties of solidarity uniting Christ with the «children» God entrusted to him; it has made those ties indissoluble. Christ's confidence consists in being able to obtain everything from God for those «children» (see Heb 7,25).

c. *INTERPRETATION*

After the short exhortation, the preacher resumes the tone of doctrinal exposé to complete the presentation on the Name of Christ. He now wishes to speak of the human aspect of that Name and to underline its capacity for being brought into relation with human beings, a «very different» capacity from that of the angels.

An «in fact» (*gar*) attaches this paragraph to what precedes. The connection can be understood in a broad sense, with the whole of what has been said, or in a more precise way, with verse 4: the fact that God so vigorously supports the announcement of salvation through Christ shows that «it was not to the angels that he subjected the world to come». The preacher wants to be satisfied for the time being with that negative statement. The positive explanation will be given gradually in the rest of the paragraph. Let us note that, to designate «the universe to come», the preacher does not use the word «world», but the term he used in 1,6, «*oikoumenē*», «inhabited region», «civilized region».

To give the positive explanation, the preacher uses Ps 8 which, along the lines of Gen 1,28, states mankind's calling to universal domination (Wis 9,2-3). So it is not to angels that that domination is promised but to mankind. In what way it will be given it is shown by the commentary on the psalm: by the glorification of a representative of mankind, a glorification obtained by accepting abasement.

Ps 8 actually expresses a contrast between an abasement and a coronation. Read in the light of the story of creation (Gen 1), that abasement beneath the angels and that coronation are not two steps succeeding each other, but two complementary ways of defining the position of the human being: man is inferior to the angels and superior to all earthly creatures. The formulation in the psalm, however, tends to distinguish two successive stages. Read in the light of the mystery of Christ, the psalm's expressions are revealed as prophetic. They correspond to two phases of this mystery: the abasement of the incarnation and the coronation of the glorification. Through the incarnation and passion, the Son of God, «splendour of his glory», was «made a little lower than the angels». Through the resurrection and the glorification, he was «crowned with glory and honour», well above the angels. In the paschal mystery of Christ, mankind's calling has therefore found its fulfilment on these two points, which inspires confidence that it will also be fulfilled on the third point, universal domination.

In his commentary (2,8-9), the preacher first stresses the universal character of the dominion conferred by God on mankind. He then points out that one cannot yet perceive the fulfilment of that divine decision. But he adds immediately that one can see in Jesus the accomplishment of the first two aspects: abasement beneath the angels and glorification above them.

In expressing that perception the preacher is careful to make two clarifications of extreme importance for his subject. The first concerns the link between the two phases of the mystery, a link that does not appear in the assertions made in the psalm: it is «for having suffered death» that Jesus was «crowned with glory and honour»; in other words it was the last degree of his abasement that gained glorification for him. The other clarification concerns the effect of this mystery. The death of Jesus was not just a glorious outcome for himself, it had an importance «for all» (literally, «for every [human being]». It was for the good of every human being that Christ fully achieved mankind's calling. Everything that follows will confirm this outlook which defines the human aspect of the Name inherited by Christ. A Name of a man, fully man and fully in solidarity with all humans. How «different» a Name «from that of the angels»! —at once inferior and superior, with the inferiority paradoxically producing a new element of superiority.

In 2,10 the preacher shows himself as a theologian, for he expresses his reflection on the coherence of God's plan. He finds that it was what was «fitting». God embraces the whole universe, but his plan was to «lead many sons to glory». That meant saving them, for they were in a state of perdition, and to save them it was necessary to give them a guide who would help them get out of that situation. This «pioneer of their salvation» had to descend into the abyss into which they had fallen, share their destiny of suffering and open for them the way to salvation. The preacher is not content with this image and it is here that his reflection as a theologian is shown to be very profound. To the idea of movement in place he joins that of personal transformation, expressed by the verb «to make perfect», and he puts the action of God himself before the action of the pioneer. What mankind actually needed to be saved was not so much a path to go along as a personal transformation to be achieved. But as this transformation had to be carried out «through suffering», sinful mankind was not in a position to accept it positively; it was always kicking out, rebelling. So the «pioneer of their salvation» had to submit himself to it, although personally he had no need to do so. And for that he had to take on a human nature which needed it, and take on «a slave's condition», as the apostle Paul says (Phil 2,7), «flesh like the flesh of sin» (Rom 8,3), and, in that flesh, accept the painful transforming action of God so as to be able to communicate it to his brothers and sisters in humanity. This way of understanding the redemption is certainly more profound than the one that understands it as a commercial buying-back operation or as a ritual expiation ceremony. It takes better into account the necessity of the passion of Christ, insistently stated in the gospels (see Matt 16,21; Mark 8,31; Luke 9,22; 17,25; 24,7.26), not an external necessity, but an internal one.

The preacher then rapidly explains the principle of solidarity (11). To be able to transmit holiness to sinful mankind, «he who sanctifies» must be part of it, a member of their race; otherwise the stream would not pass. The Son of God therefore became brother to mankind and stays so even after the glorification of his human nature. «He is not ashamed to call them brothers», Ps 21 attests; the text in Isa 8,17-18 also manifests the link of solidarity that unites Christ to mankind, for they are the «children» whom God has entrusted to him. Christ is therefore not a solitary conqueror, like the one in the canticle of David (2Sam 22,3; Ps 18,3). His triumph holds good for everyone.

Verse 14 expresses with greater precision the way in which the Son of God became brother of mankind: he took on their nature of «blood and flesh», a frail and mortal nature. He took it on precisely to face up to human death and to change its meaning radically.

Death, being a consequence of, and punishment for, sin (Gen 3,3.19; Rom 5,12), placed mankind in a fearsome state of separation from God (Ps 88,4; Isa 38,11) and oppressed them under the power of the devil (Wis 2,24). With his death, Christ broke the power of the devil, for he turned an event of terrible separation into a covenant event (9,15); he used his death to introduce his human nature into the heavenly intimacy of God (9,24) and to open up that same way to all mankind (10,19), doing so by accepting in his death the positive action of God who was «making him perfect» by inspiring him with perfect filial docility and full brotherly solidarity.

Incapacitating the prince of death means thereby freeing mankind from the fear of death which had made slaves of them throughout their lives (15). This was indeed a terrible servitude in which mankind was forced to go on, day after day, towards a fatal outcome. The psalms of supplication express the anguish involved. Since death can henceforth be a way to God, followed victoriously with Christ, it no longer causes so much fear (Phil 1,21).

After these comforting reflections the preacher brings this First Part of his sermon to a close in two ways. He comes back first to the relation of Christ to the angels which he used until 2,9 to define the «Name» of Christ; here he states, more precisely, the lack of relation. The Son of God did not become one with the angels, but with mankind, by entering into the family of Abraham (16), in conformity with the promise of God who had promised on oath: «In your descendants all the nations of the earth will be blessed» (Gen 22,18).

The other conclusion (17-18) opens up completely new prospects by introducing the subject of the priesthood of Christ, a subject completely absent from the other New Testament writings. The innovation is twofold because it also has a bearing on how to become high priest. In the Old Testament, to become high priest it was necessary to receive priestly consecration by means of solemn rites which raised the future high priest to the divine sphere and separated him from the rest of mankind: ritual bath, anointing, priestly garb and vestments and especially a whole series of sacrificial immolations for a whole week (Exod 29; Lev 8). Minute prescriptions of ritual purity then provided for the maintenance of the separation thus obtained (Lev 21); they forbade, in particular, any contact with death because there was seen to be complete incompatibility of the sanctity of the living God with the corruption of death.

The way in which Christ was to become high priest is the exact reverse. Instead of separating himself from other humans and rising above them to be closer to God, he had to «become in everything like his brethren» and to descend to their level, as far as to suffer and die like the most unfortunate of them. A greater contrast is hard to imagine. The change is obviously due to the fact that the death of Christ was a victory over death, won by means of filial docility and fraternal solidarity and which effectively obtained what the rites of old strove in vain to obtain: perfect communion with God.

To the title of high priest the author adds two qualifying phrases which thereby announce the two sections of the next part. Christ had to «become merciful and trustworthy high priest for relations with God» (17). These two phrases do not designate two individual virtues, such as courage or prudence; they express ability to establish relations which are necessary for the exercize of priestly mediation; «merciful» expresses the ability of the high priest to relate to unfortunate mankind; «trustworthy» concerns the ability to relate to God; the text says so explicitly; more precisely, it is a matter of being able to provide relations with God.

The Old Testament was concerned with this second point, but not with the first. It did not think of requiring mercy towards sinners from the high priest. Two traditions, on the contrary, require that the priest should place himself clearly on God's side and act pitilessly against sinners, enemies of God. Moses had declared to the Levites who, after the idolatry of the golden calf, had dealt severely with the idolators: «You have given yourselves priestly consecration for the Lord, each one at the cost of his son or his brother» (Exod 32,29). In Num 25,6-13 a similar episode results in a conclusion of the same kind: for having acted severely against an Israelite and his Madianite accomplice, Phinehas received the assurance of an eternal priesthood for himself and his descendants. In the old idea of priesthood all the attention was given to the relation of the priest to God and it was thought that fidelity to that relation called for severity against sinners. One episode, however, is an exception: at Moses' request, Aaron intervenes in it to save the people from extermination (Num 17,11-13; Wis 18,21-25).

In Greek, the other adjective is *pistos*, which we have translated as «trustworthy», the first meaning of this adjective. Another possible meaning, «faithful», is adopted here by many translators, but the later context (3,1-6), in which the word is explained, shows that it is not a question of fidelity here, but of trustworthiness. We shall talk about this again when commenting on this passage.

The high priest's two qualities are necessary for him «in view of blotting out the sins of the people» (17). To be sure, blotting out sins is an act of great mercy which requires, furthermore, being accredited in the matter of relations with God. The Greek verb *hilaskesthai* translated here as «to blot out» (as in Ps 64(65),4; see also Sir 3,3.30) is often translated there as «to expiate»; while being possible in other contexts, that translation is not suitable here for the verb is in the present and denotes an activity of the glorified Christ. Before his glorification Christ «offered a unique sacrifice for sins» (10,12). His unique sacrifice obtained for him henceforth the power to eliminate sins without having to «expiate» them anew.

The last verse (18) completes the thought, by moving from the theoretical level to that of what «had to» be (17), to the practical level of what actually happened. Christ has in fact «become in all things like his brethren», for «he himself suffered, having been tested» (18). In Greek, the verb to suffer is put in the perfect, which indicates that a deed in the past has present consequences. To suffer passes away, to have suffered does not pass away. Christ is *someone who has suffered*; he has gone through various trials, he even suffered death (9). His personal experience enables him to understand those who are being tested and to bring them help suited to their needs.

The two innovations introduced by the preacher in this conclusion to Part One of his sermon may seem, at first sight, to be without any connection with the foregoing context from which the liturgical and priestly categories are completely absent. But careful examination shows that these innovations have been painstakingly prepared. Verses 17-18 really do constitute a conclusion to Part One, but a conclusion which, instead of confining itself to summarizing what has been said, expresses it in new categories which will later have to be gone into in the next Part.

In Part One the preacher reminded his audience of Christ's paschal mystery in traditional terms. He first spoke to them about Christ's glorification (1,5-14), then about his passion which brought about that glorification (2,5-16). To express these two phases of the mystery he used some traditional biblical texts used by apostolic catechesis, many of which are linked with Davidic Messianism of the royal kind. When ending (2,17-18), the author shows that the same Christology can also be expressed in priestly categories and that there is no difficulty in passing from a royal to a priestly explanation of the mystery of Christ. In fact, in his glorification, Christ is proclaimed Son of God and in his passion he is shown as brother of mankind. Through his glorifying passion he entered with his human nature of flesh and blood into the heavenly intimacy of his Father and at the same time strengthened his fraternal links with us and made them indissoluble. Having brought these two relations to their perfection, he now finds himself established in a position of perfect mediator between God and us or, in other words, of «merciful and trustworthy high priest for relations with God» (2,17).

Which explanation better expresses the mystery of Christ? Is it the royal or the priestly one? Royal Messianism was more fixed in people's minds. The gospels only mention that one, but pointing out its dangers and inadequacies. To combat injustice a king certainly has recourse to force; to free his people he takes up arms and goes to war. Jesus refused to go down that road.

For Jesus to be able to be proclaimed Messiah-King was it necessary that he should undergo the worst suffering and humiliation? That does not seem evident. Did he have to be introduced into heavenly intimacy with God? That does not seem clear either. Christ is king in a way that completely transcends the normal notion of royal power and that way corresponds rather to the notion of priesthood. Priesthood is actually a form of mediation; it therefore requires the presence of a twofold relation, the most perfect relation possible, with God and mankind. Christ's passion was necessary to make him fully at one with all mankind, including people being tested and humiliated the most. The heavenly glorification of Christ was necessary to provide his human nature with a perfect and immovable relation with God.

The priestly exposé has the advantage of being on the religious plane, whereas royal Messianism is on the political plane, which is not suitable when it is a matter of relations with God. It can therefore easily be understood that the preacher ends his treatment of the «Name» of Christ with the title of «high priest». The other titles just express one aspect of Christ's position: «Son of God» his relation with God, «brother of mankind» his relation with us, «Lord» his glorification, «servant» his humiliation. «High priest» implies the twofold relation and recalls the sacrifice and the glory. Further on, the preacher will be able to point out that applying the title of high priest to Christ is based on a declaration by God himself, a more solemn declaration than all the others because it is backed up with a divine oath (7,20-22; Ps 109,4).

Part Two

Christ is a trustworthy and merciful high priest: priestly Christology, general characteristics (3,1-5,10)

Chapter 6

Trustworthy high priest (3,1-6)

Having introduced the theme of his sermon in 2,17—the priesthood of Christ—the preacher begins explaining it in a short paragraph (3,1-6), to which he immediately joins a long exhortation (3,7-4,14). To show clearly that this passage is the beginning of the exposé of his theme, the preacher introduces it with an urgent appeal for attention addressed to his listeners. He then takes up the title of «high priest», which he has applied to «Jesus», uniting with it the second of the adjectives used in 2,17: «trustworthy». The hearers can foresee that the first adjective, «merciful», is going to be the subject of a second section.

1 So then, holy brothers, who share in a heavenly calling,
consider the apostle and high priest of our profession of faith, Jesus,
2 who is trustworthy for him who constituted him,
like Moses, in his house.
3 Of greater glory than Moses, in fact, he was deemed worthy
just as he who builds the house
has greater honour than the house itself.
4 Every house is actually built by someone
and he who built all things [is] God.
5 And Moses [is] trustworthy *in* all his house as a servant
in testimony of the things that will be said,
6 he, Christ, [is so] as son, *over* his house,
and his house, it is ourselves,
if we keep confidence and pride of hope.

A. *COMPOSITION*

The limits of this short paragraph do not cause doubts for any commentator. Its beginning is in fact marked by a solemn call to the listeners: «holy brothers, who share in a heavenly calling». The subject proposed for their consideration is the «trustworthiness» of their high priest. The former is put into relation with the trustworthiness of Moses (2-6). The comparison between Jesus and Moses stops at verse 6, which then has a transition statement in a sentence in the first person plural. The end of the paragraph can be recognized there, the following verse being the start of an exhortation.

Based on a comparison between «Jesus» and «Moses», this brief exposé is constructed with parallelisms of different kinds.

The first parallelism expresses a relation of resemblance:

Jesus, who is trustworthy for him who constituted him,
like Moses, in his house.

From the relation of resemblance we go straight on to a relation of superiority, expressed grammatically by a comparative proposition of proportionality:

He was in fact judged worthy of a *greater glory* than Moses,
Just as he who built the house
Has *greater honour* than the house itself.

The parallelism between «greater glory» and «greater honour» is synonymous. Between «the house» and «he who built it» there could be a parallelism of complementarity but, in the context, it is antithetic, the house being considered as inferior, because its existence depends entirely on the builder.

1 So then, holy brothers, who share in a heavenly calling,
consider the apostle and high priest of our profession of faith, Jesus,
2 who is trustworthy for him who constituted him,
like Moses, in his house.
3 Of greater glory than Moses, in fact, he was deemed worthy
just as he who builds the house
has greater honour than the house itself.
4 Every house is actually built by someone
and he who built all things [is] God.
5 And Moses [is] trustworthy *in* all his house as a servant
in testimony of the things that will be said,
6 he, Christ, [is so] as son, *over* his house,
and his house, it is ourselves,
if we keep confidence and pride of hope.

Verse 4 introduces a reflection that examines the perspective in greater depth. It is expressed in a parallelism of complementarity that moves on from «every house is built» to «he who built everything» and from «someone» to «God».

In verses 5-6a we go back to the epithet «trustworthy» common to Jesus and Moses but this time to establish some differences. The parallelism becomes antithetic between «as *servant*», for Moses, and «as *son*», for Jesus, then between «*in* all his house», for Moses, and «*over* his house», for Jesus.

The end of verse 6 (6c) introduces a new idea, «his house, it is ourselves», which provides a good transition to the next exhortation.

The style of this paragraph is marked by its concision, which requires a constant effort on the part of the listeners to fill out the thought. The preacher alludes to Scripture texts and to points of evangelical catechesis, but without saying so explicitly. In 3,3 he makes it understood that «he who built the house» is Christ, but he does not say so and he does not explain whether «the house» is the whole of creation (see 1,10) or the sanctuary rebuilt in three days (John 2,19; Mark 14,58). The statement in 3,4b is not clear; it proclaims the divinity of «he who built all things», without making it clear that it is speaking of Christ or God. Attentive listeners will remember that the Son was called «God» in Part One (1,8-9) and that according to 1,10 he created the earth and the heavens. They will therefore understand that the preacher, in 3,4, wishes to refer to that affirmation of his faith.

B. *BIBLICAL CONTEXT AND INTERPRETATION*

This paragraph does not contain any explicit quotation from the Old Testament, but its interpretation depends entirely on two implicit references.

The most important problem is the precise meaning of the Greek adjective *pistos*, because it is the subject of the paragraph: Jesus is the *pistos* high priest. The first meaning of this word is «trustworthy», whence the transition is made to the meaning of «faithful» and even to that of «believer» (in ecclesiastical language one speaks of «the infidels» to designate «non-believers», in fact). What does the author wish to speak about—the fidelity or the credibility of Jesus? Most translators do not give a thought to the first meaning and translate it as «faithful». The commentators explain that it is a matter of fidelity of Jesus in accomplishing the will of God despite all the difficulties. As this fidelity manifested itself in his earthly life, the sentence is put in the past: «Jesus, who *was* faithful», whereas the Greek text has a present participle.

The solution to the problem is to be found in the Septuagint text to which the author alludes and which ascribes the quality of *pistos* to Moses: Num 12,7. In this passage (Num 12,1-15), there is no question of the fidelity of Moses;

what is at stake is the authority of Moses to transmit God's words. That authority is contested by Miriam and Aaron. God replies firmly to the argument by declaring «My servant Moses is trustworthy (*pistos*) in all my house» (Num 12,7).

The author of Hebrews has grasped this meaning perfectly, because he links the quality attributed to Moses with the «witness» he was to give about «the things to be said» (Heb 3,5). God declared Moses «trustworthy» in order that the words he was to transmit be received with faith. Similarly, in glorifying Christ, God presented him as «trustworthy».

To state that Jesus is «trustworthy» like Moses, the author implicitly goes back to the famous oracle by the prophet Nathan, which is the basis of the expectation of the Messiah. He does not take that oracle from its first version, the one in the Second Book of Samuel (2Sam 7), but from the formulation in the First Book of Chronicles (1Chr 17), a more clearly Messianic one. In 2Sam 7,14-15 the oracle does not actually present the son and successor promised to David as an ideal king, because it envisages the case in which «he will do evil». In 1Chr 17 that possibility disappears. Moreover—and this is the point that interests us—the promise of stability given in 2Sam 7,16 to the *house of David* in 1Chr 17,14 becomes a promise given to the *son* of David. In 2Sam 7,16 God declares to David: «*Your house* and your kingship will last for ever before me», while in 1Chr 17,14 God speaks of a promised son and declares: «I shall keep *him* for ever in *my house* and in my kingdom». In the Greek translation of 1Chr 17,14, God's promise concerning the Messiah says more precisely: «and I *shall make* him *trustworthy in my* house and in his kingdom for ever». This formulation of the oracle leads naturally to stating that, according to Scripture, Christ, in whom the promises made to David are fulfilled, is «trustworthy for him who constituted him, like Moses, in his house» (Heb 3,2), that is to say in God's house.

The connection with Nathan's oracle is confirmed by two other allusions, one to the construction of God's house, the other to the relation of sonship. In Nathan's oracle, God announces: «...one of your sons, whose reign I shall strengthen... will build a house for me... I shall be a father for him and he will be a son for me» (1Chr 17,11-13). This text provides the opportunity for two comparisons between Jesus and Moses: «Jesus was judged worthy of a greater glory than Moses», for he is «the one who built the house» of God (Heb 3,3) in his paschal mystery (see John 2,19: «Destroy this sanctuary and in three days I will raise it up»; see Mark 4,58). Then again, when Moses, in Num 12,7, is called «my servant» by God, Jesus, in 1Chr 17,13, is called «son» and therefore has authority «over his house» (Heb 3,5-6).

Another detail that comes to back up the translation of *pistos* as «trustworthy» is the relation that can be established between the title of «apostle» given to Jesus in Heb 3,1 and an oracle of Malachi on the role of the priest. The prophet Malachi expresses the serious reproaches addressed by God to unworthy priests (Mal 1,6-14) and then says:

> The lips of the priest should guard knowledge
> And from his mouth instruction is sought;
> He is *messenger* of Yhwh Sabaoth (Mal 2,7).

Malachi thus recalls an important aspect of priesthood in the Old Testament: the transmission of the word of God. The priests «teach the customs to Jacob and the Law to Israel» (Deut 33,10). When circumstances require it, they are charged with consulting God and to communicate God's replies to the authorities and the people concerning the conduct to be observed.

In the Septuagint translation, the Hebrew word meaning «messenger» is rendered by the Greek word *aggelos*, which has that meaning. But *aggelos* also has the sense of «angel» and the author of Hebrews has just used it ten times in that sense to show that Christ has a «very different» name from that of the angels. It follows from this that he could not apply the name *aggelos* in 3,1, because that would have caused serious confusion. So he chose an equivalent title, that of *apostolos*, «envoy».

Even independently of the possible relation with Malachi's oracle, the addition of the title *apostolos* to that of high priest expresses the priestly function of communicating the word of God, a function which must be recognized in the glorified Christ. In the exhortation immediately following, the preacher exhorts his hearers to listen to his voice (3,7.15; 4,7); further on he designates him as «he who speaks from the heavens» (12,25). Christ «trustworthy high priest» has the right to our entire allegiance in faith, as well as our obedience, for he has full authority «over his house» (3,6; see 5,9; 10,21).

Let us note that in the sentence in 3,6, the syntagma «his house» (in Greek: «the house *of him*») is ambiguous: is it about the house *of God* or the house *of Christ*? Grammatically, the pronoun «him» refers to «Christ», because that is the nearest antecedent. It would therefore be a matter of the house of Christ.

But in the previous context (3,2.5) where it is a question of Moses, «trustworthy in all the house of him», the allusion to Num 12,7 has to be taken to mean «in all the house of God». In Heb 10,21 the author will say clearly that «we have… a high priest established over the house of God».

There is reason to believe that the author did not feel the need to remove the ambiguity here, because, to his way of thinking, the two interpretations are valid at one and the same time. The sanctuary rebuilt in three days is at once house of God and house of Christ; house of God because built for God by Christ; house of Christ because built for Christ by God who raised Christ from the dead. The risen Christ is at once the son given by God to David as perpetual successor and the house built for God by the son of David.

The author adds: «and his house, it is ourselves», a very quick allusion to the New Testament doctrine according to which those who believe in Christ become members of his body (1Cor 12,27; Rom 12,5), branches of him who is the vine (John 15,5) and sanctuary of God (1Cor 3,16-17; 2Cor 6,16).

Chapter 7

Warning against lack of faith (3,7-4,14)

Having shown that «the apostle and high priest of our confession of faith, Jesus,» is «trustworthy like Moses» and even more so than him, the preacher issues a stern warning against lack of faith to his listeners. For this purpose he uses some verses of Ps 94(95). He quotes them in Heb 3,7-11 (Ps 94,7-11) and then begins to comment on them while applying them to his audience.

After a short introductory proposition, the words of Ps 94 are addressed to the listeners (3,7-11) and commented on in three subdivisions, the limits of which are marked by inclusions (3,12-19; 4,1-5; 4,6-11). Praise for the Word of God concludes the exhortation (4,12-13). The next sentence (4,14) concludes the whole section; it recalls the brief exposé in 3,1-6 on Jesus, the trustworthy high priest and sums up the exhortation in three words. A very perceptive inclusion puts this last sentence (4,14) into touch with the initial sentence of the section (3,1); we noted this in our first chapter.

1 *Quotation (3,7-11)*

7 This is why, as the Holy Spirit says:
Today, if you hear his voice,
8 Do not harden your hearts
as in the embitterment
according to the day of testing in the desert,
9 where your fathers underwent a testing
and saw my works
forty years
10 that is why I grew angry with that generation
and I said: They always go astray in heart,
but they did not know my ways,
11 as I swore in my anger:
If they enter into my rest!

A. *COMPOSITION*

A problem arises about the division of the sentences in 9-10. From the point of view of grammar and rhythm, «forty years» goes with what precedes: «and they saw my works, forty years». The «That is why» that follows is normally the beginning of a sentence. This «That is why» is not in the Hebrew text, nor in the Greek Septuagint. Apparently it is the preacher who adds it to get a more regular rhythm (a stich of thirteen syllables, instead of seven, after a stich of 17 syllables). But the separation into verses did not follow his intention and attached the «forty years» to what follows, as in the Hebrew text.

The psalm is constructed in more or less strict parallelisms. Complementary parallelism:

Today, if you hear his voice,
do not harden you hearts.

The voice seeks to reach into the hearts. If they are hardened, it cannot do so. The «Today» applies to the two members. In the Greek text, there is a chiasm:

if his voice		do not harden
	×	
you hear		your hearts.

Synonymous parallelism:

As in the embitterment
According to the day of testing in the desert.

«as» and «according to» are parallel, like «the embitterment» and «the testing»; «in the desert» applies to the two members.

Complementary parallelism:

where your fathers underwent a testing
and saw my works forty years

the testing results in an observation: «they saw»; as regards rhythm, «in a testing» and «forty years» correspond to each other.

I grew angry with that generation
And I said:

The second member is very short, because it is followed by a cut-off and is completed by the following parallelism which is synonymous:

They always go astray in heart
But they did not know my ways.

To «going astray» corresponds «not to know the ways».

The last distich does not offer verbal parallelism, but only a correspondence in content: the oath mentioned in the first stich:

As I swore in my anger

Is expressed in the second:

If they enter into my rest.

B. *BIBLICAL CONTEXT AND INTERPRETATION*

Ps 95(94) is composed of two very different parts. The first, verses 1-7a, is a joyous call to praise God; the second, verses 7b-11, is a severe warning, ending with a reminder of a terrible threat of exclusion. This second part the preacher quotes in appying it to his hearers. It recalls some instances of revolt by the Iraelites at the time of crossing the desert.

A difference is to be noted between the Greek translation of the psalm and the original Hebrew: the disappearance of two place-names, Meriba and Massa, where some famous incidents of argument and rebellion occurred (see Exod 17,7; Deut 6,16; 9,22; 32,51; 33,8). The Greek tanslators treated these two nouns as common nouns, which they are also, and translated them as «exasperation» and «testing». The result is that the psalm makes no allusion to the incidents at Massa and Meriba, but only to another instance of rebellion, recounted in Num 14, which ends with an announcement of punishment sanctioned by God's oath: «By my life, says the Lord, [...] your corpses will fall in this desert» (Num 14,28.29). The psalm recalls this oath in equivalent terms: «Hence I swore in my anger: Never will they enter into my rest» (Ps 95,11).

The Hebrew text says, literally: «If they enter into my rest», an imprecation formula which can be completed by saying: «May the worst things happen to me if I let them enter into my rest!» The Septuagint translated slavishly: «If they will enter into my rest», which is strange in Greek, just as in English. The TOB has filled out the meaning roughly by adding: « *We shall indeed see* whether they will enter my rest». In the Hebrew text, the proposition in verse 9 that speaks of God's works is understood as concessive: «they put me to the test, *whereas they had seen my works*», the works being the wonders God had performed to free his people from Egypt. The Greek translation rules out this interpretation. In it the works come *after* the testing imposed on God by the Israelites: «they put to the test… and they saw my works». They then designate God's punitive actions against the rebellious Israelites. It follows that one can link the «forty years» with «they saw my works», as the author of Hebrews does. In Num 14,34, after the rebellion of the Israelites, God does announce a punishment that will last «forty years». In his commentary, the author of Hebrews shows himself to be very aware of the allusion in the psalm to the incident in Num 14; for instance, he uses the expression in Num 14,29.32.33 about «the limbs» which «will fall in the desert». He could hardly find a more suitable text than that to cause a strongly dissuasive effect.

Besides, this text was open to being developed along spiritual lines, for, instead of containing, like Num 14,30, the threat of not being able to enter «into the land», promised by God, it speaks of not being able to enter «into the rest» of God. The person addressed is the same but on its own the expression does not name him and is open to another interpretation. The psalmist chose it precisely for that purpose, so that the Israelites already established in their land can nevertheless apply God's threat to themselves. The author of Hebrews will not fail to exploit that possibility with regard to his Christian listeners.

2

First subdivision (3,12-19)

After quoting the exhortation in the psalm, the preacher comments on it, using the same exhortative tone. He goes back to some words in the psalm; we put them in italics:

12 SEE, brethren, that there be not in anyone among you
a *heart* afflicted with INCREDULITY
such as to withdraw from the living God.
13 but exhort each other every day
for as long as the *Today* is proclaimed,
lest anyone among you become *hardened*
by deception of sin.
14 Sharers with Christ, in fact, we have become,
provided that the beginning of our position,
we keep it firm to the end,
15 when it is said:
Today if you hear his voice,
do not harden your hearts as in the embitterment.
16 Who, actually, having *heard, embittered*?
were they not all those who left Egypt thanks to Moses?
17 And against whom did he *get angry forty years*?
was it not against those who sinned,
whose limbs fell in the desert?
18 And to whom did he *swear* that *they shall not enter into his rest*,
if not to the indocile?
19 and we SEE that they could not *enter* because of INCREDULITY.

A. *COMPOSITION*

The boundaries of this subdivision are indicated by an inclusion: «see» and «incredulity» at the beginning (12ab), «we see» and «incredulity» at the end (19). In the middle, a repetition of the beginning of the quotation from the psalm is observable: 15bc repeats 7b.8a.

The next subdivisions will similarly have their boundaries marked by an inclusion and will take up part of the quotation from the psalm, its last sentence in the second subdivision (4,3) and its first sentence in the third subdivision (4,7) as in the first. The overall result is a concentric arrangement (beginning-end-beginning), strengthened by the relationship one notices between the inclusion of the third subdivision («indocility», *apeitheia*: 4,6.11) and that of the first one («incredulity», *apistia*: 3,12.19). More precisely, this correspondence is in the form of a chiasm:

(3,12)	*apistias*		*di'apeitheian* (4,6)
		×	
(3,19)	*di'apistian*		*apeitheias* (4,11).

Between 3,19 and 4,6 the relation is particularly close:

...they could not enter because of incredulity (3,19)
...they did not enter because of indocility (4,6).

The two halves of the first subdivision (3,12-19) are clearly distinct. Verses 12-15 do not contain any interrogative sentence, whereas verses 16-18 are a sequence of questions. To the initial questions (16a, 17a, 18a) the reply is suggested by means of other questions (16b, 17b, 18b). The collaboration of the listeners is thus constantly called for.

Verses 12-15 are exhortative. The exhortation is explicit in 3,12a.13a.15c, implicit in 3,14bc, which defines a condition to be fulfilled. In these verses, the parallelism is somewhat loose. It is synonymous between 3,12b and 3,12c:

a heart afflicted with incredulity (3,12b)
becomes detached from the living God (3,12c).

It is complementary between 3,13a and 3,13b:

exhort each other every day (3,13a)
for as long as the Today is proclaimed (3,13b)

as also between the «become hardened» in 3,13c and «through deceit of sin» in 3,13d.

In 3,14 there is no parallelism, but 3,14b contains an antithesis between «the beginning of our position» and «the end». In 3,15 there is the parallelism at the beginning of the quotation from the psalm, already noted.

Verses 16, 17, 18 are tied to each other in parallel arrangement. Both start with an interrogative pronoun: «Who?» (3,16a), «against whom?» (3,17a), «to whom?» (3,18a) and consist of a question and the answer to it; in 3,16b and 3,17b, the latter being suggested by another question: «is it not so...?», while in 3,18b it comes in the extension of the initial question: «To whom... *if not* to the indocile?».

Between verses 12-14 and verses 16-19, some correspondences that follow a concentric arrangement may be noted:

A incredulity, detaching oneself from the living God (3,12)
  B deceit of sin (3,13d)
    C sharers with Christ (3,14a)
    C' those who left … thanks to Moses (3,16b)
  B' those who sinned (3,17b)
A' the indocile (3,18b) not to enter because of incredulity (3,19).

B. *BIBLICAL CONTEXT AND INTERPRETATION*

The quotation from the psalm —as we have said— alludes to the incident of the rebellion in Num 14: having got near to the Promised Land and being called upon by God to enter it, the Israelites refused, for fear of the risks of the enterprise. An oath by God then blocked their access to it and forced them to wander in the desert for forty years, until the death of all the adults who had been indocile. This most important episode is related at length later on in an address by Moses (Deut 1,19-46) and briefly in Deut 9,23-24 as well as in two psalms (Ps 95,11; 106,24).

In Heb 3,12 the preacher directs all the rest of his commentary on Ps 95 towards a warning against incredulity, the absence of faith (*a-pistia*), which corresponds to the theme he has just expounded: Jesus is «trustworthy» (*pistos*), so we must be careful not to lack faith. For those keeping to the text quoted (LXX Ps 94,7-11), this approach may seem arbitrary, because the psalm does not speak of «a heart afflicted with incredulity», it simply says: «do not harden your hearts» (8) and «they go astray in heart» (10). In reality, the introduction to the theme of absence of faith is perfectly justified; that theme is present in the incident to which the psalm alludes. In Num 14,11 God complains of the lack of faith of his people, saying: «Until when will it refuse to believe in me?». In Deut 9,23 Moses reminds the Israelites of the episode, telling them: «You were indocile to the word of the Lord your God, you did not believe in him or listen to his voice» and Ps 106 declares: «They refused a land of delights, they did not have faith in his word» (Ps 106,24).

The Christians are therefore exhorted not to be lacking in faith or, more exactly, they are called upon to watch over each other and to exhort each other lest anyone be lacking in faith and give way to the seduction of sin. Being «sharers in

Christ», they are in a situation like that of the Israelites guided by Moses, a very favourable, but demanding, situation which requires holding firm to the end to the position (*hypostasis*) taken at the beginning, at the time of the initial profession of faith.

In 3,16-19, the preacher comes back to the text of the psalm, to explain the allusions in it. «The embitterment» came about after the exodus from Egypt under the guidance of Moses. God's anger, for «forty years» (Num 14,34), was unleashed, after the rebellion recounted in Num 14, against those who had «sinned» (Num 14,19) and had been «indocile» (Deut 9,23). God declared to them: «Your limbs will fall in this desert» (Num 14,29.32 LXX; see 14,33.35), and he swore: «You will certainly not enter into the land in which, with my hand raised, I took an oath to settle you» (Num 14,30). That prediction came about. An attempt made the next day by the Israelites to enter into the Promised Land ended in disastrous defeat (see Num 14,39-45). The preacher can conclude:

> And we see that they could not enter because of incredulity (3,19).

From the rhetorical point of view, pointing out an undeniable fact like this gives utmost power to the exhortation. God's threats come true; they must therefore be taken seriously!

3

Second subdivision (4,1-5)

1 Let us therefore fear that it does not happen
—there still being a promise to ENTER INTO his REST—
that one of you seem to have stayed behind.
2 And indeed, we have had the good news preached to us just as they have,
but the word *heard* was of no avail to them,
who did not unite in faith with those who had *heard*.
3 We, in fact, *are entering into the rest*, we who have clung to the faith,
in accordance with what he said:
As I swore in my anger:
If they will enter into my rest,
the works, to be sure, having been accomplished since the beginning of the world.
4 Concerning the seventh [day], this has actually been said:
And God *rested*, on the seventh day, from all his works
5 and here again:
If they WILL ENTER INTO my REST.

A. *COMPOSITION*

The expression «enter into rest» (4,1b) provides the transition with the end of the first subdivision (3,18a.19a). It is a link-formula. The boundaries of this second subdivision are marked by the repetition of «enter into rest» (1b and 5b). Still, this inclusion is not so clear as the preceding one, because the same expression also comes in the middle (3).

Between 1b and 1c one notes an antithetic parallelism, prepared by the «So let us fear» at 1a. To the «promise to enter» (1b) the «stayed behind» comes in opposition (1c).

Between 2a and 2b the parallelism is synonymous; to «received the good news» (2a) there corresponds «the word heard» (2b).

The join between 2b and 2c is provided by the double negation («was of no avail»: 2b; «did not unite with»: 2c) as well as by the idea of hearing («the word heard»: 2b; «those who heard: 2c).

An antithetic parallelism opposes 3a («we have clung to the faith») to 2c («who did not unite in faith»).

A synonymous parallelism unites 3a («We are entering into the rest») to 3d («If they will enter into my rest»); it reinforces the logical connection expressed by 3b («according to what he said»).

To 3d, which speaks of «rest», 3e is tied by the antithesis rest—works.

Between 4b and the two preceding stichs the relations are manifold. The repetition of «the seventh» unites 4b to 4a which introduces it. The repetition of «the works» and the antithesis «rested» and «the works» unite 4b to 3c.

A parallelism is then set up between «God rested» (4b) and «my rest» (5b), the possessive adjective «my» referring to God, who speaks in the psalm.

B. *BIBLICAL CONTEXT AND INTERPRETATION*

This part of the commentary has several surprises in store for the listeners, because the preacher brings some novelties into it. The first of these novelties is the statement concerning «a promise to enter into his rest», that is to say into God's rest. The psalm does not in fact speak of such a promise but, on the contrary, expresses a threat of not entering God's rest. It is true that the Greek translation of the psalm does not say: «Never will they enter into my rest». It says: «If they will enter into my rest», an obscure formula for anyone not knowing the meaning of the underlying Hebraism. It may be judged that it leaves open the possibility of entering.

Be that as it may, the author's statement can be justified in two ways. The first is that along with the threat, which is more exactly a decision to exclude, Num 14 actually contains a promise. The adults are excluded and will die in the desert, but the generation of small children, who have not been able to be accomplices in the rebellion, will be able to enter into the Land. God declares: «your small children, I shall have them enter and they shall know the Land that you have disdained» (Num 14,31).

The other justification is based on the psalmist's implicit intention, which is not at all to exclude the people he is addressing from God's rest but, quite the contrary, to inspire them with behaviour that results in their entering it, like the generation of innocent small children.

Another surprise is caused by the sentence that says: «we have heard the good news preached as well as they have». The psalm, in fact, does not speak of any evangelization of the Israelites in the desert. Once again, to understand the preacher's statement, we have to go back to the stories in Num 14 and in Deut 1. There it is seen that the Israelites were evangelized, that is to say they received some good news. In Deut 1,8 God himself announces it, saying: «This is the land that I delivered to you; go therefore and take possession of it». In Num 14,7 Josuah and Caleb, back from their exploration, declare: «The land that we went to reconnoitre is a good land, a very good land». This good news foreshadowed the gospel where Jesus proclaims: «The kingdom of God has come near; convert and believe the good news» (Mark 1,15). Evangelized like the Exodus Israelites —and better than them— Christians must take care not to adopt the same attitude, which makes the announcement of the gospel unproductive by not accepting it in faith. Faith, on the contrary, makes that announcement fruitful. The preacher has no hesitation in saying that adherence of faith to the word of God opens the way into God's rest now. In 11,1 he will define faith by saying that it is a way of possessing here and now the things hoped for. The great hope of Christians is entry into God's heavenly rest. Faith gives access to it. The preacher's declaration is nuanced. He does not say that through faith we have entered into the rest, but that we are entering into it. Our entry is not over and done with; it is still going on.

The rest of the text is disconcerting. It seems incoherent. The author states that our entry into rest is in conformity with the oath made by God in his anger —an oath which excludes rest. The author explained himself very badly. To arrive at a coherent explanation, it is necessary to complete the text somehow or other;

either: «We are entering the rest, for God's rest exists, as the word of the psalm says, while barring access to it to the rebellious Israelites».

or: «We, the believers, are entering into the rest, because what the psalm says has barred access to non-believers».

What is clear is that the author then explains what is meant by God's rest. When we read the psalm in the light of the Book of Numbers, we understand that «God's rest» means a place of earthly rest, the land to which the Israelites were going. The word *katapausis*, «rest», is used in that sense in Deut 12,9. In 2Chr 6,41 and Ps 131(132),14 that word more precisely designates the earthly sanctuary which God makes his place of rest. But by itself the word *katapausis* does not have a local sense, it means «act of resting» or «rest». The psalmist —as we have said— had already suggested that meaning. The preacher explicitly points to it by putting the word *katapausis* in antithetic relation to the word «works».

After work comes rest. God's rest is not a place, but a state, of which the story of creation speaks: «God rested on the seventh day from all his works» (Gen 2,2). The promise to enter into God's rest is a promise to have a share with God in that blessed state, in that peace, in that joy. Thanks to their faith, believers have a foretaste of it.

4
Third subdivision (4,6-11)

6 Since, then, it is still granted to some to ENTER INTO that
and the first to be evangelized did not enter by reason of INDOCILITY,
7 again he fixes a day, *Today*,
saying in David after such a long time
as has been said before:
Today, if you hear his voice,
Harden not your hearts.
8 In fact, if Jesus (= Joshua) had given them *rest*
he would not speak thereafter about another day.
9 A sabbath rest is therefore granted for the people of God.
10 Indeed, *he who entered into his rest*
also *rested* from his works
as God did from his.
11 So let us hasten to ENTER INTO that *rest*,
lest anyone fall into the same example of INDOCILITY.

A. *COMPOSITION*

The transition between 5 and 6 is provided by a link-formula «to enter into». This expression also helps with the inclusion marking the boundaries of the subdivision; this inclusion contains, notably, the repetition of «indocility» (6 and 11: the only occurrences in the letter).

This subdivision is more prosaic. Between the two causal propositions at the beginning (6), we notice an antithetic parallelism between the present possibility of entering into the rest and the past fact of non-entry of the first to be evangelized. A similar antithesis, but without the slightest verbal parallelism, is noticeable in the period that expresses an unrealizable condition (8) that follows the resumption of a distich from Ps 94: the supposition of an entry into the rest occurring in the past would result in the impossible denial of a present fact; that supposition is therefore unreal and a positive conclusion (9) becomes necessary. In verses 7 and 8 the words «day» and «today» are repeated in chiastic order. Verse 10 presents a parallelism between «who entered into his rest» and «he, too, rested», as well as an antithesis between —literally— «the rest of him» and «the works of him». The parallelism is prolonged by a comparative phrase, «as God from his», which gives a ternary rhythm to the whole. The last distich (11) places an entry into the rest and an example not to be imitated in antithesis. This final sentence is exhortative («Let us hasten therefore») and is thereby in relation with the initial sentence of the preceding subdivision («Let us fear therefore»: 4,1). There is at once resemblance and difference; resemblance through the exhortative genre; difference —and even antithesis— through the content of the exhortation: the beginning (1) inspires fear, whereas the ending (11) inculcates action. From the psychological and rhetorical point of view, this arrangement is completely suitable; it is better to end by inculcating action which makes it possible to avoid danger.

B. *BIBLICAL CONTEXT AND INTERPRETATION*

After warning against «incredulity» (*apistia*) in 3,12-19, the preacher now recalls the «indocility» (*apeitheia*) of the Israelites who had received the good news. He had already alluded to that indocility in 3,19. Moses —as will be recalled— had reproached the Israelites, in Deut 9,23, at once with their indocility as well as their lack of faith at the time of the episode in Num 14. The indocility of the adults had excluded them from entry into the land, but that entry had been granted, forty years later, to the young generation.

The exhortation in the psalm shows that the same possibility remains open. To convince his listeners of this the preacher uses two arguments. The first is the date of composition of the psalm, much later than the crossing of the desert, because the psalms are ascribed to David. In inspiring David to say: «*today* if you hear his voice, harden not your hearts», God showed that he was again opening the possibility of entering into his rest one day. Which day is that? The preacher does not say. Much further on, in 10,25, he will tell his listeners: «You see the Day approaching», the day of the manifestation of the Lord, the day of condemnation for the indocile and of the final entry into the rest for the faithful. It must be recognized, however, that this eschatological interpretation of the «today» in the psalm, according to which God «fixes a certain day» (7), forces the meaning of the text. The «today» in the psalm does not actually denote a definite day. It occurs any day, through the liturgical recitation of the psalm (see 3,13). But the eschatological interpretation of biblical texts was prevalent at the time; the Qumran documents bear ample witness to this.

The other argument concerns the nature of the promised rest. This is explained by means of an answer to a possible objection: Is there any reason for speaking about a future entry into the rest? Was this entry not effected in the past, with Joshua when the Israelites took posession of the promised land? To this objection the preacher quickly replies by showing that the invitation in the psalm, addressed to the Israelites who had already made their entry into the promised land, shows that that entry was not really the entry into God's rest. It was a material achievement, a simple prefiguration of the spiritual entry which gives a share in the heavenly joy of God himself. The psalm therefore attests that a «sabbath rest» of that kind is still offered to the people of God (9).

The next sentence, expressed in the past, is open to two interpretations. It can be understood as a general statement, taking the Greek aorist as «gnomic», in which case it is translated in English with a present: «he who enters into his rest also rests from all his works». One can also understand it as a precise statement applied to a past event and to a definite person. This second interpretation is preferable, the more so because it opens up the possibility expressed by the first. «He who entered into his rest» is obviously Christ, of whom it will be said several times that «he entered» (6,20; 9,12.24). «He entered inside the veil» (6,20), «he entered into the sanctuary» (9,12), that is to say «into heaven itself» (9,24). The sentence in 6,20 states that Jesus «entered as forerunner for us», which shows clearly that the application to Christ of the statement in 4,10 is by no means exclusive. Christ's entry into his rest has made our entry into God's rest possible. The preacher therefore concludes with a pressing invitation: «Let us hasten therefore to enter into that rest», the rest of Christ, a sharing in the rest of God. He knows that positive action is the best way to guard against dangers of falling.

5
Fourth subdivision (4,12-13)

To reinforce his exhortation, the preacher adds a reflection on the formidable power of the word of God which lays everything bare and penetrates. The Greek word for «word» being masculine (*logos*), it is fitting to translate it, as in French for instance, with a masculine noun, «verbe», so as not to rule out certain text ambivalences, «God» also being masculine.

A. *COMPOSITION*

This passage is enlivened with great oratorical spirit which, on the whole, corresponds more with Graeco-Latin rhetoric, but, in detail, uses Semitic parallelism.

12 Living, indeed, is the WORD of God, and energetic
and more penetrating than any two-edged sword
and penetrating until it divides soul and spirit, joints and marrow
and able to judge dispositions and thoughts of the heart
13 and there is no creature that escapes from its sight
but all are bare and vulnerable in his eyes,
he towards whom to us [is] the WORD (= to whom we must give an account).

The sentence starts with a very brief epithet for the word of God (one syllable in Greek); the next description is a little longer (three syllables) and more menacing; then the language swells (fourteen syllables and a comparative) until it gets to twenty-three syllables thanks to two pairs of nouns; the menace likewise fills out; the intensity then diminishes a little, while still maintaining a high level (fifteen syllables, fourteen and seventeen), until the sudden final drop, which falls like a cleaver (seven syllables).

An inclusion about the word *logos* («word») marks the beginning and end of the passage. It is imperfect, because the meaning of the term is not the same in both cases: at the beginning, «the word» of God; at the end, «the account» that we shall have to give.

The first stich has a concentric arrangement. In the middle, «the word of God»; on both sides, an epithet. The effect of this arrangement is to put the two epithets into relief, especially the first, «living», which is in an emphatic position.

«Living is the word of God» is much more expressive than «the word of God is living». Besides, a conjunction (*gar*, «indeed») underlines the epithet even more.

The second stich has a similar arrangement to that of the first, which gives a kind of parallelism. The two epithets occupy both ends of the stich. They are related: «more penetrating» and «two-edged».

The second distich presents a synonymous parallelism: «penetrating»/«able to judge»; «soul and spirit»/«dispositions and thoughts of the heart». But it is asymmetric, the first stich comprising two couples of complements and the second just one.

The third distich shows an antithetic parallelism: «there is no creature» is set against «but all»; «that escapes his sight» is set against «bare and vulnerable to his eyes».

B. *BIBLICAL CONTEXT AND INTERPRETATION*

This description of the Word of God does not contain any quotation from the Old Testament, but corresponds to the teaching in it on the juridical aspect of the Word. It is to this aspect that the preacher actually draws the attention of his hearers, beause he wants to reinforce his exhortation. So he does not bring out the more positive aspects of the Word: its creative power (Ps 33,6; Wis 9,1), its power to illuminate (Ps 119,105), to nourish (Deut 8,3) and to heal (Ps 107,20; Wis 16,12). He takes his inspiration more from Wis 18,15 which personifies the Word when saying to God: «From the height of the heavens your almighty Word lept from the royal throne, a stern warrior [...] bearing your irrevocable decree as sharp sword». This text well shows that the word of God is «living ... and energetic», without, however, applying these qualities to it. The First Letter of Peter (1,25) says that the Word of God is «living», but instead of then speaking of its energy, the apostle speaks of its stability: «it remains» and he quotes Isa 40,8: «The word of the Lord remains eternally». An oracle of Isaiah better expresses the efficacy of the word; in it God declares: «The word that comes from my mouth does not return to me without any result, without having done what I wanted and achieved its mission» (Isa 55,11). But the context makes no mention of any juridical action.

The word of God is «more cutting than a two-edged sword». This is to be seen in Wis 18,15, which has just been quoted, or, without the comparison to a sword, when God says of the sinful Israelites: «I put them to death with the words of my mouth» (Hos 6,5). The Letter to the Ephesians says that the word of God is «the sword of the Spirit» (Eph 6,17), but the line of thought is different: Christians are called upon to grasp that sword to use it in their spiritual struggle «against the Spirits of evil» (6,12). In our text, on the contrary, it is the Christians themselves who are implicitly under the threat of that sword. Its penetration is fearsome, since it is capable of dividing off the soul, the principle of physical life, from the spirit, the principle of spiritual life, and of reaching the joints, despite their solidity, and the marrow, despite its bony protection. The word of God has a capacity to judge that is far superior to that of a human judge, for it discerns «dispositions and thoughts of the heart» (for the Bible, as is known, the heart is the organ of thought, just as much as of affectivity). The last distich states the impossibility of escaping from the inquiry. The culprit will be discovered without fail.

Exegetes have noted that the text reverses the normal order of juridical operations so as to heighten its dissuasive effect. Instead of following the order inquiry —sentence— execution, we have, at the beginning, the sight of the sword, ready to carry out sentence, then there is the allusion to judgment and lastly the affirmations about the inquiry, which deprive the culprit of any hope of escape[1].

6
Conclusion (4,14)

14 Having therefore an eminent HIGH PRIEST,
Who has gone through the HEAVENS
JESUS, the son of God,
Let us hold firm to *THE CONFESSION OF FAITH*

A. *COMPOSITION*

The «therefore» shows that this sentence is a conclusion. Its link with what immediately precedes is weak. The whole section (3,1-4,14) is what it concludes. As we have already noted, it forms an inclusion with the beginning of the section (3,1), the most conspicuous inclusion in the whole sermon:

1 See PROULX P. - ALONSO SCHÖKEL L., «Heb 4,12-13: componentes y estructura».

[1] So then, holy brethren, who share in a HEAVENLY calling,
consider the apostle and the HIGH PRIEST of our *PROFESSION OF FAITH*, **JESUS**,

Three terms of great importance («high priest», «Jesus», «the confession of faith») are repeated in identical form and the word «heavens» is in close relation with «heavenly».

From the literary point of view this sentence is less attached to the preceding verses (12-13) than it is to the next verses (15-16). A link-formula «to have a high priest» links verses 14 and 15. There is therefore room for considering the three (14-16) as a passage of transition between the two sections of this second part (3,1-5,10).

The sentence is composed of two parts, a long part consisting of affirmations containing three elements and a very short part consisting of exhortations. The affirmation acts as foundation for the exhortation.

B. *INTERPRETATION*

The affirmation recalls the doctrine expounded at the beginning of the section (3,1-6), but it is not just a summary of it. Each of its three elements brings something new. In fact, for the first time, the preacher declares we have a high priest. This title had appeared in 2,17, in a sentence that applied it to Jesus in a very indirect way. It indicated what had to be done «to become high priest». In 3,1 the title was applied directly to Jesus, «the apostle and the high priest of our confession of faith» but in an invitation to consider him. Here (4,14), the preacher uses the verb «to have»: «Having, therefore, a high priest» and he points out that our high priest is «eminent»[2].

Our high priest «has gone through the heavens», to reach the divine Majesty which is «above the heavens» (Ps 8,1). That had not been said explicitly before either. Thus is explained the position of the son who, according to the sermon's exordium, «has sat on the right of the Majesty in the heights» (1,3). Moreover, this remark also explains what was said in the preceding exhortation about Christ's entry «into his rest» (4,10).

For the first time, too, Jesus is called «the Son of God». In the exordium the preacher spoke about a «Son» (1,2) and then defined that Son's glorious position at length (1,5-13), but without ever saying that it was a question of Jesus. At

2 Literally: «Having, therefore, a great archpriest», but in English *archiereus* is translated as «high priest».

the beginning of the present section, he declared that «Christ» is trustworthy «as Son» (3,6), but he did not specify whose son he is. Here, at last, he definitely does by adding the article «the» and the complement «of God». This slow progress is rhetorically clever. It arouses a sustained interest in the listeners and, by finally giving them the answer they were waiting for, gives them the satisfaction of knowing that they were not deceived: the Son is Jesus Christ, and he is truly «Son of God», in the fullest sense of the term, God with God, Creator with the Creator, completely trustworthy.

The three words of exhortation, «let us hold firm to the confession of faith», summarize the preceding exhortations (3,12; 4,1.11), especially the one that warned against «the absence of faith» (3,12); they point them in the direction, defined at the beginning, of «confession of faith» in Jesus, the «trustworthy» high priest (3,1-22).

This sentence therefore constitutes a perfect conclusion to the first section (3,1-4,14) of the first exposé on priestly Christology (3,1-5,10).

Chapter 8

Merciful high priest (4,15-5,10)

Having concluded, in 4,14, what he had to say about Jesus, the trustworthy high priest, to whom we must cling in faith, the preacher starts speaking of the other necessary priestly quality for excercizing mediation, mercy. He had mentioned it first in the announcement of the subject of this Second part of his sermon (2,7-18). Here he takes up the many expressions in that announcement which are connected with the theme of priestly mercy: «high priest», «being able to sympathize», «being similarly tested in everything», «merciful», «help», «with regard to the things of God», «the people», «the sins».

Much shorter than the previous section, which extended over twenty-three verses, this second section consists of an introductory verse (4,15), a verse of exhortation (4,16) and of ten verses of exposé (5,1-10). The difference in length is due to the brevity of the exhortation, which occupies only one verse instead of 17, with the exposé being, on the other hand, a little longer (10 verses instead of 6).

Introduction (4,15)

15 We do not, in fact, have a HIGH PRIEST
who cannot sympathize with our weaknesses,
but one who has been tested in all things similarly,
apart from sin.

Exhortation (4,16)

16 So let us then approach with confidence the throne of grace
that we may receive mercy
and that we may find grace
for help in due time.

Description of the high priest (5,1-4)

1 Every HIGH PRIEST, in fact, taken from among men,
is established for mankind in what concerns relations with *GOD*,
that he may *offer* gifts and sacrifices *for sins*,
2 being able to have feelings adapted to those who are ignorant and go astray
for he, too, is beset with weakness
3 and because of it he must, just as for the people,
so also for himself, *offer for sins*,
4 and one does not take for oneself honour
but [one is] *appointed by* GOD
exactly as was Aaron.

Application to Christ (5,5-10)

5 So also Christ
did not glorify himself for becoming HIGH PRIEST
but He who said to him:
You are my son; I, today, have begotten you,
6 [he appointed him] according to what he also said in another [oracle]
You are a priest for ever *like Melchisedek*
7 he who, in the days of his flesh, [having offered]
pleas and supplications to Him who could save him from death
with powerful cry and tears
having *offered* and having been heard by reason of his piety,
8 although being Son, learnt obedience from the things suffered
9 and, made perfect,
became, for all who obey him, cause of eternal salvation,
10 being *proclaimed by* GOD HIGH PRIEST *like Melchisedek*.

In this particularly carefully elaborated text, the system of the inclusions is first noticeable. The word «high priest» is used in a threefold inclusion: a general inclusion (4,15 and 5,10), another, limited to the exposé (5,1 and 10) and a third, limited to the application to Christ (5,5 and 10). The inclusion limited to the exposé is reinforced by the repetition of the name of «God» (5,1 and 10). The name of God at the same time serves as an inclusion marking the boundaries of the limits of the description of the high priest (5,1 and 4).

Several parallelisms coming at the end of certain elements are also noticeable: the end of the first element of the description that speaks of «offering for the sins» (5,1c) finds an echo in the end of the second element (5,3b). The end of the description («appointed by God» 5,4b) has a parallel at the end of the application to Christ («proclaimed by God»: 5,10). The end of the first element of this application («priest [...] like Melchisedek»: 5,6b) is repeated at the end of the last element, with a variation («high priest like Melchisedek»: 5,10).

The beginning of the section (4,15-16) has a parallel structure to that of the preceding verse (14), which contains a statement and a short exhortation. But instead of being united in one sentence, the two elements are in two distinct sentences and the exhortation is more developed.

The grammatical link with the previous sentence is provided by an «in fact», the literary link by the repetition of the link-expression «have a high priest».

The introductory verse contains an antithetic parallelism between a qualification that is denied and another that is stated. However, the antithesis is not perfect; against the incapacity to sympathize, it does not set the capacity to have mercy, but a situation which, implicitly, is such as to obtain that capacity.

A «therefore» shows that the exhortation rests upon the preceding declaration. A synonymous parallelism between «receiving mercy» and «finding grace» is in chiastic form:

so that we may receive		and that grace
	×	
mercy		we may find.

Not having noticed this arrangement, the Vaticanus copyist left out the second verb and writes: «so that we may receive mercy and grace».

The description of the high priest (5,1-4) comprises three elements. The first (1) is a general definition of the high priest as mediator between mankind and God, completed with a detail concerning sacrifices. The second element (2-3) insists on the relation of the high priest with sinful mankind, a relation manifested in the offering of sacrifices for himself and for the people. The last element (4) brings an explanation of the relation of the priest to God. The sentence is antithetic.

The last element corresponds in part to the first, for it explains how a high priest «is established for relations with God» (1), saying that he is «appointed by God» (4), but it says nothing about relations with mankind.

The application to Christ (5,5-10) likewise has three elements. They correspond, in inverse order, to the three elements of the description, which gives a concentric arrangement to the whole ABC-CBA. The first element (5-6) immediately takes up the final expression of the description: to «precisely like Aaron» (4) corresponds «So also Christ» (5). Then comes the detail about the relation of the high priest to God in an antithetic sentence as previously: to «one does not take the honour for oneself, but…» corresponds (literally) «he did not glorify himself, but…». The rest is still symmetrical in the sense that it speaks of God who appoints Christ high priest, «as Aaron had been appointed by God» (4), but the words are not the same and the proportions are very different. Instead of the simple name of God, the preacher, to designate God, here uses a long periphrasis containing two parallel oracles, one coming from Ps 2, the other from Ps 109(110) and applied to Christ. In the first oracle, God appoints him his Son; in the other, he appoints him priest. The sentence is elliptical; the periphrasis is its subject; the verb is not expressed.

At first sight, the second element of the application (7-8) corresponds very little with the second element of the description (2-3). It offers only one verbal contact, but that contact is very significant, for it involves the verb «to offer». Since «every high priest is established to offer» (1) and «must offer» (3), Christ «has offered» (7). The content of the offering is different: on the one hand, «gifts and sacrifices» (1), on the other, «requests and supplications» (7). If, apart from vocabulary, we look for relations between content, we find that the description of Christ «in the days of his flesh» (7) corresponds to that of the high priest «beset with weakness» (2), except that, for Christ, there is no question of «sins» (1 and 3), but only of an extremely distressing situation that causes «supplications, loud cry and tears» (7).

The last element (9-10) corresponds to the first (5-6), for it speaks again—and more clearly—about Christ appointed «high priest» by God «like Melchisedek», but it speaks also about the relation of Christ with mankind, for whom Christ has «become cause of salvation» (9). It thereby corresponds at the same time to the first element of the description (1), which expresses the twofold relation of the high priest with mankind and God. The thought has moved on. It goes from a vague «is established» (1) to a triumphant «proclaimed by God» (10). The kind of priesthood is explained: «high priest like Melchisedek», as well as the advantage «for mankind» (1): to secure for them an «eternal salvation». The «gifts and sacrifices» of the former worship (1) are replaced by the *teleiōsis* of Christ, «made perfect» through his suffering (8-9; see 2,10). This last relation —of continuity and of going beyond— is not immediately apparent; suggested by the symmetry of the text, it will later be confirmed by the great exposé of priestly Christology in chapters 7 to 10, announced by these verses.

Introduction (4,15)

15 We do not, in fact, have a HIGH PRIEST
who cannot sympathize with our weaknesses,
but one who has been tested in all things similarly,
apart from sin.

Exhortation (4,16)

16 So let us then approach with confidence the throne of grace
that we may receive mercy
and that we may find grace
for help in due time.

Description of the high priest (5,1-4)

1 Every HIGH PRIEST, in fact, taken from among men,
is established for mankind in what concerns relations with *GOD*,
that he may *offer* gifts and sacrifices *for sins*,
2 being able to have feelings adapted to those who are ignorant and go astray
for he, too, is beset with weakness
3 and because of it he must, just as for the people,
so also for himself, *offer for sins*,
4 and one does not take for oneself honour
but [one is] *appointed by* GOD
exactly as was Aaron.

Application to Christ (5,5-10)

5 So also Christ
did not glorify himself for becoming HIGH PRIEST
but He who said to him:
You are my son; I, today, have begotten you,
6 [he appointed him] according to what he also said in another [oracle]
You are a priest for ever *like Melchisedek*
7 he who, in the days of his flesh, [having offered]
pleas and supplications to Him who could save him from death
with powerful cry and tears
having *offered* and having been heard by reason of his piety,
8 although being Son, learnt obedience from the things suffered
9 and, made perfect,
became, for all who obey him, cause of eternal salvation,
10 being *proclaimed by* GOD HIGH PRIEST *like Melchisedek*.

A further point made in verse 9 adds a relation with the first section of this Part (3,1-4,14). It is «for all those who obey him» that Christ became cause of eternal salvation. Thus it is recalled that Christ, «trustworthy high priest», has authority «over his house» (3,6) and that any «indocility» must be guarded against (4,6-11), if it is wished to obtain «eternal salvation» (5,9) by entering, thanks to him, «into God's rest» (4,10-11).

The sentence in 5,9-10 is therefore a perfect conclusion, not only to its section, but to the whole of the Second part of the sermon. It is at the same time, as we know, the announcement of the subject of the next Part[1], for its three statements require fuller explanation.

Outline of 5,1-10: priesthood and solidarity

A a) High priest between mankind and God (1ab)
b) offers sacrifices for sins (1c)

B a) relation to sinful mankind (2)
b) offers for the sins of the people and his own sins (3)

C a) does not take the honour (4a)
b) but is appointed by God (4b)
c) like Aaron (4c)

C c) so Christ (5a)
a) did not glorify himself (5b)
b) but was appointed son and priest by God (5c-6)

B b) he offered up his human distress (7)
a) he learnt obedience from his sufferings (8)

A b) made perfect through his sacrifice (9a)
a) saviour of mankind, proclaimed high priest by God (9b-10)

B. *BIBLICAL CONTEXT*

The biblical context of this section is obviously the institution of the priesthood in the Old Testament (Exod 28-29; Lev 8-10) with this very important difference, mentioned above in connection with 2,17, that the old texts never speak

1 See chapter one.

of priestly mercy. But the preacher manages to find in these texts an attestation of solidarity in «weakness» (5,2) between the high priest and the people, a solidarity that shows itself in the need for the high priest to offer sacrifices of expiation for himself and for the people. Indeed, the first kind of sacrifice for sin, provided for in Leviticus, is the one that the «priest consecrated by anointing», that is to say the high priest, must offer for his own sin (Lev 4,3-12); after which comes the sacrifice he must offer for «all the community of Israel» (4,13-21). The same is true for the solemn liturgy of the great pardon (*Kippur*): the high priest must first offer up «the sacrifcial bull for his own sin» (16,11) and then «the goat set aside for the sacrifice for the sin of the people» (16,15). The preacher's affirmation is therefore perfectly well founded.

Another difference between this section of the sermon and the ancient texts on the priesthood is that the preacher restricts his perspective to the offering of sacrifices for sins. The Old Testament ascribes many other functions to the priests: offering other kinds of sacrifices, a special relation with the sanctuary and with the word of God, passing on the divine blessing. In the first section (3,1-6), the preacher has already borne witness to the authority of our high priest to speak in the name of God and to govern God's house; he does not return to those subjects. The insistence on the sacrifices for sins is explained by the importance given them after the harsh experience of the exile and also by the undeniable need for them in making the covenant with God possible. Sins constitute the great obstacle to the covenant; the first thing to achieve is the removal of that obstacle.

In designating sinners as «those who are ignorant and go astray», the preacher limits the perspective to a certain category of faults. The Old Testament in fact clearly distinguishes faults committed «in error» (Lev 4,2.13; 22,27; Num 15,22.24.27) and faults committed «high-handedly», that is to say in deliberate revolt against God (Num 15,30). In the first case, the offering of a sacrifice for the sin is prescribed to obtain pardon (Lev 4,20.26.35; Num 15,25.26.28). In the second case, no remission is possible; the culprit «will be cut off from the middle of his people» (Num 15,30). The expression used by the preacher is therefore precise. It is found again in 9,7.

In the verses that speak of Christ (5-10), there are firstly two divine oracles, drawn from two royal psalms applied to the Messiah. The first oracle proclaims the divine sonship of the king consecrated by God over Sion (Ps 2,6-7). The preacher already quoted it at the beginning (1,5) while applying it implicitly to the risen Christ, like St. Paul in a speech in Acts (Acts 13,33). The second oracle proclaims the priesthood of the king invited by God to sit at his right hand (Ps 109,1.4). The first verse of this psalm, as we have said, is applied to Christ in the gospels and in other New Testament writings. The preacher alluded to it towards the end of his exordium (1,3) and then quoted it in 1,13 when linking it structurally to the oracle in Ps 2, by means of a parallel introduction. Contrariwise, the oracle on the priesthood, the one in verse 4 of the psalm, makes its first appearance in the New Testament here (6). It will later be taken up, partly or completely, no less than eight times (5,10; 6,20; 7,11.15.17.21.24.28). This verse is not quoted elsewhere in the New Testament. It is evidently a discovery by the author, an extremely important discovery, because it leads to recognizing the accomplishment of priestly worship, an essential part of the Old Testament, in Christ's paschal mystery.

The dramatic description of Christ's offering (7-8) calls to mind his Passion, expressed in the language of the psalms of supplication, which speak of urgent prayers, cries, tears. Various psalms have been proposed as source of the passage: Pss 31,23 and 39,13 by Dibelius, Ps 116 by Strobel. In fact it is not possible to pin down a precise source. The author takes his inspiration freely from the prayers of the psalter and creates some original expressions. The word «supplications» never appears in the Greek translation of the psalter, nor does the word *eulabeia*, «piety», nor the expression «loud cry» nor «offering up petitions» These words and expressions do not occur either in the gospel accounts of the Passion. The author calls the Passion of Jesus to mind, but without any verbal borrowing from these accounts.

c. *INTERPRETATION*

To introduce his statement on the second priestly quality of our high priest —mercy— the preacher unites it to the first quality with an «in fact» and a double negation: « *We do not, in fact, have* a high priest *who cannot* sympathize with our weaknesses…» (4,15). He thus replies to an objection that could be raised against his invitation to cling in faith to «Jesus, the son of God», «eminent high priest, who has gone through the heavens» (4,14). This high priest, it could be objected, is too distant from us; how could he, from the height of his glory, be interested in us who are so wretched? The objection is overcome thanks to the other aspect of the priesthood of Christ, mercy. Christ's glory does not prevent him from understanding us, because he acquired it by largely sharing our pitiful fate. He was «tested in all things as we are». Like us, he experienced hunger and thirst, fatigue and sadness, temptations; more than we do, he underwent humiliations and ill-treatment, the agony of the cross. All that made [illegible] able «to sympathize with our weaknesses», in depth. The author, obviously, does not think of mercy superficially, as the attitude of a person who easily gets emotional over the misfortunes of other people. He thinks of it as a capacity acquired at the cost of hard personal suffering. To be able to sympathize really, one needs to have undergone suffering oneself and to have been interiorly tansformed by suffering. In the Old Testament, the mercy of God was expressed in many ways, not just in words full of tenderness, but also by action taken to help (Exod 3,7-10). It still lacked a dimension, that of expressing itself through a human heart, marked by suffering and thus made capable of profound compassion. That dimension is to be found in the glorified Christ, because his Passion has made him for ever one with mankind.

The assimilation of Christ to mankind was complete in the afflictions, but it did not include sin: it was achieved «in all things apart from sin» (4,15). The preacher distinguishes clearly between affliction and fault, temptation and sin. When one undergoes a painful affliction, one is tempted to rebel or to give way to discouragement (see 12,3-4). Christ was put to the test and even tempted, but he never had any collusion with sin. This clarification is important because, from the need for complete resemblance with his brethren (2,17), it might be concluded that sin was present in the life of Jesus. The occasional exegete has drawn that conclusion. The author rejects it explicitly here, as he does further on, in 7,26 and 9,14.

Far from diminishing Christ's solidarity with us, the absence of all sin in his life reinforces that solidarity, because sin undermines solidarity. Every sin is an act of selfishness, which creates division. Experience demonstrates this and Scripture bears witness to it. After the first sin, the man accuses the woman, the woman accuses the serpent (Gen 3). After the worship of the golden calf, Aaron, who showed the people how to go about it (Exod 32,2-5), later denies all responsibility and accuses the people (32,22). Real solidarity with sinners does not consist in making oneself an accomplice in their fault, which makes things worse; it consists in generously taking the disastrous consequences of the sin along with them. That is the generosity Christ had. He took on himself the fate of sinful mankind, the torment of the worst criminals, so that no guilty person can experience a painful situation without finding, next to his own cross, the cross of the crucified Christ.

The result is that, thanks to Christ, we can henceforth «with confidence approach the throne of grace» (16). The word «confidence» (in Greek *parrēsia*) does not simply express subjective confidence; it expresses a right, the freedom of access. Its etymological meaning is the right «to say all». In the Greek cities it denoted the right, reserved to freemen, to address the people's assembly. Here, as later in 10,19, it designates the right of access to the throne of God. This throne of awesome sanctity (think of Isaiah's fear when he had a vision of it: Isa 6,1-5) has become «the throne of grace», because Christ, our brother, has been called upon, because of his sufferings for us, to sit there on the right hand of God (Ps 109,4: Heb 1,13). We are sure to receive not only the «mercy» granted to the wretches we are, but also the «grace», the freely bestowed favour; both of them are manifested in the concrete by «help in time of need» (16).

The doctrinal exposé (5,1-10) appears as confirmation of the exhortation that has just been addressed to the listeners: «every high priest, in *fact...*» (1). The trustful recourse to Christ, the merciful, is justified by means of a reflection on the nature of the priesthood (1-4) and on its realization in Christ (5-10).

In fact, the author insists on the high priest's solidarity with mankind, explicitly in the general description (2-3), implicitly in the allusions to the Passion of Christ (7-8). The new element in comparison with the previous sentences and with 2,17.18 is the introduction of sacrificial vocabulary. For the first time in the sermon, the preacher speaks of «offering gifts and sacrifices» (2), «offering for sins» (3), «offering up requests and supplications» (7). In his second exposé of priestly Christology (7,1-10,18), he will continue to present Christ's paschal mystery in the category of the sacrificial offering.

The definition he gives of the high priest is innovative in comparison with the Old Testament, for it insists on the solidarity of the high priest with mankind, whereas the Old Testament marked the separation. Between the high priest and mankind a double link is affirmed; firstly a link of origin: the high priest is «taken from among men» (1), then a link of purpose: «he is established for mankind». This «*for mankind*» corresponds to the theme of the section, the one about Christ's priestly mercy. It is in contrast with the Old Testament perspective, whereby one was a priest *for God*. The institution of the Israelite priesthood begins with the following word of God to Moses: «Call Aaron, your brother to you, along with his sons among the children of Israel, so that he may be priest *for me*» (Exod 28,1). The same expression is repeated in Exod 29,1 concerning the rites of priestly consecration. In the Old Testament, all the attention was brought to bear on the special relation of the priest with God, to the extent of seeming to forget that priesthood is an institution for mediation. The Letter to the Hebrews, on the contrary, clearly shows the twofold necessary relation for mediation and insists more on the relation of the high priest with mankind; the latter is named in the first place, and twice before the relation with God is mentioned.

The high priest's role of mediation is then explained in the sense of sacrificial offerings intended to obtain pardon for sins (1c). That is indeed the first thing the high priest must do for mankind to obtain a positive relation with God for them. This point allows the preacher to insist further on the solidarity of the high priest with mankind. The ritual in Leviticus actually shows that the high priest is in the same situation as the rest of mankind; he is morally weak, he is a sinner, he must therefore offer sacrifices for sins, both for himself and for the people (Lev 9,7; 16,11.15). From this necessity there normally results a capacity for «having feelings adapted to those who are ignorant and go astray» (2). The preacher is not speaking here of «sympathizing», as in the case of Christ in 4,15. He is using a different verb, which is found only here in the Bible and the etymological meaning of which is «to have moderate feelings». In the language of the philosophers this verb expressed self-control. Philo uses it in that sense. But here, this verb has an indirect complement, which leads to its being translated «to have suitable feelings for». The preacher did not want to ascribe compassion for sinners to the high priests of the Old Testament, which is nowhere found in it; he reserved that compassion for the new high priest; to the high priests of old he merely ascribed something approaching it.

The third element in the description comes back to the high priest's relation to God (4). Instead of insisting, as in 3,1-6, on the positive aspect of that relation, the preacher on the contrary stresses the humility necessary on the part of him who accedes to the priesthood: «one does not take the honour for oneself». The requirement of humility is evidently based on the fact that the high priest is a man, «taken from among men» (1), «beset with weakness» (2), and that he therefore has no pretext for claiming a special relation with God. The initiative can only come from God alone. The priesthood is received as a gift from God. It is God who appoints a human being. The verb used here can be translated «to call» or «to appoint»; it is fitting to translate it «to appoint», because here it is not a question of a call to the priesthood, of a vocation; it is a question of an appointment. Aaron was «appointed» priest by God (4); Christ was «proclaimed» high priest by God (10).

The Old Testament clearly shows that Aaron did not ascribe the dignity of the priesthood to himself, nor was he designated by Moses; it was God who ordered Moses to take him saying: «Send for Aaron, your brother, [...] so that he may be a priest for me» (Exod 28,1). «You shall send for Aaron ...» (29,4) and God dictates all the rites of priestly consecration (29,4-21). Moreover, the Levite Kore and his party disputed the priesthood of Aaron and wanted to take that dignity for themselves, the divine answer was as clear as possible. With two miraculous signs God showed «who the consecrated one is» (Num 16,5-7) and he exterminated the ambitious people (Num 16,35). The priesthood cannot be won by a man so as to rise above his brethren. It is a gift of God that puts one at the service of others.

The application to Christ (5-10) states immediately that the requirement for humility has been met: «Christ did not glorify himself to become high priest...» (5). The preacher uses litotes here. The apostle Paul puts it more in plain terms by saying that Christ «humbled himself, becoming obedient unto death and death on the cross» (Phil 2,8). The preacher was to express himself later on in similar terms (7-8). His sentence contains a skilful oratorical progression.

After the negative part of the sentence, the positive part, introduced with a «but» (5c), is incomplete. It does not have a verb, but only a disproportionately long subject, which is a periphrasis designating God. The absence of a verb is significant. It shows that the author wanted to keep to the idea of renouncing glory. He did not imitate Paul who straightaway balances the statement about Christ's voluntary humiliation with the proclamation of his super-glorification: «God super-exalted him» (Phil 2,9). The author has kept the proclamation by God of Christ's priestly glory for the end (10).

The long periphrasis designating God contains two quotations from a psalm. The role of the first lends itself to debate. God declares in it that Christ is his Son (Ps 2,7). Some exegetes judge that this first «bears the main weight of the demonstration» of the priesthood of Christ and that the second quotation comes only «in confirmation»[2].

That opinion is debatable. No one is appointed priest by saying that he is a son, but by saying that he is a priest. The error comes from a wrong interpretation of the Greek conjunction *kathōs*, which serves to introduce the second quotation. If it is given a simply comparative meaning «just as», the second

2 BONSIRVEN H., *Saint Paul. Epître aux Hébreux*, 267.

quotation seems to be of secondary importance. But *kathōs* often has a normative sense, «according as», and serves to introduce, in particular, proofs from Scripture (Matt 26,24; Mark 1,2; 9,13; etc.). This is the meaning it should be given here. God has appointed Christ high priest in accordance with what Scripture says: «You are a priest…» (Ps 109,4). This more coherent interpretation is confirmed by the end of the passage, where it is not repeated that Christ has been declared son of God but that he has been «proclaimed high priest like Melchisedek by God» (10). The whole demonstration of Christ's priesthood in 7,11-28 will be based on the oracle in Ps 109(110),4 and not on the oracle in Ps 2.

What then is the function of the quotation from Ps 2,7? It serves to introduce skilfully the one from Psalm 109. One could paraphrase the text as follows: «You all know—I reminded you of it at the beginning of this sermon (1,5)— that in Psalm 2, God declares to the risen Christ: «You are my son, today I have begotten you». But have you noticed that in 109, which is Messianic like Psalm 2, God declares to the risen Christ, invited to seat himself at his right hand (Ps 109,1): «You are a priest for ever like Melchisedek» (Ps 109,4)? Christ does not only possess filial glory, he also has priestly glory».

Let us add that, in the author's perspective, the filial glory of Christ is part of his priestly glory, for it fully provides one of the two relational capacities necessary for priestly mediation; the Son, in fact, has the most intimate relation with God there is. But being Son is not enough to be priest; the other relational capacity is indispensable, the one concerning relations with mankind. Christ acquired that second capacity through his Passion, at the end of which he could be proclaimed high priest. To tell the truth, the two relational capacities are the ones Christ acquired through his Passion for his human nature. His obedience to God unto death gained for him, for his human nature, filial glory; his solidarity with us until death earned him, at the same time, the glory of brotherly love. But the relation with the Passion is more exclusive in this second case, for Christ had never possessed the glory of brotherly love before, whereas he had always possessed filial glory in his divinity (John 17,5.24); he had always been «splendour of the glory» of God (Heb 1,3).

In the next verses (7-8), the preacher shows how Christ became high priest: through a dramatic sharing in the human condition, the occasion of a priestly offering to God. The main statement comes at the end of the sentence; it is expressed in a personal verbal form: Christ «learned, through the things he suffered, obedience». This statement is preceded by two participles: «having offered and having been heard», themselves being preceded by a long series of complements. The author thus expresses two differents aspects of the same events: an offering up of prayers which was heard and an education through suffering. These two aspects may seem contradictory: in the first, in fact, God does the will of Christ, while in the second, Christ submits himself in suffering to the will of God. A further analysis shows that in reality they are two complementary aspects of the Passion of Christ, each corresponding to a truly human situation.

The beginning of the sentence defines the perspective: Christ was «in the days of his flesh», that is to say in the time of his mortal life, distinct from his eternal divine pre-existence and from his present situation as glorified Lord. The expression is a Hebraism. To speak of the life of a person, the Bible says: «his days» (Gen 6,3.5; 9,29; etc.; also Luke 1,5.7). Furthermore, to express the condition of weakness of mortal mankind, the Bible uses the word «flesh» (Gen 6,3; Isa 40,6; Matt 26,41). The author is therefore clearly referring to Christ's human existence, full participation in the common fate of mankind, fragile creatures doomed to die.

Then comes the description of a situation of dramatic anguish: Christ prays and beseeches Him who can save him from death, he shouts with all his strength, he weeps. The sentence explains that Christ is struggling with a very grave danger of imminent death and is imploring God's help, like king Hezekiah (Isa 38) or so many others whose cries fill the psalms of supplication. This is no ritual liturgy, but the irrepressible reaction caused by extreme distress.

The preacher here presents the Passion of Christ as an intense prayer, more precisely, as the offering up of petitions and supplications. The tragic events that threatened Jesus' existence and questioned his teaching, his work and his very person, these events are faced up to with an intense prayer which constitutes an offering. Having declared that «every high priest is established to offer» (1), the preacher states that Christ «has offered». The content of his offering is paradoxical, because he offered up «petitions». The current distinction between offering and petition is passed over here, and rightly so because all genuine prayer is at the same time an offering in the sense that it is always accompanied by a willingness to accept the solution chosen by God. The gospel accounts of Jesus' agony clearly show this aspect of his prayer. Having made his petition, Jesus adds: «However, not as I will, but as you will» (Matt 26,39). The preacher expresses this generous attitude of Jesus by speaking of his «piety». The word he uses is not the usual term, which would be *eusebeia*, but another term, *eulabeia*, which expresses an attitude of religious respect (Luke several times uses the corresponding adjective: Luke 2,25; Acts 2,5; 22,12) or a feeling of apprehension.

The prayer of Christ was heard. In a famous article, A. Harnack claimed that the original text of the sermon did not contain that statement but its opposite: Christ asked to be preserved from death and he was not heard, he had to die[3].

This conjecture has not the slightest support in textual criticism and is based on an error: the text does not say that Christ asked to be preserved from death, it does not say exactly what Christ asked for, but only says to whom Christ addressed his petition. It is true that by describing God as «He who could save him from death», the text suggests that Christ asked to be saved from death, but being saved from death does not necessarily mean being preserved from death. Three ways of being saved from death can be distinguished. The first consists effectively in being preserved from it, like king Hezekiah to whom God granted fifteen extra years of life (Isa 38,5; 2Kgs 20,6). An appreciable, but provisional, solution: after the fifteen years, Hezekiah died. The second way of being saved from death consists in being freed from it after having suffered it; this was the case, for example, of Lazarus (John 11,43-44) or of the daughter of Jairus (Mark 5,41-42). It, too, a prodigious, but provisional, solution. The third way of being saved from death consists of defeating death once and for all by undergoing it in such a way that it opens the way to heavenly communion with God. This solution is the only one not to be provisional: «Christ risen dies no more, death has no more power over him» (Rom 6,9). It is in this way that Christ was «heard».

He was «heard by reason of his piety» (7). This expression has raised much discussion, for the Greek term translated by «piety» is open to other interpretations. Some people translate it as «fear» and explain that Christ was freed from fear and could thus fearlessly face his Passion and death. This translation strains the meaning of the Greek words: *eulabeia* does not mean «fear»; this word can denote the fear of God, that is to say deep respect for God, but not a panic-stricken fear of death. Besides, after «heard», the Greek preposition *apo* never means «being freed from». Other exegetes give this preposition the meaning of «after», which it can have in certain contexts: Christ was heard *after* having undergone the anguish of death. This interpretation is the opposite of the preceding one, while having, in common with it, the inexact translation of *eulabeia* as «anguish». With the verb «to hear», the normal meaning of the preposition is not

3 HARNACK A., «Zwei alte dogmatische Korrekturen in Hebr», 62-73.

«after», but «by reason of» (see Exod 6,9 in the Septuagint). Christ was «heard by reason of his respect for God».

Indeed, the attitude of profound respect makes hearing the prayer possible because it opens up the one who prays to the action of God. A psalm clearly says so: God «carries out the will of those who fear him, he listens to their prayer and saves them» (Ps 144[145],19).

In the anguish of looming death, Jesus experiences the very human desire to escape from it. He embraces that desire and presents it to God in suppliant prayer, but with profound respect for God, that is to say without claiming to impose anything on God, leaving to him, on the contrary, the choice of solution. This attitude opens the soul to God's action. Matthew's gospel shows that during Jesus' agony a transformation occurred in his prayer. At the beginning, Jesus says: «My father, if it is possible, may this chalice pass far from me!»; he adds: «However, not as I wish, but as you wish» (Matt 26,39). At the end, Jesus gives up his first petition and says: «May your will be done!» (26,42). The formulation in the Letter to the Hebrews agrees perfectly with that gospel tradition, for, while not saying exactly what Jesus asked for, it leaves open the possibility of a development in his prayer. The sequence of events showed that the will of God consisted in granting Jesus the most perfect reply possible to his prayer: complete and definitive victory over death, by means of death itself.

Offering and being heard are the two components of a sacrificial event. The hearing is an integral part of the sacrifice, for, if God does not accept the offering, it is not really sacrificed, that is to say made sacred by God's sanctity; it was presented in vain. Thus there was an attempt at sacrifice, not an accomplished sacrifice.

The next verse (8) expresses another aspect of the event, that of education through suffering. In it one can see the first aspect of being heard. This did not consist in preserving Jesus from suffering and death, but of giving them a very positive outcome by making them serve as a transformation of Jesus himself: «he learned, from the things he suffered, obedience» and was thus «made perfect». In this sentence there is, in the Greek, the preposition *apo* from the previous verse; it serves to show the origin of a result, the means used to achieve it. These means are the sufferings, including death. The theme of education through suffering often occurs in Greek literature, where it is expressed with the help of a suggestive assonance, *pathein, mathein*, «to suffer», is «to learn»; the preacher uses it skilfully in the form of: *emathen, epathen*, «he learned from what he suffered». When the Bible takes up this theme it is not content to note a fact of experience in it; it adds a consideration on the action of God. It is God who provides suffering with positive efficacy. By means of trials which involve suffering, God makes himself known to mankind, either as a judge from whom no one can escape (Ezek 6,7; Job 19,29), or as a father attentive to the education of his sons (Prov 3,11-12 quoted in Heb 12,5-6). God transforms mankind so as to be able to set up a closer relation with it, which confers on the human being all his dignity.

In the case of Christ, the preacher is careful to note that education through suffering was not necessary for him personally. He received it «although being Son». The preacher will say further on that for us it is necessary so that we may become sons and daughters of God, worthy of that name (12,8). But the Son of God, «splendour of his glory», personally had no need of an education. It was his human nature that needed it, in so far as it was in solidarity with mankind, «flesh like the flesh of sin» (Rom 8,3).

Christ suffered, therefore, and not only did he suffer, but he was transformed by his sufferings; in them he «learned obedience». A bold statement, which one is easily tempted to overlook, but it shows all the gravity of the incarnation and the redemption. Of course, it does not mean that Jesus was disobedient at first and that God had to punish him to reduce him to submission. That interpretation was excluded in advance by the sentence stating that our high priest was tested in all things, «apart from sin» (4,15). At his entry into the world, Christ appears with an attitude of perfect adherence to the will of God (10,7.9). But there is good reason for distinguishing, in human existence, a preliminary disposition to docility to God and obedience as a tried virtue. For the preliminary disposition to become a virtue that penetrates every fibre of human nature, it is indispensable that harsh trials be faced and overcome. Having taken on our nature of flesh and blood marked with the consequences of original disobedience, Christ submitted himself to that requirement. He learned obedience through his sufferings. In the Passion of Christ, human nature was radically renewed. A new human being was created who corresponds perfectly with the divine intention because he agreed to learn obedience in the crucible of suffering.

This obedience consisted first of all in accepting the action of transformation done by God, but at the same time it constituted an extremely generous personal offering. God's action and Christ's action joined up perfectly, thus forming a perfect sacrifice. The human nature assumed by the Son of God was transformed and transfigured by this real sacrifice. And it was so for the benefit of all human persons, as the preacher said earlier on (2,9); he says it again in 5,9: having learnt, through his sufferings, obedience, Christ has «become cause of eternal salvation for all who obey him» (5,9).

The end of the sentence (9-10) expresses the consequences of the event and casts new light on it. As we have said, it contains three statements which form the conclusion to this important paragraph and announces the subject of the next part.

The first and third statements are expressed with participles: «having been made perfect», «having been proclaimed high priest by God»; the central statement has a personal verb, «he became», and thus acquires greater importance; that is not surprising, for it corresponds more directly to the theme of the section, which is one of priestly mercy. It expresses the capacity to come to help, which was acquired by Christ through his Passion. Christ, henceforth, is not simply able to help, as was said in 2,18 and 4,16; he became «cause of salvation» and of «eternal» salvation.

This conclusion is, in a sense, surprising—and to a greater extent revealing. It is surprising, because nothing led up to it explicitly in the preceding mention of the Passion of Christ (7-8). It was not said there that Christ suffered in order to become the cause of salvation of other people. It was there only a matter of his own salvation. It could certainly be seen that he had fully taken on the human condition with all its weight of suffering and that he had been made «similar in all things to his brethren» (2,17; 4,15). But nothing had been said about the outcome, for «his brethren», of that complete solidarity. It is the conclusion that reveals that outcome and shows that Christ's solidarity with us was such that by beseeching God for salvation for himself, he obtained it for all human nature at the same time and therefore for all human beings who follow him. Having been obedient until death, he has a right to their obedience, which he asks of them only in order to save them.

The salvation he obtains for them is an «eternal salvation» and not simply an occasional act of liberation. The adjective «eternal» makes its first appearance in the sermon here. When, in 2,10, Christ was presented as «the pioneer of salvation», the quality of the salvation was not specified. It is now, in visible relation to the quality of the priesthood of Christ, priest «forever» (6 and 10), who introduces believers into God's rest (4,3).

It is because he has been «made perfect» (9) that Christ has become «cause of eternal salvation». The first statement is the shortest—a single word in Greek—

but its position at the beginning of the sentence gives it decisive importance, for it presents it as fundamental. The arrangement of the text puts it into immediate relation to education through suffering. Christ learned obedience through his sufferings and was thus «made perfect». A sentence in the first part of the sermon (2,10) confirms this interpretation and further specifies that it is God who made Christ perfect. It says actually that it was fitting for God to «make perfect through suffering the pioneer of salvation». This sentence also confirms the relationship between having been made perfect and having become cause of salvation.

Then again, what is the relationship between «having been made perfect», the first statement, and «to have been proclaimed high priest by God», the third statement? The sentence implies that one is the condition of the other. If God could proclaim Christ high priest, it is because he had become so thanks to the transformation of his human nature, which «made [him] perfect». In 2,17 the preacher declared that Christ «had to be made like his brethren in all things in order to become high priest». Here he expounds the same doctrine in other terms: Christ suffered and learned obedience so as to be made perfect and to be proclaimed high priest.

One notices, however, some progress in the thought, expressed by the verb «to make perfect». By agreeing to be made like his brethren, Christ was paradoxically «made perfect», which his brethren were not. The transformation obtained by Christ is twofold: the assimilation of Christ to mankind, the gift of perfection to man in Christ. The paradox is that the gift of perfection to mankind is achieved by means of the assimilation to the radical imperfection of fallen mankind. The explanation of the paradox is to be found in the motives for the assimilation: docility towards God and brotherly love for mankind. These two generous dispositions take concrete form in the assimilation to human misery, but they are factors of profound transformation. The situation assumed is transformed from within. Thus it is that in making himself in all things like his unfortunate brethren, Christ is made perfect and communicates that perfection to them.

For a reader of the Greek Bible the word *teleiōtheis*, «made perfect», bears a connotation that did not appear in 2,10, but which begins to reveal itself here (5,9-10), thanks to its connection with the end of the sentence. In the Pentateuch, the verb *teleioun* and the noun of action *teleiōsis* always designate the consecration of the high priest. In Hebrew, the expression used means literally «to fill the hand». The Greek translators apparently judged this expression too material and so almost always transposed it to another level, a nobler one, that of perfection: instead of «to fill», they put «to make perfect» (Exod 29,9.29.33.35; Lev 4,5; 8,33; 16,32) and instead of «act of filling», they put «act of making perfect» (*teleiōsis*: Exod 29,22.26.27.31.34; Lev 7,27/37; 8,21/22; etc.).

It follows that the author's statement according to which Christ was «made perfect» through his sufferings can at the same time be understood as a statement of the priestly consecration of Christ. The transformation that Christ achieved through his sufferings made him a high priest. The logical connection with the last statement in the sentence then becomes very close: because his Passion consecrated him high priest, Christ was proclaimed high priest by God.

To complete the interpretation of this vital text, we have to go over *the connections there are between the two successive parts (5,1-4 and 5,5-10)*, that is to say between the description of «every high priest» (1-4) and the verses concerning «Christ» (5-10).

The preacher's explicit intention is clearly manifested in the middle of the text: «... just as Aaron. So also Christ...». A parallelism is stated between Christ and the high priest of the Old Testament. Like Aaron, Christ was appointed high priest by God. We, Christians, therefore have a high priest. We are not in a situation inferior to that of the Israelite people, but in a similar situation.

This affirmation of resemblance and continuity is characteristic of this Second part of the sermon. The first section began by affirming a connection of resemblance between Jesus and Moses. Our high priest Jesus is «trustworthy... like Moses» (3,1-2). The exhortation that follows affirms a connection of resemblance between us, Christians, and the Israelites of the Exodus: «we have been evangelized like them» (4,2).

In the Third part, on the contrary, the preacher will point out some differences and even some opposing aspects between the priesthood of Christ and that of the Old Testament, in order to show the originality and the novelty of the priesthood of Christ (see 7,11.27; 9,12.24-25).

Here, in 5,1-10, the preacher is not setting the priesthood of Christ against that of Aaron, but is asserting, on the contrary, their resemblance. The parallelism is particularly close between verses 4 and 5; we noted that fact at the beginning of this chapter, as well as the connections between verses 2-3 and 7-8, on the one hand, and between verses 1 and 9-10, on the other.

The preacher made the task easier for himself by the choice of components of his description. He carefully avoided entering into details that might have prevented seeing a parallelism between «every high priest» and «Christ».

The relation between the high priest and other persons is defined in an extremely vague way. «Taken from among men, he is established for men» (1). The Old Testament never expresses itself in that way. On the contrary, it specifies the tribe assigned to the service of the Temple (Num 1,50) and the family from which the high priest must come (Exod 29,9.44). All the other tribes, all the other families are excluded (Num 17,27-18,7). Provision is made for the death penalty for anyone not observing this restriction (Num 1,52; 3,10; 18,7).

The term used to designate the high priest is likewise of the vaguest. «Every high priest is established...» There is nothing specific about this verb; it can be used for any function. Nothing is said about the rites of consecration of the high priest, described with such insistence in the Pentateuch (Exod 29; 39; Lev 8-9). This omission is a hint that sanctification by means of ritual separations is not considered essential for access to the priesthood.

On the other hand, the description insists on an aspect of the priesthood that did not draw any attention in the Old Testament: the solidarity of the high priest with other human beings. Instead of speaking of being a priest for God, as in Exod 28,1 or 29,1, the author says that every high priest is established «for mankind» (1). Instead of going into raptures, as Sirach does (45,7-8; 50,5.11), over the splendour of the pontifical vestments, the author shows the high priest «beset with weakness» and finds, in favour of this point, a very strong argument in the ritual laws that require the high priest to offer sacrifices for his own sins.

The description of «every high priest» therefore takes on a new orientation which facilitates applying it to Christ. In spite of that, some differences appear which hint at a change in the way the priesthood comes about.

The application to Christ does not mention sin, whereas the description spoke about it insistently: «for sins» (1), «those who are ignorant and go astray» (2), «to offer for sins» (3). The weakness of the high priest implied sin on his part. In the case of Christ, the weakness appears clearly in his supplications, his loud cry and his tears (7), but there is no question of sin; this is in conformity with the declaration in 4,15 which excluded sin from Christ's likeness to us. In place of sin, we find its opposite, respect for God *(eulabeia)*.

Another difference between description and application to Christ is the merging of weakness and offering. In the description, weakness and offering are two dictinct realities. The high priest must offer because of his weakness (3). He cannot offer his weakness because it is tied up with sin. The high priest therefore offers «gifts and sacrifices» (1), which are external to him. Christ, for his part, does not offer external gifts and sacrifices, but, in suppliant prayer, offers God his own situation of weakness and anguish. It can be said that Christ's offering consists of his very weakness, taken on in prayer. There is thus a transition from an outward ritual sacrifice to a personal and real-life sacrifice, made possible because the weakness of Christ is completely free from any connivance with sin. It is a weakness taken on in solidarity with sinful mankind in a great burst of generous love.

Third difference: the description of every high priest speaks twice about offering (1 and 3), without saying anything about the result obtained. The application to Christ expresses the result of the offering: Christ offered and was heard (7d). In the central part, the preacher will explain this difference more clearly, which, here, is only suggested. The sacrifices of the Old Testament never really came to anything; they were only ineffective attempts. Christ's offering, for its part, was accepted by God and therefore constituted a sacrifice in the full sense of the word. Christ's human nature really was sacrificed, that is to say made sacred, taken up into the holiness of God (John 17,19). This transformation was achieved through the prayer of Christ. On its own, weakness does not constitute a sacrifice. It becomes one thanks to God's transforming action, called for by an intense prayer (7) and accepted in generous docility (8).

The most radical novelty in comparison with the priesthood of old is the personal transformation of the priest himself. The ancient rites did not bring about any personal transformation of the priest. Christ, for his part, «through his sufferings learned obedience» (8) and was thus «made perfect» (9).

According to the Old Testament, the high priest had to receive the priesthood by means of ritual sacrifices, called in Greek *teleiōsis*, «action of making perfect»; these sacrifices qualified him to offer sacrifices for the people afterwards: «Every high priest… is established… to offer gifts and sacrifices for sins» (1).

In the case of Christ, there was no ritual sacrifice of consecration, but a real-life transformation by means of distressful events submitted to in prayer. Such was the *teleiōsis* of Christ, his priestly consecration. This consecration was not followed by other sacrifices, offered later for the people. It constitutes a unique sacrifice, which is enough for all. The real-life transformation of Christ makes him the perfect mediator, «cause of eternal salvation for all who obey him» (9);

it therefore makes any supplementary sacrifice useless. Unlike the high priests of old, Christ was not established high priest «to offer gifts and sacrifices» (1). His unique offering constitutes at once a sacrifice of priestly consecration, a sacrifice of expiation, a sacrifice of covenant and a sacrifice of praise, that is to say of thanksgiving; it takes the place of all kinds of sacrifices, because it resulted in the complete sanctification of human nature, a sanctification that was not ritual, but real, not external, but spiritual and complete.

The author does not insist here on these differences, for his perspective is centred on the similarities between the mystery of Christ and the former priesthood. But he was not able to prevent the differences being hinted at. He will explain them amply in his second exposé of priestly Christology (7,1-10,18). The last statements of this first exposé (5,9-10) announce, as we have said, the themes of the second.

To this first exposé, the author has given a binary structure which corresponds to the double relation necessary for exercizing priestly mediation. As a first approximation, one can say that the first section concerns the relation with God —the priest is «trustworthy for relations with God» (2,17)— and the second section, the relation with mankind—the priest is «merciful» (2,17), «able to sympathize» (4,15). A more attentive examination, however, reveals a more complex situation, for the first section insists much on the relation of the priest to the «the house» of God, formed by the believers, and the second section speaks much about offering to God. A more exact statement of the theme of the two sections must therefore show, for each of them, the union of the two relations in the person of the mediator.

In the first section, Christ is presented as high priest accredited by God to put the faithful in contact with him (3,1-6); these must therefore listen to his voice and cling to him in faith (3,7-4,14). In the second, Christ is presented as at one with human misery (4,15) in a suppliant gesture of offering to God (5,7). His mercy is therefore not just philanthropy; it has a strong God-centred dimension. In his mercy, as in his trustworthiness, Christ is truly high priest, mediator between mankind and God.

Central Part

Christ is the perfect high priest: priestly Christology, specific characteristics (5,11-10,39)

Chapter 9

Exhortative introduction (5,11-6,20)

Shrewd listeners could realize that by concluding Part Two of his sermon at 5,9-10, the preacher announced the subject of Part Three at the same time. The three statements at the conclusion do in fact need further development. The preacher explicitly confirms the intuition of these listeners by telling them:

> On this subject we have a long speech to make,
> and it is difficult to interpret (5,11),

and he starts with an earnest introduction, in keeping with the importance of the subject. It is of the exhortative type, while only containing one explicitly exhortative sentence in it (6,1).

A. *COMPOSITION*

This section is divided into six oratorical movements: 1) reproaches; 2) declaration of intent; 3) negative perspective; 4) positive comparison, then a negative one; 5) positive statement; 6) twofold reason for hope.

An inclusion on the word «nonchalant» (5,11 and 6,12: the only occurrences in the New Testament) groups the five first movements together. The sixth actually has a different look about it; it quotes and comments on a passage from Scripture, which is never the case in the previous movements.

1) The preacher begins by shaking up his listeners to arouse their attention. He aims some cutting remarks at them, bearing on their inability to be nourished with sound doctrine:

11 On this subject we have a long speech to make,
    and it is difficult to interpret,
    since you have become NONCHALANT about listening,
12 and indeed, when you ought by this time to be masters,
you need to be taught again
    the elements of the beginning of the oracles of God
and have got to the stage of needing milk,
    not solid food.
13 Whoever takes milk
    is incompetent [when it comes] to speaking of justice,
    for he is a child;
14 but adults have solid food,
those who, through practice, have faculties trained
    for the discernment of good and evil.

This subdivision is entirely built on antithetic parallelisms.

11 On this subject we have a long speech to make,
and it is difficult to interpret,
since you have become NONCHALANT about listening,
12 and indeed, when you ought by this time to be masters,
you need to be taught again
the elements of the beginning of the oracles of God
and have got to the stage of needing milk,
not solid food.
13 Whoever takes milk
is incompetent [when it comes] to speaking of justice,
for he is a child;
14 but adults have solid food,
those who, through practice, have faculties trained
for the discernment of good and evil.

A first antithesis contrasts a difficult speech and nonchalant listeners (11). A second antithesis contrasts the situation in which the listeners do not find themselves, whereas they ought to be in it, that is to say the situation of school-masters, with the one in which they are, that is to say the situation of elementary school children (12a-c). An antithetic comparison illustrates this situation by contrasting milk with solid food (12de). The rest embellishes this contrast by adding more complex elements. It arouses the desire to reach adulthood.

2) The preacher then announces his intention:

6,1 That is why, leaving behind discussion of the beginning of Christ,
let us go forward to adult perfection,
without laying once again the foundations of
renouncing dead works and faith in God,
2 doctrine of baptisms and of imposition of hands,
of resurrection from the dead and of eternal judgement,
3 and that we shall do, if at least God allows it.

These verses are constructed in threefold parallelism: one antithetic parallelism between «leaving behind the matter of the beginning» and «let us go forward to adult perfection» (1ab), a complementary parallelism between «the matter of the beginning» (1a) and the list of the «foundations» (1cd and 2ab), and a synonymous parallelism between «let us go forward...» (1b) and «we shall do» (3).

The formula «without laying once again» introduces what Greco-Latin rhetoric calls a «preterition», a quick reference to subjects which the speaker does not wish to deal with. The lengthy enumeration of these subjects makes it difficult to perceive the synonymous parallelism between 1b and 3. When the listeners hear the «we shall do it», they may miss its connection with the «let us go forward…» which is too far back. This is clumsiness on the preacher's part; it is not the only one.

3) The preacher justifies his «preterition» with an impossibility, which makes the perspective very negative:

4 Impossible, in fact,
that those who were once enlightened
and tasted the heavenly gift
and became sharers in the holy spirit
5 and tasted God's beautiful word
and the powerful realities of the world to come
and then fell,
6 [it is impossible] to give them the renewal of a conversion,
while they are crucifying the Son of God for themselves and dishonouring him.

The impossibility is expressed forcefully from the first word. It is then justified by a double antithesis, of content and proportion, and reinforced at the end by a final observation.

As for the content, we have, on the one hand the gifts received, on the other, the fault. As for the proportion, the gifts received are indicated in a long series of five expressions (in participial form in the Greek text; 23 words in all), whereas the fault is indicated with one participle and expressed as a fall. The oratorical effect is strong.

The gifts received and the fault are situated in the past, the impossibility of a new conversion is situated in a continuing present, as is the final observation which expresses a present aspect of the fault: sinners «are crucifying the Son of God again». It is especially in that way that they make their conversion impossible.

4) An agricultural comparison is then inserted. Unexpectedly, it expresses firstly a positive vision, before the negative vision that was expected, but the negative vision has the last word:

7 When some ground, in fact, which has drunk up the rain falling on it often,
gives birth to grass useful to those for whom it is grown,
it receives from God its share of blessing,
8 but if it produces thorns and thistles,
it is reproved and is close to being cursed,
which results in being burnt.

After a preliminary fact (7a), which holds true for both cases, there is the opposition between the positive hypothesis, leading to a blessing, and the negative hypothesis, leading to a curse. The antithetic parallelism is not regular: the insistence is stronger on the result of the negative hypothesis, which further brings with it a relative proposition at the end.

5) The preacher then applies the comparison to his listeners. and again in an unexpected way. He shows himself to be aware of this:

9 Our conviction concerning you, beloved,
  [ascribes to you] the good situation, the one which is in connection with salvation,
  even if we speak like this.
10 God, in fact, is not unjust
  to the extent of forgetting your work
  and the love you have shown for his name
  by your being placed at the service of the saints and by placing yourselves at it.
11 But we wish everyone of you
  to show the same zeal for the fullness of hope
  until the end,
12 lest you become NONCHALANT,
  but imitators of those who through faith and perseverance
  inherit the promises.

After the introductory sentence (9), which contrasts the preacher's positive «conviction» with the negative remarks he has just made, verse 10 gives the reason for the positive conviction and verses 11-12 explain the intention of the negative remarks.

An antithetic parallelism contrasts the absence of injustice (10a) with an act of overlooking (10b) which would be unjust.

A complementary parallelism between «love» in 10c and service in 10d is expressed.

A last antithesis contrasts the «nonchalant» (12a) with the «imitators…» of the heroes of the faith (12b). The sentence ends with the encouraging perspective of the «promises».

6) The final word «promises» (12c) serves as transition to the next subdivision (13), which is the last in this exhortative introduction. Indeed this word is immediately repeated at the beginning of this last subdivision, in a somewhat different form, that of a participle of the verb «to promise». Here we have a transition with a link-word.

The word «promises» also defines the perspective. It occurs twice in the singular; the first time concerning Abraham, who, through his perseverance, obtained the fulfilment of the promise (15), the second time concerning Christians, called «heirs of the promise» (17). The promise arouses «hope» (18). Implicitly, this subdivision is an exhortation to hope; it gives good reasons for hoping. But it is not purely exhortative. With the explanations it gives about God's oath (13-17), it prepares for the next doctrinal exposé, especially 7,20-22.

In this text, four stages are marked out:

1 A reminder of Abraham's experience (13-15)
2 A general reflection on the worth of oaths (16)
3 God's oath to the heirs of the promise (17-18)
4 The solidity of our hope (19-20).

1. Reminder of Abraham's experience

13 To Abraham, indeed, when God made a PROMISE,
since he could not swear by anyone greater,
he swore by himself saying:
14 to be sure, blessing I shall bless you
And multiplying I shall multiply you,
15 and thus, having persevered, he obtained the PROMISE.

An inclusion marks the limits of this small literary unit; the translation reinforces it, for it puts the word «promise» at the beginning as at the end, while the Greek text has it only at the end, having the verb «having promised» at the beginning.

A parallelism between 13b and 13c is noted here: 13c repeats the expression «to swear by». In 14a and 14b, the quotation from Gen 22,17 presents a very well supported parallelism, with the Septuagint having rendered a Hebraism denoting insistence by means of two forms of the same verb and that twice.

2. The value of oaths

16 Men, indeed, swear by something greater than themselves
And for them, the oath given in confirmation
Puts an end to all argument.

These two propositions have the theme of oath in common, but it is expressed with two different words: the verb «to swear» in the first proposition (Greek *omnuein*), and the substantive «oath» in the second (Greek *horkos*). Still, a parallelism in position underlines their connection: in the Greek text, «swear» is the last word in the first proposition and «oath» the last word in the second.

3. God's oath for the heirs of the promise

17 In this way, wishing to show more clearly to the heirs of the promise
the irrevocable character of his decision,
God intervenes with an oath,
18 so that, through two irrevocable acts
in which it is impossible for God to lie,
we may take great encouragement,
we who have sought refuge by seizing the hope that is before us,

This long sentence, which then goes on into a relative proposition (19-20), has a complex grammatical structure. It starts with a participial syntagma with a causal meaning (17a-b), continues with the main proposition (17c), followed by a long final proposition (18) inside which is a relative proposition (18b); this final proposition ends with a long participial syntagma (18d) which serves as subject. This kind of construction does not correspond to Semitic rhetoric but to Greco-Latin rhetoric. However, some traits of parallelism are noticeable. The word «irrevocable» comes before and after the main proposition; the latter thereby occupies a central position, which makes it stand out. Furthermore, a complementary parallelism is perceptible between 18a and 18b: the «acts» (18a) offer a guarantee of sincerity (18b). There is also correspondence between the «encouragement» in 18c and the seeking refuge in 18d.

4. The soundness of hope

19 [the hope] that we have like an anchor of the soul, sure and firm
and which enters within the curtain [of the sanctuary],
20 where, as precursor for us, entered Jesus,
like Melchisedek having become high priest for eternity.

Christian hope is defined with a naval image; it is «like an anchor of the soul». Some explanations are then given; the first of them agree with the image: the anchor is «sure and firm». The next detail loses contact: an anchor does not enter within a curtain; it is thrown into the depth of the water. It is hope, not the anchor, that reaches Jesus where he has entered.

The author took a lot of trouble to reintroduce, when ending his sentence, the last of the three themes he announced at the end of Part Two (5,9-10). The result is that the end of this exhortation section (5,11-6,20) is parallel to the end of Part Two (3,1-5,10). The order adopted is chiastic, which reinforces the relation:

5,10		6,20
high priest		like Melchisedek
	×	
like Melchisedek		high priest

He adds, moreover, the further clarification brought by the oracle in Psalm 109: «for eternity». The announcement of the subject is thus more complete. The corresponding development starts immediately afterwards. The expression «for eternity» comes back four times in it (7,17.21.24.28).

B. *BIBLICAL CONTEXT*

With its reproach of «nonchalance» (5,11), the beginning of the exhortation evidently belongs to the sapiential genre. The Greek word *nōthroi*, «nonchalant», is found in the Septuagint only three times, solely in the Wisdom writings (Prov 22,29; Sir 4,29; 11,12). The reproach of being «nonchalant in listening» corresponds, in a negative way, to the exhortation to listen, so frequent in the Wisdom writings (Prov 1,8; 4,1.10; 5,7; etc.; Sir 3,1; 6,23; etc.).

The comparison between teaching and drink and food is traditional, too. Wisdom invites people to eat her bread and drink her wine (Prov 9,5). The antithesis between milk for babies and solid food for adults is used by the apostle Paul in 1Cor 3,2: «It was milk that I gave you to drink, not food to eat, for you were not yet fit for it, but even now you are not yet fit for it».

The first part of chapter 6 has no close connection with the Old Testament (6,1-12). It refers to Christian catechesis (1-2) and to Christian spiritual experience (4-5).

The last part, on the contrary (13-20), cites the Old Testament. The preacher there recalls firstly the oath by God pronounced after the sacrifice by Abraham: God then «swore by himself» (13). In Gen 22,16 we in fact read: «I swear by myself, says the Lord». Then the preacher explicitly quotes a passage from the divine oath, changing the end of it: «Truly, blessing I shall bless you and multiplying I shall multiply you» (14); instead of «I shall multiply you», (in Greek: «I shall multiply *you*»), the text of Gen 22,17 has: «I shall multiply *the descendants of you*». The change accentuates the parallelism of the two propositions and better concentrates attention on Abraham.

It is more difficult to discern what the author's following assertion alludes to: «and thus, having persevered, he obtained the promise» (15). On the one hand, the Old Testament never says that Abraham «persevered». On the other, «to obtain the promise» is an expression open to two different interpretations: to get someone to promise or to get someone to fulfil what he promised. In 11,33, when the author states that the heroes of the faith «obtained promises» (same Greek verb as in 6,15), the most probable meaning is that they obtained the fulfilment of promises received.

At first sight, the meaning is the same in our text: God promised, Abraham persevered and thus obtained the fulfilment of the promise. Abraham's perseverance would therefore come after the divine promise backed up with an oath, that is to say after the sacrifice or, more precisely, after the «tying up» of Isaac.

But that interpretation comes up against a strong objection: in the Bible, it is impossible for the fulfilment of a promise sworn by God to be conditional on human behaviour. When an utterance from God has been backed up with a divine oath, it is irrevocable; it cannot fail to come about. And that really is the meaning of Gen 22,16-18; this text confirms, irrevocably, the divine promises in Gen 12,2-3 and 15,5. Our author was certainly aware of this.

In consequence, the most plausible interpretation of Heb 6,15 consists in seeing Abraham's perseverance in his docility to God during his trial. Restraining the reaction of his fatherly heart, Abraham went all the way to the spot indicated for the sacrifice. He thus obtained irrevocable confirmation of the divine promise of an innumerable progeny and a magnificent inheritance.

The long sentence in verses 17 to 20 begins in a solemn way, but is lacking in clarity. Who are «the heirs of the promise» (17a)? Are they Isaac and Jacob, further on called «the co-heirs of the same promise» (11,9)? And what other divine «oath» (17c) does the preacher wish to speak about? We have to wait patiently for the rest of the sentence to discover gradually that it is not a question of Isaac and of Jacob, but of «us» (18c), that is to say the Christians, and to guess at last that the divine oath is the one connected with the proclamation in Ps 109 about the priesthood of the Messiah «in the manner of Melchisedek» (20b). The preacher actually ends with an allusion to that oracle which he quoted in 5,6 and recalled in 5,10. He does not say that the psalm introduces it with a divine oath. The listeners have to remember it on their own. If they do not remember it, the preacher will remind them of it explicitly further on, in 7,21.

All things considered, it emerges that the preacher put the divine oath given to Abraham in parallel with the one in Ps 109 from which Christians benefit, in order to call on the latter to imitate the faith and perseverance of the patriarch (see 6,12). But at the same time he prepared the explanations of the next section (7,20-22).

INTERPRETATION

To interpret this exhortative introduction correctly, it is indispensable to remember that it is part of a sermon composed to be delivered orally in a Christian assembly. The text confirms this, for the preacher reproaches his listeners for having become «nonchalant *about hearing*» (5,11). This reproach is an oratorical device aimed at arousing a great effort to pay attention on their part, necessary for properly following the doctrinal exposé which is coming next and which will be particularly rich in content. It is not a question of taking him literally and concluding that their spiritual situation is deplorable. The preacher will say the opposite a little further on (6,9). His reflections on their inability to be nourished with solid doctrine (5,12-14) are not to be taken literally either, for they are relativized immediately afterwards: in 6,1 the preacher declares that he will in fact offer them solid doctrine. If they were really incapable of assimilating it, he would not be offering it to them.

The passage on milk and solid food mixes metaphor and reality. The preacher compares his listeners to infants who can only take milk (12). Then he says: «Whoever takes milk is incompetent in speaking of righteousness» (13). That statement can be understood at two levels. On the physical level: an infant is incapable of reasoning about what is right or not. On the spiritual level: a Christian who has not gone into his faith is unable to discern spiritual realities and to reason about what is valid in that domain. As Saint Paul writes, «he does not accept what is of the Spirit of God, for him it is folly and he is unable to know it» (1Cor 2,14).

The next sentence (14) can likewise be understood at two levels and even more easily since the Greek word designating adults also means «perfect»; that is even its first meaning. On the physical level, adults take solid food; they are not content with milk. On the spiritual level, «perfect» Christians, adults in the faith, are not content with elementary doctrine, but wish for further instruction. They look for «God's mysterious wisdom» (1Cor 2,6-7). On the physical level, adults have the capacity to discern what, for them, is good or bad; they do not absorb just anything. On the spiritual level, «perfect» Christians are no longer «children» who let themselves be «tossed around and carried off by every wind of doctrine» (Eph 4,14). They are capable of «discerning what the will of God is, what is good, what pleases him, what is perfect» (Rom 12,2); they can reach «full knowledge of his will, in all Wisdom and spiritual intelligence» (Col 1,9).

The «that is why» which introduces the next subdivision (6,1-3) affirms a logical connection, which in fact is not there. The preacher has just told his hearers that they are still at the stage of «needing milk, not solid food» (5,12). Logically, he ought to have said then: «That is why I abstain from expounding profound doctrine to you...». In fact he says exactly the opposite: he refrains from expounding elementary doctrine and announces an exposé of great depth. This oratorical incoherence shows that the reproaches were an oratorical device aimed at arousing the listeners' *amour propre* and stimulating attention.

On the other hand, the imperfect correspondence between the list of the «foundations» (1b-2) and the formula that introduces it (1a) may cause surprise. Whereas the latter speaks, literally, about «talking about the beginning *of Christ*», the list contains no mention of Christ. The formula that concerns conversion, «renouncing dead works and faith in God», expresses the two complementary aspects of it, negative and positive, but has nothing specifically Christian; it differs in that respect from the appeals to repent and believe the gospel (Mark 1,15), or appeals to «conversion to God and faith in our Lord Jesus» (Acts 20,21). The expression «dead works» to denote sins is peculiar to the author (here and in 9,14).

The allusion to baptism, also, is lacking in clarity, for the author does not use the ordinary word, *baptisma*, he uses the word *baptismos*, with a vaguer meaning, and puts it in the plural, perhaps to distinguish several kinds of baptism, that of John the Baptist and Christian baptism. In 9,10 the same plural will serve to designate Jewish ritual ablutions, «rites of flesh, left in place until the time of redressment». The «imposition of hands» is, on the contrary, put in the singular, whereas there are various kinds of it: gestures of blessing (Mark 10,16), healing (Luke 4,40; Mark16,18), transmission of the Holy Spirit (Acts 8,17; 19,6), ordination to a ministry (Acts 6,6; 13,3). Faith in the resurrection of the dead and eternal judgement is expressed already in the later writings of the Old Testament. Christian faith is more precise; it is faith in the risen Christ who will judge the living and the dead. It can therefore be seen that, in his list, the author kept to really elementary points of doctrine on conversion, rites and eschatology. The doctrine which he is getting ready to expound will, on the contrary, be an unprecedented thorough investigation into Christology.

In the next subdivision (4-6), the preacher returns to a negative perspective. He justifies his decision not to start teaching «the subject of the beginning» by saying that would serve no purpose, for it is impossible to convert hardened sinners again.

Their first conversion is described in glowing terms. It was a decisive event that happened «once». The Nicene creed echoed this fact by expressing faith in «one baptism». That event was an illumination, for Christ said: «I am the light of the world; whoever follows me will surely not walk in darkness» (John 8,12). To Christians it can be said: «You were once darkness, but now you are light in the Lord» (Eph 5,8). In the second century, Saint Justin says that baptism «is called illumination» (*Apology* I, 61). To the metaphor of light, the author twice adds that of food: at the time of their Christian initiation, converts «tasted the heavenly gift»; they «tasted the fair word of God». The second expression is clear: the word of God is Christian preaching proclaiming the accomplishment of the Old Testament in the person of Christ. The first expression, which speaks of the «heavenly gift», is open to several interpretations. It can be taken in a general sense meaning the grace of God, or in a more concrete sense meaning the «Lord's meal» (1Cor 11,20), during which the believers receive «the bread come down from heaven» (John 6,58). To the «fair word of God» are added «the powerful realities of the world to come». The resurrection of Christ has inaugurated a new world, the «world to come» that was expected. This new world manifests itself in Christian life through powerful events, miracles of all kinds (see 2,4). Saint Paul reminded the Galatians that God «worked powerful deeds» among them (Gal 3,5). He also reminded them that God «gave the Spirit» (Gal 3,5), the source of charismatic gifts, to them. Our author likewise says that the new converts have become «sharers of holy spirit».

The hypothesis that emerges is that these marvellous gifts were followed by a culpable fall, while their superabundance makes that fall inexcusable. The author does not specify the nature of this fall. He simply says, at the end of the sentence, that it was equivalent to «crucifying again the Son of God and dishonouring him». It is therefore an extremely serious fall and not a matter of faults of weakness which the mercy of Christ generously forgives (see 2,17). This fall completely contradicts clinging to Christ in faith.

Hence it follows that, in this hypothesis, «it is impossible to give them the renewal of a conversion». This fearsome impossibility comes from the fact that «they are crucifying the Son of God again». The author says no more about this, because he wants to produce a powerful dissuasive effect to preserve his listeners from any serious fault.

His words would be different if he were addressing Christians who had actually fallen. Then he would exhort them to stop crucifying the Son of God and thus make the renewal of a conversion possible. The change in rhetorical situation would bring about a change in oratorical tactics. The attitudes adopted might seem contradictory, but they would not really be, for they would not be in connection with the same circumstances.

The subdivision that follows (7-8) proposes an agricultural comparison in which the author's intention stands out. He actually applies the treatment reserved by God for human conduct to the earth's produce: blessing for those who produce good works, a curse for the others. In fact, it can hardly be said that that God gives its share of blessing to a field that produces grass and denies it to the field next to it that produces thorns. The Sermon on the Mount teaches, on the contrary, that God «lets rain fall on the just and the unjust» (Matt 5,45). What is true is that people treat fertile land and barren land differently. Thorns and thistles are in fact destined for «burning».

In the next verses (9-12), the preacher declares to his audience his conviction that they are in «*the* right situation». By putting the article «the» he shows that he wants to speak about the positive situation described in verse 7, the one that provides the divine blessing and which is therefore «in relation to salvation». The way in which the preacher had insisted on the negative situation gave the opposite impression. The effect of happy surprise thus achieved is part of his oratorical tactics. He then gives the reasons for his conviction by recalling his listeners' merits, merits which God cannot overlook, for he is not unjust. These merits consist of activity and love. Without the activity, the love would not be genuine; it would remain superficial and illusory. Without the love, the activity, even apparently generous, would be worthless; Saint Paul said that clearly in 1Cor 13,3. The love that the faithful have shown by their activity comprises two closely united dimensions: love for God and love for neighbour. It is in fact by placing themselves at the service of their Christian brothers and sisters that the faithful have shown their love for the name of God, that is to say for God to the full extent to which he has made himself known. Christian men and women are here called «the saints», as often in Paul's letters, for they have been sanctified by faith and baptism.

The preacher then explains the reason for his urgent exhortations and his severe warnings. He wanted to stimulate his listeners to continue their efforts. Less demanding than Saint Paul, who exhorts his Christians to «abound more» (1Thess 4,1.10; Phil 1,9.26; Col 2,7), the author asks only for perseverance in «the same zeal». But he points them towards a «fullness», that of «hope», for hope communicates a powerful spiritual dynamism, which sustains the effort «right to the end», that is to say until «eternal salvation».

By saying «lest you become nonchalant», the preacher fits in an inclusion with the beginning of his exhortation (5,11), where he used the same expression, «become nonchalant», but he seems to contradict himself at the same time. If he is talking to them so that they should not become nonchalant, it implies that they are not so, whereas at the beginning he told them: «you have become nonchalant» and the form of the verb —a perfect— indicated that they still are. This inconsistency has nothing surprising about it in a oratorical kind of text, which is a text in motion. It is better not to interpret it as a philosophical or juridical text. When he wants to be encouraging, the orator does not express himself in the same way as he does when he wants to warn. The interpretation must not therefore take every statement in an absolute sense, but, on the contrary, relativize it, taking account of its situation and the aim in sight.

Instead of becoming «nonchalant» (11), the listeners make themselves «imitators of those who, by faith and perseverance, inherit the promises» (12). By speaking of inheritance and promises, the preacher stays in the perspective of hope. «Inheriting the promises» obviously means entering into possession of the good things promised. These things are not of the same kind in the Old Testament and in the New. The author does not go into details on this point, but he points out the conduct necessary to inherit the good things promised: one must behave with faith and perseverance. That is what many men and women in the past did and what many courageous believers are still doing. We must imitate them.

The author could have mentioned many persons here who deserve to be taken as models. He does not do so. He will do so later on, in a long section of the fourth part of his homily, which presents the heroes of the faith of whom the Old Testament speaks, from Abel up to the martyrs in the Books of the Maccabees (11,4-40). For the moment (6,13-15) the author quotes only one example of them, but it is an example that has a fundamental importance, that of the patriarch Abraham. He does not speak explicitly of the faith of Abraham —he will speak of it in 11,8-10.17-20— he only stresses his perseverance, having noted that the promise made by God to the patriarch was reinforced with a divine oath, which he quotes (Gen 22,17).

The discussion then revolves upon the value of the guarantee given by an oath. In human affairs, this guarantee has supreme value, for the oath takes as witness «someone greater», God, most often. Being greater than all, God could swear only by himself and he actually swore by himself to back up his promise to Abraham (13-14); he swore again, on another occasion, to show clearly «the irrevocable character of his decision».

As can be seen, the author makes a clear distinction between a divine oath and a simple divine utterance. He does not adopt Philo's position, who, reasoning as a philosopher, denies that there is any difference and declares: «All the utterances of God are oaths», that is to say have the same value as an oath[1].

Philo explains at length that ascribing oaths to God is an anthropomorphism, just like ascribing hands and feet to him. The preacher does not follow Philo in his philosophical reasoning; he shows himself more faithful to biblical revelation, which uses all the subtleties of human language. Between the simple utterance of God and a divine oath, the Bible makes a distinction which must be observed. A simple utterance by God can be revoked. This is the case, for example, of the utterance transmitted by Jonah to the Ninevites, an utterance that had all the appearances of a definitive divine decision: «Still forty days and Nineveh will be destroyed» (Jonah 3,4). but the Ninevites generously do penance; that brings God to go back on his decision (Jonah 3,10). Contrariwise, an utterance supported by an oath by God cannot be revoked. In the episode of the rebellion in the desert (Num 14), God swears that the guilty will not be able to enter the promised Land (Num 14,21-23; Ps 95,11; Heb 3,11); they repent (Num 14,40), but God maintains his decision: «they were not able to enter» (Heb 3,18; Num 14,44-45).

The preacher is therefore quite right in speaking of the irrevocable (literally: «immutable») character of the divine decision. God wishes to show it «to the heirs of the promise». Who are these heirs? We have to wait until the end of this long sentence to be able to identify them: a first person plural («in order that … *we may have* strong comfort») then gives one to understand that the heirs of the

1 PHILO, *The Allegories of the Laws* III, 204; see also *On Sacrifices*, 93-96; *Abraham*, 273; *On the decalogue*, 82-95; *On Dreams* I, 12-13.

promise are the Christians. This «we» designates in the first place the «I» of the preacher and the «you» of his listeners, with whom he associates himself, but it also takes in all who have «seized the hope» offered by Jesus; this «we» therefore means I + you + they.

The preacher is not just speaking of one irrevocable act, but of «two irrevocable acts» guaranteed by the absolute sincerity of God. The context shows clearly that one of these two irrevocable acts is an oath by God, but he does not say which oath and he does not indicate what the other irrevocable act is. The listeners need much perspicacity to understand immediately what will become clear later on. The last words of the long sentence will give them the key to the enigma, for by saying that Jesus has «like Melchisedek become high priest for ever», these words refer to the priestly oracle in Psalm 109, which was quoted in 5,6 and recalled in 5,10. The listeners can remember that in the Psalm this oracle is introduced by a declaration of a divine oath. For those who might not remember, the preacher will say it explicitly in the next section of his homily (7,21). The «two irrevocable acts» are therefore the oracle in the psalm and the divine oath that backs it up. These two acts bring «strong comfort» to the believers, for they assure them that they have a high priest fully accredited by God and able to save them. Their problem, actually, is to gain salvation, in spite of all the dangers that threaten them. To escape from them, they have «sought refuge by seizing the hope» which was in front of them.

The preacher then defines Christian hope and proclaims its soundness (19-20). He compares it to a ship's anchor. This comparison is never found in the Old Testament, the Israelites not being navigators, but it is found in the Greek authors. The anchor provides safety for the ship, preventing it being carried adrift by the wind. The anchor of hope is going to attach itself «inside the curtain», that is to say in the holy of holies in the Temple. The end of the sentence makes it clear that it is not a question of the Temple in Jerusalem, for it says that it is a question of the place Jesus entered, that is to say the heavenly sanctuary, the place of God's presence (see 9,24). Jesus is here called «forerunner»; this is the only use of this word in the New Testament; John the Baptist never receives that title in it; it was conferred on him later by Christian tradition, for it corresponds to his function, «to go forward in the presence of the Lord to prepare his ways» (Luke 1,76). John the Baptist was Jesus' forerunner, but Jesus was everyone's forerunner, for, in his paschal mystery, «he has opened a new and living way for us» (Heb 10,20) which brings us into intimacy with God.

It is as «high priest» that Jesus opened this way; he is indeed the high priest solemnly accredited by God, in accordance with the oracle in Psalm 109. By taking up the terms of that oracle, the preacher —as we have said— reminds his listeners of the last statement in the announcement of the subject of Part Three (5,10) and he intimates to them that he is now going to develop that point.

Chapter 10

A different kind of priesthood (7,1-28)

In this first doctrinal section of the central part of his sermon, the preacher expresses the novelty of the priesthood of Christ, very different from the Levitical priesthood. He finds this novelty announced in the oracle in Psalm 109, verse 4, when it is taken in a Messianic sense and when it is seen fulfilled in the glorification of Christ. As this oracle speaks of the priesthood of Melchisedek, the preacher starts by examining the short account in Genesis which introduces this personage and he considers the relation of his priesthood to the Levitical priesthood (1-11); he then very precisely analyses the oracle in the psalm (12-28).

A. *COMPOSITION*

This section, which concerns the scriptural basis of the author's doctrine, is composed with the greatest care. A system of inclusions indicates the boundaries of the two great paragraphs (1-10 and 11-28) and of their subdivisions.

The boundaries of the section as a whole are not marked by an inclusion in the strict sense but by a similar procedure, that is to say by a parallelism between the final subdivision (26-28) and the initial subdivision (1-4). On the one hand, there is an inclusion on the word «priest» and, on the other, on the word «high priest».

7,1-3	7,26.28
[1] This Melchisedek, in fact, king of Salem, PRIEST of the Most High God,	[26] Such a HIGH PRIEST, in fact, was fitting for us
[3] remains a PRIEST forever.	[28] The law, in fact, established HIGH PRIESTS...

For paragraph 1-10 which comments on Gen 14,18-20 the inclusion is constructed on the name of Melchisedek and the verb «to meet» (arranged in chiastic form):

1 This MELCHISEDEK, in fact, king of Salem, priest of the Most High God,
who MET Abraham,
10 ...when he met MELCHISEDEK.

For paragraph 11-28 which comments on Ps 109,4 LXX, the inclusion is made between «made perfect» and «perfection»:

11 To be sure, if PERFECTION were given by the Levitical priesthood …
28 … a Son MADE PERFECT forever.

Melchisedek (7,1-3)

1 This Melchisedek, in fact, king of Salem, PRIEST of the Most High God,
who met Abraham on his return from the defeat inflicted on the kings,
and blessed him,
2 to whom also Abraham gave as share the tithe of everything,
who first is translated king of justice,
who, then, is king of Salem, that is to say king of peace,
3 without father, without mother, without genealogy,
having neither beginning of days, nor end of life,
but made like the Son of God,
remains a PRIEST forever.

This long sentence is really included between the subject at the beginning: «This Melchisedek… *priest* of the Most High God» and the verb at the end: «remains a *priest* for ever» All the intermediary items refer to the subject of the sentence and prepare the final statement.

The events mentioned after Melchisedek's titles and before the explanation of those titles form a small concentric structure: two long formulas that contain the name of Abraham (1b and 2a) frame a short formula, from which that name is absent (1c). The short formula mentions blessing given by Melchisedek to Abraham. This blessing will likewise be at the centre (6-7) of the next subdivision (4-10), which shows its particular importance for expressing the priesthood of Melchisedek.

A complementary parallelism is then noticeable between 2b: «king of justice» and 2c: «king of peace», then between 3a: «without father, without mother, without genealogy» and 3b: «having neither beginning of days, nor end of life» (with chiastic arrangement in 3b: «neither beginning of days, nor end of life»), lastly between 3c: «but made like the Son of God» 3d: «remains a priest in perpetuity» because it is necessary to be made similar to the Son of God in order to remain a priest in perpetuity.

Melchisedek and the Levitical priesthood (7,4-10)

4 See how great he is,
to whom ABRAHAM gave a TITHE of his booty,
he, the patriarch,
5 and those of the sons of Levi who receive the priesthood
have orders to collect the tithe from the people according to the law,
that is to say from their brethren,
although proceeding from the loins of Abraham;
6 but he, without genealogical relation to them,
collected the tithe from Abraham
and blessed him who had the promises;
7 now, without any argument,
it is the inferior who is blessed by the superior,
8 and here, from people who die receive tithes,
whereas there, someone who is testified to as living.
9 And, one might even say, with ABRAHAM as intermediary,
even Levi, who collects TITHES,
was liable to pay TITHE;
10 he was, in fact, still in the loins of his ancestor,
when he met Melchisedek.

The inclusion of this subdivision is obtained by the repetition at the beginning and at the end, of the name of Abraham and of the word «tithe» or of the verb derived from it.

This is not a very clear-cut inclusion, because this name and these words are repeated several times within the subdivision; they characterize it.

The inclusions are more clear-cut when the word comes only at the beginning and at the end of the literary unit they mark out, which is often the case.

The first sentence (4) is doubly emphatic: at the beginning, where it is about Melchisedek, with «how great», and at the end, where the title of Abraham, «the patriarch», is placed separated from the name of Abraham, which puts it in relief.

We then have two antithetic parallelisms, one in 5-6, the other in 8; the first lacks clarity because it begins with an overloaded sentence (5). These two parallelisms concern the theme of the tithe. They are separated by a reflection on the theme of blessing (6c-7). The join between 6b and 6c is in the form of a chiasm:

6b		6c
He collected the tithe	×	and he who had the promises,
from Abraham		he blessed him.

The second antithetic parallelism (8) is made more expressive by means of a daring stylistic move: instead of saying: «and here, *mortal* men receive tithes», author puts: «men *who die*»; he thus obtains a complete antithesis between «who die» and «he lives».

The last sentence (9-10) is introduced by a Greek formula expressing oratorical caution, «one might even say», for it expresses a daring idea that consists in saying that Levi, who came into the world three generations after Melchisedek, nonetheless paid the tithe to that person, for he was in a sense present in his ancestor Abraham. Two antithetic situations: one of the person who collects the tithe and one of the person who pays it are thus paradoxically ascribed to the same person.

Disqualification of the Levitical priesthood and of the Law (7,11-19)

11 If, surely, PERFECTION had been given by the Levitical priesthood
—on it in fact was based the LAW received by the people—
what need [would there have been] still that
    another priest like Melchisedek should arise
    and that he be not appointed like Aaron?
12 With the priesthood changed, in fact,
necessarily a change in law also happens,
13 He about whom these things are said,
actually belongs to another tribe,
no member of which had anything to do with the altar.
14 It is clear, in fact, that it is from Judah that our Lord descended,
a tribe about which Moses said nothing [in his laws] on priests,
15 and it is even more evident,
if it is like Melchisedek that another priest is raised up,
16 who did not become so according to a law of carnal order
    but according to a power of indestructible life;
17 he indeed receives this testimony:
you are a priest for ever in the manner of Melchisedek.
18 There is in fact an abrogation of an earlier precept,
    because of its weakness and uselessness,
19 —the LAW, in fact, made nothing PERFECT,—
and the introduction of a better hope,
    through which we approach God.

The transition between the end of the first paragraph (9-10) and the beginning of the second (11) is achieved by passing from «Levi» (9) to «Levitical» (11). The boundaries of the subdivision are indicated by an inclusion on the subjects of «perfection» and of the «Law» (11 and 19); the Greek words are not identical, but closely related.

To show clearly that he is arguing a case, the preacher punctuates his text with the repetition of the conjunction *gar*, «in fact». It comes no less than seven times (11.12.13.14.17.18.19). The last occurrence (19) corresponds to the first (11), because it coincides with the inclusion on the theme of the law and perfection. The penultimate occurrence, which speaks of «abrogation of a precept» (18) corresponds to the second, which mentions a «change in law» (12). Is there any correspondence between the fifth (17) and the third occurrence (13)? It may be thought so, because verse 17 speaks of the same person as verse 13 does and states what things «are said» (13) about him, quoting the oracle in Ps 109,4 (17). The central occurrence (14) introduces the sentence which names «our Lord»; the central place really suits him! The central element (14-16) is much longer than the others; it contains the strongest argument, the «resemblance» with Melchisedek, based on «a power of indestructible life»(16).

From the logical point of view, The author actually offers two arguments to show that the Levitical priesthood and the law are disqualified; the first argument is the change of priestly order: the oracle in Ps 109 moves from a priesthood «according to the order of Aaron» to a priesthood «according to the order of Melchisedek» (instead of «according to the order of» the English translation has «in the manner of», to avoid its being understood as «according to the commandment of» because it is a matter of two kinds of priesthood and not of two commandments). The second argument is the resemblance with Melchisedek (15b); it corresponds to «for ever», another expression from the psalm; the «power of indestructible life» (16b) makes priest «for ever».

A remarkable feature of this text is the connection of the theme of the law with that of the priesthood. The oracle in the psalm does not speak of the law, but the author, on his own initiative, expressed the close link that exists between priesthood and the law. He expressed it right from the beginning (11b), then points out its consequence (12), comes back to it in the long central element (16a) and, with insistence, in the conclusion (18a and 19a), in very negative terms.

A complementary parallelism is established in 11ab between the «priesthood» and the «law received»; it is taken up more clearly in 12ab. An antithetic parallelism is expressed in 11de between the order of Melchisedek and the order of Aaron. A mainly synonymous parallelism links 13 and 14, the «other tribe» to which the priest in the oracle belonged (13b) being that of «Judah» (14a) and this priest (13a) being «our Lord» (14a); moreover, 13c and 14b are two ways of saying that Judah was not a priestly tribe.

A parallelism exists between «it is clear» (*prodēlon*) in 14a and «it is more evident (*katadēlon*)» in 15a, but this parallelism is deceptive because the most evident point does not refer to the same fact. In 14a it is a matter of the tribe from which Jesus descended, whereas in 15a it is a matter of his relation to Melchisedek. 15b is not parallel with 14, but with the statement in 11d about the other priest raised up according to the order of Melchisedek; this parallelism is close, only one word is different («resemblance» instead of «order»). In the interests of stylistic elegance, the author changed the order of the words: «another arising priest» in 11d, «arising priest another» in 15b.

In verse 16, an antithesis contrasts «according to a law of carnal precept» with: «according to a power of indestructible life», a very significant antithesis because a «power of life» is quite different from an inert law text, and an «indestructible» reality is quite different from a fragile «carnal» reality. Besides, in the author's mind, 16b corresponds to 17b: to be «priest for ever» it is necessary to have become one «according to a power of indestructible life»

Verses 17-18 present the antithesis between «abrogation» and «introduction», between a «precept» and a «hope» and between the weakness and the uselessness of the precept, on the one hand, and the efficacy of the hope, on the other. To the critique of the precept (18b), the author has added an interpolation in which he criticizes the law (19a) and in which at the same time he places the two words that form an inclusion with the beginning (11ab).

Superiority of the new priesthood (7,20-28)

20 And to the extent that where there is no OATH-TAKING,
— these, in fact, became priests without taking an oath,
21 but he with taking an oath by him who said to him:
The Lord has sworn and will not repent:
You are a priest for ever—
22 to that extent exactly Jesus has become guarantee
of a better covenant.

23 And those who became priests were many in number,
because death prevented them from continuing,
24 but he, because he remains *for ever*,
he has a priesthood that does not pass away,
25 whence it results that he can save completely
those who through him approach God,
ever living to intercede for them.

26 It is indeed a HIGH PRIEST like this that was fitting for us,
holy, innocent, spotless,
who was separated from sinners and is more exalted than the heavens,
27 he who has no need every day, like the high priests,
first for his own sins to offer sacrifices,
then for those of the people;
that, in fact, he did once for all, by offering himself.
28 The law, in fact, established as HIGH PRIESTS men
who have weakness,
but the utterance about OATH-TAKING that came after the LAW
[established as high priest] a Son MADE PERFECT *for ever.*

This second half of the second paragraph has as inclusion a rare word, «oath-taking»; it is repeated three times at the beginning (20-21) and is taken up again at the end (28). These are the only occurrences in the New Testament. It is found only three times in the Septuagint.

Three subdivisions (20-22.23-25.26-28) can be distinguished in this text, each of which expresses an antithesis between the priesthood of old and the new priesthood. The boundaries of the last subdivision are marked by an inclusion on the word «high priest» (26 and 28), which reappears here after a long absence; it was never used before in this section. Its last occurrences are in 5,10 and 6,20.

Let us recall that verse 28 also contains the end of the inclusion of the whole paragraph (11-28), with the words «Law» and «made perfect». This verse therefore contains the ends of three inclusions, all three very visible, for they use words that are absent either from all the rest of the sermon («oath-taking»), or from all the rest of the section («high priest»), or words that are only used in the two inclusions («law» and «perfection»), 11-19 and 11-28.

The first subdivision (20-22) has a complex construction. The main sentence is cut in two by a very long interpolation. It expresses a parallelism, because it is a sentence expressing a comparison of proportionality: «to the extent that…, to that extent…». The interpolation expresses an antithesis between two ways of becoming a priest, without any oath on God's part or with an oath and it quotes the divine oath in the psalm.

The second subdivision (23-25) uses the additional qualification given in the psalm, «priest *for ever*» and establishes an antithesis between priests whose priesthood was interrupted by death and the priest who remains for ever. The effectiveness of this priesthood is then stressed.

The third and last subdivision (26-28) concludes the paragraph. It comprises three elements: firstly an enthusiastic description of the new high priest (26), then an antithesis between this high priest and the former high priests as regards the offering of sacrifices (27) —this antithesis prepares the theme of the following section— lastly an antithesis between the law and the oracle in the psalm or, more precisely, between the high priests established by the law and the high priest established by the oracle, the weakness of the former and the perfection of the latter (28). The last word, «made perfect», is a reminder of the first assertion in the announcement of the subject, made at the end of the preceding part (5,9). The author thus announces the subject of the next section.

B. *BIBLICAL CONTEXT*

This section quotes and comments on the two texts of the Old Testament that refer to Melchisedek, Gen 14,18-20 and Ps 109(110),4. In the Hebrew Bible, they are the only ones. In the Greek Bible, a third occurrence comes in Sinaiticus, in 1Chr 10,2, but that is in order to designate one of the sons of Saul, called *Malkîšûa*ʿ in Hebrew.

In Gen 14,18-20, the short passage on Melchisedek appears as an insertion added to the story of a warlike action by Abraham (Gen 14,14-17.21-24). To complete this insertion, which does not say that Melchisedek «met Abraham on his return from the defeat inflicted on the kings», the author of Hebrews uses verse 17, which says that about the king of Sodom. After the insertion, the story goes back to the king of Sodom (Gen 14,21).

The author faithfully reports in 7,1-2b what the text of Gen 14,18-20 says about Melchisedek, his titles and actions; he only omits mentioning the bread and wine that Melchisedek «brought out».

The name of Melchisedek is translated «king of justice», according to the meaning of the two Hebrew words *melek* and *ṣedeq*. Philo of Alexandria and the historian Josephus interpret it in the same way, «just king». That interpretation is accepted by certain modern commentators, but rejected by others, who give the letter *yod* (in *malkî*) the value of a first-person suffix: «the king of *me*», «my king». Moreover, *ṣedeq* could designate a god. The name would then mean «*Ṣedeq* is my king», just as *Malkiyyāhû* means «*Yāhû* (*Yhwh*) is my king» (Ezra 10,3; Jer 38,6).

The name of the city, *Salem*—*Šālēm* in Hebrew—is understood as an equivalent of the word *šālôm*, «peace». The same symbolic interpretation is proposed by Philo. The Targums and Josephus on the other hand see in *Salem* an equivalent of Jerusalem. This is also suggested, in Ps 76,3 (Hebrew), by the parallelism between *Salem* and *Sion*. Ps 122(121),6-8 places the name of Jerusalem (*Yerûšālaim*) in relation with that of peace (*šālôm*).

The titles «king of justice» and «king of peace» place Melchisedek in relation to the Messianic ideal. The relation of the Christ-king to justice was referred to by the preacher in Part One of his homily by means of a quotation from Ps 44(45) where the psalmist says to the ideal king: «you loved justice» (Ps 44,8; Heb 1,9). More than one Messianic oracle announces that the Messiah will establish justice and peace. In Isa 9,5 the promised king is called «Prince of peace»; the next verse announces «infinite peace» and the strengthening of the throne of David «in righteousness and justice». The oracle in Isa 11,1-9 likewise speaks of a work of justice and describes a situation of perfect peace in which «the wolf will dwell with the lamb». Concerning «he who is to reign over Israel» the oracle in Micah declares: «He himself will be peace» (Mic 5,1-4). When speaking of the ideal king, Ps 72(71) announces: «In his days, justice will flourish and great peace until the end of the moons» (Ps 72,7). Melchisedek is therefore presented as prefiguring the Christ-king, king of justice and of peace.

In verse 3, the preacher adds some negative features to the text in Genesis: «without father, without mother, without genealogy, not having either beginning of days, or end of life». These features correspond to some omissions: the text of Genesis presents Melchisedek without speaking of father, or mother, or genealogy. As it is a matter of a king who is at the same time a priest, this omission is surprising, because according to the law of Moses, one can only be a priest if one has a priestly genealogy. In Num 3,10 the Lord says to Moses: «You shall enlist Aaron and his sons, who will fulfil their priestly charge. But any layperson who approaches will be put to death». The same injunction is repeated in Num 3,38. It was taken very seriously. Witness to this is the decision, on the return from the Exile, to remove from the priestly functions the priests who could not produce family documents showing they belonged to a priestly lineage (Ezra 2,61-63). There could be no doubt about Melchisedek's priesthood because it was attested to by Scripture, but the conclusion had to be that it was a question of a different priesthood.

On Melchisedek, the text in Genesis does not give any chronological indications either, while it does do so for the birth and death of the patriarchs, Abraham, Moses and Aaron, and the death of the high priest is given as the limit of validity of certain legal prescriptions (see Num 35,25.32). The result is that the image of Melchisedek that is conveyed is that of a personage whose existence is without limits. The preacher concludes from this that, in the biblical text, he is «made like the Son of God», for the Son of God has «neither beginning of days, nor end of life». The biblical image of Melchisedek corresponds to that of a perpetual priest.

As can be seen, the preacher is reading the text of Genesis in the light of the oracle of the psalm and, in that oracle, he establishes a very close relationship between the two expressions «priest for ever» and «like Melchisedek»; it is by being a «priest for ever» that one is a «priest like Melchisedek». Moreover, the mystery of Christ, «the Son of God» (4,14), casts light on the «everlastingness» of the priesthood.

In verses 4 to 10, the preacher argues at length about the tithe received by Melchisedek from Abraham's booty; he compares it to the tithes received by the sons of Levi (Num 18,21.24) and draws an argument from it to show Melchisedek's superiority over the Levitical priests. He also speaks about the blessing given to Abraham by Melchisedek and observes that it implies that Melchisedek is superior to Abraham.

The second big paragraph (7,11-28) passes from Gen 14,18-20 to Ps 109,4; it comments on each expression in the psalm or, more exactly, he argues on the basis of each one of them. He introduces two wider subjects as well, one on perfection and one on law. The inclusions, as we have seen, draw attention to these two themes.

On perfection, the preacher commences by questioning whether it was ever bestowed «by the Levitical priesthood» (11), then he declares that «the law has never made anything perfect» (19), lastly he ends by attributing perfection to the «Son» proclaimed high priest by the oracle in the psalm.

To understand these texts properly, it must be noticed that the Greek term used in verse 11 does not denote a quality, but an action, the action of «making perfect». This term is used 13 times in the Greek translation of the Pentateuch and there it designates exclusively the consecration of the high priest. It comes 5 times in the prescriptions concerning the sacrifice at that consecration (Exod 29,22-35) and 6 times in the corresponding account in Leviticus (Lev 8,22-33). In the rest of the Greek Bible, it has only 4 other occurrences, spread over 4 books: 2Chr 29,35; 2Macc 2,9; Sir 31,8; Jer 2,2.

In the oracle in the psalm, the author sees the announcement of a change of priesthood: the priestly order of Melchisedek must succeed the priestly order of Aaron. That was not the original meaning of the psalm. By expressing a difference of priestly order, the oracle wanted rather to make the co-existence of two different priesthoods possible, that of the king, who had the upper hand in the accomplishment of worship, and that of the priests who performed it. Read at the time of the Hasmonean sovereigns, who were at the same time high priests, the oracle added the dimension of royal priesthood to their Levitical priesthood. But applied to Christ, who was not of the tribe of Levi, the oracle takes on a new meaning, which corresponds to one of its potentialities: the proclamation of a different priesthood which comes to replace priesthood «in the manner of Aaron», an ineffective one.

That the priesthood is the basis of the law received by the people (11) is an affirmation that corresponds to the nature of the law of Moses. This law, actually, is not on the merely earthly plane of the organization of a nation, but it is the law of the Covenant with God. Its basis therefore really is the priesthood, because the latter is officially entrusted with relations with God. Immediately after the conclusion of the Covenant on Sinai (Exod 24), the first laws to be given concern the construction of the sanctuary (Exod 25-27) and the consecration of the priests (Exod 28-29).

If the priesthood is the basis of the Law, it follows logically that a change of priesthood has as consequence a change of Law (12). But such a conclusion is nowhere expressed in the Old Testament, which never explicitly envisages a change of priesthood and still less a change of Law. «The Law of the Lord is perfect» (Ps 19,8); there is therefore no reason to change it. In speaking of changing the Law, the preacher manifests extreme boldness, liable to cause scandal. A text in the Old Testament, however, allowed him to defend himself: the oracle in Jeremiah announcing a change of Covenant (Jer 31,31-34). The prophet declares explicitly that the new Covenant will be different from that of Sinai (Jer 31,32). The Covenant of Sinai being defined by the Law, the announcement of a new Covenant implies a change of Law; instead of an external Law inscribed on stone, an internal Law, inscribed on hearts. But it is especially the teaching of the apostle Paul that allowed the preacher to justify his boldness, because Paul asserts that the Law had only a provisional validity until the coming of faith (Gal 3,19.23-25) and that believers are no more under the Law, but under grace (Rom 6,14).

The application of the oracle in the psalm to Jesus confirms that the change of priestly order happened, because Jesus is a descendant of Judah (Matt 1,2-3; Luke 3,33; Rev 5,5) and the tribe of Judah did not have access to the priesthood «according to the order of Aaron», reserved to the tribe of Levi (Num 3). The priesthood of Christ could therefore only be placed in the priestly «order» (*taxis*) of Melchisedek. That it really is placed there results from the fact that, being «for ever», it is «in the likeness of Melchisedek» (15). In the context of the Old Testament, the expression «for ever» was not taken literally; in reality it meant «for as long as you live». But applied to the risen Christ, who «dies no more, death has no more any power over him» (Rom 6,9), it takes on its full meaning. The risen Christ is truly a «priest for ever».

In verses 20-22, the preacher argues from the oath taken by God which supports the oracle in the psalm. This oath, according to the explanations given earlier, in 6,16-18, makes the oracle irrevocable and therefore provides perfect validity for the priesthood «in the manner of Melchisedek». Not having been backed up with a divine oath, the Levitical priesthood has not the same validity.

The sentence in verse 27 arouses debate because it affirms the need, for the former high priests, every day to offer sacrifices «first for their own sins, then for those of the people». The need was there (see 5,3), but the Law never says that it was daily. There were indeed daily sacrifices, morning and evening (Exod 29,38-39), which were offered under the authority of the high priest and could therefore be ascribed to him (see 2 Kgs 16,15; Sir 45,14), But they were holocausts (Exod 39,42) and not sacrifices of expiation. To be sure, the difficulty is easily overcome, because expiatory value can be allowed to the holocaust (see Lev 1,4), «odour of appeasement for the Lord» (Lev 1,9.13.17).

c. *INTERPRETATION*

To interpret this section correctly, it is important to observe in what light the preacher presents it. His purpose is not to offer a commentary on the text of Gen 14,18-20 considered in itself, but to explain this text in the light of the glorification of Christ. It is actually of the risen Christ that the final sentence of the exhortative introduction speaks; it declares that our hope «enters within the curtain» of the heavenly sanctuary, «where, as forerunner for us, Jesus entered, having become high priest for ever like Melchisedek» (6,19-20). This sentence is a partial reminder of the announcement of the subject made in 5,9-10, which likewise says that after his Passion, Christ, «made perfect», was «proclaimed high priest like Melchisedek».

The author therefore sets out from a vision of the glorified Christ. In this light he reads the priestly oracle in Ps 109 and as that oracle mentions Melchisedek, the author, in this perspective, considers the text of Genesis that speaks of that personage. It is only in this framework that it becomes fully clear how the author comments on the text of Genesis and especially how he uses what it does not say.

Knowing that Christ is the incarnate Son of God (1,2-3b; 2,14), that his Passion gained all his filial glory for him (1,3c-13; 4,14) and that he is at the same time «priest for ever» (Ps 109,4), the author examines the image that the Book of Genesis gives of Melchisedek. He finds that it is explicitly the image of an ideal, «king of justice» and «king of peace», who is at the same time a priest. He notices that his priesthood is of a particular kind, because it is not attached to a priestly line, the text mentioning neither father, nor mother, nor genealogy. The image does not contain any limits of time either, «nor beginning of days, nor end of life», and corresponds therefore, in a way, to the «priest for ever» in the oracle in Ps 109. It corresponds at the same time to an image of the Son of God, for the Son of God has «neither beginning of days, nor end of life», and only the Son of God could become «priest for ever» With all these traits, the biblical image of Melchisedek constitutes a prefiguration of the glorified Christ, Son of God and priest for ever.

Only a prefiguration, because Melchisedek was not really Son of God, nor priest for ever; he was only «made like the Son of God» by the way he is represented in the text of Genesis, and not in reality. Likewise, his priesthood is not truly eternal but has only, in the text of Genesis, an appearance which has something of eternity about it. To express this important nuance, the author avoids using, concerning Melchisedek, the expression of the psalm, «for ever», but uses an expression with a weaker sense, which can be translated as «continually» or «in perpetuity».

Of whom exactly is Melchisedek a prefiguration? He is not a prefiguration of the Son of God before the incarnation, for the latter is not «without father», he has God as father, and he is not a priest, for he lacks the fraternal link with mankind.

Nor is Melchisedek a prefiguration of the incarnate Son of God and living his earthly life, because then he is not «without mother», he is the son of Mary; he is not «without genealogy», being of the tribe of Juda. And he has not yet been proclaimed priest by God.

Melchisedek is the prefiguration of the risen Christ, for the resurrection is a new creation, in which neither human father, nor human mother, nor genealogy have any part. The human nature of the risen Christ is the «the greater and more perfect tent, not made by hand of man, that is to say not of this creation» (9,11) by means of which Christ entered into intimacy with God and into God's eternity. In the resurrection, the human nature of Jesus received the fullness of filial glory but that glory does not break the links of Christ with mankind, for it is through complete fraternal solidarity with them that it was obtained (see 2,9-18). It follows that the glorified Christ, Son of God and brother of mankind, is «priest for ever». This is what the author sees prefigured in the biblical image of the perpetual priesthood of Melchisedek.

In verses 4-10, the preacher argues from two facts mentioned in the Genesis story: the tithe received by Melchisedek from Abraham's booty and the blessing given by Melchisedek to Abraham. These two facts put Melchisedek in a position of superiority over the patriarch. The preacher comments by suggesting this superiority in connection with receiving the tithe, which shows «how great» Melchisedek is (4). But he goes on immediately to considerations about another receipt of the tithe, done «according to the Law» by the Levitical priests. His purpose is to show that Scripture shows the superiority of Melchisedek not only over Abraham, but to the Levitical priesthood. To this effect he compares the two receipts of tithe and points out some significant differences which point towards Melchisedek's superiority.

He uses the two main aspects of the interpretation he has just given about what Scripture does not say about Melchisedek: the absence of genealogy and life without limits.

In the case of the Levitical priests, the tithe is received in a context of genealogical ties, in relation with Abraham (5). In the case of Melchisedek, on the contrary, the tithe is received in the absence of genealogical ties (6). The bearing of this difference does not appear clearly; so the preacher adds another element that suggests the superiority of Melchisedek more clearly: the latter collected the tithe from the genealogical ancestor of the Levitical priests. There is not only no genealogy in the case of Melchisedek, therefore, but power exercised over a genealogy right from its origin.

At this point (6c-7), the preacher inserts a reflection on the other fact mentioned, which allows him to speak explicitly about superiority. Melchisedek blessed Abraham, «now, without any argument, it is the inferior who is blessed by the better» (7). At first sight, contrary to what the preacher says, argument is possible. It is not rare actually in the Bible for indigent people to bless their rich benefactors (see Deut 24,13; Job 31,20) and human beings are often called upon to bless God, who, assuredly, is not inferior to them. Melchisedek himself, after blessing, blesses «the most high God» (Gen 14,19-20).

There is good reason to distinguish two very different kinds of blessings, those which may be called ascending and the others, descending. The first express simply sentiments of praise of thanks or desires. The others come down from God, directly or through authorized intermediaries, and they transform the situation; they bring fecundity, prosperity, victory and success. These descending blessings are the ones that can and should be spoken of: the inferior is blessed by the better. The father of a family transmits the divine blessing to his children (Gen 27,28-29.39-40; Heb 11,20-21); the king transmits it to his people (2Sam 6,18; Kgs 8,14.55).

The power of blessing in the name of God belongs especially to the priests, whom God establishes «to serve him and bless in his name» (Deut 21,5; 1Chr 23,13; Sir 45,15). In blessing Abraham, the king-priest Melchisedek manifests a power received from God who makes him superior to the patriarch.

The preacher then returns to the tithe and to the comparison between Melchisedek and Levitical priests (8). This time he uses the second feature in the image of Melchisedek, the one of a life that has no limits. To make the contrast more striking, instead of saying that the Levitical priests are mortal men, he says that they are «men who die», whereas, of Melchisedek, the biblical text states «that he lives». To tell the truth, this affirmation is an exaggeration, because the biblical text does not contain this affirmation explicitly. It is only implicitly that it presents Melchisedek as living and it is only by arguing from what it does not say that one can speak of a life that has no limits. But the preacher's sentence produces an oratorical effect full of vigour.

A final consideration expresses a reversal of the situation that cannot fail to arouse a delightful surprise among the listeners. The preacher skilfully shows that «even Levi, who collects tithes, was subject to the tithe» (9). How does he show that Levi was subject to the tithe by Melchisedek, whereas he did not yet exist? The preacher here has recourse to the principle of family solidarity: what the ancestor does determines the situation of all the descendants. Instead of expressing this principle in the abstract, the preacher expresses it concretely, which strikes the imagination better: Levi had not yet been born, but he existed in a certain way in the body of his ancestor, from which he was to come forth; he therefore took part in the homage paid by Abraham to Melchisedek. The preacher says no more about it, but it is clear that the principle of solidarity that holds for Levi in relation to Abraham also holds for the Levites in relation to Levi. If Levi was subject to the tithe, all the Levites find themselves in this situation of inferiority with regard to the priesthood of Melchisedek.

Thus ends this paragraph (7,1-10). With a very clever exegesis, the author managed to sap the foundations of a conviction anchored in the Jewish mentality, that of the excellence of the Levitical priesthood. He has shown that even before the birth of Levi, the Old Testament presents the image of a different and superior priesthood to which Levi himself paid homage. The way is thus prepared for the reflection on the oracle in Ps 109,4.

In 7,11 the preacher moves on from his reflections on Melchisedek to a consideration of the «Levitical priesthood». The transition is easy, because he has just spoken about a relation between Melchisedek and Levi (9). The tone immediately becomes polemical. The preacher questions whether «the action of making perfect» was done by the Levitical priesthood. According to the texts of the Pentateuch —as we have seen— that name was given to the sacerdotal consecration of the high priest (Exod 29; Lev 8). The preacher here disputes the use of that name. He gives us to understand that the rites of consecration of the high priest did not really correspond to it. They did not make the one for whom they were carried out perfect. Being external rites, they did not transform in depth (see 9,9). Those rites were prescribed by the Law, which had nothing better to offer. Their inefficacy therefore showed the inefficacy of the Law. The preacher takes advantage of this to extend his argument to the Law.

What is the basis of this argument? It is the existence of the oracle in Psalm 109 which, read in the light of Christ, announces another priesthood. If the priesthood «in the manner of Aaron» had given full satisfaction, the word of God would not have had to announce «another priest» —«other» in the sense of «different»— now the oracle certainly speaks of a different priestly «order», according to Melchisedek and not according to Aaron. The existence of the oracle revealed that the former priesthood left something to be desired.

To speak of the appearance of the other priest, the author chose a significant verb that suggests an allusion to the resurrection. This verb, in fact, (*anistēmi*), which means «to make to rise», can also mean «to resurrect» and very often has that meaning in the New Testament. The other priest was «made to rise» whereas Christ was «resurrected».

The former priesthood constituted the basis of the Law of Moses, for it had to regulate the relations of the people with God first of all. If, by reason of a radical change, this basis no longer exists, the whole edifice collapses and must be replaced (12). The author does not hesitate to express this conclusion. His critique of the Law is as vigorous as that of the apostle Paul, but it sets out from a different point of view, that of priestly mediation, whereas Paul adopts a juridical perspective, that of justification. Paul criticizes the Law because it is incapable of making a sinner just. Our author, for his part, criticizes the Law because it is incapable of establishing a good mediator between the people and God.

To the theoretical argument, based on the formulation of the priestly oracle, the preacher adds the observation of a fact that comes to confirm it (13-14). The one in whom the oracle is accomplished did not belong to the tribe of Levi, to which God exclusively reserved the priesthood «in the manner of Aaron»; «it is clear, indeed, that our Lord came from the tribe of Judah» (14), since he is a descendant of David, a member of the tribe of Judah. His priesthood can therefore only be one of another order. The change of priesthood is effective.

The change of priestly order could be just superficial, nominal, like a change of label. In reality, it is very profound. The new priest does not belong only to the category of Melchisedek; he is «in the likeness of Melchisedek»; he corresponds profoundly to the image that the Book of Genesis gives of this personage, an image of a life that has no limits. Indeed, he has become a priest «according to a power of indestructible life» and not, like the former priest, «according to a law of carnal precept» 16). The author, here, takes the regime of the Law to task. The latter made the priesthood depend on carnal affiliation; one had to be born into a priestly family, have a priestly genealogy, which implied a succession of generations and therefore a limited life.

With the «law of carnal precept» the author contrasts «a power of indestructible life». This contrast is full of meaning. It shows to what extent the author is aware of the new Christian reality, like Saint Paul, who expresses more than once this kind of contrast. The Old Testament is characterized by an external Law which gives orders, but does not bring salvation, because it does not communicate an interior strength; it leaves the human person to its congenital weakness (see Rom 7,14-15). The New Testament is characterized, on the contrary, by an interior strength, the power of the Spirit which ensures salvation, because it communicates new life to the person who receives it.

The Pauline text to which our author comes closest is the one in Gal 3,21 which presents as unreal the hypothesis according to which «a law able to give life» would have been given. In Rom 8,2-3 Paul declares likewise that the Law lacked strength and «was weak because of the flesh».

A question arises over the moment when Christ became priest «according to a power of indestructible life». Is it from the first moment of his incarnation? Is it at the moment of his resurrection? A renowned commentator, C. Spicq, favours the first solution. The other, equally qualified, O. Michel, remains undecided. In reality, the theory according to which Christ would have become priest at the first moment of his incarnation because, at that moment, he possessed «a power of life indestructible», does not correspond to the outlook of the Letter to the Hebrews. It is not true that, as from this first moment, the divine eternal life completely penetrated the human nature of Jesus. On the contrary, that human nature was weak, subject to suffering, mortal. Far from being in a divine condition, it had «slave form» (Phil 2,7) and it was to transform it by his paschal mystery that the Son of God had assumed it. It was at the moment of the resurrection that the «power of life indestructible» completely penetrated the human nature of Jesus and made it become immortal.

The terms chosen by the author all have this meaning. The word «*power*» is in relation to the declaration of Saint Paul according to which Christ was «established Son of God with *power* according to the Spirit of holiness *by reason of his resurrection from the dead*».(Rom 1,4). The word «*life*» reminds one of the *new* life of the risen Christ, which is communicated to believers (Rom 6,4) and ensures their salvation (Rom 5,10). The expression «*power of life*» recalls that Christ «was crucified by reason of his weakness, but he *lives* by reason of the *power* of God» (2Co 13,4). The word «indestructible» is not found elsewhere in the New Testament (nor is it met with in the Old Testament in Greek), but it is a derivative of the verb «to destroy», which is often connected with the paschal mystery of Christ; after the destruction of the «sanctuary made with hand of man», the construction «in three days» of a «sanctuary not made with hand of man», and therefore indestructible is announced (Mark 14,58; see John 2,19-22).

Other passages from the sermon show that it is at the conclusion of his Passion that Christ became high priest (2,17-18; 5,7-10). The incarnation was not enough for that. It was the indispensable basis, but it was not the accomplishment. On this point, the author's doctrine corresponds perfectly with that of the gospels, which on several occasions affirm the necessity of the Passion (Matt 16,21; Mark 8,31; Luke 9,22; 17,25; 24,7.26; John 12,23-24).

The preacher links the «power of life indestructible» to the announcement of a «priest» established «for ever» (16-17). To remain priest «for ever», a «power of life indestructible» is indeed necessary. A mortal human nature can only exercise the priesthood for a limited time and in an imperfect way.

The «power of life indestructible» that he received in his resurrection means that Christ is priest «in the manner of Melchisedek». A reversal of relations is noticeable here which may appear incoherent. At the beginning it is said that Melchisedek was «like the Son of God» (3); now it is said that Christ is a «priest like Melchisedek». Is there not a contradiction? No, because we are in a context of typology, in which relations are complex. There is reason for distinguishing three stages, that of God's design, that of its manifestation through a prefiguration and that of its practical accomplishment. God's design was to give us a priest who would be a perfect mediator thanks to his filial relation with him in his glory and to his fraternal relation with us. This design was then expressed in the biblical image of Melchisedek, «made like the Son of God» and «priest of the most high God», «priest who remains for ever». For the accomplishment achieved in Christ to be recognized as genuine, it has to correspond to this biblical prefiguration. Christ must therefore be «like Melchisedek». Let us add that he is at the same time superior to him because he has a fullness of reality that the image could not have.

The conclusion drawn by the preacher can hardly be clearer. It asserts the «abrogation of an earlier precept» (18), the one that established the Levitical priesthood, and «the introduction of a better hope», the one that results from the establishment of a priest who is a perfect mediator and therefore gives us the possibility of «approaching God» (19). Here, as at the beginning of the paragraph (12), the preacher insists at the same time on putting the Law under the hammer of his polemic. After justifying the fate of the earlier precept for «its weakness» —it was unable to bestow perfection— and «its uselessness» —due to the very fact of its inability— he extends his criticism to the Law by saying that it «did not make anything perfect». This observation is very negative, but Saint Paul is even more negative, when he states that «the Law came in so that the fault might be multiplied» (Rom 5,20).

In speaking of a «*better* hope», verse 19 makes explicit an aspect of the situation that could be easily perceived but which remained implicit: the situation has not just changed (12), it has definitely improved: the priesthood in the manner of Melchisedek did not simply set up «a different priest» (11.15), but a priest of greater worth.

The following verses (20-22) continue along the same lines by stating that «Jesus became guarantor of a *better* covenant» (22). This statement of superiority is based on a difference: no divine oath confirmed the establishment of the Levitical priesthood, whereas the priestly oracle in Psalm 109 backs up the establishment of a «priest for ever» with a divine oath. The preacher here quotes the attestation of the divine oath, which is particularly solemn, because it is given in a positive and negative form: «The Lord has sworn and will not repent». In other episodes, the Bible sometimes recounts God «repented» of a decision he had taken, that is to say he gave it up. Thus it is that in 1Sam 15,35 it is said about Saul that «the Lord had repented making him king over Israel» and in 1Chr 21,15 about Jerusalem that «at the moment of exterminating it, the Lord looked and repented of this evil; he said to the exterminating angel: Enough. Withdraw your hand». The oracle in Psalm 109 gives an assurance, on the contrary, that the Lord «will not repent» because he has sworn and a divine oath —the preacher recalled it in 6,13-18— makes the decision taken «irrevocable». The priesthood of Christ «in the manner of Melchisedek» is therefore irrevocable, which the priesthood «in the manner of Aaron» was not.

This irrevocable character means that Jesus is «guarantor of a better covenant» (22). The preacher here introduces the theme of the covenant which will occupy much space in the next section (8,1-9,28), in which the word occurs 12 times. Let us say at once that the Greek term used, *diathēkē*, does not have, strictly speaking, the sense of «covenant»; it means «disposition»; but in the Greek Bible, it usually designates the provisions of a covenant, which calls for it to be translated this way.

The author, conceiving -as we have seen- priesthood as a form of mediation, closely links priesthood and covenant. Later he will say of Christ the high priest that he is «*mediator* of a new covenant» (9,15), here he calls him «guarantor of a better covenant». The difference in the titles corresponds to a difference of point of view. «Mediator» is used in the context of the work accomplished by Christ; by means of his sacrifice, Christ re-established the relation between mankind and God: he is therefore mediator (8,6; 9,15). «Guarantor» is used in the context of the divine proclamation: because God solemnly proclaimed that Christ is priest for ever, the very person of Christ is an attestation of the covenant, which gives every guarantee. If, by any remote chance, God were to prepare to denounce the covenant, it would be enough to present him with the person of Christ and God would have to admit that revoking the covenant is impossible, for he himself proclaimed Christ high priest and deprived himself of the right to change his mind on that point.

In verses 23-25 the preacher comes back to the expression «for ever» which qualifies the priesthood «in the manner of Melchisedek». He has already commented on it in 7,15-17; he takes it up from a different point of view. In 7,15-17 he presented it as expressing a new quality of priesthood, no more a priesthood fixed by carnal origin, but a priesthood produced by a «power of life indestructible». Here, he considers it from a quantitative point of view: on the one hand, priests who succeed each other and are therefore many; on the other, a unique priest, «because he remains for ever».

The quantitative difference actually comes from the qualitative difference; tied to the flesh, the former priesthood is inexorably conquered by death; animated by a life force that no longer fears death, the new priesthood is a priesthood «that does not pass away». The Greek adjective translated in this way, *aparabatos*, has only this occurrence in the Greek Bible. Its etymological meaning is: «beside whom one cannot walk»; applied to a prohibition, it means «which cannot be transgressed». Here, it has often been understood as meaning «who can have no successor», but several occurrences in the Greek authors show that it simply means «immutable», «permanent».

The author shows the consequence of this permanence. The work of the former priests remained necessarily incomplete, because it was interrupted by death. On the contrary, nothing prevents the work of Christ from being complete. «He is capable of saving completely those who through him approach God» (25). This work is accomplished by means of intercession. The risen Christ is «always living» and can therefore always «intercede». Saint Paul likewise declares that Christ «has risen, is at the right hand of God, intercedes for us» (Rom 8,34). «To intercede» is to approach an authority in favour of someone. The priestly ministry of the glorified Christ does not now consist of offering, but of interceding. This intercession must not be confused with the «pleas and supplications» that Christ offered to God «in the days of his flesh» (5,7). He was then in a condition of humility. Intercession presupposes on the contrary an elevated position. The one interceding for others must enjoy real power of influence.

Instead of «to save *completely*», the Greek expression can signify «to save *for ever*»; that is how the Vulgate understood it, in connection with the sentence in 5,9 that speaks of «eternal salvation». In fact, the two significations imply each other. To be saved completely, one has to be saved for ever, and conversely, one cannot be saved for ever if one is not completely saved.

The last verses of the section (26-28) form a solemn conclusion in which great admiration is expressed for the new priest. Here he is called «high priest», a title which is not in the oracle in Psalm 109, for it was only introduced very late into the language of the Jews. But because of its already established use the author had to ascribe it to Christ. If he had only given him the title of priest, he would have seemed to ascribe to him an inferior rank of priesthood. The application of the title of high priest to the «priest in the manner of Melchisedek» is easily justified because Melchisedek was at once king and priest, a situation that corresponds to the two components of the title *archi-hiereus*, which means «head-priest».

Here, as several times elsewhere, the preacher manifests a theologian's frame of mind, which reflects on the data of revelation and notes a correspondence between God's plan and the situation of mankind: «it is such a high priest that suited us».

In saying «such a high priest», the preacher is referring to what he has just said: a priest established for ever and able to obtain salvation perfectly; but at the same time he introduces the description he is going to present. This starts with three epithets, continues with two expressions in participial form and ends with a long relative proposition. Its rhythm builds up therefore, which produces a powerful oratorical effect.

The high priest that suited us had to be «holy, innocent, spotless» (26b). To say «holy» the author does not use the most usual word, *hagios*, «holy», «consecrated» but another word, *hosios*, which expresses moral holiness, in correspondence with the will of God. The second adjective, *a-kakos*, «innocent», expresses the absence of wickedness; the third, *a-miantos*, the absence of uncleanness. The insistence on moral integrity is something new with regard to the former high priest, from whom perfect physical integrity was required (Lev 21,17-23) and absolute ritual purity (Lev 22,1-9), but not perfect moral integrity; provision was made for his failings, none the less, and the need to offer sacrifices for his sins. It is clear that a high priest who was a sinner was not «suitable» for exercising mediation between the people and God.

The position of our high priest is then defined by two expressions in participial form, the first with a negative meaning: «being separated from sinners», the second with a positive meaning: «having become higher than the heavens». They are both applied to the glorified Christ. In his earthly life, Christ was not «separated from sinners», he accepted contact with them and even sought it out, for he had «not come to call the just, but sinners» (Matt 9,13). On the other hand, he could undergo opposition from sinners who were hardened in evil and underwent it to the point of «enduring the cross» (Heb 12,2-3). But his Passion ended in his glorification in the sight of God, which puts him altogether out of reach, for it made him henceforth to be «higher than the heavens».

In the Bible it is usually said that God lives «in the heavens» (Ps 11,4; 123,1; etc.), but Solomon declares that «the heavens and the heavens of the heavens cannot contain him» (1Kgs 8,27) and the psalms sometimes place the divine Majesty «above the heavens» (Ps 8,2; 113,4). Our author likewise varies his expressions. Sometimes he says that Christ is «in the heavens» (8,1), and that he has entered «into heaven itself» (9,24); another time he says that Christ «has gone through the heavens» (4,14); here, to express the priestly glorification of Christ better, he proclaims him «higher than the heavens». The very variety of the expressions shows that the author is not at all interested in cosmological speculations; he freely uses spatial metaphors to express the divine transcendence. This transcendence does not restrict relations with the world, rather it broadens them. The Old Testament was already declaring that the Lord, who «sits on high», «lifts up the weak from the dust» (Ps 113,5-7). Christ, likewise, «having become higher than the heavens», is at the same time «merciful high priest» (2,17; see 4,14-15).

Having defined the qualities and the glorious position of Christ high priest, the preacher speaks of his activity or rather, paradoxically, of his absence from sacrificial activity (27). The case of Christ, actually, is very different from that of «every high priest» because «every high priest is established to offer gifts and sacrifices» (5,2), whereas Christ, proclaimed high priest at the end of his sacrifice of priestly consecration, does not have to offer other sacrifices.

Former high priests continually found themselves in need «of offering sacrifices first for their own sins, then for those of the people» (27). This need is expressed explicitly at the time of the priestly consecration of Aaron (Lev 9,8.15) and during the liturgy of the great Expiation (Lev 16,11.15), but the author does not hesitate to say that it is daily, because he does not accord any efficacy to those sacrifices.

This need does not exist for Christ, because his sacrifice was perfectly efficacious. What the high priests had to do continually, Christ «did once for all» (27d). The preacher here imperfectly expresses himself, because his sentence can be understood as meaning that Christ offered «first for his own sins, then for those of the people». But this interpretation is excluded, because the beginning of the sentence affirms the innocence of the new high priest (26b) and because in 4,15 the absence of sin was pointed out.

It is «by offering himself» that Christ obtained the remission of sins. In saying that, the preacher is preparing the next section, in which he will introduce Christ's personal offering (9,11-14.24-28). To speak here of this offering, he uses a somewhat different Greek verb which, instead of meaning «to bring to» (*prospherein*), means «to take up» (*ana-pherein*). This nuance is fitting at the end of this section which has introduced the priesthood of the glorified Christ, «having become higher than the heavens».

Verse 28 concludes the whole section (we pointed out above that it contains three inclusion endings: 11-28; 20-28; 26-28). It expresses an antithesis between the priesthood established by the Law and the priesthood established by the oracle in Ps 109,4. To designate the oracle, the author calls it «the word of the oath-taking», so as to underline its definitive value. He adds that this oath-taking came «after the Law»; it revealed its unsatisfactory character (7,11) and foreshadowed the abrogation of its priesthood institution (18) and therefore its own change (12). In the Greek sentence, the expression «who have weakness» may also refer at the same time to «men» and to the «high priests». The Law takes «men who have weakness» and makes «high priests who have weakness» of them. Priestly consecration leaves these men in the state they were in, that is to say «surrounded with weakness» and with a weakness that involves sin (5,2-3). This consecration was called «action of making perfect» (7,11), but it did not correspond with its name, for «the Law did not make anything perfect (7,19). On the contrary, the high priest established by the oracle was «made perfect» (28), by his Passion (2,10; 5,7-9) which was his sacrifice of priestly consecration. This perfection was implicitly announced by the reference in the oracle to eternity: «priest for ever». Only what is perfect can in fact be eternal. Then again, this reference also announced, implicitly, that the new priest would not simply be a human being like the former priests, but that he would be at the same time «Son», that is to say «the Son of God» eternal, foreshadowed by Melchisedek (3). The eternal Son of God alone can be «priest for ever». but for him to be priest, he must also be man, for «every high priest» is «taken from among men» (5,1); furthermore, he must also be a man «made perfect» by means of the sufferings of human existence (2,10) and thus raised to filial glory. Such is the situation of the glorified Christ.

Chapter 11

Critique of the former worship and of the first covenant (8,1-9,10)

In beginning the second section of his central exposé, the preacher refers to what he has just said in the conclusion to the preceding section. He declares: «*this is the kind of high priest* we have» (8,1), that is to say a high priest who has been «made perfect» (7,28) by his sacrifice, a very different sacrifice from the immolations of animals carried out in the Old Testament. Made perfect through his sufferings, Christ could be admitted into heaven itself, where he was invited to sit «on the right of the throne of the divine Majesty» (8,1; Ps 109,1). The preacher then announces how he will present the sacrifice of Christ. He will present it as a liturgy of which the parameters are «the sanctuary and the true tent which the Lord planted, not a man» (8,2). This formulation hints at an exposé in two great paragraphs, the first of which will speak about the former worship, characterized by a tent a man planted, and the second will present the intervention by Christ, characterized by a tent the Lord planted. The development that follows does in fact correspond to this announcement. It begins with a critical exposé of ancient worship (8,3-9,10) and then contains a positive exposé of the sacrifice of Christ (9,11-28). Christ is named only in this second exposé; he is named four times in it (9,11.14.24.28).

An important feature, which the formula in 8,2 does not reveal, is that to the theme of worship the author closely associated the theme of covenant, in the middle of each of these two paragraphs. We therefore have the sequel worship-covenant-worship twice and the section is composed of six subdivisions which correspond to each other according to a concentric plan:

a. 8,3-6: exclusion of former worship, of an earthly nature
b. 8,7-13: former imperfect covenant, to be replaced by the new
a. 9,1-10: former worship, ineffective sanctuary and rites
A.: 9,11-14: oblation of Christ, perfectly effective
B. 9,15-23: new covenant, founded on blood like the former one
A. 9,24-28: worship of Christ, heavenly nature.

Introduction (8,1-2)

1 Main point of what we are saying:
we have such a high priest,
who has sat down on the right of the throne of the Majesty in the heavens,
2 a LITURGICAL officiant in the sanctuary and in the true tent,
that the Lord planted, not a man.

Exclusion of the former, earthly worship (8,3-6)

3 Every high priest, in fact, is established
to OFFER GIFTS AND SACRIFICES (9,9)
hence the need for himself, too,
to have something to offer.
4 If, assuredly, he were on earth,
he would not be a priest at all,
for there are those who offer gifts according to the Law;
5 these perform the worship of a figure and sketch of heavenly realities,
according to the oracle received by Moses, when he was to construct the tent:
See, he actually says, you shall do all things
according to the model that was shown to you on the mountain.
6 Indeed, he obtained a very different LITURGY,
to the extent that the covenant of which he is mediator is better,
which was established on better promises.

An inclusion on «*leitourgos*» (2) and «*leitourgia*» (6) unites the introduction (1-2) and the first subdivision (3-6). The introduction offers a complementary parallelism: it is because he was a «liturgical officiant in the sanctuary and in the true tent» that our «high priest» could «sit at the right of the throne of the Majesty in the heavens». The author, in fact, will declare further on that the «sanctuary» into which Christ entered is «heaven itself» (9,24). The remark added about the tent («that the Lord planted, not a man») announces, as I have said, the division of the section into two great paragraphs. Then, the order of the text is in chiastic form with the announcement: there, in the first place, it is a matter of the tent planted by a man, announced in the last place.

An inclusion insisting on «to offer gifts and sacrifices» (8,3 and 9,9) marks the boundaries of the first great paragraph.

In the first subdivision, the author refrains from naming Christ, although he speaks of him in verses 4 and 6. The result is that his text lacks clarity, especially in 6, which comes after some reflections on Moses. The translators feel the need to add the name of Christ, which the author has kept for the paragraph with positive content (9,11-28).

The two sentences in verse 3 offer a parallelism between «every high priest» and «he also» in the action of «offering». The second sentence is vague: «something to offer», because we are in the preparatory paragraph. We have to wait for the other paragraph to find out what our high priest had to offer.

3 Every high priest, in fact, is established
to OFFER GIFTS AND SACRIFICES (9,9)
hence the need for himself, too,
to have something to offer.
4 If, assuredly, he were on earth,
he would not be a priest at all,
for there are those who offer gifts according to the Law;
5 these perform the worship of a figure and sketch of heavenly realities,
according to the oracle received by Moses, when he was to construct the tent:
See, he actually says, you shall do all things
according to the model that was shown to you on the mountain.
6 Indeed, he obtained a very different LITURGY,
to the extent that the covenant of which he is mediator is better,
which was established on better promises.

Verse 4 expresses, on the contrary, a contrast between our high priest and «those who offer gifts according to the Law». The latter take up all the room on earth. Our high priest's priesthood must therefore be of another kind.

In verse 5, the earthly worship is counted out because of being simply figurative. Correspondence is asserted between this initial assertion and the oracle received by Moses, but the parallelism is hardly visible, because the terms are different: «figure and sketch» in the initial affirmation, «according to the model», in the oracle; the relation between «the mountain» and «the heavenly realities» is not one of identity.

Verse 6 places a parallelism between a threefold superiority, that of the «liturgy» of our high priest, that of the «covenant» established by that liturgy and that of the «promises» which confer value on that covenant. The adjective is special for the liturgy, which is «very different», it is identical for the covenant and promises, which are «better», of greater force (*kreittōn*). The term of the three comparisons is not spelled out, but the previous context shows that it is a question of the institutions of the Old Testament, for it speaks of «the tent» constructed by Moses and of «all the things» of the former worship. The next verses confirm this interpretation: they speak of the covenant of Sinai (7-9).

The former covenant imperfect and replaced (8,7-13)

7 If, in fact, this FIRST were irreproachable,
a place for a second would not be sought.
8 He reproaches them, in fact, saying:
Behold, days are coming, says [the] Lord,
and I will conclude for the house of Israel and for the house of Judah
a new covenant,
9 not like the covenant that I made for their fathers
on the day I took them by the hand
to bring them out of the land of Egypt;
because they did not remain in my covenant,
I, in turn, neglected them, says [the] Lord;
10 because that [will be] the covenant that I shall draw up for the house of Israel
after those days, says [the] Lord:
giving my laws,
in their intelligence and on their hearts I shall write them
and I shall be for them [their] God
and they will be for me [my] people,
11 and they will no longer teach
each one his fellow citizen
and each one his brother
saying: Know the Lord,
because all will know me
from the small to the great among them,
12 because I shall be indulgent over their iniquities
and their sins I shall remember no more.
13 By saying «new», he made the FIRST one old,
now what becomes ancient and grows old will soon disappear.

The way the preacher presents the oracle from Jeremiah and comments on it does not bring out its main message, which is very positive; it consists solely of a criticism of the first covenant. It is of «this first one» that the introductory sentence speaks (7) and the concluding sentence does likewise (13); in this way an inclusion for subdivision is arranged. In the introduction, a parallelism is noticeable between «irreproachable» in an unreal context and «he reproached them», a real fact. This parallelism is imperfect, because the unreal «irreproachable» refers to an institution, the first covenant, whereas the reproaches are addressed to persons, designated by a personal pronoun, without further explanation; it is understood that it is a question of the Israelites.

The concluding sentence (13) offers a progressive parallelism between «making old», «becoming ancient and growing old» and «soon to disappear».

The oracle in Jeremiah has a simple and harmonious composition, according to a general plan ABA', in which the last element, A', much fuller than the ones before, is itself constructed according to this plan.

(8)	A.	positive, future:	I will conclude a new covenant,
(9)	B.	negative, past:	not like the covenant I made for their fathers,
(10)	A'.	positive, future:	this is the covenant that I shall draw up:

(10)	a.	positive, future:	I shall write my laws on their hearts
		positive, future:	I shall be their God, they shall be my people
(11)	b.	negative, future:	they will no longer teach each other
		positive, future:	all will know me
(12)	a'.	positive, future:	I shall be indulgent over their iniquities
		negative, future:	their sins I shall remember no more.

Also noticeable is the alternation of the grammatical subjects, the «I» of God and the «they» of mankind:

in A, the subject is «I»;	in B, «I…they…I…»;	in A', the subject is «I»
in a, «I…I…they…»;	in b, «they… they…»;	in a', «I… I…».

The presence of the divine «I» at the beginning, in the centre and at the end, stresses that the new covenant comes from a very generous initiative on God's part.

The oracle from Jeremiah is marked out regularly by the repetition of the interpolation «says Lord», in which «Lord» is without any article, because considered as a proper noun, the proper name for God. This noun in effect replaces the Hebrew word of four letters YHWH which is the proper name of God and which, for fear of profaning it, the Jews gave up pronouncing. In Hebrew, they replaced it with the word *'ădōnāy* meaning «Lord». In Christian manuscripts of the Old Testament in Greek, it is replaced by *Kyrios*, usually without the article.

After the short introductory formula (8b), the oracle expresses an antithetic parallelism between the new covenant, promised by God (8cd) and the covenant of the time of the Exodus (9abc). Then comes a synonymous parallelism between two negative attitudes (9de), that of the Israelites unfaithful to the covenant and God's corresponding reaction. The new covenant is then defined at length (10-12).

In verse 10, the Greek translation differs from the Hebrew text by putting the word «law» in the plural (instead of «my Law», God says: «laws of me») and breaking the parallelism. Instead of saying:

I will put my law inside them
and on their heart I will write it

the translation given in the Letter to the Hebrews puts a participle at the beginning:

Giving my laws

(in the Septuagint, some manuscripts have: «Giving I shall give…», which keeps the parallelism). It follows that in good Greek syntax, one should then put:

in their intelligence and on their hearts I shall inscribe them.

It is not entirely impossible to keep the parallelism in part by translating:

Giving my laws in their intelligence,
also on their hearts I shall inscribe them,

but this construction is not normal, for the Greek conjunction *kai* as it is situated in this text. The next parallelism (10ef) is, on the other hand, perfectly balanced. The turn of phrase is a Hebraism, literally:

I shall be for them *to God*
and they will be for me *to people*

In verse 11, there is first of all a small chiastic structure (a b b' a'): «they will no longer teach» (a) is given further precision by «saying: Know the Lord» (a') and «everyone their own fellow citizen» is echoed by (b) «and everyone his brother». (b') The chiasm is imperfect, because instead of being attached one at the beginning and the other at the end, the central elements both depend grammatically on the beginning. By the verb «to know» the next distich (11ef) is linked to what precedes.

Verse 12 is built in synonymous parallelism, in chiastic form: to the declaration at the beginning, in positive form («I shall be indulgent»), there corresponds the one at the end, in negative form («I shall no more remember»); in one case, the «iniquities» follow the verb; in the other case, the «sins» precede it. Elegant Semitic style.

The former sanctuary and its ineffective rites (9,1-10)

The transition from the preceding subdivision is achieved by link-word: «the first» (8,13 and 9,1).

An inclusion on the word «rites» (1 and 10) marks the boundaries of this subdivision. The introductory sentence (1) announces two subjects, the description of the «rites of worship» and of the «holy» place. They are discussed in reverse order: firstly the holy place (2-5), then the rites (6-7); the parallelism at the beginnings helps to distinguish them: «a tent…was set up» (2), «These things being set up thus» (6). The subdivision ends with a critical reflection on the holy place (8) and on the rites (9-10).

The description of the holy place is divided into two very unequal parts concerning two tents in succession (2 and 3-5). These two parts are united in chiastic form by the qualification given them: the first tent is described firstly and then given a qualification («it is called holy»), the other tent is first given a qualification («called very holy») and then described at length.

9 1 The first [covenant] also had, assuredly, RITES of worship
and the holy [place] which was of this world.
2 A tent was actually *set up*, the first,
in which were the candlestick, the table and the presentation of the loaves
it is called holy,
3 after the second curtain, a tent called most holy,
4 containing a golden incense-burner,
and the ark of the covenant all covered in gold
in which was a golden vase containing the manna
and Aaron's rod, which had blossomed,
and the tablets of the covenant,
5 and above it the cherubim of glory
overshadowing the mercy seat;
about these things this is not the place to speak in detail.
6 These things being thus *set up*,
into the first tent, at all times, enter the priests
accomplishing the ceremonies of worship,
7 but into the second, once a year, only the high priest,
not without [taking] blood,
which he offers for himself and the failings of the people,
8 the holy Spirit showing this:
the way of the sanctuary has not yet been manifested
as long as the first tent is in place.
9 This is a symbol of the present time,
according to which GIFTS AND SACRIFICES ARE OFFERED (8,3)
which are unable to make perfect in conscience
those who offer worship;
10 only, on, drink and various ablutions,
RITES of flesh which are there until the time of redressment.

In the introductory sentence, the preacher expresses the relation between the covenant and the worship, a relation which does not appear in the ritual laws in Leviticus. To the holy place, he gives an epithet, *kosmikon*, «of this world», which is connected in meaning with the specification excluded in 8,2 in the case of «the true tent». The latter is not of this world, for it was not planted by man. Being «of this world», perishable as it is (see 1,11-12 and 12,26-27), the holy place of the first covenant is not the true tent.

The description of the first tent (2) is very sober: a simple relative without verb presents a short list without any qualifying phrases; it is followed by a second relative clause which indicates what the first tent is called. The description of the other tent is, on the contrary, complex (3-5). After the qualifying phrase «very holy», we have a participial expression beginning with a Greek adjective meaning «golden» (4). Emphasized by being in this position, this adjective then recurs twice. The participial expression comprises two long complements. Attached to the second of these is a relative clause that contains another list. At the end, a personal pronoun (*autēs*, «of it» (5) takes over from the relative pronoun to introduce the «cherubim of glory».

The relative clause in verse 4 («in which...») is like the one in verse 2 («in which...»), but it is not really parallel to it, because it is not connected to the «other tent», but to the ark of the covenant which is in it. This subdivision (2-5) does not therefore offer a regular structure, but a kind of unpredictable cascade.

The description of the worship (6-7), in contrast, offers a very clear parallelism which is mainly antithetic. There is a parallelism between «in the first tent, on the one hand (*men*)» and «in the second, on the other (*de*)»; there is a contrast between «at all times» and «once a year», then between «the priests» and «only the high priest». The parallelism is much less apparent between «accomplishing the ceremonies of worship» and «not without blood, which he offers for himself and the failings of the people».

The critical reflection (8-10) follows an order parallel to the description (2-7): it is first concerned with the holy place (8) and then with the rites (9-10). But it is at the same time in relation with the beginning of the section. In verse 8, there is actually a relation between the tent and the sanctuary as in 8,2, but the relation is negative, because it is not about the «the true tent», it is about a tent planted by a man, which cannot therefore be «the way of the sanctuary». In verse 9, we come back to the expression in 8,3 «to offer gifts and sacrifices», accompanied, this time, by a critical evaluation and going on to make various remarks. In speaking of a «time of setting things right» (10), the end of the last sentence prepares for the positive paragraph (9,11-28) which follows immediately.

BIBLICAL CONTEXT

Introduction (8,1-2)

By declaring that our high priest «sat on the right of the throne of the Majesty in the heavens» (1), the introduction again recalls, as in 1,3, the beginning of Psalm 109: «The Lord said to my Lord: Sit on my right». The terms here are similar to those in the exordium (1,3): a verb of movement, «he sat», replaces the verb of position used in the psalm and God is designated by the word «Majesty». Two details are different: the word «throne» is added, which makes the sentence more solemn; instead of the expression «in the heights», open to several interpretations because «the heights» can be earthly, we have «in the heavens», which is more precise.

The rest of the sentence is in relation to the other oracle in Psalm 109, the priestly oracle: «high priest» (1) instead of «priest», as before in 5,10; 6,20; 7,26; «liturgical officiant», in Greek *leitourgos* (2); «the sanctuary», in Greek a neuter plural *ta hagia;* «the tent». These last two words are characteristic of this section. *Ta hagia*, literally «the holy things», is a frequent translation, especially in the book of Ezekiel, of the Hebrew *miqdāš*, which means «holy place», «sanctuary» (Lev 20,3; 21,12; Ezek 5,11; 8,6; 9,6; etc.) As for «the tent», in this worship context, it is in connection with the sanctuary in the time of the Exodus, which was actually a tent, called in Greek «the tent of testimony» (Exod 40,2.5.6. etc.). But the preacher distinguishes two sorts of sanctuary and tent, the priesthood of Christ not being tied to the earthly sanctuary and to the earthly tent. The whole section must be read to grasp his thinking on this subject.

2. Exclusion of the old, earthly worship (8,3-6)

In verse 3, in a shortened form there is again the affirmation in 5,1 about «every high priest», an affirmation that corresponds to the sacrificial function of the high priest in the Old Testament (Lev 1-5; 16; Sir 45,16). That our high priest cannot be a priest on earth (4) is based on the Law of Moses, which keeps priestly functions for the tribe of Levi (Num 3,38); this exclusiveness was mentioned earlier in 7,13-14.

To define the worth of the former worship, the author bases himself on the instruction given by God to Moses in Exod 25,40, but he changes this text (5).

The Septuagint says: «See, you shall do according to the model shown to you on the mountain» after «you shall do», the author adds «all things», which indicates an extension to the instruction; the latter admits of no exception. In Exod 25,9 another divine instruction contains this further detail. Moreover, instead of «which has been shown to you», in Greek a perfect participle, connoting an aspect of permanence, the author has «which was shown to you», an aorist participle that limits the action to a moment in the past.

In verse 6, establishing a relationship between «liturgy», «covenant» and «promises» is not without foundation in the Old Testament, in which the covenant on Sinai is established by means of sacrifices (Exod 24,4-8) and in which a «new covenant» is defined by promises (Jer 31,31.33-34). But the explicit union of these three elements is something new.

Another novelty appears in the next verse: the idea that the first covenant was not irreproachable (7). This idea is never expressed in the Old Testament. However, the oracle in Jeremiah comes close to it when saying explicitly that the new covenant will not be like the covenant concluded with the fathers. To justify his attitude, the author relies effectively on that oracle.

3. The former, imperfect and superseded covenant (8,7-13)

The oracle in Jeremiah itself indicates the circumstances in which it was uttered: in a situation of violation of the Sinai covenant. The Hebrew text expresses this situation in harsh terms: «they have violated, they have broken my covenant» (Jer 31,32); the Greek translators have toned down the expression and put «they did not remain in my covenant». The conjunction that follows in Hebrew (*waw*) is open to several interpretations: it can be concessive («*although* I am their master») or consecutive («*so that* I made them feel my power»). The Greek translators took it as consecutive and put: «and I, I neglected them», that is to say did not defend them against their enemies. It is a matter of the situation described at the end of the second Book of Chronicles: «All the chief priests and the people were exceedingly unfaithful [...] so that the Lord's anger against his people was such that there was no remedy for it. He aroused the king of the Chaldeans [...] God delivered them all into his hands» (2Chr 36,14-17). Jerusalem is besieged, it is taken and devasted the Temple razed, the survivors are deported.

This is the tragic context in which God promises a new covenant, more marvellous than the one that did not hold up. The oracle is part of a positive section of the Book of Jeremiah (Jer 30-31 or 30-33), which contains prophecies announcing the restoration of the kingdom of the north. The oracle about the new covenant has given rise to debate. W. Rudolph thinks that it dates from the first period of the prophet's activity and that it concerned the kingdom of the north, which, a century ago, had undergone the Assyrian invasion and the deportation. A. Gelin, however, places it later, at the time of the siege of Jerusalem and concerning both kingdoms. Yet other exegetes come down in favour of an even later epoch and attribute it to a disciple of Jeremiah. One thing is certain: in its present state, the oracle applies to all the people, Israel and Judah, and reflects a terrible situation of covenant violation.

All commentators agree in admiring the depth and beauty of this prophecy. In the commentary in the «Anchor Bible» series, J. Bright declares that it «represents what may be considered the peak of Jeremiah's theology. It certainly has some of the most profound and most moving texts in the whole Bible» (*Jeremiah*, p. 287). Different from many other promises of restoration announcing the return of material prosperity, the oracle about the new Covenant is not interested in that aspect, but expresses only a very pure religious aspiration, one of personal relation with God.

As is his custom, the author quotes the oracle in the Greek translation of the Septuagint. He changes some details, in particular in the expressions used in connection with the covenant. While the Septuagint regularly says «to arrange an arrangement» (the word used in Greek, *diathēkē*, literally means «arrangement»), the author puts a stronger verb in verse 8 to announce the new covenant: «*I shall conclude* a new arrangement», and a less strong verb in verse 9 to speak of the first covenant: «the arrangement *I made* for their fathers»; in verse 10, to speak about the new covenant, he keeps the expression constantly used in the Septuagint: «the arrangement that I shall arrange». These details are significant: the author disparages the first covenant and gives importance to the new one. Other details are along the same lines: to speak about the first covenant, the author usually leaves out the noun and simply says «this first» (8,7) or «the first» (8,13; 9,1), as if he wished to insinuate that it did not really deserve the name covenant; he only puts the noun when it is a question of the «transgressions committed under the first covenant» (9,15), transgressions which disqualify it.

4. The former sanctuary and its ineffective rites (9,1-10)

The description of the holy place is based on the Torah and does not therefore refer to the Temple of Herod that existed at the time of the author, nor even to the Temple of Solomon, but to the «tent» in the desert, set up by Moses; the author has already alluded to it in 8,3. The divine prescriptions about this are in Exod 25-31; their execution is reported in Exod 35-39. The erection of the sanctuary is prescribed in Exod 40,1-15 and carried out in Exod 40,16-33.

The author insists on the division of the tent into two parts and even seems to speak of two distinct tents, which he calls «the first tent» (9,6), and «the second» (9,7), but in Greek, the expressions used can designate the first and the second part of one and the same tent. Indeed, the detail given in 9,3, which speaks of a «curtain» of separation suggests this interpretation.

The qualifying phrases added to the two parts of the tent give rise to problems. The solution depends on a question of accentuation. The oldest manuscripts do not show the accentuation and therefore leave open the possibility, in the present case, of two different accentuations for the word *hagia*, a form of *hagios*, «holy». With the accent on the «i» the word is a feminine singular: «a tent, the first, [...] which is called *holy*», «a tent called very *holy*» (literally: «holy of holies», a Hebraizing form of the superlative). With the accent on the first «a», the word is a neuter plural; «a tent, the first, [...] which is called *holy* things», «a tent called *very holy things*». Almost all the manuscripts that show the accentuation have chosen the second solution, because the copyists thought they recognized in the text the name of the two parts of the sanctuary, «the holy»and «the holy of holies»: the first tent «is called the holy» the second is «called the holy of holies». But this option comes up against great difficulties, because as it stands in Heb 9,3, that is to say without any article, the expression in the Septuagint never designates the *debir*, the innermost part of the sanctuary. What is usually found is the singular with two articles, *to hagion tōn hagiōn* (Exod 26,33.34; Lev 16,33; 2Chr 3,8; Ezek 41,4); sometimes we find the plural, with two articles, *ta hagia tōn hagiōn* (3Kgs 8,6; 2Chr 4,22; 5,7) or with one article (Ezek 45,3); the expression is not reserved exclusively to the holy of holies; it can be applied to another place (Num 18,10) or to other things (Lev 21,22). Without the article, the expression is a superlative, qualifying the victims immolated (Lev 6,17.25), the altar (Exod 30,10; 40,10), a perfume (Exod 30,36), the loaves of proposition (Lev 24,9). In our text, it must therefore be understood as an adjective in the superlative (Heb 9,3). With greater reason, the simple *hagia* in verse 2 must be understood as an adjective in the feminine: «a tent, the first: [...] which is called holy». To see here the neuter plural *ta hagia* here causes inextricable difficulties, because elsewhere in the sermon, this plural does not designate the first tent, but the second, the one into which only the high priest can penetrate: *ta hagia* in 9,25 and 13,11 corresponds to «the second» in 9,7. In our text, 9,2-3, the presence of many textual variants shows that the copyists were aware of these difficulties and attempted to remedy them, without realizing that the simplest remedy —which was obvious— was to adopt the other accentuation.

The preacher quickly enumerates the objects that were in the two parts of the tent. «The candlestick» with «six branches» is described in the priestly tradition of the Pentateuch (Exod 25,31-40; 37,17-24; 40,4.24); if one includes the central stem, it has seven branches and is therefore furnished with «seven lamps» (Exod 25,37, 37,23). Its symbolism is not explained. It has to be lit before «the Lord, from evening to morning, permanently» (Lev 24,2-4), which leads on to thinking about the symbolism of vigilant presence «before the Lord».

«The table» is described at length and orders are given to make «the presentation of the loaves» on it (Exod 25,23-30; 37,10-16; 44,4.22-23). Leviticus points out that it is a matter of «the food offered in memory, a dish for the Lord» (Lev 24,7). When the loaves are removed the following Saturday, only the priests can eat them, in a holy place (24,9).

«The second curtain» is the one separating «the holy (*to hagion*) from the holy of holies (*to hagion tōn hagiōn*)» (Exod 26,33). It was of precious material (Exod 26,31-33; 36,35). Philo of Alexandria and Josephus speak of it at length. The preacher is content with naming it. He does not name the first curtain made «for the entry to the tent» (Exod 36,37; LXX 37,5).

The «incense-burner» raises problems, because the preacher places it in the second tent, whereas the altar of incense was situated in first tent, where a priest came morning and evening for the offering of incense (Exod 30,1-10; 40,5.26; see also Luke 1,11). But does the preacher mean the altar of incense? He uses a word, *thymiatērion*, which, in the Septuagint, never designates that altar, called *thysiastērion*, but designates a censer (2Chr 26,19; Exod 8,11; 4 Macc 7,11). According to Lev 16,12, at the time of the liturgy of Kippur, the high priest entered the second tent with a censer full of burning charcoal, on which he burnt incense. The preacher could be alluding to that rite. It should be noted, however, that in Lev 16,12 the word used to designate the censer is not *thymiatērion*, but a synonym much more frequent in the Septuagint, *pyreion*.

In the history of the priesthood during the Exodus, attention is drawn several times to the censer. At the time of Korah's dispute over the priesthood, the censers are used in a trial whereby the Lord makes it known «who is his, who is the consecrated one» (Num 16,4-7.17-19). Later, to bring about the end of a divine scourge, Aaron receives the order to take his censer and «to hasten to go to the community to perform the rite of expiation over it» (Num 17,11). Aaron's action was effective. Its importance is stressed in the Book of Wisdom (Wis 18,20-21); it is also recalled in 4Macc 7,11, a text in which the censer, called *pyreion* in Num 17,11, is called *thymiatērion*.

In the opposite direction, it is noticeable that Philo and Josephus use *thymiatērion* to designate the altar of perfumes and that it would be strange if the author should not mention that altar, the place of which was important in worship. The remark according to which the *thymiatētion* was «golden» calls to mind the altar of perfumes, for the description of it that is given in Exod 30,1-5 says that it was plated with pure gold, surrounded with a golden moulding and fitted with two golden rings on its two sides. Nothing like this is said about the high priest's censer.

It is difficult to draw any conclusion. The situation is not clear. In declaring, at the end of the sentence, that «about these things now is not the time to speak in detail» the preacher shows that he is not concerned with perfect precision.

«The ark» is described at length in Exod 25,10-22 and 37,1-2. Its importance was capital. In these texts and in many others, it is not called «ark of the covenant», but «ark of the testimony», for it was designed to contain «the testimony», that is to say the two tablets of the Law, an attestation of the will of God and of the commitment entered into by the people to observe it (Exod 24,3-8). The expression «ark of the covenant» is equivalent; it is sometimes found in the Pentateuch (Exod 31,7; 39,15 LXX...), and often elsewhere (Josh 3,3-17; 1Chr 15,25-29). The preacher mentions its contents. In it he first places «a golden vase containing the manna» interpreting in this sense the text in Exod 16,33-34 in which Aaron receives the order to take a vase (the Septuagint specifies: «golden»), to fill it with manna and to place it «before God» Aaron carries out the order and places the vase «before the testimony».

The position is similar in the case of «Aaron's rod which had blossomed», a sign of the divine choice after Korah's dispute (Num 17,23). The Lord orders Moses to place this rod «before the testimony».

The situation is clear only in the case of the «the tablets of the covenant». To be sure, the most important texts do not use this expression; they speak of the «testimony», but other texts clearly show that this noun designates «the tablets of the covenant» on which were engraved the ten commandments of God. In

Exod 25,16, God orders Moses to «place in the ark the testimony»; this order is repeated in Exod 25,21 and its execution is stated in Exod 40,20. But to report this same fact, Deuteronomy says that Moses placed «in the ark the tablets» on which God had engraved the Decalogue (Deut 10,1-5). In Exod 31,18 and 32,15 these tablets are called «tablets of the testimony», in Deut 9,9.11 «tablets of the covenant». In the time of Solomon, the Bible records that «there was nothing in the ark, save the two tablets of stone that Moses had deposited there at Horeb, the tablets of the covenant which the Lord had concluded with the Israelites on their coming out of Egypt» (1Kgs 8,9). The preacher takes no account of this text, perhaps because it concerns the time of Solomon, different from the time of the Exodus.

What gave the ark great importance, was not only its content, but also and above all its cover, named «the mercy seat», a place where God manifested himself. To Moses, God had declared: «That is where I shall meet you» (Exod 25,22; see Lev 16,2). At each end of the mercy seat there was a golden cherub with wings extended upwards; these two cherubim «shaded the mercy seat with their wings» (Exod 25,20) and with it they formed the throne of God. «The Lord who sits on the cherubim» was invoked there (Ps 80,2; 2Kgs 19,15). The preacher completely omits all mention of God. He confines himself to an allusion by adding a qualifying phrase about the cherubim, whom he calls «cherubim of glory». Then he breaks off.

The way in which worship was performed is summarily recalled, especially as regards the first tent; no detail is given (2). For the worship in the second tent, however, some specific points are added (3-5); they correspond to some prescriptions in Leviticus for the celebration of Kippur, the only occasion in the year (Lev 16,34) when the high priest, and he alone (16,17), was authorized to go into the holy of holies, to perform various rites there, especially sacrificial ones. Of these rites, the preacher mentions only the use of the blood of immolated victims. Leviticus actually prescribes rites performed with blood. Aaron has to take the blood of the bull offered for his own sin and sprinkle the mercy seat with it (16,15). But the preacher parts company with Leviticus when he speaks of an *offering* of the blood and when he says that this offering is made for «the failings (literally «the ignorances») of the people». Leviticus does not speak about offering, but of an expiation rite performed with the blood and he extends its intention to the «impurities of the children of Israel, their iniquities and all their sins» (16,16.34). The preacher, on the contrary, applies the rule in Num 15,22-30 to the Kippur expiation, a rule according to which only the faults committed «in error» can be taken away by a sacrifice; the sins committed «high-handedly», that is to say with full knowledge of their gravity, cannot be taken away by a sacrifice; they entail the death penalty.

The appraisal of the place of worship and the rites (8-10) is made in the light of Christ; it does not have an explicit foundation in the Old Testament. When ending, the preacher places sacrificial worship in relation to the prescriptions of ritual purity concerning «food, drink and various ablutions» (10). The Law of Moses contains many prescriptions of this kind. Leviticus gives a whole list of impure animals of which it is forbidden to eat the meat (Lev 11,1-47); it also forbids eating the fat and the blood of the other beasts (Lev 3,17; 17,10-14). Some sacred foods are reserved for priests and forbidden to laity (Exod 29,33; Lev 10,12-15; 22,10; Num 18,8-19). Abstinence from wine and other fermented drinks was imposed on priests at certain periods (Lev 10,8-11) and on people, men or women, who had taken the Nazirite vow (Num 6,1-4).

Besides, in many cases in which ritual impurity had been contracted, for example by touching a corpse, ablutions were prescribed (Num 19,11-22). Ritual impurity ruled out taking part in worship (Num 9,6).

C. *INTERPRETATION*

1. Introduction (8,1-2)

The solemn sentence in 8,1-2, which introduces the whole of the section (8,1-9,28), well shows its importance, because it defines it as the «main point» of the homily, which corresponds fully to its central position in the structure.

Another translation, it is true, is grammatically possible: «a point in addition to what is said»[1].

But when one has recognized the literary structure of the homily, one can see that this translation is altogether improbable. The point that is actually going to be dealt with in this central section concerns the sacrifice whereby Christ was «made perfect» and has therefore become mediator of the new covenant. This point is by no means a «point in addition», added to a discourse already complete without it. On the contrary, it is an integral part of the discourse, because the author prepared it earlier with the important sentence in 2,10, he placed it in

1 This is the option taken in the new edition of the Bible of Jerusalem (1998), which translates: «a chapter to be added to these discourses», thereby following the position of P. GARUTI, *Alle origini dell'omiletica cristiana. La lettera agli Ebrei.*

the first position in the announcement of the central part (5,8-9), treated it in a negative way in 7,11.19 and recalled it with the last word in 7,28, to which the expression in 8,1 refers: «it is a high priest like this that we have», a high priest «made perfect» (7,28). It will be mentioned again in 10,1.14.

About the expression «high priest like this», some commentators think they have to choose between a reference to what precedes, «a high priest as described in 7,26-28», and a reference to what follows, «a high priest as will be described in 8,1-2» and pronounce in favour of this second possibility (Westcott, Spicq). In reality, it is not necessary to choose; it is more a question of adopting both possibilities together, for they do not in any way exclude each other. The first is suggested by the parallelism linking 8,1 with 7,26. «It is a *high priest like this* that we have» (8,1) obviously refers to «it is *a high priest like this* that was fitting for us» (7,26). The second possibility follows from the rest of the sentence, which adds other particulars, altogether in harmony with the preceding ones: according to 7,28, the high priest who was suitable for us is the one of whom the oracle in Ps 109,4 speaks; the same psalm reveals that he was invited to sit at God's right hand (Ps 109,1; Heb 8,1) and that his priesthood is therefore in relation with the heavenly sanctuary (2).

Sitting at God's right hand is not expressed as a present situation, but as the result of a past action: our high priest has gone to sit at God's right hand. This detail makes way for the theme of the section which is going to say that Christ «entered» into the sanctuary (9,12) thanks to the sacrifice he «offered» when offering himself (9,14).

Sitting on the right is situated explicitly «in the heavens», which excludes an earthly interpretation of the expression. This point corresponds to the prediction made by Jesus during his trial before the Sanhedrin, a prediction that closely links sitting on the right hand with the heavenly apparition of the Son of man (Dn 7,13): «You will see the Son of man seated on the right hand of the Power and coming on the clouds of heaven» (Matt 26,64; Mark 14,62). It likewise corresponds to the statement made by Peter in his speech on the day of Pentecost (Acts 2,34) and to other texts of the New Testament (Ep 1,20; Col 3,1-2). The preacher will describe later on and in the same way the entry of Christ into the sanctuary, not a sanctuary built on earth by men, but «heaven itself» (9,24).

To the royal aspect of sitting on the right hand, the psalm adds the priestly aspect a little further on. The preacher, too, expresses these two aspects and does so by uniting them more closely: he suggests that the sitting on the right hand was obtained by liturgical activity. It is in the capacity of «liturgical officiant of the sanctuary and the tent» that our high priest went to sit at God's right hand. To tell the truth, the preacher's expressions are rather obscure; they raise some questions, which is a way of introducing the subject; another way consists in briefly giving the answers beforehand, but here, to have the answers we have to wait for the development that follows.

«Liturgical officiant» (2) translates *leitourgos*, a Greek word which does not usually have this sense but simply means «servant». Its adjuncts here give it a worship nuance, as in some other texts, for example Rom 15,16. The corresponding verb, *leitourgein*, the primitive meaning of which is «to perform a public service» and could be applied to a religious service, is specialized in this second sense in the Septuagint and likewise the substantive *leitourgia* which marks the end of the inclusion of which *leitourgos* marks the beginning; this structural relationship confirms the worship meaning of *leitourgos*.

Of itself, this substantive does not specify the moment or the moments in which the liturgical activity of our high priest must be placed. At first sight, one might think of continual activity «in the heavens» but this interpretation does not agree well with the seated position taken by our high priest. Actually, in 10,11-13, the preacher will make a contrast between the priests who stand and celebrate their liturgy every day and Christ who offered a unique sacrifice and henceforth remains seated. Christ is called a «liturgical officiant» not in the sense of a liturgy continually celebrated in heaven, but in the sense that some liturgical activity caused him to pass from earth to heaven.

That liturgy has as its co-ordinates «the sanctuary and the true tent that the Lord planted, not a man» (2). Here again the listeners may be perplexed. What is this «sanctuary»» and what is this «tent»? Do these two words, which make their first appearance here, designate two different realities or the same reality? The immediate context does not shed any light, for it only speaks of a tent «that a man planted», «Moses» (5). The commentators themselves are in an embarrassing situation. More than one—and not the least of them (Westcott, Spicq)—reckon that it is a matter of one and the same reality, designated in two different ways. This opinion comes from a lack of attention given to the structure of the text. These exegetes have not made out the structural role of Heb 8,1-2, which is to announce an exposé divided into two long paragraphs, the first on the tent planted by a man (8,3-9,10), the second on the sanctuary and the tent planted by the Lord (9,11-28). If, therefore, one wants to find the solution to the problem posed by the expression «the sanctuary and the tent», one has to look for it in this second paragraph. One then realizes that the preacher clearly distinguishes between the sanctuary and the tent, because he says that «through the tent» Christ entered «into the sanctuary» (9,11-12) and he defines the tent and the sanctuary in two different subdivisions: the tent in 9,11-14, the sanctuary in 9,24-28. Doubt is therefore not possible: the sanctuary and the tent do not designate the same reality, but two realities that are distinct, while being closely connected.

Exclusion of the former, earthly worship (8,3-6)

This first subdivision begins by specifying in what sense «liturgical officiant» must be taken, that is to say in a sacrificial sense (3); then, somewhat laboriously, it moves on (4-5) to the theme of this long paragraph (8,3-9,10), which is the critical description of the priestly worship of the Old Testament.

«Liturgical officiant» is to be taken in liaison with an offering of sacrifice, because, as was stated in 5,1, «every high priest is established to offer gifts and sacrifices»(3). The application of this principle to our heavenly high priest is made in a rather indeterminate way, because the preacher at this moment does not want to deal with the subject of the sacrifice of Christ, reserved for the other long paragraph; he only wants to prepare it. He does not therefore clearly name Christ, he only puts a demonstrative pronoun, «this one». He does not specify what he offered, but only says «something». He does not put any verb in the indicative, but speaks only of a «necessity», without saying whether it still prevails in the present or prevailed in the past and prevails no longer. To be informed about all these points, we have to wait for the positive paragraph (9,11-28). One detail, however, points the perspicacious listener in the right direction. This detail is only noticeable in the Greek text. It concerns the verb «to offer». The preacher did not use the same tense of the infinitive with «every high priest» as with «this one». With «every high priest», he put the present infinitive which indicates that a continual or repeated action is in question: the complement in the plural, «gifts and sacrifices», shows that it is a question of a repeated action. With «this one», on the contrary, we have the aorist infinitive, which designates a definite action, and does not allow for its repetition. Elsewhere in his homily, the preacher constantly expresses the same distinction: present of repetition for the former worship, aorist of something done once only for the sacrifice of Christ (see 5,1-3.7; 7,27; 9,6.14; 9,25-26; 10,11-12). Here, in 8,3, the perspicacious listener can understand already that the preacher is implicitly excluding the idea of a continual sacrificial offering or one repeated in heaven.

Yet he does not exclude every heavenly aspect in the sacrifice of Christ. The next sentence (4) makes it clear that, on the contrary, he does include a heavenly aspect in it, because he points out that, if our high priest were on earth he would not even be a simple priest there, since, on earth, the Law reserves the priesthood to people other than our high priest. The same observation has already been made, in other terms, in the previous section (7,13-14). The former priesthood is a privilege of the tribe of Levi, now Jesus belonged to the tribe of Judah. Without stating precisely in what the heavenly aspect of the sacrifice of Christ consisted, the preacher passes on to the critique of the former worship (5).

Here, as often, he bases his criticism on the Old Testament itself, of which he fully recognizes the authority as divine revelation. To minimize the value of the former worship, he uses a word of which the purpose was, on the contrary, to lay the foundations of that value, guaranteeing that the whole organization of the worship corresponded to the model shown by God. The preacher does not deny that at all, but he points out that it is not therefore a matter of the heavenly realities themselves, but of their representation. The expression he uses can bear a very pejorative meaning, because «worshipping a representation» could be understood as an attitude related to the worship of idols, forbidden by the Decalogue (Exod 20,4-5; Deut 5,8-9). This possibility, however, is still very questionable. What is certain is that God is never named in the description of the former worship. In his homily, the preacher uses the verb *latreuein*, «to pay worship» 6 times; when Christians are involved he states that worship is paid «to God» (9,14; 12,28); when the Old Testament is involved, this qualification is never added (8,5; 9,9; 10,2; 13,10).

When speaking of «figure and sketch», and not of «copy» —a frequent error in translation— the preacher opens up a perspective which is not suggested by the text he is quoting (Exod 25,40). The latter asks for a «model» (*typos*) to be reproduced and therefore for a copy to be made. In 9,24 the preacher will actually present the former «sanctuary» as a «copy» (*antitypos*) of the true sanctuary. But here, where there is talk of the «tent», he speaks of «figure and sketch», which means that the copy of the heavenly model of the tent is the prefiguration of a perfect reality. The heavenly model, in fact, is not the perfect reality, it is simply a model.

Here and in other passages, the preacher unites a Platonic conception, according to which a perfect heavenly idea precedes in time an imperfect earthly reproduction, with a biblical eschatological conception according to which a first imperfect earthly reproduction precedes and announces the perfect fulfilment of God's plan. The tent raised by Moses preceded and announced «the greater and more perfect tent» which will be spoken of in 9,11 in connection with Christ's offering.

The preacher terminates this subdivision by actually mentioning the «liturgy» celebrated by Christ (6). His assertion is very dynamic and positive, but it resembles the one in verse 6 about Christ's offering: the verb «has obtained» does not have a subject expressed, Christ is not named. His name will only appear for the first time in 9,11, the beginning of the positive paragraph.

Our high priest's «liturgy» is said to be «very different» from the former liturgy. Here we find the Greek adjective *diaphoros* in the comparative of intensity, as in the exordium concerning the «name» received by Christ at the end of his paschal mystery (1,4). this comparative expresses at once difference and superiority, which is also the meaning of an emphatic «very different» in English. The difference and the superiority of Christ's liturgy are placed in relation with the greater value of the covenant of which he is the mediator. Making this relation constitutes a new approach with regard to worship in the Old Testament, because the laws governing worship in Leviticus know hardly anything about this relation; they contain the word «covenant» only once (in Lev 2,13, about the salt that has to be added to the oblation). However, the Book of Exodus records that sacrifices were offered at the time of the conclusion of the covenant on Sinai (Exod 24,5). According to the preacher, the value of the covenant depends on the value of the promises on which it was established. In the Old Testament, the emphasis was rather on the value of the Law of the Covenant. The change of perspective is apparently brought about by the oracle about the New Covenant which the preacher is about to quote. The New Covenant, in fact, is defined there only by promises.

Our high priest is called «covenant mediator» here. A mediator (*mesitēs*) is someone who stands in the middle (*mesos*) and attempts to set up good relations between two parties. This term is rare in the Bible. It has only one occurrence in the Old Testament (Job 9,33); it has six in the New (Gal 3,19.20; 1Tim 2,5; Heb 8,6; 9,15; 12,24). The expression «covenant mediator», which is very coherent, is found only in Hebrews; it comes three times in it. To say that a high priest is a covenant mediator corresponds very well with the definition the preacher gave in 5,1 of «every high priest», in a perspective which —as we have seen—

was hardly noticed in the Old Testament; the latter was more inclined to insist on the functions of the priesthood connected with worship than on its role of mediation.

3. The former imperfect and superseded covenant (8,7-13)

In speaking of a «*better* covenant», the preacher is alluding implicitly to the existence of a covenant that is not so good. His hearers immediately understand that this covenant that is not so good was the one on Sinai. To contest its value was daring, because many were convinced that it was perfect. The preacher is therefore expecting objections and he answers them by saying that if it had been irreproachable, God would not have announced that he would replace it with another one. The Sinai covenant is called «this first», despite the existence, in the Old Testament, of other covenants which preceded it: God's covenant with Noah (Gen 6,18), then with Noah, his descendants and all living beings (Gen 9,9-17), and the covenant of God with Abraham (Gen 15,18; 17,2-15). But the Sinai covenant is the first to have been concluded between the people of Israel and God (Exod 24,3-8) and that is the one that the oracle in Jeremiah mentions in his announcement of another covenant. Further on, the preacher will explicitly recall the foundation of this «first» covenant (9,18-21).

Here, he bases himself on the oracle in Jeremiah to criticize the Sinai covenant. A slight incoherence is noticeable in his text. To show that the first covenant was not irreproachable, he ought to be able to say that the oracle contains reproaches against it; he cannot, because the oracle does not explicitly contain any; it contains only one against «them», that is to say against the Israelites. The preacher must therefore be content to say: «he makes reproaches against *them*», which makes his remarks shaky; he has not shown that reproaches were made against the covenant.

Yet one can justify his line of argument by saying that, to be recognized as irreproachable, the covenant ought to have made those who had entered into it irreproachable; it did not have the capacity to do so, it therefore left something to be desired. The new covenant, for its part, will make those who accept it irreproachable.

The way in which the author introduces the oracle in Jeremiah is very one-sided. It only stresses the short passage with reproaches in it and says not a word about its magnificent positive perspectives. This way of proceeding corresponds to the orientation of the whole paragraph in the direction of a critique of the institutions of the Old Testament. The conclusion will be similar (13).

The oracle commences with an indication of time, which concerns the future, without being explicitly eschatological: «days are coming». The Lord announces that at that time, he will conclude «a new covenant» with the two components of the people of Israel. To express the idea of novelty, Greek has two adjectives, one of which, *neos*, expresses the idea of novelty in time (for example, «new wine», Matt 9,17, has recently fermented wine), whereas the other, *kainos*, can designate a new kind of thing (a «new» wine, Matt 26,29, no longer earthly, but heavenly). The Septuagint chose *kainos*, which suggests that it will be a matter of a new kind of covenant. This choice is perfectly justified, because the oracle immediately states that the new covenant will be different from the one on Sinai. The description then given of it confirms this difference.

The Sinai covenant is mentioned in moving terms. It was made by God for the fathers, that is to say for the ancestors of the Israelites, the day when God took them by the hand in a fatherly way to bring them out of Egypt, where they were oppressed. This generous initiative on God's part ought to have been greeted with gratitude and fidelity. In fact, the beneficiaries were not faithful to the covenant. After the account of the conclusion of the covenant (Exod 24), the first narrative episode —the intervening texts are legislative texts— is the one that relates the adoration of the golden calf (Exod 32), a violation of the Covenant symbolized by Moses' action of breaking the two tables of the Covenant (Exod 32,19). The lack of fidelity is thereafter repeated indefinitely in the course of the next generations; in the Book of Jeremiah, God relates the sad fact: «From the day their fathers left the land of Egypt until today [...] they have stiffened their neck, they have been worse than their fathers» (Jer 7,25-26; 2Kgs 21,15). The formula in the oracle extends implicitly to all these epochs, both as regards God's reaction and as regards the infidelity of the people and its leaders. The expression in the Septuagint, which has God saying: «I, too, neglected them» is not so vigorous as the one in the Book of Judges, which declares that God «handed them over» to their enemies (Judg 2,14; 6,1; 6,13; 13,1) or the one in 2Chr 36,17, according to which God «raised up against them the king of the Chaldeans, who put them to the sword». «To neglect» does not express an active deed of punishment, but only the absence of any intervention: God ceased to provide protection, peace, prosperity; he no longer put the promises of the covenant into effect; he conformed to the state of violation.

But he announces that he is not resigning himself to this situation and that he will establish a new covenant of which he defines the salient features, implicitly opposed to those of the Sinai covenant:

1) instead of being written on tablets of stone, the laws of God will be written by him on hearts (10 cd);
2) in this way there will be a perfect reciprocal relation between the people and God, never achieved by the Sinai Covenant (10ef);
3) instead of a collective institution, there will be a personal relation of every one with God (11);
4) God's pardon of all faults, which seemed impossible under the Sinai Covenant, will be generously granted (12).

The first words announce that God *will give* his laws. The Hebrew verb used here (*nātan*) does not always mean «to give», it often has the sense of «to put» and this sense is more suitable here because of the context: «I shall put my law at the bottom of their being», but the Septuagint preferred the other meaning, probably to insist on the aspect involving a precious gift. Jewish tradition greatly insists on the gift of the Law. This aspect is still more marked in the new covenant where God's gift is of unequalled generosity.

Instead of the singular «my law» the Septuagint put the plural without any article, literally «laws of me». This allowed the preacher to make a distinction between those laws of God, written on hearts, and the Law of the first covenant, written on stone. He has already strongly criticized the Law by declaring that it «has not made anything perfect» (7,18); further on, he will again criticize its inefficacy (10,1).

The new laws of God will be inscribed «in their minds and in their hearts». At first sight, this double formula corresponds to a complementary parallelism between intellectual capacity and affectivity. But for the Hebrew it is more a question of synonymy. In the Bible, the heart is before all the organ of thought. Sirach declares that to mankind God «gave a heart to think» (Sir 17,6). The Hebrew word *lēb*, «heart», is often translated in Greek by *dianoia,* «intelligence» but it is true that the signification of the word *lēb* extends beyond the intellectual aspect; this word designates the whole interior of the person, memory, will and affectivity. God will act so that his will is fully understood by people and sincerely accepted, with love. The whole inner part of the human being will thus be transformed.

It can be easily seen that the opposition to the Sinai covenant, expressed explicitly in the preceding verse (9), continues here implicitly. The outward promulgation of the Law, on two tablets of stone (Exod 24,12; 31,18; 34,1; etc.), proved to be ineffective. God therefore provided another way of manifesting his will, which is a will of love, and of having it accepted.

The result will be the establishment of a perfect reciprocal relation, a real covenant (10ef). The formula «I shall be their God and they shall be my people» does not come in the account of the conclusion of the first covenant; it is imposed later as an ideal never reached. It is met with 6 times in the Book of Jeremiah and 5 times in that of Ezekiel, with variations of detail. What prevented the achievement of this ideal was the hardness of heart of the chosen people, constantly indocile. «Their heart ever goes astray» (Ps 95,10; He 3,10). By writing his laws on hearts, God will overcome this obstacle and the ideal will become reality.

To express the personal and interior character of the relation with God in the new covenant better, Jeremiah boldly announces the end of religious instruction which will have become useless (11). In Greek, a double negation insists upon this declaration. There will no longer be any instruction concerning the most important point of all: knowledge of God. It will no longer be necessary nor even useful to exhort each other «to know the Lord». As often in the Bible, the verb «to know» does not refer here simply to intellectual knowledge, but to a personal, real-life relation. The essential problem for each person is that of their relation with God, a relation that should be profound and vivifying. Every effort made by the prophets tended therefore to bring the Israelites to «know the Lord» in that sense. It was not, on the part of the prophets, a matter of theoretical instruction, based on ideas and proofs, but of an urgent appeal to follow the ways of the Lord to be in a genuine relation with him. The prophets had continually to observe bitterly that Israel did not know the Lord. «They go from one sin to another and do not know the Lord» (Jer 9,2-3). The prophets receive the mission to shout in the ears of the people. God tells them: «Shout at the top of your voice, do not spare yourself, like the trumpet lift up your voice, announce their revolts to my people, to the house of Jacob its faults» (Isa 58,1). «Go, shout in the ears of Jerusalem» (Jer 2,2). An indispensable mission, but an ineffective one. God himself predicts it to Jeremiah: «You can repeat these words, they will not listen to you; you can cry out, they will not answer» (Jer 7,27).

Situated in this context, the prediction in verse 11 manifests all its paradoxical novelty. It announces a complete reversal of the situation. Instead of an ever indocile people despite the prophets' pressing exhortations, there will be a people every member of which will be in an intimate relation with God, without needing to be exhorted to it. This is the realization of Isaiah's ideal vision: «The knowledge of the Lord fills the earth, as the waters fill the sea» (Isa 11,9).

A «because» introduces the last element of the description of the new covenant This fourth and last «because» is not simply connected with the declaration that immediately precedes it; its bearing extends to everything that was predicted in the oracle. All this is clear because God will pardon the faults.

Indeed, once the violation was noted (9de), a positive situation seemed impossible. Between the people and God, everything was finished. The people had not remained in the covenant; it therefore had no further right to any divine blessing. It had only to wait for the terrible curses pronounced against rebels (Lev 26,14-38; Deut 28,15-68). Does the positive description therefore constitute an enormous paradox and raise a question: how will that become possible?

The answer is given at the end, as a last surprise, giving the key to everything. That will become possible, because, in his boundless generosity, God will remove all the obstacles: he will pardon. The divine promise of pardon is expressed with insistence, twice, the first time with a positive formula, «I shall be indulgent», the second time with a negative formula, still more expressive (in Greek a reinforced negation), «their sins, no, I shall no longer remember them».

The extraordinary nature of this divine pardon appears in all its clarity when one reads over the previous oracles of the Book of Jeremiah, who declares pardon to be impossible (Jer 5,1.7; 6,28-29; 9,1-8; 18,13.17). The situation had got so bad that God forbade the prophet to intercede for the people: «And you, do not intercede for that people, do not send up any suppliant prayer for them, do not insist with me, for I do not wish to listen to you» (Jer 7,16). But, in the long run, the divine mercy prevailed none the less and won a complete victory: God promised pardon and, with pardon, not only the re-establishment of the covenant, but the foundation of a much more perfect covenant.

The conclusion (13) returns to the perspective of the introductory sentences (7-8a), a perspective of criticism of the first covenant. Of the very long quotation, the preacher takes up only one word, but a very important word, the one qualifying the covenant announced: it will be «new»; the preacher does not at all stress the positive content of this word, so well expressed in the oracle; on the contrary, he shows the negative implications resulting from it for the first covenant. He goes from the idea of being new to the antithetic one of being old, from being old to old age and from old age to passing away. One cannot be more negative.

The subject of the sentence is not expressed, but the context indicates it very clearly. The one who *said* «new», is obviously «the Lord», the subject of the verb «to say» in the sentence announcing the new covenant (8) and in two other sentences in the oracle (9 and 10). The one who «made old» the first covenant is therefore God himself. The Greek verb is in the perfect, which expresses a completed action the effect of which is still present. In itself, being old can be understood positively —it makes the person or thing venerable— or negatively —it makes them outmoded, out of date. The preacher wants to present it in this second way so to «made ancient» he adds «and growing old». Ancient things —including the institutions— sometimes stay in existence indefinitely, but old age, for its part, ends inexorably in «passing away», in Greek *aphanismos.* This Greek term is found only here in the New Testament, but it is frequent in the Greek translation of the Old Testament, especially in the Book of Jeremiah, where it is met with 18 times. It is therefore quite at home here, after a long quotation from Jeremiah. It recalls that the mission of this prophet comprised two aspects, the first, of destruction and demolition, the other, of planting and of construction. Announced in Jer 1,10, in the account of the prophet's calling, this mission is recalled in Jer 31,28, three verses before the oracle about the new covenant.

The preacher does not say directly that the first covenant is «close to passing away»; he states only a general principle, suggesting that this principle applies to the first covenant. In exactly what way does he think it applies to it? It is not easy to pin down. Several answers can be proposed, for example:

1) in saying «new» at the time of Jeremiah, God then made the Sinai covenant old and close to disappearance. Its disappearance was not late in coming: the holy City was besieged and conquered by the pagans, the Temple, a sign of the Covenant, was destroyed, the priestly worship suppressed.
2) The Sinai covenant was made close to its disappearance by the effective foundation of the new covenant. Its disappearance will not delay in coming, because Jesus announced the destruction of the Temple and of it one can see «the Day approaching» (Heb 10,25).
3) The Sinai covenant remains indefinitely close to its disappearance —and therefore indefinitely valid.

This third answer does not agree very well with the author's outlook, expressed by the metaphor of old age; one does not stay old indefinitely. However, it is upheld at present by authors anxious to find the least offensive possible interpretation for Jews who do not believe in Christ.

The first answer has the disadvantage of setting the disappearance in the remote past, which is not at all suggested by the author's sentence.

The second answer, or another of the same kind, seems to be the most probable, especially if we take this text along with the passage in which the preacher declares that a change of priesthood necessarily entails a change of Law (7,12): now the proclamation by God of the priesthood of Christ «according to the order of Melchisedek» (5,10) indeed constituted a change of priesthood. Add to that the sentence in 10,9 which declares the abolition, by Christ, of the sacrificial worship paid according to the Law. The preacher appears convinced of the end of the first covenant as a legislative institution also dealing with worship (which in no way means the end of the bond of love between God and his people, see Rom 11,28-29) and appears just as convinced of the permanent validity of the Old Testament as revelation. In this passage as elsewhere, it is on the Old Testament as revelation that he takes his stand to declare the end of the role of the first covenant as an institution.

4. Ineffective former worship, sanctuary and rites (9,1-10)

In 9,1 the preacher passes from the theme of the covenant to that of worship, by stating the link that unites them: «The first also had, assuredly, rites of worship…». This passage from the covenant to worship was not at all suggested by the oracle in Jeremiah, which does not contain the slightest allusion to worship. It is the preacher here taking up this idea, which he introduced earlier, in 8,6. The «also» is in relation with this verse: just like the better covenant, the first «also» had a liturgy. This «also», however, is absent from the Vaticanus and, it seems, from Papyrus 46, which makes the explicit relation uncertain, but there then remains a relation of parallelism. The imperfect «had» is due to the fact that the author is referring to the organization of worship at the time of the exodus, when «a tent was set up» (2). What he says is based on the Torah and not on the situation at the time of the second Temple. He never uses the word *hieron*, «temple», or *naos*, «sanctuary». Here, he speaks, literally, of «the holy thing», *to hagion*, to designate the holy place, as does the Septuagint sometimes. He adds an epithet, in an attributive position: this holy place is «worldly» or «of this world». The bearing of this epithet is not at once evident; it seems simply objective, but it will be seen further on that it serves as ground for argument: a holy place which is «of this world» cannot place anyone in genuine relation with God (see 9,11 and 24). The only other occurrence of this epithet in the New Testament makes it even more negative, for it is a reference to concupiscence and impiety (Titus 2,12).

The description of the holy place is summary (2-5). It insists on its division into two parts, called «the first tent» and «the second». This insistence on the division corresponds to a system of sanctification by means of ritual separations. The holy place is a place separated from profane ground and in this holy place a separation distinguishes two degrees of holiness: the first tent «is called *holy*», the second «*very holy*». By means of these separations, an attempt is made to get closer and closer to the holiness of God.

The contents of the first tent are mentioned very sparingly, without any qualifying expressions and without the least commentary: «the candlestick, the table and the display of loaves» (2). The second tent is described at length (3-5) and its description contains qualifying phrases: a triple mention of objects in gold and a double mention of the covenant. No commentary. The insistence on gold gives an impression of splendour, but of material splendour. The insistence on the covenant seems deliberate, for —as we have seen— other expressions could have been used, both for the ark and for the tablets of the Law. The ark is often called «ark of the testimony» or «ark of the Lord», the tablets are also often called «tablets of the testimony». But the author wants to underline again the link between covenant and worship and therefore puts «of the covenant» twice.

The most notable detail in this description is an omission: the name of God is never found in it, whereas the Old Testament says and repeats that the Lord makes himself present in his sanctuary and that he sits on the cherubim. This omission is significant. It implicitly contests the value of the organization of worship in the Old Testament. The same omission will be found in the description of the revelation on Sinai in 12,18-21.

Parallel to the description of the holy place, the one concerning rites of worship (6-7) offers the same characteristics. It insists on the division into two tents, is brief on the rites celebrated in the first tent and more detailed about the celebration in the second tent. A contrast is expressed between what the priests do in the first tent and what the high priest does in the second. On the one hand, there is a multiplicity of celebrants and ceremonies. On the other, there is one celebrant and one annual celebration, which necessarily involves an expiatory offering of blood. That obviously gives the greatest importance to this celebration, which is as it were the high point of sanctification by ritual separation: the most sacred person, in the most sacred place, at the most sacred moment. But, on the other hand, the result is that if this liturgy ends in failure, the whole system is disqualified. That is indeed the conclusion the preacher draws immediately.

He first of all questions the value of the holy place (8) and then that of the rites (9-10). The questioning of the holy place is presented as a revelation of the Holy Spirit himself. The preacher can say so, because the description he has given of it is based on Scripture inspired by the Holy Spirit. Decided upon by the Holy Spirit, the organization of the holy place and the rites that take place there show that «the way of the sanctuary has not yet been manifested as long as the first tent is still in place» (8). In this sentence the two terms linked together in the introductory sentence are found (8,2): «the sanctuary» (literally: «the holy things») and «the tent», but here it is not a matter of «the true tent, which the Lord planted», it is «the first tent», which has just been spoken of, and this first tent was set up by a human being.

One may ask oneself what the expression «the first tent» means exactly here. Is it, as in verses 2 and 6, the first part of the holy place built by Moses or is it the whole of this place, called «the tent» in 8,5? One might be tempted to chose this second interpretation, so as to have a contrast in the sentence between the genuine, divine «sanctuary», and «the tent» put up by a human being. But an examination of the context shows that the first interpretation must be chosen (see 9,11-12; 9,24-25; 13,11). In theory, «the first tent», that is to say the first part of the holy place, was the way to the sanctuary, that is to say that it ought to lead to God's dwelling, but in reality, it was not the way to it, because, built by a human being, it could not really lead into intimacy with God; it led only to a second tent, it, too, built by a human being and therefore not really God's dwelling. The situation was no different in the case of the Temple in Jerusalem, Solomon himself recognized this (1Kgs 8,27).

The preacher is not simply saying, as some translations have it, that the way to the sanctuary was not open; he is saying that this way had not yet been «manifested», which brought about the complete impossibility of communication. One did not know which direction to take to make contact. Instead of leading the high priest into the presence of God, the whole system of ritual separation ends up in an impasse. But this situation was not to last for ever; in saying «*not yet* manifested», the preacher hints that a change took place since then.

After the dispute over the value of the holy place comes the dispute over the value of the rites (9-10). The Greek text presents some difficulties. It starts with a relative feminine pronoun which can be construed grammatically in several ways. It could refer to the word «tent»: «the first tent [...] which [i.e. the tent] is a parable...». This meaning is hardly satisfactory. An object is not a parable. It is therefore better to understand the relative as a neuter that has become feminine through the attraction of the gender of «parable»; the meaning then is: «that which is a parable…». It is a matter of the situation that has just been described, that is to say of the way in which worship was organized: the division of the holy place into two tents and all the restrictions imposed on access to them constituted a symbolic way of expressing the inefficacy of the worship.

Another difficulty concerns the next relative, which is governed by the preposition «according to». The majority of the manuscripts put it in the singular; it then refers to the word «time»: «the time being according to which…»; but the oldest manuscripts put it in the feminine, thus referring it to the word «parable» or «figuration», which gives it a more coherent meaning, because we are waiting for some clarification on what is meant by the «figuration».

The preacher therefore presents the organization of the former worship as «a figuration for the time being». Instead of «for the time being», one could also translate «for the present time». What does he mean by that? To understand it, it must be noted that this expression is related, in the sentence, to a correlative expression which comes at the end : «until a time of redressment». Here we have a distinction, current in Judaism, between «the present time or world», in which evil is widespread, and «the time or world to come», in which the kingdom of God will be established. This distinction appears in the New Testament with some new clarifications. The resurrection of Christ, in fact, was the inauguration of the world to come; however, it did not put an end to the present defective world. Christians already share in the «powers of the world to come» (6,5), but their life still goes on in the «present world», although they no longer belong to it by virtue of their baptism. The «figuration» constituted by the organization of the former worship does not therefore apply to the new life of Christians, but to the religious situation of pre-Christian life.

This figuration shows that the gifts and sacrifices offered in it do not have power to «make perfect in conscience the one who pays the worship». This expression is very interesting, because it defines in an original way the result that the sacrifices ought to obtain and which they do not obtain in the worship of the first covenant. Spontaneously, the sacrifices are understood as a means of pleasing God and thus obtaining his favours or, in other words, as a means of changing God's dispositions. This way of looking at things is naïvely expressed in connection with the holocausts of Noah after the end of the flood. God breathes in the pleasant odour and that makes him change his attitude: «He says within himself:

Never again will I curse the earth because of mankind» (Gen 8,20-22). Certain people even imagine that abundant sacrifices can help to bribe God, just as money can help to bribe politicians. Sirach warns against this ungodly illusion (Sir 35,11). The sentence in Heb 9,9 suggests a completely different perspective: instead of God's dispositions, it is the dispositions of mankind that sacrifices must change. They must «make perfect in conscience the one who pays worship».

Some idea of the transformation of the person was already there in the Old Testament in the case of one category of sacrifices, those for the consecration of the high priest. We have already noted that, to designate this priestly consecration, the Septuagint uses the word *teleiōsis*, the etymological meaning of which is «action of making perfect», but it was a matter of making the hands perfect, and not the conscience. The rites were exterior, whereas what is needed is an interior transformation. The preacher explains that every sacrifice ought to be a *teleiōsis*, an «action that makes perfect interiorly» the person offering it, which implies interior action by the Holy Spirit, for only the Holy Spirit can purify and sanctify the «conscience».

Very rare in the Septuagint, and absent from the gospels, the word «conscience», *suneidēsis*, has 20 occurrences in the Letters of Paul, 5 in Hebrews and 3 in the First Letter of Peter. Here, it does not denote psychological conscience, a witness to the person's dispositions and actions, nor moral conscience, which passes judgement on actions and dispositions, but it denotes the inner situation resulting from them. In this sense, conscience can be sullied (Titus 1,15) or «pure» (1Tim 3,9), «bad» (Heb 10,22) or «good» (13,18). The preacher declares that the sacrifices of the first covenant were unable to effect a transformation at this level.

It may be noted that, in his analysis of the situation, the preacher uses two ways of expressing himself in succession. In verse 8, he adopts a vocabulary of space and movement; he speaks of the «way to the sanctuary»; to reach the presence of God, the right way must be found. In verse 9, on the contrary, he speaks about conscience and uses a vocabulary of personal transformation. Of the spatial vocabulary, he says that it is figurative. Indeed, to progress towards God, local movement has no effect. What is needed is a profound transformation of the person. The spatial vocabulary, however, has its uses; it helps people to become aware of the difficulties of the situation and to perceive the need of an effort to overcome them. Besides, it is suggested by the symbolism of the worship.

At the beginning of the positive paragraph (9,11-14), the preacher will take up the two formulations and show the close connection between them.

The reason for the inefficacy of the former worship is given in verse 10, which begins with a significant «only»[2]. The gifts and sacrifices were «only [...] rites of flesh», rites in which the Spirit did not act, external and material forms of worship, unable to remedy the interior evil. The word «flesh» can have various connotations. In certain texts, the flesh is presented as the source of bad tendencies (Gal 5,19; Rom 7,14); other, less negative, texts insist on its fragility: «All flesh is as grass» (Isa 40,6). Here, the context suggests rather the opposition between the outward, the flesh, and the inward, the conscience. «Rites of flesh» are incapable of making the conscience perfect. They are not even on the same anthropological level and, obviously, the most important level is that of conscience; that of the flesh is common to us and the beasts.

With the sacrifices, the preacher associates the ritual observances concerning «food, drink and various ablutions». The relation between sacrificial worship and these various observances is expressed by the preposition *epi* followed by the dative. This can mean «in addition to» or «above», «on». In consequence, the relation may be understood either as not very close—sacrificial worship is added to the observances— or, on the contrary, as very close: the worship is established on the observances, the latter are its foundation. This second interpretation agrees better with the context, because the observances of ritual purity lay down conditions for sharing in the sacrificial worship (see Lev 7,20-21; Num 19,13.20). The preacher presents the religious system of the Old Testament like a pyramid of which the base is made up of the observances of ritual purity. On this base rise the various kinds of sacrifice, the summit of which is the Kippur sacrificial rite (Lev 16).

All this is declared ineffective, because it is incapable of changing the sinful man's heart. For the same reason, it was also provisional and was to last only «until a time of redressment», a time when the religious situation of mankind would no longer be lamentably at fault.

Meanwhile, this system was not without its uses, for it witnessed to the fact that mediation was necessary. In fact, it did constitute an attempt at mediation, an ineffective attempt, but it was important that there should have been at least this attempt, to arouse the expectation of an effective mediation, the foundation of an authentic covenant between the people and God.

2 The grammatical construction of this part of the sentence lacks clarity, which results in the appearance of textual variants. The most common one links «rites of flesh» with the preceding nouns and therefore makes it depend on the same preposition; the text then becomes somewhat lame.

The criticism expressed by the preacher touches on a fundamental point and is connected with a change effected in the New Testament in the way of conceiving religion. This change had been prepared in certain texts in the Old Testament, but it was not readily admitted, because it went against a spontaneous tendency in religiosity. It conditions the universalism of the new covenant.

Religiosity, in fact, expresses itself spontaneously in outward rites and observances, which are at the same time sociological determinations, useful to the human group in defining its identity and avoiding confusion with other groups. The history of religions discovers this sociological function especially in observances concerning food. The prohibitions serve to reinforce the cohesion of the tribe by differentiating it from the others. Thus it is that the laws governing ritual and worship in Israel guaranteed its cohesion and formed a «wall of separation» (Eph 2,14) between Israel and the other peoples. It therefore meant a closed religion, tinged with particularism and a source of antagonism.

The early Church acknowledged —but not without difficulty— that the death of Christ had overthrown the wall of separation. Henceforth it was no longer possible to ascribe an absolute value to a sociological distinction (see Gal 3,28). In more than one passage, the gospels take a stand against the former way of conceiving religion, in particular in the controversy in Mark 7,1-23, which contains the same elements as our text in Heb 9,9-10 and in the declarations in Matt 9,13 and 12,7; Luke 9-41. In the Acts of the Apostles, the problem is officially faced (Acts 5). The apostle Paul struggled more than all against those who wanted to impose Jewish particularism on Christians coming from the pagan nations; he showed that «justification» is not acquired by means of legal observances. The author of the Letter to the Hebrews has a similar argument, starting out from another point of view, that of priestly mediation. In Heb 9,9-10 he ends the first long paragraph (8,3-9,10) of the central section (8,1-9,28) by noting the inefficiency of the former ritual and sacrificial system; the latter did not set up an authentic relation with God. The first covenant was therefore defective.

The last words in the sentence (Heb 9,10) prepare the next paragraph (9,11-28), by opening up the perspective in «a time of redressment», which will remedy the situation. This time —one can forsee— will be the time of the «liturgy» of Christ, mentioned at the beginning of the section (8,2.6), a sacrifice of a genre radically new, capable of «making perfect in his conscience the one who pays worship».

Chapter 12

A new kind of sacrifice and a first covenant (9,11-28)

At the beginning of this second paragraph, the name of Christ, which has not been mentioned since the beginning of the chapter, appears solemnly with his title of «high priest», as opposed to the high priest of the former worship.

COMPOSITION

Oblation of Christ (9,11-14).

11 But Christ, having come as high priest of the good things to come,
+ through the greater and more perfect tent,
- not made with hands, that is to say not of this creation,
- 12 and not through the blood of goats and calves,
+ but through his own blood
entered once for all into the sanctuary,
having found an eternal redemption

This sentence resumes, in an antithetic perspective, the elements in verses 7-8: another priest, another tent, another blood, another entrance. In parallelism with the former high priest in verse 7, who entered «once a year» into the second tent, Christ is presented as having entered «once and for all» not into a tent, but «into the sanctuary». The parallelism is therefore in part synonymous and in part antithetic.

The sentence is composed in concentric symmetry: at the beginning, the name «Christ» with its qualification «high priest of the good things to come»; at the end, Christ's action and its result. The «eternal redemption» is in synonymous parallelism with the «good things to come» and the two are in relation with the «redressment» announced at the end of 9,10.

In the central interval the means used by Christ for his action are indicated: «the greater and more perfect tent» and «his own blood». The qualifications given to these means are in concentric order: positive qualifications then negative ones for the tent, a negative then a positive one for the blood. The tent and the blood are thus closely united.

These two means are in antithetic relation with the «blood» offered by the high priest (7) and with «the first tent» (8), which was not «the way to the sanctuary». The entry of Christ into the sanctuary manifests that the tent which he uses is the way to it.

13 If, indeed, the blood of goats and bulls
and the ashes of a heifer
sprinkled on defiled persons
sanctify them for purity of the flesh,
14 how much more the blood of Christ,
who through Spirit eternal offers himself immaculate to God
will purify our conscience from dead works
to pay worship to the living God.

This long sentence presents an *a fortiori* piece of reasoning (called *qalwa-homer* in rabbinic exegesis). It therefore contains a parallelism, accompanied by a progression. To the «blood of goats and bulls» there corresponds, much better, «the blood of Christ». To the sanctification «for the purity of the flesh» corresponds, and much better, the purification of «our conscience».

Other elements in the sentence are in parallelism of position, but not of content, because, on the one hand, there is the mention of the rite performed with the ashes of a heifer, an aspersion rite, and, on the other, the mention of Christ's offering which confers incomparable efficacy on his blood.

Two further amplifications are observable: to the blood of animals is added «some heifer ashes», the effect of which is to stress the materiality of the former rite; to the efficacy of the blood of Christ for the purification of consciences is added the mention of the relation established with God. The name of God is absent from the first half of the sentence; it appears twice in the second half. This difference is not without significance. It corresponds to the absence of the name of God in the description of the holy place and of worship in the first covenant (9,1-10).

Verse 14 is at the same time in antithesis with verses 9-10: with the outward «gifts and sacrifices» offered in the former worship is contrasted the personal offering of Christ; with the «rites of flesh» is contrasted an offering raised up by «the eternal spirit»; with the inability to «make perfect in conscience» is contrasted the ability to «purify our conscience».

The foundation of the new covenant (9,15-23)

15 And for that reason he is mediator
of a new covenant-TESTAMENT,
so that, a death having occurred as redemption of the
transgressions committed under the first testament,
those called may receive the promised eternal inheritance.
16 Indeed, where there is a testament,
of *necessity* the death of the testator must be certified;
17 a TESTAMENT actually takes effect in the case of the dead;
for it is never in force while the testator is living.

18 This is why the first testament
was not inaugurated, either, WITHOUT BLOOD.
19 In fact, having proclaimed to all the people
every commandment according to the Law,
Moses, taking the blood of goats and calves
with water, scarlet wool and hysop,
sprinkled the Book itself and all the people with it
20 saying:
This is the blood of the covenant-testament
which God has ordained for you.
21 He likewise sprinkled with the blood
the tent and all the objects of worship.
22 Almost everything is purified with blood, according to the Law,
And WITHOUT shedding of BLOOD there is no remission.

23 There was therefore *necessity*
that the figures of the heavenly realities be purified by these means
and that the heavenly realities themselves be so by sacrifices
of greater value than these.

The composition of this subdivision is complex. Two pieces (15-17; 18-22) and a conclusion can be distinguished (23). The first piece is characterized by the repetition of the word *diathēkē*, taken in its usual sense in Greek, «testament», and by the repetition of the corresponding verb, in the form of a participle (in English, «the testator»). One can say that *diathēkē* forms an inclusion between the beginning (15) and the end (17) of this first piece.

The second piece (18-22) is confined within an inclusion between «without blood» (18) and «without bloodshed» (22).

Marked with a «therefore» (23), the conclusion takes up the word «necessity», occurring towards the end of the first piece (16b), which makes up a parallelism of final clauses and contributes to unifying the whole.

In the first piece, the initial sentence (15) does not contain any Semitic parallelism. Its syntax is typically Greek. A short main clause is followed by a long subordinate clause which includes a genitive absolute weighed down with a cascade of complements. The sentence ends in Greek with the word «inheritance», which introduces the subsequent reflections on the notion of testament, an inheritance being passed on by a will.

These reflections are arranged in parallelism. A first parallelism (16) is complementary: a transition is made from the «testament» to «the death of the testator». The second parallelism (17) is synonymous, but with an antithetic aspect: an affirmation, «taking effect in case of death», is resumed in the form of a negation: «never in force while the testator is alive».

To this is added a parallelism between the two verses: their first stich (16a, 17a) contains the word «testament», the second (16b, 17b) ends with the word «testator», but with antithetic references, «death» in 16b, life in 17b.

In the second piece, the words of Moses that speak of «the blood of the covenant-testament» (20) are made to stand out by a concentric disposition: they are, in fact, preceded (19e) and followed (21) by a reference to a sprinkling performed with this blood, as well as a reference to law («according to the law» 19b and 22a), to which is added the inclusion about the words «without blood» (18) and «without bloodshed» (22b):

- without blood (18)
  - according to the law (19b)
    - sprinkled with it (19e)
      - This is the blood of the covenant-testament (20)
    - sprinkled with the blood (21)
  - according to the law (22a)
- without bloodshed (22b).

The conclusion (23) expresses a parallelism of progression. The initial word, «necessity», is there as common factor, as is the verb «to be purified». There is then a relation of progression between «the figures of the heavenly realities» and «the heavenly realities themselves», as between «by these [means]» and «by sacrifices of greater value than these». The progression is made particularly explicit in the last case, thanks to the use of a comparative.

Heavenly and definitive outcome of Christ's offering (9,24-28)

24 It is not indeed into a sanctuary made with hands
that Christ entered,
into a representation of the true [sanctuary],
but into heaven itself,
to appear now in the presence of God in our favour,
25 nor is it any more to offer himself many times,
as the high priest enters into the sanctuary every year
with the blood of another [living creature],
26 for then he would have had to suffer many times since the foundation of the world;
in reality, it is once only, at the end of the ages, that he has manifested himself
for the abolition of sin through his sacrifice.
27 And as it is appointed for mankind to die once,
and after that [there is] a judgement,
28 so also Christ,
having been offered once only to take away the sin of a multitude,
a second time will appear without [connection with] sin
to those who await [their] salvation.

The first sentence (24) affirms the heavenly outcome of Christ's oblation. The link with the preceding subdivision is provided by the relation between «heaven itself» (24) and «the heavenly [realities]» mentioned twice in the previous verse.

The statement about the heavenly outcome is reinforced by an antithetic parallelism between «a sanctuary made with hands», a simple «representation of the true [sanctuary]» and «heaven itself» into which «Christ entered». A surprising detail in the arrangement of the sentence is the place chosen for the words «Christ entered», placed between the two qualifying phrases of the earthly sanctuary. The second qualifying phrase («representation of the true») makes it better understood why Christ could not be content to enter an earthly sanctuary and, besides, it prepares the listeners to apply the name of «true sanctuary» to «heaven itself».

The next sentences (25-28) add that Christ's entry into heaven has a unique and definitive character.

A first parallelism is an antithesis between the negation of the «many times» in the case of Christ's offering (25a) and the statement about «every year» as regards the entry of the Jewish high priest into the sanctuary (25b). We then have an antithetic parallelism between «suffering many times since the foundation of the world» (26a) and «being manifested once at the end of the ages through his sacrifice» (26bc). Verses 27-28 explicitly state a parallelism between the fate of mankind, which is to «die once» and Christ's offering, which was made «once», but then the parallelism is imperfect, because Christ's oblation has a purpose that the death of simple human beings does not have and instead of the «judgment» (27b) which comes after the death of human beings, there is, in the case of Christ, a second appearance, which will be «without connection with sin» (28c), but in relation to «salvation» (28d).

In all this subdivision, the parallelisms suggest some instructive correspondences between Christ's entry into heaven (24bc), the offering he made of himself (25a.26c), his passion (26a) and the death of human beings (27a).

B. *BIBLICAL CONTEXT*

1. Oblation of Christ (9,11-14)

To express the meaning of the paschal mystery of Christ, the preacher uses the metaphor of sacrificial worship and, more precisely, of the liturgy of Kippur, which he has just mentioned (7). He has his own way of naming the two parts of the holy place; he does not say «the Holy» and «the Holy of Holies», but «the tent» and «the sanctuary» (literally: «the holy things») as in 8,2 and 9,8. «The tent» is the way, the means of reaching the «sanctuary», which is the purpose to be achieved.

For the first time, he makes it clear that the blood used in the former sacrifices is the blood of beasts,—«blood of goats and calves» (12), «the blood of goats and bulls» (13). The expression calls to mind Isa 1,11 in which God declares: «The blood of bulls and goats, I want none of it» (see also Ps 50/49,13).

The quality of the tent is noted by saying that it is not «work-of-hands—that is to say not of this creation». The translations specify «not made with hand *of man*», but this specification is debatable because the author distinguishes two creations of God here; the tent is not part «of this creation», which is «work of the hands» of God (Ps 101,26 quoted in Heb 1,10) and which will perish (1,11); the tent is therefore part of the new creation, announced by Isaiah (Isa 65,17; 66,22; 2Pet 3,13; Rev 21,1), which will be «unshakeable» (Heb 12,27), like the «eternal redemption» found by Christ.

The word translated as «redemption», *lytrōsis*, has 11 occurrences in the Septuagint; there it designates a right to redeem. The verb from which it derives is very frequent. Psalm 129(130),7-8 declares that with the Lord «is grace, abundance of atonement (or: «of redemption»), he will redeem Israel from all its faults». From the idea of redeeming, that is to say of freeing by paying a ransom, there is an easy passage to that of setting free with another form of action.

In verse 13, the preacher puts the blood of sacrifices and «the ashes of a heifer» together, an allusion to the rite of lustral waters described in Num 19. The expression used is incorrect, because it was not with the ashes that the sprinkling was done but with water containing the ashes. When a ritual impurity had been contracted by touching, for instance, a dead body, sprinkling was indispensable: «An impure man who would omit purifying himself in this way would be cut off from the community, for he would defile the sanctuary of the Lord» (Num 19,20).

The qualifying description given to Christ, who «offered himself *immaculate*», corresponds to the prescription laid down in Leviticus concerning animals offered in sacrifice (Lev 1,3.10; 3,1.6.9; etc.), but the meaning is obviously different. For the animals, it was about the absence of physical blemish; for Christ, it is about moral and spiritual integrity. The rest of the proposition has no equivalent in the Old Testament. This sacrificial expression is not found in the other writings of the New Testament either. The latter uses other verbs about Christ: «to give oneself» (Gal 1,4), «to give oneself in ransom» (1Tim 2,6), «to give one's life as ransom» (Matt 20,28; Mark 10,45), «to give oneself up» (Gal 2,20; Eph 5,2.25), «to lay down one's life» (John 10,11-18; 1John 3,16) as one «lays down one's garments» (John 13,4).

The expression «eternal spirit» is never found anywhere else in the whole Bible. «Offering oneself by eternal Spirit» may be associated with «sacrificing by perpetual fire» (1 Ezra 6,23; absent from Ezra 6,3 Hebrew).

«Living God» is an Old Testament expression: Josh 3,10; 2Kgs 19,4.16; Ps 83(84),2; Hos 2,1; Isa 37,4.17: etc. It is related to the formula of an oath by God: «I am living, says the Lord» (Num 14,21.28; Deut 32,40; etc.) and with that of human oaths: «He is living, the Lord,…», frequent in the historical books (1Sam 14,39.45; 19,6; 20,3; etc.).

2. The foundation of the new covenant (9,15-23)

The reflection on the word *diathēkē* in the sense of «testament» (15-17) depends on the Greek language and not on the Hebrew Old Testament. Yet it finds a certain foothold in the latter thanks to the frequent notion of «inheritance». In Gen 15,2-3 Abraham complains to God at not having an heir. God replies by promising him heirs and an inheritance (15,4-7). The «covenant with Abraham» (15,8) concerns the inheritance. The departure from Egypt and the Sinai covenant are closely related to this gift of an inheritance (see Deut 4,37-40; 6,23-24).

The way in which the foundation of the Sinai covenant is recalled (19-21) takes its inspiration above all from the story in Exod 24,3-8. The words of Moses are freely quoted, with some changes. Instead of: «Here the blood...» we have «This [is] the blood...», perhaps under the influence of the words of Jesus over the cup, at the last Supper: «This is the blood...» (Mark 14,24; Matt 26,28). The preacher then avoided, here as in the oracle in Jeremiah, using for the Sinai covenant the insistent formula «the arrangement that he has arranged» (he keeps it for the new covenant); instead of «has arranged», he put «has ordered». The name «Lord», *Kyrios* without the article, a translation of YHWH, is replaced by «God» (in Greek *ho Theos*, with the article). The lasts words, «concerning all these words», are omitted, so as to concentrate attention on the blood.

The preacher also widens the perspective, to take in other rites and thus be able to assess the whole of the worship. To the «calves» in Exod 24,5, he adds «goats», which are used in other sacrifices. To the blood, he adds water and he points out that for sprinkling, Moses took «some scarlet wool and hysop», which Leviticus speaks of concerning the purification of lepers (Lev 14,4-7) and the Book of Numbers concerning lustral water (Num 19,6). The sprinkling extended to the «book itself» (19), as well as to «the tent and all the objects of worship» (21). According to Exod 40,9 Moses, in different circumstances, received the order to consecrate the tent and all the objects of worship, but by using «the oil of anointing» and not the blood; according to Lev 8,11 Moses carried out this order. In the Kippur ritual, however, a sentence orders that what is done for «the expiation over the sanctuary» be done «for the tent of the meeting» (Lev 16,16), now that expiation is done by sprinkling blood (Lev 16,15).

In Heb 9,22 the preacher concludes with two statements of principle; the first concerns purifications, the second speaks of «remission». On the purifications, the statement is qualified: «almost everything»; on «remission», however, no exception is admitted.

The use of blood for «purifications» is actually prescribed in the Pentateuch in many cases, according to the LXX (the Hebrew text often uses different terms). Blood is used for the purification of the altar (Exod 29,36-37; Lev 8,15; 16,19), of the vestments of the high priest (Lev 8,30) and of the tent (Lev 16,20). Not only things, but persons also are purified by means of blood: the priests, according to Lev 8,23-24.30, and the lepers according to Lev 14,7.14. A bloody sacrifice is prescribed for the purification of women when they have given birth to a child (Lev 12,6-8). According to Lev 16,30 the bloody rites of the Kippur celebration obtained purification: «On that day the rite of expiation will be performed for you to purify you; before the Lord, you shall be purified of all your sins».

The preacher then declares that «without blood-shedding, there is no remission». The Greek word *haimatekchusia*, «blood-shedding», is not in the Septuagint, nor in the Greek authors, but it was easily comprehensible, because it corresponds to the expression «to shed blood» (*haima ekchuein*), which is in current use.

There is good reason for distinguishing, in the Bible, several kinds of bloodshed, because bloodshed can be ritual, or criminal, or penal. It is ritual in sacrifices (Exod 29,12; Lev 4,7.18 etc.) and also, in a less strict sense, when it is carried out according to the precept forbidding the blood of beasts to be eaten with their flesh (Deut 12,16.24). One must then «pour the blood on the ground, like water» (Deut 12,16.24).

It is criminal when it is a case of murder, and penal, when it is a matter of punishment for murder or other crimes. «Whoever sheds the blood of man, by man will have his blood shed» (Gen 9,6).

Add to this the case in which the shedding of human blood is neither criminal nor penal, either because it is accidental (Deut 19,4-5), or because it is an act of war; David, for example, «shed much blood when fighting great battles» (1Chr 22,8).

The word «remission» is used here without any complement, which leaves open the possibility of several interpretations. The context suggests that the author wants to speak of remission *of sins*, obtained by the shedding of *sacrificial* blood. Actually, in the sacrifices of expiation, the Old Testament gave utmost importance to the use of blood. In the other kinds of sacrifice (holocausts, thanksgiving sacrifices), they just let «the blood flow around the perimeter of the altar» (Lev 1,5; 3,2), but in sacrifices for sin, many rites were performed with blood; it was used for repeated aspersions, it was placed on the horns of the altar of incense, it was poured out at the bottom of the altar of holocausts (Lev 4,5-7; 4,16-18). The foundation of these rites was what God said: «The life of the flesh is in the blood. This blood, I myself gave you, to perform the rite of expiation for your lives on the altar; for the blood atones for the life» (Lev 17,11). The blood of sacrificed animals was therefore used to obtain the remission of sins. However, the Old Testament never says that «without bloodshed, there is no remission». Jewish tradition says so in the Talmud: «Expiation is achieved only in blood» (Zebahim 6a), but the exact bearing of this principle is the object of discussion, with Judaism admitting, in other texts, other means of expiation. Witness to this is found actually in the Greek Bible: Sirach declares that «he who honours his father expiates his faults» (Sir 3,3) and that «almsgiving will expiate sins» (Sir 3,30) the Book of Tobit expresses the same conviction in slightly different terms: «Almsgiving [...] will purify from all sin» (Tob 12,9).

Because the preacher refrains from stating that he intends to speak of remission *of sins* and of shedding *sacrificial* blood, his formula leaves the door open to another interpretation; it can apply to the impossibility expressed by the text at Num 35,33: «For the homeland there is no other expiation for blood shed than the blood of whoever shed it». In case of criminal bloodshed, the only solution is the shedding of penal blood. The context of the Book of Numbers explicitly excludes the hypothesis of pecuniary compensation: «You shall not accept any ransom for the life of a murderer subject to the death penalty; he must die» (Num 35,31).

3. Heavenly and definitive outcome of Christ's offering (9,24-28)

The biblical context of these verses is the one that has already been given for the previous passages. In speaking of «representation» (*antitypa*: 9,24) of the true sanctuary, the preacher refers to the text of Exod 25,10 which he has quoted in the symmetrical subdivision, in 8,5, a text which speaks of a «model» (*typon*) shown by God for the construction of the tent.

The next sentence (9,25) refers to the liturgy of the great expiation, mentioned in Heb 9,7.

«The foundation of the world» (9,26) was mentioned in Heb 1,10 in terms of Ps 101. The expression was taken up in Heb 4,3. It is not found in the Old Testament, but is quite common in the New (Matt 13,35; 25,34; Luke 11,50; John 17,24; Eph 1,4; 1Pet 1,20; Rev 13,8; 17,8).

«The end of the ages» (9,26) corresponds to «the end of the days», a biblical expression used in Heb 1,2. It, too, was mentioned, in Heb 1,11-12, in terms of Ps 101. The Old Testament never says «the end of the ages». In the New Testament, «the end *of the* age» is met with several times in Matthew's gospel (Matt 13,39.40.49; 24,3; 28,20), that is to say «the end of the present period», distinct from «the coming period», that of the reign of God (see Matt 12,32; Mark 10,30; Luke 20,34-35).

In Heb 9,28 the purpose of Christ's offering is expressed by means of an allusion to the famous prophecy of the Servant of the Lord (Isa 53,12); this declares hat he «has taken away the sins of a multitude»; Heb 9,28 takes up the same Greek words and says that Christ was «offered to take away the sins of a multitude». The same allusion comes in the first Letter of Peter (1Pet 2,24), but with «*our* sins» instead of the «sins of a multitude».

Waiting for «salvation» (9,28) is a very frequent theme in the Old Testament, in particular in the psalms (Ps 3,7; 6,4; 7,1; etc.). It is precise in the New Testament, where the return of Christ is expected «for salvation» (see 1Thess 1,10; Phil 3,20; Rom 5,9-10).

INTERPRETATION

Oblation of Christ (9,11-14)

To the liturgy of the Old Testament, which he has just criticized, the preacher opposes the perfectly efficacious liturgy of Christ, because Christ «entered», with his human nature, «into the sanctuary», that is to say into the heavenly intimacy of God, and he found an «eternal redemption». The means of this efficacy are «the greater and more perfect tent» and Christ's «own blood».

The sentence, as can be seen, expresses the three phases of an act of priestly mediation. The ascending phase is characterized by the means used to enter into the sanctuary: «through the tent» and «through his blood». The central phase is the entry into God's dwelling. The descending phase is the «eternal redemption» obtained for the believers.

It is in this original way that the preacher presents the paschal mystery of Christ, passion and glorification, by using a spatial and liturgical image. In the Fourth gospel, a spatial image is used by Jesus himself. To speak of his passion, Jesus says that he is going away (John 8,21; 13,33), that he is setting out (14,2) and that his way takes him to the father (16,10.17), therefore to his glorification, at the same time gaining great graces for his disciples (14,2-3; 16,7). No great effort is required to express this spatial image in a liturgical sense, since it is a question of going to God. The liturgical language expresses more explicitly the direction of the move towards God.

The paschal mystery of Christ made him the perfect high priest, who carried out the priestly mediation to perfection. What, in the liturgy of the Old Testament, was only a prefiguration, has become fully realized in Christ.

The name of Christ, as we have seen, stands out clearly here, as the first word of the positive paragraph. The preacher kept us waiting for it, because he has not mentioned it for more than three chapters, the last occurrence being in Heb

6,1, a not very significant text. The absence of any article reinforces the effec produced. The word is not given here as a title, but as a proper name of a person A particle (*de*) contrasts it—and, with it, the whole sentence— to what has jus been said about the inefficacy of the former worship. The steps taken by th high priest succeeding Aaron being unable to come to anything, Christ came a high priest of a new kind.

The qualifying phrase applied to him is not the same in all the manuscripts Some say «high priest of the good things *that have come* (*genomenōn*)», other say «high priest of the good things *to come* (*mellontōn*)». It is not easy to decid between these two formulas, because both are attested to in some excellen manuscripts. The critical editions are hesitant. The *Greek New Testament* of th «United Bible Societies» comes down in favour of *genomenōn*, but gives thi choice a letter C, which indicates «a considerable degree of doubt» about th validity of this choice.

As regards internal criticism, those who favour *genomenōn* say that since it is a matter of the Messianic good things Christ obtained by his sacrifice, they should be called «the good things that have happened». This reason seems decisive. It may be objected that in Heb 10,1 the other expression, «the good things to come» is found, in all the manuscripts, but this objection does not carry much weight, because in Heb 10,1 the discussion is not about Christ, but about the Law of Moses, which was imposed at a time when the Messianic good things were still «to come». Other objections are stronger. The expression with *genomenōn* does not correspond well to the author's usual language and seems ambiguous, because it could be translated as «the past good things». Contrariwise, to designate the Messianic good things, even present ones, the author elsewhere uses «to come», because he takes this expression in a qualitative and not simply a chronological sense; it denotes the definitive eschatological realities which belong to the world inaugurated by the resurrection of Christ. In Heb 2,5 this new world is called «the universe to come»; in Heb 6,5 he says that believers have already been able to taste «the powerful realities of the age to come». It should be noted, however, that for Christians during their earthly life, the Messianic good things are not all present, because Christians have not yet entered with Christ into «the rest» of God (see Heb 3,7-4,11); they do not yet possess all the good things promised (see Heb 10,36), they do not have an «abiding city» on this earth but are on the way to the city «to come» (Heb 13,14). For Christ himself, there is still something «to come», because, according to Ps 109,1, «he is waiting until his enemies are placed under his feet» (Heb 10,13). For all these reasons, the expression «high priest of the good things to come» is more probably the one the author used. But in both cases, it is about the Messianic good things that Christ obtained by his offering.

The sentence insists above all on the two means used by Christ to be able to enter into the divine sanctuary: «the tent» and «the blood».

The interpretation of the second means is not difficult: to say that Christ entered into the sanctuary «through his own blood» means that Christ gave his death on the cross the value of a sacrifice that united his human nature to God in heavenly glory in a perfect and definitive way. This transformation of the death was the fruit of a double disposition —as the author showed in the second section of the previous part of his sermon (Heb 4,15-5,10)— a disposition of perfect docility to God and of complete solidarity with us.

As given by the apostle Paul in 1Cor 15,34, the primitive formula of the Christian kerygma did not speak of the blood of Christ, it spoke of his death, because it was not sacrificial, but a matter of fact. In contrast, when speaking of the blood of Christ, the author of Hebrews expresses a sacrificial perspective, made obvious by the simultaneous mention of the «blood of goats and calves» (Heb 9,12), blood of animals offered in sacrifice, and by the parallelism with the entry of the high priest into the sanctuary, which was made with «blood» (Heb 9,7). In this paragraph (9,11-28), the author insists repeatedly on the blood. Before, the word *haima*, «blood», was used only twice (2,14; 9,7); in 9,11-28, it comes ten times.

This insistence does not arise from the account of the Passion. The death of a crucified person is not actually caused by the loss of blood, but by the asphyxiation due to the tetanisation of the muscles of the chest. The word «blood» is completely absent from the account of the Passion according to Saint Mark; in Luke's account, it is found only at the moment of the agony, to say that Jesus' «sweat» «became like drops of blood» (Luke 22,44); in Saint Matthew's account the word occurs five times, but never in its concrete sense, always in a metaphorical sense, to designate a violent death. The concrete sense, but not without symbolism, is found in John 19,34; from Jesus' pierced side, «there came forth blood and water»; this loss of blood obviously did not cause the death, because that had already happened, but it testified that it had happened and that it was transmitting the living water of the Spirit.

The author's insistence on the word «blood» is not therefore explained by the accounts of the Passion, but by his intention to express the sacrificial character of the Passion and death of Jesus in contrasting parallelism with the former sacrifices. Perhaps he was at the same time going on the words of Jesus at the Last Supper, words pronounced over the cup of wine which speak of «blood shed» in «covenant» sacrifice (Matt 26,28 and parallel).

Being perfectly efficacious in giving access to the heavenly sanctuary, the blood of Christ replaces the «blood of goats and calves» which was used in the ritual of the great Expiation. To be able to enter into the earthly sanctuary, the high priest had to offer a calf, or a young bull, for himself, the priests and, besides, a goat for the people. The principal rite consisted of aspersions of the blood of the immolated victims over the mercy seat and in front of it, in the holy of holies (Lev 16,11-16). The preacher will later explain the inefficacy of these rites, already pointed out in the Old Testament itself (see Heb 10,1-11). The Old Testament actually expresses two contradictory positions with regard to the blood of sacrifices: this blood, on the one hand, is given by God himself to be used in expiation sacrifices (Lev 17,11), to which the Law of Moses ascribes great importance, but in other texts, God rejects the immolation of animals and the blood of victims: «The blood of bulls and goats repels me» (Isa 1,11). «Am I going to eat the flesh of bulls? Goats' blood, am I going to drink that?» (Ps 50/49,13). The Letter to the Hebrews makes the prophetic argument over the immolation of animals fully its own, but it does not stop at this argument; it opens up a positive perspective. It is not content with a solution that would consist in replacing the blood of animals with an interior disposition of personal offering. It maintains the decisive importance of the role of blood. Christ's oblation has no less real consistency than the former liturgy, which made blood flow. Here the three dimensions necessary for the accomplishment of God's design are recognized: resemblance (blood is shed), difference (no longer the blood of unwitting animals), superiority (it is the blood of a person, who sheds it out of love). The preacher will complete his thought later on, in Heb 9,14.

It is fitting here to note that the text does not speak at all about a heavenly ceremony in which Christ would have offered God his own blood. Certain commentators imagine this kind of ceremony, but the text does not suggest it. Blood is represented as a means used to enter into the sanctuary, and not as a biological reality used for a rite inside the sanctuary. The author is using an image to speak, not of a ceremony, but of the death and glorification of Christ and to express its religious meaning.

It is as easy to understand what the mention of blood means as it is hard to determine what another means used by Christ to enter into the sanctuary, «the greater and more perfect tent», refers to. The preacher certainly has something precise in view, not «any tent», but «*the* tent». He has already spoken of it in the introduction to this section, when he defined the co-ordinates of the liturgy of Christ, «the sanctuary and the tent» (Heb 8,2). He then called the tent «true» and added: «that the Lord planted and not a human». Here, he calls it «greater and more perfect» and specifies «not made with hands, that is to say not of this creation». The context shows that this tent corresponds, in the liturgy of Christ, to «the first tent», which served the former liturgy (9,2.6.8). This first tent, as we have seen, was not the way of the sanctuary»; it only led to «the second» tent. «The greater and more perfect tent» is, on the contrary, the way to the sanctuary, since, through it, Christ entered into it. The image does not lack clarity, but what reality does it conceal?

Despite all the details given by the preacher, the commentators are divided over the identification of this tent. Some propose a mythological interpretation, others a cosmological interpretation, still others a Christological exegesis.

The mythological interpretation is the simplest. It takes the text as it stands and ascribes to the author the idea that there actually exists in heaven a sanctuary divided into two parts, like the earthly sanctuary of the Old Testament. To reach the second part, which is God's dwelling, Christ had to cross the first part. Such is the position held, in desperation, by Michaelis, in the *Theologisches Wörterbuch zum N.T.*, VII, p. 378. A position open to criticism, because it does not take account of the author's insistence and the many qualifications he gives to this tent. Nor does it correspond to the author's Alexandrian mentality, by no means given to materializing metaphors.

More common is the interpretation according to which «the tent» represents heaven or, more precisely, the intermediate heaven, situated between the earth and the highest heaven where God dwells. Christ crossed this intermediate heaven to reach the throne of God. This way of conceiving the glorification of Christ is traditional. It is mentioned in the gospels: after the resurrection, Jesus «was taken up to heaven and sat at the right hand of God» (Mark 16,19; Luke 24,51); the Acts of the Apostles give some details on this subject (Acts 1,9-11); the Letter to the Ephesians declares that Christ «went up above all the heavens» (Eph 4,10). Moreover, the Letter to the Hebrews itself adopts this representation and states that Jesus is «an eminent high priest who went through the heavens» (Heb 4,14) and that he is «raised higher than the heavens» (7,26). Besides, a psalm praises God saying: «You spread out the heavens like a tent» (Ps 104/103,2). There is therefore much to be said in favour of this cosmological interpretation.

Yet this interpretation comes up against some strong objections.

About «the greater and more perfect tent» the author specifies that it is not «of this creation», now the intermediate heaven is «of this creation»: «In the beginning, God created heaven and earth» (Gen 1,1).

The author recalled it in the first part of his sermon by quoting Psalm 101 (Heb 1,10). Heaven is part of the first creation and will perish with it. The same perspective is expressed in the last part, by using, this time, an oracle of the prophet Haggai (Hag 2,6.21 in Heb 12,26).

«The tent», on the other hand, does not belong to this perishable creation, but to the new creation inaugurated by the resurrection of Christ. It must constitute a new revelation, for it is «the way to the sanctuary» which —the author clearly says so in 9,8— had not yet been «manifested» before the coming of Christ. Representing the intermediary heaven as an expanse to be crossed to reach God is not at all a new revelation, but an idea that came spontaneously from the remotest antiquity.

We have also seen that the structure of the sentence very closely unites, at its centre, the two means used by Christ to enter into the sanctuary: «the tent» and «the blood». This suggests that these two realities are related. What relationship is there therefore between the intermediary heaven and the blood of Christ? None, obviously. Is it coherent to say that Christ entered into the sanctuary «through the intermediary heaven and his own blood»? No, of course not.

There is therefore good reason for thinking about a Christological interpretation. Greek patristics offer us one: «the greater and more perfect tent» is none other than the body of Christ. Without the slightest hesitation, Saint John Chrysostom declares: «Here it denotes his flesh»[1].

But suddenly there is an objection: the text says that Christ went through the tent; can it be said that, to reach God, he went through his own body? The answer is that here two possible meanings can be given for the Greek preposition *dia*; they also exist in English for the preposition «through»; the local sense and the instrumental sense. On the level of the image, in the expression «through the tent» the sense is local: Christ is compared to the high priest who went through

1 St. John Chrysostom, *Enarratio in Ep. ad Hebraeos*, PG 63, p. 119.

the first tent to enter into the second; but the sense is at the same time instrumental, for the first tent was a means, a means of access to the second. For the parallel expression, «through the blood», the sense is not local—the high priest did not cross a stream of blood— it is solely instrumental, which suggests seeing here, too, the instrumental sense of the expression «through the tent», which is closely linked with «through his blood». Hence nothing prevents us, as regards the application to Christ, from no longer stopping at the local sense: Christ entered *by means of* his body.

Can the qualifying phrases applied to «the tent» be applied to the flesh of Christ? Chrysostom responds: «It is with good reason that he calls it greater and more perfect», since God the Word and the whole power of the Spirit dwell in it». But can one say that it is «not of this creation»? Chrysostom replies: «It is not one of the creatures, but it is spiritual, for it was constructed by the Holy Spirit». Not a satisfactory answer, but it points the way to the right solution.

Not satisfactory, because it denies the realism of the incarnation, forcefully asserted by the author, who says about Christ: «Thus then, since the children have blood and flesh in common, he also likewise took part in the same realities» (2,14); «he had, in all things, to be made like his brothers» (2,17). During the earthly life of Jesus, his human nature was not fully spiritual, for he had emptied himself and had taken «slave form» (Phil 2,7), «a flesh like that of sin» (Rom 8,3). It is at the end of his paschal mystery that his human nature was completely renewed by the Spirit and received all filial glory (see Rom 1,4; 1Cor15,45). Thanks to his sacrifice he became high priest «according to a power of life indestructible» (Heb 7,16).

These data suggest the right solution to us. «The greater and more perfect tent», is not the dead body of Jesus, because he had not yet been made perfect, it is the body of Jesus glorified (see 2,9), «made perfect» (5,9; 7,28) by his passion, experienced as an offering of filial and fraternal love (2,10; 5,8).

This interpretation is in close relation with the gospel tradition about the body of the risen Christ, presented as the new sanctuary built in three days. This catechesis shows, in the paschal mystery of Christ, the perfect accomplishment of the theme of God living in the midst of his people, so important a theme in the Old Testament. To the «tent» of the Exodus there succeeds the temple of Solomon, built, destroyed, rebuilt. The synoptic gospels mention this theme insistently in their account of the passion (Matt 26,21; 27,40; 27,51 and parallels). The Fourth gospel says explicitly that the words of Jesus about the destruction and the resurrection of the sanctuary referred to the «sanctuary of his body» (John 2,19-22).

It is more than likely that those listening to the sermon knew these traditions and could therefore understand what the preacher was alluding to when, after mentioning «a time of redressment» (9,10), a time of resurrection, he is speaking of «the greater and more perfect tent» (9,11), which took, as regards relations with God, the place of «the first tent» (9,2.6) of the former sanctuary.

All the qualifying phrases applied by the preacher to «the tent» are understood perfectly of the glorified body of Christ. That body is «the greater tent», both in the sense of a greater glory, the one the prophet Haggai announced for the new sanctuary (Hag 2,9), and in the sense of a greater capacity to receive people. The glorified body of Christ, in fact, is not a sanctuary to which access would remain closed to the people, as the former one was; on the contrary, it is a house open to all believers, even more than that, a house formed by all believers, who, in union with the risen, «living stone», become its «living stones» (1Pet 2,4-5), becoming «partners of Christ» (Heb 3,14), «his house» (3,6).

Calling it the «greater tent» has inspired some exegetes (Cornely, for example) with an ecclesiological interpretation, according to which the expression would designate the Church. This interpretation is not directly possible, because it cannot be said that Christ entered through the Church into the sanctuary, but it is possible indirectly, in relation to the glorified body of Christ, which in a certain sense, contains the whole Church.

Moreover, the tent is «more perfect» than the former sanctuary, because Christ was «made perfect» (5,9) through his sufferings. This allusion to the theme of perfection is particularly significant, because the author has greatly insisted on it (2,10; 5,9; 7,11.19.28; 9,9).

The tent was «not work of hands». This qualification is found only once in the gospels and it is to qualify the sanctuary built by Christ in three days (Mark 14,48). In the other New Testament writings, the use of this phrase is constantly related to the destitution of the former worship and its renovation in the paschal mystery of Christ (see Acts 7,48; 2Cor 5,1; Eph 2,11; Col 2,11-12). Because it is not the work of hands, the tent is a perfectly adapted means of access to the true sanctuary, because the latter is not «work of hands» (Heb 9,24). The same could not be said of the first tent made by Moses.

The introductory sentence (8,2) further explains that it is a question of «the true tent which the Lord made, not a human being». The tent is «true», because it is not, like the tent erected by Moses, a simple prefiguration of God's plan, it is the full achievement of it.

This plan was carried out by «the Lord». The words of the gospels indicate that «the Lord» is to be understood as a designation of Christ, for it is to himself that the latter attributes the construction of the sanctuary in three days.

Yet one may hesitate, for many are the texts in which the resurrection of Jesus is presented as God's work. Between these two interpretations, let us note, there is no incompatibility, because Jesus receives the works of the father and «what he does, the Son does likewise» (John 5,19).

The tent is «not of this creation», for the resurrection of Christ is the first act of the new creation. Saint Paul declares that «if anyone is in Christ, he is a new creation» (2 Cor 5,17), which obviously implies that the risen Christ is, before anyone else, «a new creation». His resurrection, in fact, was not at all a return to earthly life, but the inauguration of an entirely new kind of existence, independent of all earthly contingencies.

In basic agreement with the gospel tradition, the presentation in the Letter to the Hebrews differs from it nevertheless on two points. The first is that it makes no reference to the Temple in Jerusalem, but to the «tent» in the desert. The body of the glorified Christ is the new «tent». This detail actually makes the application of the metaphor easier, because it is easier to compare the human body to a tent that can be carried from one place to another than to a building that cannot be transported. Seeing himself near to death, king Hezekiah exclaimed: «My dwelling is torn up and carried far from me like a shepherd's tent» (Isa 38,12) and the apostle Paul speaks of the mortal body as a tent and a garment (2Cor 5,1.4).

The other detail is that instead of speaking in general of «sanctuary» (*naos:* Matt 26,61; Mark 14,58; John 2,19-21), the author shows himself to be attentive to the distinction between first and second tent and identifies the body of Christ only with the first tent, presented as the means of entering into God's dwelling. This distinction does not lack coherence. In fact, God's heavenly dwelling had existed from all time; it did not have to be re-created by the resurrection of Christ. The problem was only how to replace the first tent, which did not give access to it, with a new creation that could provide this access. In other words, the problem was one of effective mediation. Here, as in his definition of the high priest (5,1), the author considers priesthood before all as mediation. Jesus is «the way»; he declares: «No one goes to the father if not through me»

(John 14,6). In Heb 10,19-21, the author will express this perspective more clearly, which will confirm the interpretation of «the greater and more perfect tent» as the body of Christ «made perfect».

It is with his human nature, made perfect by his passion, that Christ entered into heavenly intimacy with God. He entered it «once for all», which makes him at once like the Israelite high priest and yet different. Like, because the high priest entered «once» into the second tent (9,7); different, because, for the high priest, it was «once *a year*» and not «once and for all». Having entered into the second tent, the high priest actually had to come out of it quite quickly again after accomplishing the prescribed rites, and he could only go back in again a year later, on the feast of Kippur the next year, for a few moments. Another extremely important difference is that of the sanctuary: it is not into an earthly sanctuary that Christ entered, but into the heavenly sanctuary. That difference is not expressed explicitly for the moment; it will be in the complementary subdivision, in 9,24.

Christ's entry into the sanctuary is not just an extraordinary advantage for his human nature, which is there «crowned with glory and honour for having suffered death» (2,9), it is an act of priestly mediation which shows that he has «found an eternal redemption» (9,12) for the whole people. The verb «to find» suggests that the situation seemed without any outcome and that a solution was not easy «to find». Redemption acquired by the blood of Christ is indeed an astonishing novelty, as the author will show in the next sentence. This redemption is radically different from the liberation at the Exodus and other temporary divine interventions that occurred in the course of history, because it is «eternal»; it is on a level that transcends time; it leads into the eternity of God and is therefore definitive and complete, which implies effectiveness at the deepest level of the human conscience.

A conjunction (*gar*, «in fact»: 9,13) presents the next sentence (9,13-14) as an explanation of the affirmation about the «eternal redemption»; it means that the extraordinary efficacy of the blood of Christ obtained this redemption. The sentence contains, as we have seen, some *a fortiori* reasoning; instead of showing a relation of interruption between the liturgy of Christ and the former worship, it shows a relation of continuity and resemblance. Whereas in 9,9 the author denounced the inefficacy of the former worship, in 9,13 he sees a certain efficacy in it, but he is careful to point out that it is an efficacy on the level of «the flesh», an external level, very inferior to the efficacy of the blood of Christ.

The author starts with a repetition of the expression he used in the previous sentence concerning blood. By way of stylistic elegance, he brings in a slight variation: instead of the «blood of goats and *calves*» (9,12), he puts «*the* blood of goats and *bulls*» (9,13). In 9,19 he will put «*the* blood *of the* calves and *of the* goats» and in 10,4 «blood of bulls and goats». The expression is never the same. This shows the care he took over his style.

Another variation is more important: instead of a negation, «*not* with the blood of goats and calves» (9,12) we have a statement, but it is restricted. To make this restriction easier for himself, the author skilfully adds a reference to the «ashes of a heifer» to the blood of the immolated animals, ashes which went into the production of the lustral water. Certain texts of the Law ascribed an efficacy extending to the remission of sins to the blood of animals (Lev 4,20.26.31.35; 16,30); by putting together the lustral water and the blood, the author confines this efficacy to the elimination of ritual impurity contracted by contact with a dead body (Num 19). This corresponds with his conviction, according to which it is «impossible that the blood of bulls and goats take away sins» (10,4).

The blood of Christ, on the contrary, is capable of «purifying the consciences» (9,14). It owes this efficacy to the value of the oblation in the course of which it was shed. This oblation was very different from the former sacrifices, for it was (1) a *personal* oblation, (2) of an «*immaculate*» human being, (3) made under the impulse of the «*eternal spirit*».

These three specifications establish a complete contrast with the former worship in which the high priest (1) did not offer himself, but offered animals, for (2) he was not «immaculate»; (3) the rites he performed were «rites of flesh» (Heb 9,10), in which the Spirit did not act.

The high priest could not offer himself, because he was not a victim worthy of being offered and he was not capable of offering himself either. To be worthy of being offered to the three times holy God, a victim must be «immaculate», without any blemish; the word *amōmos*, «immaculate» occurs more than 40 times in the ritual prescriptions of Leviticus and of the Book of Numbers. The high priest was not «immaculate», he was a sinner, the Law ordered him to offer sacrifices for his sins (Lev 9,7; 16,6); he could not therefore offer himself. He was not capable of it either, for to offer oneself, one had to be animated with perfect generosity, now a sinner does not have perfect generosity in him, sin being always one form of selfishness or another.

Christ, on the contrary, was an altogether worthy victim to be offered and a priest quite capable of offering himself. Christ, indeed, was truly «immaculate». In the case of animals offered in sacrifice, this qualification meant only the absence of physical blemish (see Mal 1,13-14). In the case of human persons, it obviously meant perfect moral and religious integrity (see Ps 14/15,2; 17/18,24; 18/19,14; etc.). Christ possessed this integrity; he was and is «holy, innocent, immaculate» (Heb 7,26). The first Letter of Peter calls him «immaculate lamb» (1Pet 1,19) and states that he «committed no sin and, in his mouth, no deceit was found» (2,22).

Being «immaculate», Christ did not need, like the former high priests, to look for animals physically without blemish in a herd; he had no need to have recourse to the «blood of goats and calves». He could offer himself, sure to be accepted by God.

A worthy victim, Christ was at the same time a capable priest, for it is under the impulse of the «eternal Spirit» that he accomplished his oblation, which was not therefore a simple «rite of flesh» (Heb 9,10).

The expression «eternal Spirit» is found only here in all the Bible. In the absence of parallel texts, it is difficult to define its exact meaning. Three main interpretations are offered: 1) *pneuma*, «spirit», would designate here an interior disposition, as in 1Cor 4,21, where the apostle Paul asks the Corinthians whether they want him to come to them «with rods or with charity and in *a Spirit of sweetness*»; 2) «eternal spirit» would designate the divine nature of Christ, which is spiritual and eternal; 3) «eternal Spirit» would be another way of designating «the holy Spirit» (Heb 3,7; 9,8; 10,14); quite a large number of Greek manuscripts and early translations have here «Holy Spirit» instead of «eternal Spirit», which shows a spontaneous tendency in favour of this third interpretation.

The first interpretation comes up against a strong objection: it is not clear what kind of interior disposition can be called «eternal spirit», because «eternal» is an ontological quality not a moral one.

Against the second interpretation, it can be objected that it has recourse to theological distinctions which had not yet been drawn when the author wrote his sermon.

The third interpretation seems more probable. Opposed to it is the absence of any article. The author did not write «by the eternal Spirit», which would have made the reference to the Holy Spirit evident; he wrote «by eternal Spirit», which makes the reference uncertain. But it does not at all make it impossible, because the omission of the article is frequent in the New Testament, when it mentions the Holy Spirit.

In the Letter to the Romans, for example, we never have «the holy Spirit», with the article, but always «Holy Spirit» (5,5; 9,1; 14,17; 15,13.16. 19), without the article, and likewise «Spirit of God» (8,9.14), «Spirit of Christ» (8,9). In Hebrews, we also have «Holy Spirit» (2,4; 6,4), without the article, just as we have «the holy Spirit» (3,7; 9,8; 10,15) with the article. The absence of any article is therefore not an obstacle to the third interpretation: «eternal Spirit», without the article, can perfectly well designate the Holy Spirit, who is actually eternal.

This interpretation corresponds to the gospel tradition, which recounts that the «Spirit of God» came down upon Jesus at the time of his baptism (Matt 3,16) and then led him into the desert (Matt 4,1). «Filled with holy Spirit, Jesus came out of the Jordan» (Luke 4,1); «in the power of the Spirit, Jesus returned to Galilee» (Luke 4,14); coming to Nazareth, he applied to himself the oracle in Isaiah which proclaims: «[The] Spirit of 'Lord' is upon me» (Luke 4,18; Isa 6,1).

Saint Paul, too, affirms the presence and the action of the Holy Spirit in the mystery of Christ. It is «with power according to [the] Spirit of holiness» that Christ was «established Son of God by resurrection from the dead» (Rom 1,4; see Rom 8,11).

The sentence in Heb 9,14 completes the perspective indicating that it is also «in the power of the Spirit» that Jesus confronted his Passion, which is something the gospels do not say—they speak of the Spirit only in connection with his ministry— nor does Saint Paul, who only speaks of the Spirit in connection with his resurrection. The explanation given in Heb 9,14 is very coherent, for the baptism of Jesus foreshadowed his death (see Mark 10,38-39; Luke 12,30); if the Spirit came down upon him then, it is obviously to accompany him when he had to confront death. Moreover, the Spirit was able to produce the resurrection of Jesus only by first acting in his death itself and by making it a death victorious over death.

When speaking of the action of the Spirit in Christ's sacrificial offering, Saint John Chrysostom suggests that the Spirit there fulfilled the function attributed to the fire on the altar in the sacrifices of the Old Testament, an extremely important function. It is the fire on the altar, actually, that sent up to heaven, in the form of smoke, the sacrifices offered to God. This was no ordinary fire, but fire coming from God (Lev 9,24; 2Chr 7,1), for only fire coming from God is capable of going back up to God (see John 3,13) and carrying the sacrifices to him. It was never allowed to go out (Lev 6,5), so that it was always the same fire from heaven that was used for the offering of sacrifices. A picturesque story in 2Macc 1,18-36 says that even during the exile the fire on the altar was preserved miraculously, so that on return from the exile, it could carry out its function again.

The Old Testament expresses in this way a profound intuition about the nature of the sacrifices, to get us to understand that simple humans are not able to offer sacrifices, a heavenly force, an intervention by God is needed. A human being can present God an offering, but is not able to sacrifice it, because «sacrificing» means «making sacred» and God alone is capable of «making sacred», by communicating his holiness, which he does by fire which comes from him. The sacrificial transformation is therefore the work of the fire from heaven.

While being perfectly sound, the intuition still only went half way, for the divine fire was conceived in a material way; it was confused with the lightning, falling in times past from heaven, that had set fire to the pile of faggots prepared for the sacrifice (2 Chr 7,1). The author of Hebrews left this rudimentary concept behind and, reflecting on the Passion and glorification of Christ, discovered the true meaning of the symbol: the fire from God, which is not lightning, it is the Holy Spirit, alone capable of effecting the true sacrificial transformation that impregnates the offering with holiness.

The sacrifice of Christ is therefore not made «with [the] continual fire» (*dia pyros endelechous:* 1Ezra 6,23 LXX) which burnt on the altar of the Temple in Jerusalem, but «with [the] eternal Spirit» (*dia pneumatos aiōniou*: Heb 9,14); the parallelism of expressions is significant; it expresses the three aspects of the accomplishment of the Scriptures: resemblance, difference and superiority.

No material power, not even that of fire, can make an offering mount up to God, because it is not a matter of a journey in space, but an interior transformation which extends to the entire being, a transformation made possible and effective by the action of the Holy Spirit. Animated by the interior force of the Holy Spirit, Jesus had the spiritual drive he needed to transform his own death as one condemned into an offering of himself to God, for the salvation of all mankind. Other passages in the sermon show that the force of the Spirit carried out the sacrificial transformation by inspiring Jesus with two closely connected spiritual attitudes: perfect docility towards God (Heb 5,8) and complete solidarity with us (4,15). The human nature of Christ was thus raised up to God, that is to say it passed from the plane of flesh and blood, where it was by reason of the incarnation (Heb 2,14), to the plane of perfect and definitive union with God in heavenly glory (9,24).

For the choice of the expression «eternal Spirit», instead of «Holy Spirit», several reasons may be given. The author may have wanted to suggest the comparison which we have just indicated with the *continual* fire which was used in sacrifices in the Temple. The eternal Spirit fulfilled the role attributed to the continual fire and did so infinitely better.

Moreover, the author has just said that Christ found «an eternal redemption» (9,12) and is getting ready to mention obtaining «the eternal inheritance» (9,15). In order that Christ's oblation might have such efficacy, it required all the strength of the «eternal Spirit».

In saying that Christ «offered himself to God», the author affirms the sacrificial character of the paschal mystery of Christ, Passion and glorification. In the context, actually, the verb «to offer oneself» does not just express an attitude of availability, as in Heb 10,7.9; it expresses the effective performance of a sacrifice; the mention of the «blood of Christ» in the same sentence leaves no doubt about this.

Representing the death of Jesus as a sacrifice did not go without saying, because the event had nothing of the ritual about it and was even quite the opposite of sacrifice, since it had been the execution of someone condemned to death. Between the execution of a condemned person and a sacrifice offered in the Temple the contrast was complete. Jesus being innocent, his execution was, moreover, a scandal. His resurrection had turned things round.

At the beginning, the event was therefore not represented as a ritual sacrifice, but as a series of real facts: the Jews put Jesus to death, God raised him up (see Acts 2,23-24; 3,15; 4,10; 5,30; etc.). In these facts, the accomplishment of God's plan, announced in Scripture, was recognized (1Cor 15,3-4). It has been pointed out that Jesus was not a passive victim, but that he assumed a generous attitude which has been expressed in factual terms: he came «to serve and give his life in ransom for a multitude» (Matt 20,28); he appeared as «the good shepherd» who «lays down his life for his sheep» (John 10,11); he «gave himself for our sins» (Gal 1,4); he «gave himself as ransom for all» (1Tim 2,6); he «delivered himself up» (Gal 2,20).

In Eph 5,2 this last factual expression is completed by some sacrificial terms: «Christ loved us and delivered himself up for us as an oblation and sacrifice to God like a sweet-smelling perfume». The verbs, «loved and delivered himself up», remain factual. The Letter to the Hebrews goes a step further: it uses the sacrificial verb, «to offer», but in an expression, «to offer oneself», never used in the ritual laws of the Old Testament. The use of sacrificial terms to speak of the paschal mystery of Christ offers a double advantage: on the one hand, it expresses the religious dimension of this mystery directly and, on the other, it puts it into touch with the worship tradition of the Old Testament, which is fundamental to it. It shows that it is the fulfilment of it. The use of sacrificial terms was indispensable for it to be said that Christ is the full accomplishment of all Scripture.

The personal oblation of an immaculate human being, accomplished under the impulse of the eternal Spirit, the sacrifice of Christ was fully efficacious, not only in making human nature perfect in him and uniting it to the heavenly holiness of God, but also in communicating perfection to all believers (see 10,14). This spiritual efficacy, very different from the ritual efficacy of the lustral water, which was limited to «the purity of the flesh» (9,13), is transmitted by «the blood of Christ» (9,14).

The insistence on blood corresponds to the perspective of the Old Testament, according to which the blood of victims immolated in sacrifice carried out the purification, because the blood contains a vital force, capable of victoriously opposing the forces of evil and death. God himself declared: «The life of the flesh is the blood. This blood I myself gave you to perform the rite of purification on the altar for your lives» (Lev 17,11; see Deut 12,23). But in the sacrifice of Christ, the relation between blood and sacrifice is reversed: whereas in the Old Testament it was the blood which gave value to the sacrifices, in the case of Christ, it is his sacrifice that gave value to his blood. This inversion of meaning is due to a profound change in the conception of the sacred: from a biological conception —blood being thought sacred because it contains the *nepeš*, «the soul», that is to say the vital principle that comes from God— the passage was made to a spiritual concept: the blood of Christ is sacred, because it was shed in docility to the Holy Spirit, who had it shed for love of God and mankind.

The insistence on «the blood of Christ» corresponds also to the logic of the incarnation which is opposed to a complete spiritualization. The author did not say that what «will purify our conscience» are the merits of Christ; he said that it is his «blood». The blood of Christ, shed for us, gained redemption; this same blood transmits it to us. This is so because it does not simply contain a biological force, but it is wholly impregnated with holy Spirit. Here one can make a comparison with what happens in breathing: the living being breathes in the air of the atmosphere to bring oxygen into his blood, which can then revive all the cells in the organism; similarly Christ, in his Passion, breathed in the Holy Spirit by means of an urgent prayer and generous docility to the will of God (5,7-8); the result is that his blood is fully laden with holy Spirit and can communicate it to all the members of his body.

The efficacy of the blood of Christ is twofold: it purifies the conscience and makes the person fit to «serve [the] living God». The construction of the sentence here is clumsy. In principle, the subject of the verb «to serve» ought to be the same as that of the main verb «will purify»: «the blood will purify to serve», but the context shows that it should be understood: «the blood will purify us so that *we* may serve».

The future «will purify» can be understood in two ways: either as a future of logical conclusion: «if the ashes sanctify..., how much more the blood will purify...», or as a future stating that the efficacy of the blood of Christ will never cease.

Purification is achieved, as in the former rites, but it is of another nature. Instead of «the purity of the flesh» (9,13), the purification of «the conscience» is obtained (9,14). Instead of being just exterior, the efficacy is interior. This difference in the effects corresponds to that in the causes: «rites of flesh» (9,10) can only get «purity of the flesh» (9,13); they are incapable of reaching the «conscience» (9,9). Being made, on the contrary, in inward docility to the Spirit (9,14), the sacrifice of Christ is in a position to reach «our conscience» and to purify it.

It will purify it «from dead works». This expression was already used by the author in Heb 6,1, where «renouncing dead works» was mentioned among the elementary themes of catechesis. The «dead works» are obviously sins. They are never named in this way elsewhere in the Bible. Here, these «dead works» form an antithesis with the «living God», an antithesis full of meaning: the «dead works» make a positive relation with the «living God» impossible; their elimination is indispensable. The expression is, besides, in implicit relation with the rite of lustral water, mentioned in the first part of the sentence. This rite actually was used to free oneself from ritual impurity contracted by contact with a dead body (Num 19,13). The author makes it clear that impurity of conscience, contracted by committing moral faults, which are «dead works», is much more serious, but «the blood of Christ» has the capacity to eliminate them, for it comes from the personal sacrifice of an «immaculate» being (9,14) and contains the cleansing force of the «eternal Spirit», which is decisive for the remission of sins (see John 20,22-23; 1Cor 6,11). The affirmation in Heb 9,14 is close to that in 1John 1,7: «The blood of Jesus his son, purifies us from all sin» (see also Rev 1,5). Moreover, the efficacy of the blood of Christ for the «remission of sins» is stated in Matt 26,28 and in Eph 1,7).

To the efficacy, which can be called negative, in eliminating faults, there is added the positive efficacy in relating people with God. The «blood of Christ» makes people fit to «pay worship to the living God», which the blood of goats and calves was quite unable to do. Let us recall that when he speaks of the former worship and of its sacrifices, the author never says that it was paid «to God».

This end of the sentence well shows the author's basic concern and his profoundly religious mind. He is above all concerned with the relation with God. His ultimate aim is not purification, nor perfection, nor salvation, but this vivifying relation with the living God. He thus shows a theocentric orientation, and not a Christocentric one, although, materially speaking, he put the name of Christ at the centre of the literary composition of his sermon (9,11). But Christ is there as the one who opens up the way to God. The name of Christ has only 12 occurrences in Hebrews and the name of Jesus 14, whereas the name God has 68, a significant difference.

On the subject of the blood of Christ, let us note in finishing an important difference with regard to the blood in former sacrifices. At that time a life force was seen in the blood and it was not at all placed in relation with suffering and death. In the former ritual, there is never any question of making the animals offered in sacrifice suffer and no value is set on their death. It is not mentioned; immolation is spoken of and the sacrifice does not consist in immolating the victim, but in performing the rites with the blood obtained by means of the immolation. In the case of Christ, on the other hand, his sufferings and death are an integral part of his sacrifice, because that consisted in confronting suffering and death out of love, in the twofold dimension of loving docility towards God (Heb 5,8; John 14,31) and of generous solidarity with sinful mankind (Heb 2,17-18; 4,15; Eph 5,2). Christ thus transformed his sufferings and death into an offering that leads to God. Christ's sacrifice was not a rite added to his Passion; it consisted in his Passion itself and in its glorious outcome. The blood of Christ represents his death, transformed into an offering which made it a victory of love over death and therefore a source of life.

In the former worship, it was the blood, considered as sacred, that gave value to the sacrifices; in the case of Christ, on the contrary, it is the sacrifice that gives value to his blood and makes it fully sacred, impregnating it with Holy Spirit. The transition is made from a biological concept of the sacred to an authentically spiritual concept of real-life and incarnate spirituality.

Mediator of a new covenant (9,15-23)

In Heb 9,15 the author passes to another consequence of the oblation of Christ. Because of the efficacy of his sacrifice, Christ is henceforth «mediator» of a new «disposition», which is at once «covenant» and «testament». The author, as we have observed, exploits here the polysemy of the Greek word *diathēkē*, the etymological meaning of which is «disposition» and which can therefore serve to designate various kinds of disposition. The Greek text of this passage shows a sort of fluidity which unsettles the reader and translator. At the beginning, the meaning of «covenant» is suggested, by the title of «mediator». One does not speak of a mediator in drawing up a testament. The expression «new *diathēkē*» confirms the sense of covenant, because it refers to the oracle in Jeremiah, which the author quoted in 8,8-12, and in which it is certainly a question of a covenant between God and the people: «I shall be for them [their] God and they will be for me [my] people» (8,10). Christ is the mediator of the new covenant, because his blood removes the obstacle of sins, «dead works», which oppose the relation with the «living God», and because he gives the ability to «pay worship» which brings with it a positive relation with God (9,14). «For this reason» therefore, Christ «is mediator of a new covenant» (9,15).

After this statement, the author adds some complementary explanations in a different way of speaking. He passes from sacrificial language, «the blood of Christ who offered himself to God» (9,14), to factual language, «a death having occurred» (9,15), which confirms that the sacrifice of Christ was achieved by his death. But there is also the aspect of a legal penalty to his death, undergone «as redemption for transgressions [committed] under the first covenant». The word «transgressions» represents the faults as violations of the Law. The author said earlier that the first covenant was not without reproach (8,7). The establishment of a new covenant required the «redemption of transgressions» committed. The oracle in Jeremiah indeed announced pardon for sins (Jer 31,34; Heb 8,12), but, not indicating how the new covenant would be founded, it did not specify the way in which this pardon would be obtained either. One might think that it would be a matter of a completely gratuitous divine initiative. The Calvary event shatters this illusion: «Christ died for our sins» (1Cor 15,3) —which in reality is also a gift of God, an even more generous gift.

The author's formulation is not so general as that of the kerygma reported by Saint Paul in 1Cor 5,3. In fact it seems to restrict the redemptive value of the death of Christ to faults committed earlier against the Law by the Jews. But it is easy to show that here the author is speaking *affirmative, non exclusive.* Since the new covenant had to be established between God and the people of Israel, the obstacle constituted by the faults committed earlier had to be removed. That is what Jeremiah's oracle promised; it announced the pardon of faults committed by Israel before the establishment of the new covenant. The author asserts the accomplishment of this prediction. That does not mean that he wants to contradict what he has just said in the previous sentence: «the blood of Christ [...] will purify our conscience of dead works» (9,14), nor what he said in Heb 2,17 about Christ becoming «merciful high priest [...] to blot out the sins of the people» (in the present continuous, the verb «to blot out» expresses a continuing action of the risen Christ).

From mentioning a «death» the author passes on to the idea of an «inheritance», giving us to understand that the death of Christ is not simply a death which obtained the pardon of faults, nor a death that founded the new covenant, it is at the same time a death that gave access to a «promised inheritance». (The author says literally: «the promise of the inheritance», but here as in Heb 11,13 «to receive the promise» means «to receive what has been promised»). The author several times associates «promise(s)» and inheritance (6,12.17; 9,15; 10,38; 11,19). Here he makes it clear that it is a question of «the eternal inheritance» (9,12); further on he will say that the blood of Christ is «blood of eternal covenant» (13,20). All that, evidently, because Christ, in and through his sacrifice, overcame the obstacle of death and entered into the eternity of God, not only for his own good, but also for the good of «all who obey him» (5,9).

The notion of inheritance is different from those of «salvation» and «redemption», for it does not connote the idea of a danger from which one escapes nor slavery from which one is redeemed, it expresses the idea of a transfer of goods conditional upon the death of a testator. Christ has not only saved and redeemed us, he has acquired inestimably good things for us by his death. In the perspective of the Old Testament, the action of «saving» and of «redeeming» corresponds to the departure from Egypt, obtaining «the inheritance» correponds to the entry into «the land of promise» (11,9). Where did the author find a promise of «eternal inheritance» in the Old Testament? In the Septuagint, the expression is found only once, in the prayer of Esther, but it is to say that Israel is the eternal inheritance of God (Esth 4,17m). A similar expression is to be read in Gen 17,8 and 48,4, however; this time it is to express the promise made by God to give the land of Canaan to the descendants of Abraham «as an eternal possession». We can see in Heb 4,1-11 and 11,9-10.13-16 that, for the author of Hebrews, this promise by God is in the last analysis the participation in «God's rest» in eternity, a participation already taking place, «for we the believers are entering into the rest» (4,3; see 12,22-24). The author could also rely on the passages of the psalms that promise the faithful victory over death and «unending delights» (Ps 15/16,11) with God, who will welcome them into his glory (Ps 72/73,24). Moreover, the author found the promise of «eternal life» in Dan 12,2 and 2Macc 7,9; he is to refer to it in Heb 11,35 in speaking of the expectation of a «better» resurrection which will not be, like some miraculous resurrections, a return to life on earth.

In speaking of «death» and of «inheritance», the author modifies the way of understanding the word *diathēkē*. He moves it from the sense of «covenant» to that of «testament». The *diathēkē* founded by Christ is at once covenant and testament; covenant, because it puts the people of the believers in relation with God; testament, because it is established by a death which opens up access to the inheritance. In the gospel of Luke, a saying of Jesus at the Last Supper suggests a perspective of this kind. Jesus declares to his disciples: «I confer on you the kingdom, as my father has conferred it on me» (Luke 22,29). The Greek verb, used in the middle voice, is the one that means «to give as an inheritance»; it is found twice in Heb 9,16-17; it is a participle, «he having given as an inheritance»; translated as: «the testator».

The author insists on the link between testament and death. His expressions are not of the clearest and have therefore aroused debate. Literally, the author says at first: «Where [there is] testament, [there is] need that [the] death of him who makes the will be brought». The meaning, obviously, is that a death certificate be produced. The author adds: «A testament, in fact, [is] about dead [people] [which is] firm». The adjective «firm» (Greek *bebaia*) can be understood in different ways. If it is translated by «valid», the author's statement lends itself to dispute, because, for a testament to be valid, it is not necessary that the testator be dead. It is necessary and sufficient that the testament was done in correct and due form. But «valid» is not a good translation, for as long as the testator is alive, his testament, even if valid, is not yet really «firm»; the testator can still change or even annul it completely and replace it with another. Only the death of the testator makes the testament definitively «firm». Nothing can be changed in it any more, it must be executed. To reproduce the author's thought, it is better therefore to speak of a testament that is «executable» and not simply of a «valid» testament. The sentence in 2,2, which uses the same Greek adjective confirms this sense, because what it attributes to «the word announced by the angels» —that is to say to the Decalogue— is not a simple theoretical validity, it is power to execute. This word «became firm», in the sense that «every transgression and disobedience received just retribution»; the parallelism of the sentence is significant in this matter; it shows that «became firm» means «came into force» by imposing legal penalties.

The death of Christ put an extremely generous testament into effect. Actually, it was not simply, as in ordinary cases, a death undergone passively, a sufficient condition for the good things promised to be properly distributed; it produced those good things itself, because it was an extraordinary demonstration of love. The author does not say so in this passage, but he shows elsewhere all the fruitfulness of the death of Christ.

For the moment, he is concerned to show that the idea of a testament conditional upon a death was already present, in one way, in the foundation of the Sinai «disposition». He perceives this idea in the use of blood. On Sinai, to establish the «disposition», Moses used the blood of immolated animals. To tell the truth, this blood did not represent death, it was used as a force of life. However, to obtain it animals had to be put to death. In the author's eyes, that was enough for there to be seen here an analogy with the function of the death which makes a testament executable. The author therefore stresses the importance of the blood in the rites on Sinai. In these five verses (18-22), the word «blood» is repeated five times and it comes back a sixth time, at the end, in the compound word «shedding-of-blood».

The author does not restrict his point of view to just the relation between death and testament, between blood and covenant. He adopts, as we have observed, an overall perspective, carrying out a kind of fusion between several things in Scripture (testament, covenant, expiation, purification, remission). He brings in, in particular, the Law. He recalls that before performing the rites of blood, Moses proclaimed to all the people «each commandment according to the Law» (19). He changes the solemn formula of the establishment of the covenant in the same sense. Instead of saying with the Septuagint: «the blood of the disposition which the Lord *disposed* for you», he says: «the blood of the disposition which God *ordered* for you» (20), which does not go well with the meaning of «testament» (one does not order a testament) and which likens the covenant on Sinai to a law, whereas the new covenant is characterized by promises (8,6).

The conclusion (23) takes the point of view of purification by means of sacrifices and expresses the need for a progression between two levels of reality, «the figures of the heavenly things» and «the heavenly things themselves». If one admits the necessity and utility of sacrifices for the purification of the first, one must admit the necessity, for the purification of the second, «of sacrifices of greater worth». Logical in principle, the affirmation is none the less surprising for two reasons. Firstly, because it speaks of a need of purification for «the heavenly things themselves», which implies that they were soiled. How could there have been impurity in heaven?

The other reason is the use of the word «sacrifices» in the plural for the second category as for the first. We can immediately understand, actually, that the second case is the one of the worship paid by Christ, but the plural, then, is surprising, because the author is always insisting on the uniqueness of the sacrifice of Christ, who «offered himself once and for all» (7,27) and does not have to repeat his sacrifice (7,27; 9,25.28; 10,12.14). In reality, the plural can be explained without great difficulty by the nature of the sentence. The latter is a logical deduction, a statement of principle, and not a registering of accomplished facts. The statement bears upon the change of quality. In the second case, the sacrifices must be «of greater value». One speaks spontaneously of sacrifices in the plural, because there were many of them in the first case. All the same, one does not exclude the fact that, in reality, the need could have been satisfied by one sacrifice, of which the unique nature had more worth than any amount of them. One can also add that the unique sacrifice of Christ itself has an air of multiplicity about it: Christ «offered up pleas and supplications» (5,7) and he bore «sufferings» (2,10; 5,8) which made him perfect (5,9).

The other cause of astonishment finds its solution thanks to rhetorical analysis and, more precisely, thanks to the parallelism in the sentence. To define «the heavenly things», we have to start with the «figures» with which they are placed in relation. According to the context, what are those «figures» that have been purified by the blood of former sacrifices? On the one hand, they are «the

Book itself and all the people» (19) and, on the other, «the tent and all the objects of the liturgy» (21). We gather therefore that the heavenly things, thus foreshadowed, are: 1) the gospel revelation and the people of the new covenant, 2) «the greater and more perfect tent» (9,11) and the Christian liturgy. The parallelism shows that it is not a matter of a purification of realities which were already with God in heaven, but of heavenly realities by calling (see 3,1), which needed Christ's sacrifice to come with him «to heaven itself» (9,24), in the presence of God. Without Christ's sacrifice, in fact, the gospel revelation remained earthly, incomplete, enigmatic (see John 16,25); it is Christ's sacrifice that gave it all its meaning and made it heavenly. Henceforth, the believers are in relation with «a blood that speaks louder than that of Abel» and with a «mediator» who speaks «from the height of the heavens» (12,24-25). The people of the new covenant have a «heavenly vocation», as the author declared explicitly in 3,1; thanks to the «blood of Jesus» (10,19), this vocation now finds a first accomplishment: the believers have free access to the heavenly sanctuary (10,19), to the «heavenly Jerusalem» (12,22). As regards «the tent» that helped Christ himself to enter into the sanctuary, it is also thanks to Christ's sacrifice that it has become «greater and more perfect» (9,11; see 5,8-9) and that it was able to fulfil its heavenly function. This tent, as we have shown, is none other than the humanity of Christ. Made of flesh and blood by virtue of the incarnation (2,14), it needed a complete sacrificial transformation to be able to give access to the heavenly sanctuary, for «flesh and blood cannot inherit the kingdom of God» (1Cor 15,50). The whole Christian liturgy receives its full heavenly value from the sacrifice of Christ: it is «into the death of Christ that believers are «baptized» (Rom 6,3-4); it is his body delivered up and his blood shed that they receive in the Eucharist (Matt 26,25-28 and parallels). The requirement expressed in the sentence in Heb 9,23 has therefore been perfectly fulfilled.

That sentence, as we have seen, prepares the way to the last subdivision (9,24-28), which defines the outcome of Christ's sacrifice, a heavenly and definitive outcome. In the sentence in 9,11-12, the author had defined the means used by Christ for his entry into the sanctuary: «the tent» and «the blood»; he had described them positively and negatively. He had not then described the sanctuary itself. He does so now, first negatively: this is not a «*handmade* sanctuary»; then positively: it is «heaven itself», «to appear before the face of God». The negative description is the same as the one that was given to the tent: «not handmade». It is easy to understand that a sanctuary built with human hands is not

God's real dwelling, but a simple «representation». «The Most High does not live in constructions» (Acts 7,48; 17,24; 2Chr 6,18). The real sanctuary where God dwells is of a very different nature. It follows that to get to it a tent made by human hands was completely inadequate and, likewise, a nature of flesh and blood. A radical sacrificial transformation was indispensable, in the crucible of divine holiness, in order to obtain a tent «not handmade», which would lead into the true sanctuary, which is not «handmade».

Concerning the tent, the author points out that it is not of this creation (9,11). This point is also true of the heaven into which Christ entered by his sacrifice. This heaven is not to be confused with «the heavens» which were created «in the beginnings» at the same time as the earth; they are «work of the hands» of God and «will perish» (1,10-11; Ps 101,26-27). This heaven is, on the contrary, the divine heaven which does not belong to this creation. Christ presents himself there now «before the face of God» and he does so «for us». His glorification, actually, is not simply individual, it is priestly, because it results from a sacrifice which was an act of complete solidarity with sinful mankind and in their favour. It is in the capacity of high priest «established for mankind» (5,1) that Christ is received into the glory of God.

He is received there definitively. His sacrifice did not have to be repeated «many times», for it succeeded perfectly. The author here completes his vision of the relations between Christ's sacrifice and the liturgy of Kippur. Earlier on, he expressed a relation of resemblance: the high priest went only once a year into the holy of holies (9,7), Christ entered once into the sanctuary (9,12). Now the author expresses a relation of difference; he observes that in the case of the high priest, the uniqueness was very relative: «once a year» which, in the long run, meant «many times», since it comes to twenty times in twenty years, thirty times in thirty years.

In the case of Christ, on the contrary, any repetition of the sacrifice is excluded. To show this, the author presents two arguments. The first is that the repetition of the sacrifice would have implied the repetition of the Passion of Christ in every period of the world's history; we would have stayed in a cyclical system. In reality, the sacrifice of Christ is an eschatological event which leads out of the cyclical system. It took place «once, at the end of the ages». Christ was thus «manifested» as an entirely new reality «for the abolition of sin by his sacrifice», which introduces a radical change in the world where sin went without remedy. The other argument is that the sacrifice of Christ was achieved by his death, an irreversible event: one dies only once. This was not simply a death, but a death transformed into a sacrificial offering and therefore efficacious against sin, as the prophet Isaiah had announced (Isa 53,12), a death all the same, unrepeatable. «Raised from the dead, Christ dies no more, death no more has power over him» (Rom 6,9). However, he will come back, but his return will not be a return to mortal life; Christ will certainly not have to die again «for our sins» (1Cor 15,3); he did it once and for all. It is to bring «salvation to those who wait for him» that he will come back in his glory.

It may be noticed here that in these verses the author passes very spontaneously from the idea of «offering oneself» (25) to that of «suffering» (26) and to that of «dying» (27), to come back later to that of «being offered» (28). It is clear that for him «offering oneself» consisted, in the case of Christ, in voluntarily facing suffering and death, out of docility towards God, his father (see 5,8; 10,7.9) and out of loving fraternal solidarity with us (see 2,14; 4,15). The relation between the personal offering of Christ and his death was already implicitly present in the sentence in 9,14, which put Christ's personal sacrifice in relation with his blood; it was understood, in fact, that it was about blood *shed*, like that «of the goats and calves» (13). The next allusion to the «death» (15) of Christ confirmed this. Verses 25-28 give a further confirmation of it.

Thus ends this central section, presented as the «main point» (8,1) of the whole sermon. It has shown that Christ was «made perfect» (5,9; 7,28) by a sacrificial offering, a «liturgy» (8,6), «very different» (8,6) from the former worship, for it made his human nature perfect, which became «the greater and more perfect tent» (9,11), it brought him from earth «to heaven itself», «into the presence of God (9,24) and made him the «mediator of a new covenant» (9,15), «of greater worth» than the first (8,6), because it ensures entry into «the eternal inheritance» (9,15). Each of these aspects is connected with *accomplishment* of the institutions of the Old Testament, that is to say in a threefold relation: of continuity, of breaking away and of outreaching (or: of resemblance, of difference and of superiority), of continuity for the purpose in view, of breaking away as regards the means used and of outreaching as regards the achievement reached.

The section ends on the eschatological perspective of the second coming of Christ (9,28). It would be hard to find a more appropriate theme for a conclusion. To claim that this section does not end at 9,28 but goes on until 10,18 is an obvious error. Some commentators fall into this error, because they are only attentive to the elements common to the two sections (8,1-9,28 and 10,1-18) due to their belonging to one and the same part. They are not alert to the conclusion aspect of 9,28 nor to the new beginning aspect of 10,1 and especially they have not noticed the structural role of the words *hē skēnē*, «the tent», and *ta hagia*, «the sanctuary». These two words appeared for the first time in the sermon in 8,2, in an expression which stated the theme of the section: Christ is «minister of the sanctuary and of the tent, the true tent». The word «tent» later has 7 other occurrences in the central section and the word «sanctuary» 5 others, whereas these two words are completely absent from 10,1-18. «The true tent» is described in 9,11, in the first subdivision of the positive paragraph (9,11-14), which speaks of the means used in the liturgy of Christ; the sanctuary is described in 9,24, in the third and last subdivision (9,24-28), which defines the outcome of the sacrifice of Christ. The author proceeds in an orderly and methodical fashion, according to the rules of Semitic rhetoric. These rules have to be followed faithfully if one wants to understand his thought properly.

Chapter 13

The only efficacious sacrifice (10,1-18)

The last word of the previous section, «salvation» is a reminder of one of the affirmations in the announcement of the subject, according to which Christ «has become for all who obey him *cause of eternal salvation*» (5,9). Of the three affirmations in the announcement of the subject, this one has not yet been developed. It is developed in this third section of doctrinal exposé.

COMPOSITION

Four subdivisions (1-3; 4-10; 11-14; 15-18) are distinguished, arranged in chiastic order: A B B' A'.

Hesitation is possible over the boundary between the first and the second subdivision. In many editions, verse 4 is attached to what precedes, but several literary pointers show that it must be attached to what follows. An inclusion, in fact, formed by the repetition of the expression «every year», encloses verses 1 to 3; another inclusion, formed by means of the verb «to take away» and of the word «offering», goes from verses 4-5 to verses 9-10. Verse 4 is a transition verse by link-word, the word «sins» in verse 3 being resumed in verse 4. Besides, the expression «Impossible, indeed,» at the head of a sentence, is more suitable for the beginning of a literary unit than for the end of one (see 6,4).

Inefficacy of the law (10,1-3)

1 The law, indeed, having a sketch of the good things to come,
not the expression itself of the realities,
EVERY YEAR, with the same sacrifices,
that are offered in perpetuity
can never make those who approach perfect.
2 Otherwise, would they not have ceased to be offered,
due to the fact that they would no longer have had any awareness of sins
who offer the worship,
having been purified once and for all?
3 but in these [sacrifices, there is] reminder of sins EVERY YEAR.

The inclusion based on «every year» has already been pointed out. A first antithesis between a «sketch» (1a) and «the expression itself of the realities» (1b) disqualifies «the law» (1a). A second antithesis contrasts the «perpetual» repetition of the same sacrifices (1cd) with the «never» reached result (1e).

The next sentence is a rhetorical question which suggests an affirmative answer: if the law and its sacrifices had been effective, the sacrifices would have ceased being offered (2a). «To cease being offered» (2a) contrasts with «to offer perpetually» (1d). A synonymous parallelism, in antithetic form, joins a negative statement, «would no longer have had any awareness of sins» (2b), to a corresponding positive expression, «having been purified once and for all» (2d). Then there is an antithetic parallelism between «reminder of sins every year» (3) and «no awareness of sins any more» (2c).

Ineffective sacrifices and effective offering (10,4-10)

4 Impossible, indeed,
that the blood of bulls and goats TAKE AWAY sins.
5 This is why, entering into the world, he says:
Sacrifice and OFFERING, you did not WISH,
but a body you fitted me with;
6 holocausts and [oblations] for sin, you did not accept,
7 then I said: See, I have come,
—in the scroll of a book, it is written of me—
to do, O God, your WILL.
8 Saying above: Sacrifices and offerings,
holocausts and [oblations] for sin,
you did not want nor did you accept them,
—these are things offered according to the law—
9 then he said: See, I have come
to do your will.
He TAKES AWAY the first [worship], to establish the second.
10 In that will we have been sanctified
by the OFFERING of the body of Jesus Christ once for all.

The inclusion marking the boundaries of this subdivision is not perfect, because its two terms are not arranged in chiastic order. They follow each other in the same order: «takes away…», at the end as at the beginning. Besides, the verb «to take away» is not identical in the Greek text but has two different prefixes: *aph-airein* and *an-airein*.

A secondary inclusion is noticeable in the quotation from Psalm 39 (LXX) between the «not want» at the beginning (5b) and the «will» at the end (7c). There is opposition between what God did not want (5b) and what he did want (7c). He rejected the ritual sacrifices and wanted the real accomplishment of his will.

The quotation from the psalm contains various kinds of parallelism. The two first stichs express an antithesis between what God did not want (5b) and what he fitted up (5c); this antithesis suggests an opposition between the ritual sacrifices and the body of the chosen one of God, but this opposition is still obscure. It is made clearer by the following verses. Stichs 6 and 7a are parallel to the two previous ones (5bc). The parallelism is synonymous between 6 and 5b: divine rejection of ritual sacrifices. It is complementary between 7a and 5c: in response to God's action comes the person's attitude, an attitude of willingness, still imprecise. It is given precision by the next two stichs which are in complementary parallelism between what «is written» (7b) and the «will» of God (7c). All things considered, what must replace the various kinds of ritual sacrifices is the personal fulfilment of the will of God.

Verses 8 and 9 take up the content of the quotation from the psalm. They bring together the elements of stichs 1 and 3 (5b and 6): firstly the four nouns, then the two verbs; they then insert a remark on the relation between the sacrificial rites and the law, which corresponds to the perspective of the beginning (10,1), and they leave out 5c and 7b, which results in bringing together the two most important expressions: «See, I have come» (9a) «to do your will» (9b). The contrast between the two ways of appearing before God is thus made clearer. A lapidary formula summarizes the situation and gives it precision: there is suppression of the first state of affairs and establishment of the second (9c).

A final sentence (10) goes back to the word «will» in 7c and 9b as well as the word «offering» in 5b and 8a, and the word «body» in 5c, but it innovates by linking the latter to the word «offering», while in the text quoted «body» is in opposition to «offering». Several further points are added: a statement about our sanctification, mention of the name of «Jesus Christ» and the unique character of the offering of his body.

This final sentence (10) is in close relation with the initial sentence. The impossibility of any expiation stated at the beginning is contrasted with the accomplished fact of sanctification. The «blood of bulls and goats» is opposed to «the offering of the body of Jesus Christ». This offering does more than «take away sins»; by it «we have been sanctified», a marvellous achievement.

Busy priests and the enthroned priest (10,11-14)

11 And every priest stands
busy every day with the liturgy
and offering many times the same sacrifices,
which can never blot out sins,
12 while this person,
having offered for sins one sacrifice,
in perpetuity has sat at the right hand of God,
13 henceforth waiting
for his enemies to be placed as a footstool for his feet.
14 By one offering, in fact,
he made perfect in perpetuity those who receive sanctification.

This subdivision is built entirely on an antithetic parallelism which contrasts the priesthood of Christ with the former priesthood. While «every priest is standing», «this one», that is to say «Jesus Christ» who has just been named (10), «sat». While every priest offers «many times the same sacrifices», Christ «offered for sins one sacrifice». The former sacrifices «can never blot out sins», whereas Christ «with one offering, made perfect in perpetuity those who receive sanctification» (14b).

Between verses 12 and 14 a significant correspondence is noticeable. If Christ could sit «in perpetuity» at God's right hand (12c), it is obviously because he made perfect «in perpetuity» those who receive sanctification (14b).

One can also notice a parallelism between this subdivision and the previous one. The contrast between the busy priests and the enthroned priest completes the contrast between the ritual sacrifices of the busy priests and the personal offering of Christ.

Lastly, this third subdivision offers links with the first (1-3). In it are found the expressions «the same sacrifices» and «in perpetuity», and especially an antithesis between «the law» which «can never make perfect those who approach» despite the perpetual repetition of the same sacrifices, and Christ who «by one offering made the faithful perfect in perpetuity».

New covenant and end of sacrifices (10,15-18)

15 The Holy Spirit also bears witness to this;
for, after saying:
16 This is the covenant that I shall arrange for them after those days,
[the] Lord says:
17 Giving my laws,
on their hearts and on their thought I shall write them
and their sins and their iniquities I shall not remember.
18 Where [there is] pardon of the latter,
[there is] no more offering for sin.

The preacher concludes this last section and therefore all his great exposé by quoting again the oracle of the new covenant which he quoted in full in the central section, in 8,8-12. Here, he quotes only two passages, the one on the laws written on the hearts and the one on the forgiveness of sins. These are the most important. He does not quote them exactly. In the first passage, he inverts the order of the complements and puts the same preposition twice: «on their hearts and on their thoughts». these two complements obviously depend on the verb that follows, «I shall write». This confirms that in 8,10 the author did not construct the Greek sentence according to the parallelism we find in the Hebrew.

A particular feature of this text is that it is grammatically structured by means of two correlative elements («after saying:... [the] Lord says: ...), the first of which comes from the author, while the second is part of the text quoted. Not noticing this feature, some scribes felt the need to add another correlative element before the last part of the quotation («*later he said:* and their sins etc»., or else: «*then he said*: and their sins etc.»). They were wrong.

The grammatical structure establishes a complementary parallelism between the announcement of the covenant (16ab) and its content (17abc).

In his way of abbreviating the content of the covenant, the author, by omitting a verb, has ruined the synonymous parallelism of the passage on pardon and has, at the same time, constructed a parallelism of form between the two passages, which both consist of two synonymous complements followed by a verb in the future. The two verbs are in antithesis; the first, «I shall inscribe it», expresses the positive aspect of the intervention by God; the second, «I shall no longer remember them», expresses its negative aspect.

The final sentence (18b) is in complementary parallelism; it expresses a logical correlation between the presence of pardon and the antithetic absence of sin.

This fourth subdivision (15-18) is in antithetic relation to the first (1-3). With «the law» of former times it contrasts the new «covenant», which will inscribe the laws of God on the hearts; with sacrifices that only cause «the remembrance of sins», it contrasts the promise of God no more to remember sins; with the continual repetition of these sacrifices, «that are offered in perpetuity» —while, if they had been efficacious, they would have «ceased being offered»—- it contrasts the effective cessation of every «offering for sin».

This section, as can be seen, is composed with the greatest care; the synonymous or antithetic parallelisms are very numerous in it and many multiple relations are established in it between the four subdivisions.

B. *BIBLICAL CONTEXT*

For the first subdivision (1-3), which speaks of sacrifices offered «every year» (1),

the biblical context is obviously the liturgy of the day of Kippur, which has already been mentioned in the central section, first in 9,7 with the expression in Lev 16,34 «once a year», then in 9,25 with the expression «every year» repeated here. Moreover, the idea of offering these sacrifices «in perpetuity» corresponds to the insistence in Leviticus, which three times stresses the point that the celebration of Kippur is required by a «perpetual law» (Lev 16,29. 31.34): «That will be for you a perpetual law; once a year the rite of expiation for all their sins will be performed over the children of Israel» (Lev 16,34). That «in these sacrifices, there is a reminder of sins every year» (3) is incontestable: the word «sin» is repeated 13 times in Lev 16.

The second subdivision (4-10) quotes Ps 39,7-9a according to the Septuagint. All the Greek manuscripts of the latter, in verse 7, depart once from the Hebrew text. This last says to God: «You have opened my ear», which means: «You made me docile to your word». Apparently finding this expression strange, the translators put: «You fitted out a body for me», which corresponds to the account of the creation (Gen 2,7)... and which admirably suits any mention of the incarnation of the Son of God, to whom God gave a body of «blood and flesh» (Heb 2,14).

The author interrupts his quotation in the middle of verse 9 of the psalm. This verse declares:

> To do your will, my God, I have desired
> And your law in the middle of my breast

the author has simply:

To do, O God, your will.

The reason for the omission is easy to understand: in a passage in which the author is criticizing the Law (10,1), the positive mention of the law did not suit him. But it must be pointed out that, in another context, nothing would have prevented the author from taking this sentence for his own purposes, because in saying «Your law in the middle of my breast», it corresponds to the description of the new covenant, in which God announces that he will write his law on the hearts.

The rejection by God of the immolations of animals is a recurrent theme in the preaching of the prophets and in the psalms. In Isaiah, God declares:

What importance do your many sacrifices have for me [...]
I am surfeited with holocausts of rams and the fat of calves.
The blood of bulls and goats repels me (Isa 1,11).

In Jeremiah, he says likewise:

Your holocausts do not please me,
your sacrifices are not acceptable to me (Jer 6,20).

Hos 6,6 may also be quoted:

Love is what I want, not sacrifices.

As well as Amos 5,22:

When you offer me holocausts, your oblations, I do not want them;
your sacrifices of fat beasts, I pay no attention to them.

In a psalm, God asks ironically:

Am I going to eat the flesh of bulls?
the blood of goats, am I going to drink it? (Ps 50,13).

In the next psalm, the «Miserere», the repentant sinner says to God:

You would take no pleasure in sacrifice;
if I offer a holocaust, you do not want it.

And he adds:

My sacrifice is a broken spirit;
for a broken, crushed heart you do not have contempt (Ps 51,18-19).

Yet the end of this psalm, clearly added at the time of the exile, gives back an important place to sacrifices:

You will rebuild Jerusalem in its walls.
Then you will take pleasure in the right sacrifices, holocaust and whole oblation;
then young bulls will be offered on your altar (Ps 51,20-21).

This ending is significant. It shows that the situation was complex, and that the rejection of sacrifices of animals proclaimed by the prophets could not be absolute, firstly because the law required them, then and especially because sacrificial mediation was indispensable to remedy sin. But where was effective sacrificial mediation to be found?

The author of the Letter to the Hebrews, without any hesitation, made the prophetic critique his own, for he understood that the paschal mystery of Christ perfectly brought the solution of the problem. The author chose Ps 39 (Ps 40 in Hebrew) from the Septuagint, in which he found the rejection by God of all kinds of sacrifice and, at the same time, a replacement solution: the complete readiness of a person to do the will of God. That person is Christ, who did the will of God offering his body.

The third subdivision (11-14) does not refer, as does the first, to the liturgy of Kippur, celebrated by the high priest, but to the daily sacrificial worship, celebrated by «every priest» (11), which provides a far more eloquent contrast between the daily repetition of manifold sacrifices and the complete absence of multiplicity and repetition. To show this absence in the case of Christ, the author skilfully falls back on the first oracle of Ps 109, which calls upon the Messiah to stay seated on the right hand of God, until God has subjected his enemies to him.

Earlier, in 1,13 the author had drawn an argument from this situation of quiet expectation.

The fourth subdivision (15-18) quotes freely, as we have seen, part of the oracle of Jeremiah announcing a new covenant. It introduces this oracle as testimony by «the Holy Spirit» (15), although it represents itself as word of the «Lord» (16). The author thus manifests his conviction that it is the Holy Spirit that communicates the words of God to the inspired authors (see also 3,7).

INTERPRETATION

In the central section, the author criticized the worship of the Former Covenant, saying that its priests «pay worship to an image and a sketch of heavenly [realities]» (8,5). Here he takes up the word «sketch» (in Greek skia, of which the primary meaning is «shadow») to criticize, this time, «the law» (10,1). The procedure is similar to that in ch. 7, where the author passed on from a criticism of the priesthood (7,11) to a criticism of the law (7,11-12.19). The criticism of the law is similar, here and there; as in 7,19, in 10,1 it bears on the incapacity of the law to «make perfect». The point of view is not identical: ch. 7 spoke of the priesthood, ch. 10 speaks of the sacrifices, that is to say of the means to be used to make the human person perfect and thus provide him with access to God.

In the central section, the author denounced the impotence of the sacrifices «to make perfect in his conscience the one paying worship» (9,9); in this section, he shows that this impotence has repercussions on the law (10,1).

The law has only «the sketch of the good things to come», it does not have «the expression of the realities itself» (literally: «the image of the realities itself»). This distinction manifests quite a different perspective from Platonic idealism. The latter is not actually interested in «good things to come», but in «ideas», which are perfect and have always existed, and puts shadows and images in the same inferior category. Biblical revelation, on the contrary, turns towards the future and concrete achievement, which comes about in several stages, to result in perfect accomplishment. God's plan is perfect, but no more than a plan; it is destined to become incarnate; that it is carried out in the flesh is not understood as a downfall —which is the case of Platonism and in the gnostic theories— but on the contrary as plenitude, a necessary accomplishment.

The law has only the sketch of this accomplishment, for —as the author has shown— it has neither valid priesthood, nor effective worship, nor irreproachable covenant. Its perspective is still confined to the earthly plane. It prescribes a repetitive sacrificial worship. In this requirement of repetition, the author detects an admission of inefficacy.

To tell the truth, his argument is questionable. The annual repetition of the great expiation did not necessarily mean that it did not obtain pardon of the faults committed in the year; it only showed that after its celebration, other faults had been committed and made a new celebration necessary. What is correct is that this requirement for further repetitions showed that the persons had not been «purified once and for all», that is to say completely freed from their attachment to sin and made capable of sinning seriously no more.

Finally, what appears here especially is the double conviction the author has, on the one hand, of the inefficacy of the immolation of animals and, on the other, of the perfect efficacy of the sacrifice of Christ, which effectively makes people capable of not sinning seriously any more. This second conviction is clearly expressed by the apostle Paul when he writes to the Romans: «Sin will no longer rule over you, for you are no longer under the law, but under grace» (Rom 6,14); «The law of the Spirit of life in Christ Jesus has freed you from the law of sin and death» (Rom 8,2). In different language, the first Letter of John takes the same position even more vigorously (1John 3,9).

The first conviction, for its part, is immediately expressed by the author, who declares: «impossible that the blood of bulls and goats take away sins» (10,4). This declaration does not lack boldness, because it seems to contradict the law of Moses which several times affirms the remission of sins obtained by the immolation of animals, for example in Lev 4,20.26.35. But to this difficulty it could be answered that the law never says the blood of bulls and goats took away sins and, besides, in the prophets and the psalms, God expresses his disgust with this worship: «The blood of bulls and goats repels me» (Isa 1,11).

The author then quotes a passage from a psalm belonging —as we have seen— to this prophetic tradition, Psalm 39,7-9 in the Septuagint. The way he introduces the quotation shows that he is applying it to a person whose identity he does not reveal, leaving it up to his listeners to guess it. He will show it later on, in verse 10, explicitly naming «Jesus Christ».

The passage in the psalm is therefore applied to Jesus Christ, which does not mean that all the psalm is considered Messianic; a verse is opposed to this possibility, for it alludes to faults committed by the one praying the psalm (Ps 39,13).

It is while «entering into the world» that Christ pronounces these words. What precise moment does this expression refer to? The author expresses himself vaguely; he does not put the verb «to say» in a historical tense, he puts it in the non-temporal present: «he says», which gives this text from Scripture perpetual relevance. The listeners are called upon to contemplate the Son of God «entering into the world» and expressing his attitude of entire readiness to do the will of God. Concretely, this entry into the world can hardly mean, as is sometimes said, the first instant of the incarnation, for, at that moment, Christ could not have said to God: «you fitted out a body for me», his body not yet having been formed. Nor can it have been the moment of birth, because a newly born child is not in a position to decide the direction its life will take. It will therefore be later, when Jesus has sufficiently «grown in wisdom, stature and grace» (Luke 2,52). But, let us repeat, the author is not concerned with pinning down the time. He is interested only in the attitude.

The latter is based on knowledge of the attitude of God himself, that is to say of the rejection by God of all forms of sacrificial worship, to which God opposes the creation of the body of the one praying to him. In the application to Christ, the variant introduced by the Septuagint —«you fitted out a body for me» instead of: «you opened my ear»— admirably brings to mind the incarnation of the Son of God. This case is similar to the one of the Greek translation of Isaiah 7,14 —«a virgin will conceive and bear a son» instead of: «the girl is pregnant and will bear a son»— announcing the virginal conception of the son of Mary.

The message of the psalm corresponds to the word addressed by Samuel to Saul: «obedience is better than sacrifice» (1Sam 15,22), but it is more vigorous, for it sets up opposition between all kinds of sacrifices and the will of God. Sacrifices, God did not want any. In conformity with the perspective the author took when beginning (10,1), a parenthesis points out the link there is between sacrifices and the law: they are offered «according to law» and yet God did not want any. The opposition is therefore also between the law and the will of God. A very paradoxical situation, but which is part of the Old Testament revelation. Yet it may be remarked that the text of the psalm does not express opposition in principle. It does not say that the sacrifices of the law were never willed by God. It says only that, in the circumstances, God did not want them. This leaves open the possibility of admitting that the law corresponded to the will of God for a certain period, that is to say until the entry of Christ into the world (see Gal 3,19.23-25). This interpretation is confirmed by the declaration in v.9 where it is said that Christ «takes away the first [worship], to establish the second». This was already the perspective of ch. 7: «with the priesthood changed, there necessarily also comes a change of law» (7,12).

The final sentence (10) has several surprises in store for us, for it introduces the theme of our sanctification («we have been sanctified»), of which the psalm makes no mention at all, and it resumes the notion of «offering», by making it go from a negative context (5 and 8) to a positive context (10) and by tying it to the word «body», while in the psalm, the word «body» came in opposition to «sacrifice and offering» (5). All this is very significant.

This final sentence actually corresponds to the theme of the section, which is about the efficacy of Christ's offering; it affirms this efficacy, which contrasts with the lack of efficacy of the «blood of bulls and goats», denounced at the beginning of the paragraph (4). The thought progresses, because the author is not simply saying that Christ's offering «takes away sins», an efficacy, so to speak, of removal, of which the blood of bulls and goats was not capable, whereas, according to 9,14, the blood of Christ is capable of doing so; going further, the author here expresses a positive efficacy, one of sanctification, and he does not hesitate to say that this efficacy is henceforth acquired: «we have been sanctified».

In 10,29 and 13,12 the efficacy of sanctification is attributed to the blood of Christ; here, because of the psalm, the author attributes it to the body of Christ or, more precisely, to «the offering of the body of Jesus Christ, once and for all». In the light of the passion of Christ, the author has understood that the will of God, of which the psalm speaks, meant, concretely, Christ offering his body up to suffering and death, out of filial obedience and fraternal solidarity, so that there was not simply a suppression of the former sacrificial worship, but its replacement with another sacrificial worship, of far greater worth, being real-life and personal.

The next paragraph (11-14) continues to treat the theme of the efficacy by stressing a new contrast, a contrast of situation between «every priest» (11) and «this one» (12) that is to say «Jesus Christ», who has just been named (10). On the one hand there is a priest standing up, a liturgical service performed «every day», the repeated offering of the same sacrifices, of which the author again highlights the inefficacy, which continually makes the repetition of new attempts necessary. On the other hand, in complete contrast, there is a priest in a seated position, «in perpetuity»; he has offered only one «unique sacrifice for sins», but this sacrifice was perfectly efficacious, firstly for him, because it meant that he was accepted «at the right hand of God», for those, next, «who receive sanctiication», for, with his unique offering, he «made them perfect in perpetuity». No repetition of this unique sacrifice is to be envisaged, since its efficacy was perfect. This new priest therefore only has to wait «until his enemies are placed as a footstool for his feet» (13). To define the position of Christ, the author uses the first oracle in Ps 109, which he recalls in its entirety, as in 1,13.

The efficacy of the offering on the faithful, which was expressed by the verbs «to purify» (9,14) and «sanctification» (10,10), is here expressed by the verb «to make perfect», which was used in 2,10; 5,9 and 7,28 for Christ. We know that God made Christ «perfect through suffering» (2,10), because «through what he suffered he learnt obedience and was thus made perfect» (5,8-9) and established as high priest «made perfect» (7,28). The great new feature here is that it is the faithful who have been made perfect and made perfect by Christ by means of his unique offering. As in 5,9 and 7,28, Christ is the subject of the verb «make perfect», but instead of being in the passive, «made perfect», the verb is in the active, «he made perfect». In his sacrificial offering, Christ was therefore at once passive and active. He himself was made perfect in his humanity, but this perfection he received he passed on to his brothers and sisters at the same time. As we have seen, it is a priestly perfection which gives access to God. It really is this priestly perfection that Christ passed on «to those who receive sanctification»; there will be confirmation of this some verses later, when the author declares that believers enjoy a privilege superior to that of the high priest: they have «full freedom to enter into the sanctuary», without any time limit (10,19). There is therefore here an implicit affirmation of what is called «the common priesthood of the faithful».

Concerning sanctification, there is a difference in this sentence from the one in verse 10: the Greek verb in verse 10 was a perfect participle, expressing an already existing state: «we have been sanctified» and we are so from now on, while in verse 14 there is a present participle, which expresses a state which is being reached: «those who are being sanctified». It is not difficult to account for this; it corresponds to two different points of view, that of the work of Christ and that of Christian existence. The work of Christ is henceforth over; it was accomplished «once and for all» (10); from that point of view, our sanctification has already been achieved. But the application of this work to our existence is not over, it is still going on. Here we find the tension, common in the New Testament, between the «already» and the «not yet».

Unexpectedly, the author, to confirm what he has just said, ends this section (10,15-18) by calling on the testimony given by the Spirit in the oracle of the new covenant. From this oracle, he takes the two main promises again, the one about the laws written on hearts and the one about the forgiveness of sins. The relation between these two promises and the preceding context is not obvious at first sight, because they do not speak either of sanctification or of perfection as do verses 10 and 14. With the reference to «sins», they are, however, in verbal relation with the negative sentence in verse 4. But a little reflection is enough to show some closer relations. Sanctification actually presupposes or includes the forgiveness of sins and the perfection in question involves welcoming the laws of God into the heart. This perfection is, in fact, a sharing in the perfection of Christ and that consisted, according to 5,8, in learning «through his sufferings obedience». When the author tells us in 2,10 that God made Christ perfect through suffering, we can express the same idea by saying that through the passion God wrote his laws in a new way in the human heart of Christ and thus brought about the new covenant for our benefit.

The order of the sentences in the oracle does not correspond to the logical order of the actions, according to which the remission of sins must come first, so that in the purified hearts God can then write his laws. The author followed the order in the oracle and therefore ends by mentioning the remission of sins. He adds a final reflection which expresses a consequence of this remission for sacrificial worship: «Where there is remission, there is no more any offering for sin» (10,18). This consequence corresponds to the declaration in verse 9 which said that Christ «takes away the first worship» and it describes a situation in complete contrast with the former worship: instead of a multitude of expiatory sacrifices, always repeated, because always ineffective, there is a complete absence of expiatory sacrifice, because a unique, perfectly efficacious, sacrifice has been offered.

Thus ends the long exposé commenced at the beginning of ch. 7, an admirable synthesis of priestly Christology. From the literary point of view, one would have expected a far more ample conclusion. The brevity of the last verse and its negative aspect are surprising. But there are tell-tale signs there. They show that this last sentence is not the end of this part; the latter continues with an exhortation which is in close relation with the exposé. The author is not a professor of theology; his sermon is not a theological treatise; the author is a pastor, his work is apostolic preaching which closely unites faith and Christian life. Faith provides the basis, but on that basis Christians must build their lives. Being an excellent preacher, the author is therefore going to call upon them to do so, with great insistence.

Chapter 14

Exhortative conclusion (10,19-39)

Having expounded his doctrine on priesthood and the sacrifice of Christ, the preacher describes its consequences for the life of believers. This exhortative conclusion of the third part of the homily is parallel to his exhortative introduction (5,11-6,20). The relation is particularly close between their second paragraphs (6,4-8 and 10,26-31), which are severe warnings, and between their third paragraphs (6,9-12 and 10,32-35), which both contain praises.

.. COMPOSITION

This text divides clearly into four paragraphs. The first (19-25) describes the special situation of believers and the attitudes corresponding to it. The second (26-31) is a severe warning against obstinacy in sin. The third, on the contrary (32-35), is an encouraging reminder of the generosity of the early days after conversion. An inclusion on the word *parrēsia*, «assurance» (19.35), groups these three paragraphs together and shows that the fourth (10,36-39) has a particular status. In fact it contains the announcement of the two themes of the next part: «endurance» (36) and «faith» (38.39).

Situation of believers (10,19-25)

19 Having therefore, brethren,
full assurance for entry into the sanctuary
in the blood of Jesus,
20 the new and living way he inaugurated for us through the veil,
that is to say his flesh,
21 and a high priest [established] over the house of God
22 let us approach with a sincere heart in fullness of *faith*,
having hearts purified, by aspersion, of evil disposition of conscience[5]
and, having the body cleansed with pure water,
23 let us unflinchingly maintain the confession of *hope*,
for he is faithful, the one who promised,
24 and let us watch over each other with a view to an increase of *charity*
and of good deeds,
25 not deserting our own assembly,
as some usually do,
but encouraging each other
the more so because you see the day approaching.

This very long sentence has a very clear overall structure, although some details may cause hesitation. Governed by the participle «Having», the first part lists three privileges possessed by Christians; they have:

1 Literally: «having been sprinkled, as regards the hearts, from bad conscience».

1) right of entry into the sanctuary,
2) a way to get to it,
3) a priest to guide them.

The second part of the sentence is then marked out by three imperatives:

1) «let us approach in fullness of faith,
2) «let us maintain confession of hope,
3) let us look out for an increase of charity».

Hesitation is possible over the grammatical function of the word «way». In the Greek text, this part of the sentence begins with the relative proposition and the word «way» is fitted into it. Literally there is: «Having… that he inaugurated for us new and living way…». In which case, one can take it as: «Having… the new and living way which he inaugurated for us» or else: «Having… full confidence for entering the sanctuary *through* the new and living way…». The first construction seems more probable because of the co-ordination that follows: «and a high priest…».

Another possible hesitation concerns the participial phrases in verse 22: should both of them be attached to the previous imperative: «let us approach… having hearts sprinkled…and having the body cleansed…»? Or should the first participle be attached to the preceding imperative and the second to the following imperative? Many editions choose the first construction, because both phrases clearly refer to baptism, considered in view of its spiritual efficacy (22b) and its ritual aspect (22c). But the Greek sentence normally requires the second construction, because nothing in it suggests a definite break before the verb «let us maintain» (23a). It is therefore better to admit a construction in the form of a chiasm:

Let us approach		and, *having the body cleansed,*
	×	
having the hearts sprinkled		let us maintain… the hope

In this way, the relation is not solely between baptism and faith, but it is also between baptism and hope, and the union between these two theological virtues is thereby strengthened.

In verses 10 and 20 a complementary parallelism between «the blood of Jesus» and «his flesh» is noticeable. In Greek, there is also parallelism between «the entry» and «the way» (*eis-odos* and *hodos*).

Moreover, a relation of content exists between «the sanctuary» (19b), «the veil» (20) and «the house of God», since, in the three cases, it is about the temple, considered from various points of view.

The two first stichs of verse 22 present a synonymous parallelism: «the hearts purified through aspersion» (22b) correspond to the «sincere heart» (22a) and the elimination of the «bad conscience» (22b) makes the «fullness of faith» (22a) possible.

The next stichs (22c and 23ab) bring some complementary notations: «the body cleansed» (22c) completes «the sprinkled hearts» (22b) and «the pure water» (22c) contrasts with the «bad conscience» (22b). Again, the «firm confession of hope» (23a) is parallel to the «fullness of faith» (22a) and is in close relation with the faithfulness of «he who promised» (23b).

The parallelism is not so close in the case of the exhortation to «an increase of charity», because the thought moves from the relation with God to the reciprocal relation between Christians. Verse 25 places an attitude of desertion not to be adopted in antithesis to an attitude of mutual encouragement to be adopted. For each one, a note is added, which produces a parallel arrangement; the latter is imperfect, because the content of the two notes is not parallel; the scheme is ABA'C.

Warning against sin (10,26-31)

26 If voluntarily, indeed, we continue to sin,
after receiving the full knowledge of the truth,
no sacrifices for sins remain,
27 but a terrible wait for judgement
and the heat of a fire which is to devour the adversary.
28 If anyone has violated a law of Moses,
without pity, on [the deposition of] two or three witnesses, he dies.
29 How much worse, do you think, will be the punishment deserved
by him who has trodden the Son of God underfoot
and considered the blood of the covenant profanity,
in which he had been sanctified,
and outraged the Spirit of grace?
30 We know, indeed, the one who said:
Mine is the vengeance, I myself shall repay,
and again:
[The] Lord will judge his people.
31 [It is] TERRIBLE to fall into the hands of the living God.

After the introductory sentence (26), an inclusion on the word «terrible» marks the boundaries of what is said about the fate awaiting the sinner (27-31).

The beginning of the paragraph expresses an antithesis between sin committed «voluntarily» (26a) and «full knowledge of the truth» (26b) which ought to have made it impossible. Then comes an antithetic parallelism between the inexistence of a sacrifice for sins (26c) and the existence of a «terrible wait for judgement» (27a); a synonymous parallelism (27b) makes this prospect more frightful.

The next verses (28-29) present, in a structure in chiastic form, an argument *a fortiori (qalwahomer)*:

A violation of the law of Moses (28a)
    B death sentence (28b)
    B' worse punishment (29a) for the
A' fault of the Christian (29b-e).

A marked dissymmetry highlights the last element (A'), much longer than the three previous ones. It helps to show the extreme gravity of the fault of the Christian. A triple antithesis insists on this gravity; in the Greek text, the order of words is more expressive than in the translation: «the Son of God, trodden underfoot; the blood of the covenant, held as something profane; the Spirit of grace, outraged». The central antithesis is more developed than the two others —which is common in concentric structures— it contrasts, not only «the blood of the covenant» and «profane», but also «sanctified» and «profane», which makes the antithesis more explicit.

Verses 30 and 31 return with more insistence to the prospect of punishment, which had not been explained at length in 28a. At the beginning there is a threatening periphrasis that mentions «the one who said: Vengeance is mine» (30ab); to this corresponds a clear designation at the end: it is referring to the «living God» (31). In the centre, two citations from the Old Testament are placed in parallel (30bd). The final sentence resumes, as we have seen, the word «terrible» of 27a; it produces a powerful dissuasive effect.

Recalling the generosity of former times (10,32-35)

32 But remember the former days,
when, having been illuminated,
you *endured* a great struggle of suffering,
33 on the one hand, being publicly exposed to abuse and tribulation,
on the other, partners with those who were in this situation,
34 and you have indeed suffered along with the prisoners
and with joy accepted the confiscation of your possessions,
knowing that you possess something better and lasting.
35 Do not cast of your assurance,
which gains a great reward.

After the warning against sin comes the encouragement to positive generosity, presented as corresponding with past conduct. To the preceding reference to three aspects of sin (29b-e), an antithetic parallelism contrasts four manifestations of generosity. These are arranged as a chiasm, ABB'A'. At either end, the sufferings endured personally (33a and 34b); in the centre, two attitudes of solidarity with the harsh fate of other Christians (33b and 34a). B' and A' are more precise than A and B. The last element is augmented by a explanation (34c).

The initial sentence (32) and the final sentence (35) are the only ones to be explicitly exhortative. There is a progression from one to the other, because the initial sentence only calls upon the faithful to remember their past generosity, whereas the final sentence concerns their present attitude.

In 32b we have the allusion to the illumination at the beginning of the conversion, present in 6,4 (they are the only occurrences of the word in Heb), but the context is antithetic: a context of fall in 6,6, of generosity in 10,32-34. In 6,4-5 the preacher insists on the gifts received with the illumination, so as to get people to see the illogical and scandalous character of the fall. In 10,32 he does not mention any of these gifts, but soon shows the good results produced by the illumination in the conduct of Christians.

The word «assurance» (35), as we have said, makes an inclusion with the «assurance» at the beginning (19). We go from an affirmation («Having therefore... full assurance») to a warning («Do not cast away your assurance»). The verb «to endure» (32) prepares for the call for «endurance» (36).

Announcement of the subject: endurance and faith (10,36-39)

36 *Of endurance*, indeed, you have need,
so that having done the will of God,
you may obtain [the fulfilment of] the promise.
37 Yet a little more [time], in fact,
[and] the one who is coming will arrive and will not delay.
38 Now, my righteous one by faith shall live
and if he falters,
my soul takes no pleasure in him;
39 we, for our part, are not [people]
who fall away for their ruin
but of faith for the salvation of [our] soul.

The two first stichs place «endurance» (36a) and «doing the will of God» (36b) in synonymous parallelism. The two stichs of verse 37 are in complementary parallelism. Verse 38 expresses an antithesis between the «faith» (38a) and «defection» (38b), as well as between the positive «shall live» (38a) and the negative «my soul does not take pleasure in him» (38c), but there is a disproportion between this negative phrase of eleven syllables (in Greek) and the positive one, which has only three syllables. Verse 39 presents a very clear, but elliptical, antithetic parallelism, the subject pronoun and the verb not being repeated in the second member; there we find the antithesis in verse 38 between «faith» and «defection», but these words are arranged in reverse order, which produces a chiasm:

38		39
faith		*defection*
	×	
to commit defection		faith

The antithesis between «for [the] perdition» (39b) and «for [the] salvation of [the] soul» (39c) is added to this.

These verses, let us remember, announce the double subject of the Fourth part. As always, the exposé starts with the last subject announced: faith. This theme was placed in relation with the priesthood of Christ in 10,19-22. The theme of endurance was prepared for by the reminder of what was endured (32) in the past and is in relation with the hope that does not weaken (23). Further on it will be put in relation with the endurance of Christ in his Passion (12,2-3).

In 10,19-21, to describe the Christian situation, the author uses the image of the liturgy of Kippur, that is to say the entry of the high priest into the holy of holies (Lev 16), an image spoke about in 9,7.25 and applied to Christ in 9,11-12. In 10,20 he recalled this application to Christ by saying that Jesus «will inaugurate the way through the veil».

By grouping the three theological virtues together in 10,22.24, the author allies himself with the Pauline doctrine, already present in 1Thess 1,3 and 5,8, and repeated in a particularly clear way in 1Cor13,13 and again in Col 1,4-5.

The way of alluding to baptism in 10,22 conveys an allusion to the Sinai covenant, because the author says in it that Christians have been «sprinkled»; in 9,19 the author recalled that according to Exod 24,8, Moses «sprinkled» the people with the blood of sacrificed beasts, saying: This is the blood of the covenant... This allusion to the former covenant twins up with an allusion to what may be called the oracle of the new covenant according to Ezekiel, that is to say the oracle in which God promises to give a «new heart» and «a new Spirit» (Ezek 36,26). The author is actually using the expression «a pure water» which comes in this oracle—it is extremely rare in the Old Testament; it is united with the verb «to sprinkle», God says: «I will sprinkle a pure water over you and you shall be purified of all your impurities» (Ezek 36,25 LXX). This suggests that baptism is the sacrament that leads into the new covenant.

The allusion to the «day» in 10,25 («you see the day approaching») is in connection with the important prophetic tradition about the coming of the «Day of the Lord» (Joel 1,15; Isa 13,6; Ezek 7,3; 30,3). This will be a «Day of anger» (Zeph 1,15). There was already a «Day of anger», when Jerusalem was devasted (Lam 1,12; 2,1). Jesus predicted another day of anger for Jerusalem (Luke 21,20), the city will be besieged and captured; of the Temple «there will not remain a stone upon a stone» (Matt 24,2; Mark 13,2; Luke 21,6). That is the day that could be seen approaching about the years 66-68, at the time of the first uprisings in Palestine which caused the Jewish war, the capture of Jerusalem and the destruction of the Temple in the year 70.

In 10,27 the expression «the heat of a fire which is to devour the adversaries» is inspired by a threatening oracle in Isaiah: «A heat will overtake a stupid people and now a fire will devour the adversaries» (Isa 26,11 LXX).

On the subject of the violation of a law of Moses (10,28), the author recalls the prescription of Deut 17,6 which says literally in Greek: «On two witnesses or on three witnesses shall die he who dies; he shall not die on one witness». Num 35,30 likewise says that the testimony of one witness is not enough to make a death sentence possible. The author of Hebrews adopted a different perspective: it must rather be noted that the deposition of two or three witnesses is already enough for a death sentence, which therefore becomes very menacing.

Verse 30 cites two sentences from the great Canticle of Moses (Deut 32). The first: «Vengeance is mine; I myself will repay» is found again in this form in Rom 12,19; it corresponds to the Hebrew text of Deut 32,35 and not to that of the Septuagint, which says: «In the day of vengeance, I shall repay». The second sentence: «Lord will judge his people», is that of the Septuagint which, this time, faithfully translates the Hebrew (Deut 32,36). It is found again in Ps 134,14 LXX. The author interprets this sentence as a terrible menace; in its context it is rather a promise: God will deal justice to his people; but quoted in isolation, it does have a menacing tone 1Pet 4,17-18).

Verses 37-38 contain a composite quotation. The beginning takes up a very rare Greek expression (literally: «a little how much how much», that is to say «a little bit of time»); it is found in Isa 26,20 LXX: «Go, my people, [...] hide for a little bit of time, until the anger of Lord is over». The rest of the quotation is taken from an oracle in Habakkuk, which calls for waiting with endurance for the coming of the saviour and then says: «coming he will arrive and will not delay. If he falters, my soul does not take pleasure in him; but the just person will live by my fidelity» (Hab 2,3-4 LXX). The author introduced several changes into this text: instead of «coming, he will arrive» he has «the comer (that is to say: he who is coming) will arrive», thereby getting an expression designating the Messiah (see Matt 11,3; Luke 7,19.20). Next, he has reversed the order of the two last sentences, putting the one that speaks of defection in second place. He thus achieves a twofold result: on the one hand, he corrects an imperfection in the Greek text, in which the possible defection seems to be attributed to the saviour, the grammatical subject of the preceding verbs; on the other, he makes the theme of faith placed first stand out better. Another change concerns the possessive (in Greek, an enclitic pronoun: «of me» which refers to God); instead of coming after the word *pistis*, which gives this word the sense of «fidelity of God», it is placed after «the just person». It follows that the word *pistis* has the meaning of «faith», the faith of the human person. (in Rom1,17 and Gal 3,11, the apostle Paul obtains the same result by simply omitting the pronoun «of me»). The author has in this way skilfully introduced the subject of the next section.

Addressing his listeners, whom he calls «brethren», the author describes their situation, as it emerges from the priestly Christology he has just expounded, a really privileged situation because Jesus has shed his blood for them, he has inaugurated a way leading to the sanctuary for them and he himself acts as guide for them. These are just so many allusions to the content of the two previous sections.

Christ entered into the sanctuary «by his own blood» (9,12). United to Christ by faith and baptism (10,22), Christians have the *parrēsia* to enter into the sanctuary «in the blood of Jesus» (19). The Greek word *parrēsia* does not only express a sentiment of confidence, it expresses a recognized right; in Greek cities, it had to do with the right to take part in the deliberations of the assembly of the people and to speak freely in it. In the New Testament, it often also has to do with freedom of speech (Acts 4,13.29.31; 28,31), but in Eph 3,12 it deals, as here, with free access to God. «The sanctuary», in fact, is obviously the divine sanctuary, and not «a sanctuary made by hands» (9,24). Christians therefore enjoy a privilege doubly superior to that of the former high priest: they have free access to the true sanctuary and this right is not limited to «once a year» (9,7), it is always valid, because they have been sanctified in the blood of Jesus (10,29), which is really «the blood of the covenant» (10,29), since it abolished all separations, not only the one that existed between the high priest and God, but also the one that separated the people from the high priest. The priestly «perfection» that Jesus acquired by his sufferings is communicated by him to «those who receive sanctification» (10,14).

Right of access is not enough; a way is also needed. Christians have «a new and living way», inaugurated for them by Jesus. The specifications given show that the author is speaking of the way to the true sanctuary that «had not yet been manifested» (9,8) for as long as the tent was in place. The latter, in theory, should have been the way to the sanctuary, but in reality it was not, because it gave access only to a «second tent», it, too, made by humans, and therefore not God's true dwelling. It is therefore understood that «the new way» is another name for «the greater and more perfect tent» (9,11), through which Christ «entered into the sanctuary» (9,12), and which, as we have seen, is his glorified human nature. The other qualifying phrase given to the way —it is «living»— confirms this interpretation, for the risen Christ is «the living one» *par excellence* (Luke 24,5), «death no longer has power over him» (Rom 6,9); he has become «living stone» (1Pet 2,4); he is «for ever living to intercede» (Heb 7,25); he is therefore at once the way and the «great high priest [established] over the house of God» (10,21). The author here uses the same expression as in the passage where he states that Christ is «trustworthy high priest» (3,1-2.6). The mention of Christ as «high priest» felicitously completes the designation given him earlier, because «way» is an impersonal appellation, whereas «priest» clearly designates a person.

Christians therefore have right of entry, a way and, to guide and present them to God, a person. Nothing is lacking to them. In consequence, they are called upon «to approach», which in the Old Testament was forbidden under penalty of death (see Num 3,10.38; Lev 16,2). The preacher says to them: «Let us approach», as he said already in 4,16, having presented Christ as «high priest, who is not unable to sympathize with our weaknesses». According to 7,25, it is God that Christians approach. In the context, the invitation to approach directly concerns a spiritual attitude, but it is permissible to think that at the same time it concerns Christian liturgy and, more precisely, eucharistic liturgy, in the course of which the preacher was addressing the Christian community. He tells it, in fact, that it has at its disposal the flesh and blood of Jesus, and his priestly presence. Where else is that verified other than in the eucharistic celebration?

The author then specifies the dispositions one must have when one «approaches». He is not delivering a moral exhortation, but a theological one to faith, hope and charity, because the theological virtues are directly connected with the relation to God, which the moral virtues are not. According to Rom 10,9-10 it is with the heart that one believes; the author therefore calls upon Christians to approach «with a sincere heart in fullness of faith» (10,22). But how can Christians have «a sincere heart», when humans, even the members of the chosen people, «always stray in heart» (Ps 94,10 LXX, quoted in Heb 3,10)? The explanation is given immediately by a double allusion to baptism which Christians have received. Two Greek participles, in the perfect passive, which expresses an actual situation, remind Christians that they have been «sprinkled» and «cleansed». Unexpectedly, the author says that the sprinkling reached their hearts. It freed them from any «bad disposition of conscience» (literally: «of bad conscience»). In sealing the faith, baptism also laid the foundations of hope, which must not weaken when trial comes along, but count on the fidelity of God to his promises. Faith, moreover, «operates through charity» (Gal 5,6). The author therefore calls «for an increase (literally: for a paroxysm) of charity»

(10,24), practised on a community basis thanks to mutual stimulation; charity must not be a sterile sentiment, but express itself, on the contrary, in «good deeds». On this matter, the author warns against any lack of community spirit which was manifesting itself in «certain people» and was driving them to «desert the Christian assembly». This probably met every Sunday, «first day of the week [...] for the breaking of bread» (Acts 20,7), that is to say for the celebration of the Eucharist. To give his exhortation more persuasive force, the author mentions at the end the approach of the «Day», which could then be observed. Christians could see that the day of the Lord was approaching. It is possible to give this affirmation a weak interpretation, in the sense of Rom 13,12: «The night is far on, the day has come near». But here, the text is more urgent and makes a strong interpretation more probable: the author wants to tell Christians that events are showing them that the day of the destruction of Jerusalem and of its Temple predicted by Jesus is approaching. That would place the composition of the homily in the years 66-68, just before the beginning of the Jewish War or even at its beginning. It should be admitted, however, that this is only a hypothesis based on a weak clue[2].

The paragraph that ends thus is of very great importance, because it establishes a close connection between the exhortations of the homily and its priestly Christology. The exhortation to faith, hope and charity resumes all the preceding exhortations and announces all the rest of the homily. On faith, we have earlier had the long warning against lack of faith in 3,7-4,14. On hope, we have had the call to trust in 4,15-16, the exhortation to walk with zeal «towards the fullness of hope» in 6,11 and the definition of hope as an «anchor of the soul», which enters heaven, where Jesus has preceded us (6,18-20). On charity, there is the sentence in 6,10, which names it and shows its two dimensions: love of God and love of neighbour, demonstrated in service.

Then all the rest of the homily is announced by reference to the three theological virtues. The first section of the part will actually be a long eulogy of the faith of the ancestors (11,1-40); the second section (12,1-13) will be an exhortation to «endurance» (in Greek *hypomonē*), closely bound to hope: 1Thess 1,3

2 Other, more consistent, clues tend to date the homily before the destruction of the Temple, but they do not indicate whether it is a short time before, or a long time before. The sentence in 10,11, for example, which, speaking of the worship celebrated in the Temple, says that «every priest stands, every day occupied by the liturgy», can hardly have been written in those terms, when the Temple was destroyed and the sacrificial liturgy could therefore no longer be celebrated. See also 10,2 and 13,10-11.

speaks of «the endurance of hope» and Rom 15,4 says that «through endurance we have hope». Lastly, the one section of the last part (12,14-13,18) will be an exhortation to live in the two dimensions of charity: on the one hand «peace with all» (12,14) «fraternal love» (13,1) and, on the other, union with God by reason of the «sanctification» (12,14). Thanks to paragraph 10,19-25, all the rest of the epistle is in relation to priestly Christology.

Having opened a fearsome prospect in 25, the author continues with an extremely severe warning (10,26-31), like the one in 6,4-8. Here, as there, the interpretation takes carefully into account the literary genre of the passage and actually sees that it is not a matter of a sentence passed upon the guilty, nor of a doctrinal definition, but of an oratorical development intended to have a strong dissuasive effect against any very grave failings. The case is hypothetical; the preacher includes himself in it by speaking in the first person plural: «If… we sin…». This shows that the case really is quite hypothetical.

The case envisaged is not one of sins committed in the past and still less one of repentant sinners, but of obstinacy always present in fully voluntary sin, sin made unpardonable because it is committed «after receiving [not only knowledge (*gnōsis*), but] the full knowledge (*epignōsis*) of the truth», that is to say of Christian revelation. Verse 29 gives other particulars which show that the sin in question is complete apostasy, or is equivalent to complete apostasy from the Christian faith. The sinner has, in particular, «held the blood of the covenant to be profane», he has rejected the blood of the sacrifice of Christ. It is obvious, then, that for him «there no longer remains, for sins, any sacrifice» (26). The author has said that Christ abolished the sacrificial worship of the former covenant (10) and that henceforth «there will be no more offering for sin» (18), the only still effective sacrifice being that of Christ (see 9,14). The obstinate sinner has got himself into a situation from which there is no escape.

For the hypothetical obstinate sinners, there is therefore nothing else than a «terrible waiting for judgement», for God «will pay back everyone according to their work» (Prov 4,24; Matt 16,27; Rom 2,6) and for obstinate sinners, «adversaries» of God, the punishment will be to go «into eternal fire» (Matt 25,41); the author makes the threat more impressive by drawing, as we have seen, on a text from Isaiah (Isa 26,11).

Then, pursuing his plan, the preacher asks a rhetorical question, calling upon his listeners to imagine for themselves the punishments deserved by the sinner. An *a fortiori* piece of reasoning suggests a fearsome answer to them: in the case of a violation of a law of Moses, in fact, it was the death penalty that was readily inflicted on the culprit; for that it was enough, according to Deut 17,6, that two or three witnesses be there to accuse him. Now, the sin of the Christian is much more serious than an infraction of the law, because it is equivalent to «trampling on the Son of God», which means inflicting the most contemptuous treatment on the person most worthy of honour, a divine person. Furthermore, the sinner has shown the most complete contempt for the blood of Christ, «blood of the covenant»; he has «considered profane» this source of his own sanctification. Lastly, «he has done violence to the Spirit of grace». It is not possible to go further in giving offence and contempt. The listeners can therefore only give an answer full of fear. Worse than the condemnation to death inflicted by the law of Moses, punishment will be terrible.

The preacher was careful not to state the concrete nature of the sin he has stigmatized. The dissuasive effect is thereby reinforced. The listeners may think that any serious fault is an act of contempt for the Son of God and for his blood shed for them and for the Spirit of love.

The preacher concludes by calling on the anger of God, but first without naming God explicitly. He uses a periphrasis, much more impressive than the simple name of God: «We know the One who said: Vengeance is mine» (30). Then comes the title «Lord» used without the article as a proper name in place of YHWH: «Lord will judge his people» and in last place, the expression «living God», prepared for by some threatening words: «[It is] terrible to fall into the hands of the living God». (31). Thus ends this short paragraph, a masterpiece of oratory in motion.

The preacher gets his breath back and then expresses himself in a completely different tone, a tone of praise (10,32-34). Such changes of tone manifest great rhetorical ability. They would not be normal in a letter.

The preacher calls upon his listeners to recall their generosity in earlier times, when they received their «illumination», that is to say when they accepted faith in Christ, «light of the world» (John 8,12; 9,5; see Heb 6,4). Like the first Christian communities, in Jerusalem (Acts 8,2), Antioch in Pisidia (Acts 13,50), Philippi (Acts 16,22-24; 1Thess 2,2), Thessalonica (1Thess 2,14), the listeners' communities faced persecution, a frequent fate of the first Christians; Jesus had predicted it (see Matt 10,17-24 and parallels; John 15,20). Paul also predicted it (Acts 14,22; 1Thess 3,4). The author in this case does not use the verb «to persecute» or the noun «persecution»; he speaks of «great struggle of sufferings» (32), a combination of themes also found in 2Tim 2,3-5. By saying that Christians have «endured» this struggle, the author is getting ready the announcement of the subject which is coming some verses further on about «endurance» that has again become necessary (36).

The sufferings mentioned have had two aspects, a personal aspect and an aspect of solidarity with others, both expressed twice, in a chiastic arrangement ABB'A'. «Exposed as a spectacle» (33a), Christians have publicly suffered «abuse and tribulation» (A). When recalling the 8th Beatitude (Matt 5,10-12), the apostle Peter would have told them: «If you *suffer abuse* for the name of Christ, happy are you, for the Spirit of God rests on you» (1Pet 4,14). As regards tribulation, Paul and Barnabas tell the disciples: «We must pass through many *tribulations* to enter into the Kingdom of God» (Acts 14,22). At the other end of the chiasm (A') Christians are reminded of «the confiscation of their goods» (34b). In between, the author has a double reference (BB') to the solidarity of Christians with their persecuted brethren (33b) and to their compassion for prisoners (34a). On the question of the confiscation of goods the author stresses the great generosity of Christians, saying that they accepted this cruel privation «with joy» (34b); he adds that this joy was founded on a conviction of faith, that of «possessing property of greater value» than material goods, that is to say spiritual richness, the possession of which is not provisory, like those goods, which one must finally abandon completely when one dies; it is, on the contrary, permanent even after death (34c).

The paragraph then ends with an exhortative conclusion («therefore») (35). To be consistent with their past generosity and with their conviction of faith, Christians avoid «rejecting their confidence (*parrēsia*)»; on the contrary, they must keep it firm, since it gains them «a great reward» (35). The author does not say that it will gain it for them; he does not use the future, but the present. This "great reward» has already been acquired. This statement corresponds to the proclamation by Jesus of the 1st and 8th beatitudes: «Blessed are the poor in Spirit [...] blessed the persecuted for justice, [...] because the kingdom of heaven *is theirs*» (Matt 5,3.10). Similarly, the author said earlier on that believers are now entering into «God's rest» (Heb 4,3) and in 6,4-5 he listed the gifts they have already received, the heavenly gift, the sharing of Holy Spirit, the beautiful word of God, the powers of the world to come». Believers are in a privileged position (10,19-21). It would be absurd to give it up.

The tone of the last paragraph (36-39) is no longer explicitly exhortative, but it is implicitly, because to say: «Of endurance you have need» (36) is a nicer way of saying: «Show you are patient, you must do so», and to say: «We are not people who fall away... but people who have faith...» (39) is a way of warning against any falling away and of exhorting people to be firm in faith.

The author thus announces the two themes of the next part. Coming at the start of the sentence, the word «endurance» attracts attention. It will come again in 12,1 and be accompanied three times by the verb «to endure» (12,2.3.7). The word «faith» is then repeated (38.39) and is highlighted by means of an antithesis with «defection».

To go from one theme to the next, the author uses a passage from Habaquq (2,3-4 LXX) which unites them effectively, but he cuts off the passage of the sentence that contains the verb «to endure», because that sentence causes a lack of coherence in the text; it says: «*If he is late*, wait for him with endurance; he who is coming will arrive and *will not be late*»; presented as possible at the beginning, delay is denied at the end. The author avoids this incoherence, more especially because he has himself denied at the start the possibility of any delay by introducing the text from Habaquq with the expression: «just a little more time yet».

Endurance is placed in relation, on the one hand, with the accomplishment of the will of God and, on the other, with the fulfilment of the promise. The perspective is thus doubly completed. For Christians, endurance does not consist simply, as in the text in Isa 26,20, in hiding until the anger has passed over, it consists, as in the case of Christ, who offered himself to do the will of God (10,7.9), in doing that will in spite of the difficulties. That is also the outlook of the letter of James, when it says: «let endurance be accompanied by a perfect work» (Jas 1,4) or the letter of Peter which summons «those who suffer» to continue «to do good» (1Pet 4,19).

Moreover, endurance is upheld by the hope of the fulfilment of «the promise» and itself strengthens that hope, because Jesus said: «Whoever endures to the end will be saved» (Matt 10,22) and the apostle Paul: «If what we do not see we hope for, with endurance we wait for it» (Rom 8,25); «If we endure, we shall also reign» (2Tim 2,12).

Verbally, defection (*hypo-stolē*) is the opposite of endurance (*hypo-monē*), but the Habaquq text the author is quoting motivates him to contrast defection more with faith, which is quite possible conceptually, and even verbally, if one defines faith *hypo-stasis* as the author does immediately (11,1). Defection leads to «perdition», faith to the «salvation of the soul», as the author clearly showed in his long warning against lack of faith (3,7-4,11). No one defecting can enter into God's rest; only those enter, following Christ, who have faith, for he alone is the «cause of eternal salvation» (5,9), he alone ensures the «salvation of the soul».

Part Four

Union with Christ the high priest through faith and endurance (11,1-12,13)

Chapter 15

The faith of the elders (11,1-40)

Announced in the last sentences of the final exhortation of the third part (10,38-39), the theme of faith is taken up immediately at the beginning of Part Four (11,1), while the theme of endurance, announced first (10,36), is only developed later (12,1-13). Being normal in Hebrew, this inverse arrangement offers the advantage of facilitating the transition. The word «faith» serves as a link-word between the end of the exhortation (10,39) and the beginning of the new exposé (11,1).

After a definition of faith, the theme is stated: the preacher is not speaking of the faith of Christians, but of the faith of the «elders» (11,2). By «elders» he does not mean only the ancestors of the Israelites, but he goes back to Abel (4) and even to the creation of the world (3).

COMPOSITION

This section has a pronounced unity through the constant repetition of the word «faith». After the initial definition of faith, this word comes back at the head of 18 sentences in the form of the dative *pistei*, which translates as: «through faith». In addition to this there are some other uses: «without faith» (6), «according to faith» (7.13), «by means of faith» (33.39):

The section is divided into four long paragraphs:

1) definition of faith and first examples: 1-7
2) the faith of Abraham and the patriarchs: 8-22
3) the faith of Moses: 24-31
4) overall picture of the next periods: 32-40.

A general inclusion marks the limits of the section by means of the words «faith» (1 and 39) and «to receive testimony» (2 and 39). Although the word «faith» characterizes all the section, the general inclusion is still perceptible, for, in 11,39, the word «faith» returns after a long absence, from 33 to 39, a unique case in that section.

The word «faith» also serves as a partial inclusion (1-7), because it comes at the end of verse 7, while its position before that is always initial; besides, it is introduced by the preposition «according to», which is not used in the other occurrences, except in verse 13. The inclusion is reinforced by a double allusion to the things «that are not seen».

The paragraph on the faith of Abraham (8-22) does not have any very clear inclusion. There is noticeable only a correspondence between Abraham's departure, who had «to go away», literally «go out», a verb used twice (8), and the «departure» from Egypt, mentioned in verse 22.

In the third paragraph (23-31), the verses concerning Moses are enclosed within a very insistent inclusion. At the beginning, the parents of Moses «saw» that their child was beautiful and «they did not fear the king's edict» (23); at the end, Moses did not «fear the king's rage», for he «saw» the one who is invisible (27). This inclusion is arranged as a chiasm, AB-BA, which makes it more perfect, the last element corresponding to the first.

The fourth and last paragraph (32-40) is marked out with the help of the expression «by means of faith», used in verses 33 and 39 and never before or after. In Greek, the expression that comes back very often in this section and is translated «through faith» is different; it has no preposition and consists simply of an instrumental dative, *pistei*. This dative is completely absent from the last paragraph, which makes the inclusion more easily perceptible.

1

Definition of faith and early examples (1-7)

1 FAITH is a way of possessing what is hoped for,
  a way of knowing realities which ARE NOT SEEN;
2 in it, indeed, the elders *received testimony* (v. 39).
3 By faith, we understand
  that the worlds were put in place
  by a word of God,
  so that it is not from visible things
    that visible things took their origin.
4 By faith, Abel offered a more valuable sacrifice than Cain,
he thereby received testimony that he was just,
God himself bearing witness over his gifts,
and by faith, after his death he still speaks.
5 By faith, Enoch was transferred in order not to see death
and he was not found, because God had transferred him;
before the transference, in fact, he received testimony
    that he had been acceptable to God;
6 now, without faith, it is impossible to be acceptable,
for he who approaches God must believe that he exists
  and that, for those who seek him, he becomes a rewarder.

7 By faith, Noah, warned of things that WERE NOT SEEN yet
taking care, built an ark for the salvation of his house;
with it, he condemned the world
and of righteousness according to FAITH he became heir.

COMPOSITION

In the definition of faith (1), we notice a complementary parallelism between «a way of possessing what is hoped for» and «a means of knowing what is not seen». The apostle Paul remarks that «we hope for what we do not see» (Rom 8,25).

After its beginning, verse 3 is built in parallelism. This parallelism is in part synonymous and in part antithetic; the arrangement is concentric. In the centre, there is the antithesis between a «word of God» and «not of things visible»; at the ends, in Greek there are the two verbs «were put in place» and «took their origin», which correspond as do «the worlds» and «what is visible». The consecutive clause (3cd) contains an antithesis between «not of visible things» and «that are visible».

The passage about Abel (4), in the middle contains a very clear parallelism between two affirmations on the testimony given to Abel. The first affirmation gives the content of the testimony: it testifies that Abel «is just»; the second indicates the author of the testimony, «God himself», and its basis, «the gifts» offered by Abel.

The sentences concerning Enoch (5-6) are linked to each other by link-words: «Enoch was transferred… God had transferred him… before the transference…»; «he had been acceptable to God… to be acceptable…»; «without faith (*pistis*)… he must believe (*pisteuein*)…».

The first two sentences (5ab) are parallel and in chiastic order: to the beginning of the first: «Enoch was transferred», corresponds the end of the second; «God had transferred him»; to the negative ending of the first: «in order not to see death», corresponds the negative beginning of the second: «he was not found».

What follows has some elements of parallelism, but is especially drawn up in a logical way: «before the transference, *in fact*», «*now*, without faith, …», «*for* he who…».

The final passage, on Noah (7), contains the end of the double inclusion with the beginning (1), in chiastic order: literally «the things not yet seen» (7a) are related to the «realities not seen» (1b); the word «faith (1) is present at the end of the passage (7d) in addition to its use at the beginning (7a), which makes it different from the other passages in which it is present only at the beginning (1a.3a.4a.5a.6a):

The passage itself has elements arranged in complementary parallelism and others in antithetic parallelism. The parallelism is complementary between «warned» (7a), in Greek *chrēmatisthēis*, and «taking care» (7b), in Greek *eulabētheis*. It is antithetic between the «salvation of his house» (7b) and «he condemned the world» (7c), then again between this expression and «righteousness according to faith» (7d).

B. BIBLICAL CONTEXT

The definition of faith from its effects (1) is original. It has no precedent in the Old Testament. Its first part, however, corresponds to the Old Testament outlook, which closely links faith and hope. Isaiah, for example, proclaims: «If you do not believe, you will not stand at all» (Isa 7,9) and: «Whoever believes will not stumble» (Isa 28,16). The other part of the definition, which presents faith as a means of knowing, sees it rather from a Greek perspective.

That, in faith, «the elders received testimony», that is to say praise from God (2), is an opinion of the author which has no explicit foundation in the Old Testament, except in the case of Abraham (Gen 15,6), but it corresponds to the religious outlook of the Old Testament.

In verse 3, the author expresses in a personal way the faith of the Old Testament in the creation of the world. Instead of saying «to create» (Gen 1,1 in Hebrew) or «to make» (Gen 1,1 in Greek), he uses the verb «to put in place», «to put in order», and instead of speaking of heaven and earth, he speaks of «worlds», literally «aeons».But his statement corresponds substantially to the story of creation as it is summarized in Psalm 33(32),6: «*By his word* the heavens were made», or, still better, by the prayer to obtain wisdom, which addresses God, saying: «You who, *by your word*, made the universe» (Wis 9,1). The story of creation declares, in fact, that «God said: … and that was» (Gen 1,3.6.9.11.14-15.20.24).

The expression «not from things seen» is related to the expression «not of existing things» in 2Macc 7,28, where the mother of the 7 persecuted brothers says to one of her sons that «it is not from existing things» that God made heaven and earth. The author of the letter to the Hebrews could not use that expression, because his sentence would then have expressed an equivalence between «word of God» and «not existing things»!

On Abel (4), the author freely interprets the Genesis account (Gen 4,1-11). The latter does not speak of the faith of Abel and does not say that Abel was declared just; it says simply that «the Lord accepted Abel and his offering, but did not accept Cain and his offering» (Gen 4,4-5). Besides, in the Genesis account, it is not Abel who speaks after his death, it is his blood which, from the ground, cries to God (Gen 4,10). In this statement, the author sees a kind of prefiguration of the resurrection of Christ.

On Enoch (5-6), the author follows what Genesis says: «Enoch walked with God, then he disappeared, for God took him away» (Gen 5,24). Instead of speaking of taking away, with the Hebrew text, the author speaks of transference, with the Septuagint. The latter does not say that Enoch «walked with God», but that he «was acceptable to God» (Gen 5,22.24). The author follows it on this point also and adds a reflection to justify the attribution, which he made, of faith to Enoch: «without faith, it is impossible to be acceptable [to God]».

That «for those who seek him [God] makes himself rewarder» (6c) is a statement that corresponds to a frequent teaching in the Old Testament, which promises the faithful the divine blessings (see Lev 26,3-13; Deut 28,1-14). Psalm 33(34) declares: «Whoever seeks the Lord lacks nothing» (Ps 34,11).

The passage on Noah (7) resumes the long biblical story concerning the flood (Gen 6-8) in a few words. This story does not speak explicitly of the faith of Noah, but only of his perfect docility to God: «All that God had commanded him, he did» (Gen 6,22; 7,5). This docility obviously presupposes faith in the truth of God's words. The author adds his interpretation of the event, saying that, by faith, Noah «condemned the world and became heir of righteousness according to faith» (7cd). The story says only, right at the beginning, that «Noah was a just man» (Gen 6,9). Sirach stresses that «Noah was found perfect and just» (Sir 44,17). «Righteousness according to faith» recalls the doctrine of Paul; the expression, however, is not Pauline; Paul uses other prepositions. He speaks of the righteousness that comes «*through* faith» (Rom 3,22), or which comes «*from* faith» (Rom 9,30; 10,6), or which is based «*on* faith» (Phil 3,9); he also uses the simple genitive, «the righteousness of faith» (Rom 4,11.13).

c. *INTERPRETATION*

Being a splendid fresco of everything faith achieved in the world, before the coming of Christ, this section gives a very positive idea of the Old Testament and thus corrects the negative impression that the parallel section (3,7-4,11) might give. It had recalled «the lack of faith» (3,12.19) and «the indocility» (4,6.11) of the Exodus generation and had warned against those attitudes. A multitude of encouraging examples is now offered to the listeners of the sermon.

The preacher gives a definition of faith that does not make the essential point (faith is before all a relation between persons); he contents himself with defining faith by its effects. The terms he uses are open to several interpretations. The first, *hypostasis*, can mean «substance», it has that meaning in the exordium (1,3); it can also mean «position» (3,14), but, in the papyri it often has the sense of «guarantee» or «title deed» and it is this sense that fits here because of the complement that relates this term with «things hoped for». By faith, we already possess, in a way, what God has promised and what in consequence we hope for. The second term, *elenchos*, does not have the sense of «inward conviction» that some exegetes give it here. It means «proof», «means of knowing». The preacher expresses two aspects of the effects of faith; the first, more dynamic corresponds more to the biblical mentality; the second, speculative, corresponds to the Greek mentality, hungry for knowledge. The examples given refer, sometimes to one, sometimes to the other.

The first example is of a speculative order: «by faith we understand» (3). It concerns faith in creation, faith which relies on the revelation contained in the first chapter of Genesis.

The second example is, on the contrary, a real-life one (4). It recalls the action that faith gave rise to on the part of Abel. It impelled him to offer God a more generous sacrifice that that of Cain. The sacrifice of Abel is, in the Bible, the first prefiguration of the sacrifice of Christ, the full importance of which the preacher has stressed in the previous chapters. Unlike Christ, Abel did not rise from the dead, but the preacher was nevertheless skilful enough to find a kind of prefiguration of the resurrection of Christ in the story of Abel: after the death of Abel, the blood of Abel, poured out on the ground, «cried out» to God (Gen 4,11) and thus continued to manifest the faith of Abel. It can therefore be said: «by means of faith, Abel, after his death, still speaks». The relation between the blood of Christ and that of Abel, while being implicit here, will be made explicit further on when the preacher speaks of «Jesus, mediator of a new covenant» and a «blood of sprinkling that speaks louder than Abel» (12,24).

The mysterious episode of the «transference» of Enoch (5-6) can be related to the ascension of Christ, the conqueror of death. «By faith» it was granted to some characters in the Old Testament to live out in anticipation one or other aspect of the mystery of Christ. Their faith was necessarily still at an elementary stage. The preacher does not ascribe an explicit faith in Christ to them, but faith in the existence of God and in his generous attitude towards «those who seek him».

The faith of Noah (7) for him was, in the first place, «a means of knowing realities» «not yet seen», but it did not remain inactive contemplation. Noah thereore began to act. His activity took on the appearance of church fecundity: «he built an ark for the salvation of his house». Besides, it showed, in contrast, the culpability of the world, inattentive to the divine warnings, and showed posiively that faith gives the believer justice as an inheritance.

This set of three examples is not without significance. In them one can actually see the three phases of priestly mediation. The sacrifice of Abel corresponds o the upward phase of the mediation. The transference of Enoch is related to he central phase, the one of being admitted into the presence of God. Lastly, the story of Noah corresponds to the downward phase, the one of graces received for the «house», the «salvation» phase.

Although it seems non-existent here, the principal theme of the sermon, the theme of priesthood, appears in filigree form.

2

The faith of Abraham and of the patriarchs (8-22)

8 By faith, Abraham, being called, obeyed and SET OUT
    for a place he was to receive as inheritance
and he set out not knowing where he was going to arrive.
9 By faith he went to dwell in the land of the promise
    as [in a land] foreign
living in tents
    with Isaac and Jacob, co-heirs of the same promise.
10 He was in fact waiting for the city that has its foundations,
    of which the architect and builder is God.

11 By faith, Sara, too, received power for the foundation of a progeny,
    and [that], outside the suitable span of age,
    because she deemed the one who had made the promise trustworthy.
12 That is why from one were born —and it was from a cankered person—
    like the stars of the sky in number
    and like the sand on the seashore, innumerable.
13 In conformity with faith all those people died
    without receiving the promises,
    but having seen and greeted them from afar
    and having recognized they were foreigners and immigrants on the earth.
14 Those indeed who tell of these things
    show that they seek a homeland
15 and if they were thinking of the one they had left,
    they would have had time to go back to it;
16 but in fact, they are aspiring to a better one,
    a heavenly one, that is to say.
That is why God does not blush to be called their God;
    he is actually preparing a city for them.

17 By faith, Abraham offered Isaac, being put to the test,
and he offered his only son, he who had received the promises
18 and to whom it had been said: in Isaac a progeny will be named for you,
19 having thought that even from the dead God is capable of raising,
whence it comes that he obtained him in prefiguration.
20 By faith also, in connection with things to come, Isaac blessed Jacob and Esau.
21 By faith, the dying Jacob blessed each of the sons of Joseph
and he bowed down over the top of his staff.
22 By faith, Joseph at life's end spoke of the DEPARTURE of the sons of Israel
and gave orders concerning his bones.

A. *COMPOSITION*

With Abraham's departure (*ex-ēlthen*) from his country (8) the departure (*exodos*) of the Israelites from Egypt (22) forms an inclusion.

This long paragraph is constructed in concentric symmetry around a long central subdivision (13-16), which offers general reflections on «all those people» —that is to say on all the patriarchs— whereas before and after, particular cases are considered. From the point of view of logic, these general reflections would be better placed at the end; the reader is surprised to be taken back then to Abraham, but he or she must realize that Semitic rhetoric prefers to place in the middle whatever clarifies the whole subject.

There is in succession:

a) Abraham's departure for the land of the promise (8-10)
  b) the foundation of an innumerable progeny (11-12)
A) the aspiration of all for a heavenly homeland (13-16)
  b') Abraham sacrifices Isaac, his offspring (17-19)
a') transmission of the blessing and foretelling the departure from Egypt (20-22).

The central subdivision (A) is in closer relation with the initial subdivision (a). Their theme is the «place» (8) where the people have to go, «the land of the promise» (9), the final «homeland» (14-16), the «city» prepared by God (10.16). This theme is not explicit in the subdivision (a'), but it underlies the mention of «things to come» (20), in the mention of the «departure» for the land of the promise and in the one about the «bones» (22) of Joseph, which had to be taken back to it (see Gen 50,24-25).

The final subdivision (a') is in relation to the initial subdivision (a) with the mention of the names Isaac and Jacob and the theme of the «departure», for, implicitly, the same land.

The theme ensuring the unity of the whole is that of the promises of God. Already there implicitly, from the first sentence, with the mention of an «inheritance» to be received (8), this theme is made explicit on two occasions in verse 9 and reappears in the subdivisions b (11) and A (13). It is then relayed, in the final subdivision, by the theme of the blessing (20.21). The blessing given by the father to his son actually ensures the transmission of the divine promises.

The details of style do not call for any important remarks. A complementary parallelism can be seen in the first sentence (8). After saying that Abraham obeyed the order to «set out towards a place he was to receive as inheritance», the author repeats the verb «to set out» to make it clear that he «set out not knowing where he was going to arrive».

In verse 12, the author quotes the synonymous parallelism in Gen 22,17, but he accentuates it by adding, at the end of each member, a reference to quantity:

like the stars of the sky *as regards quantity*
and like the sands of the seashore, *innumerable.*

A complementary parallelism can be noticed in verse 17 where the verb «to offer» is repeated. The first stich names «Isaac» and speaks of the test undergone by Abraham. The second stich shows the generosity of Abraham by saying that he «offered *the only son*» and hints at the strength of his faith, because the test seemed to contradict «the promises». These are then recalled; this addition unbalances the parallelism of the two stichs; the style becomes prosaic again.

BIBLICAL CONTEXT AND INTERPRETATION

The Book of Genesis declares once that «Abram believed in the Lord, who reckoned it to him as righteousness» (Gen 15,6). Saint Paul often quotes this sentence (Gal 3,6; Rom 4,3.9), on which he bases his doctrine of justification by faith. The latter produces obedience to God's call and starts Abraham off. God commands Abraham to «set out» (Gen 12,1 LXX) from his country, his family and from his father's house to go towards the land that would be shown him. «Abraham set out as the Lord had told him to» (Gen 12,4). That really is an attitude of true faith which entrusts itself to God without requiring any details from him concerning his plans, or any guarantees. On reaching the land of Canaan, Abraham learns that that is «the land of the promise» (see Gen 12,7), but that it is not to him, but to his progeny that it is promised (Gen 12,7; 15,18). For dozens of years, Abraham moves around this land like a nomad and likewise his son Isaac and his grandson Jacob, «co-heirs of the same promise» according to Gen 26,3-4 and 28,13. The preacher explains that this situation of uncertain waiting deepened the patriarch's desire, bringing him to an ideal fulfilment, that of a city built by God himself and which would therefore bring about a perfect relation with God.

This theme is taken up and developed in the central subdivision (13-16), which generalizes it. The preacher argues from what Abraham says when he introduces himself to the inhabitants of Canaan «as an *émigré* and a guest» (Gen 23,4), a statement amplified by king David in a prayer addressed to God: «We are foreigners in your sight, guests like all our fathers» (1Chr 29,15). In Psalm 38(39), the psalmist likewise extends the same description to all his fathers (Ps 38,13).

By adding «on the earth» after «foreigners and immigrants», the preacher plays cleverly on the words. In the story of the patriarchs, it is about the land of Canaan. In the preacher's thought, this reference to «the land» prepares for, by antithesis, the idea of a heavenly homeland. A long discussion excludes any aspiration after an earthly homeland. One must grant the preacher the fact that the account in Genesis reveals, in the life of the patriarchs, the capital importance of their relation with God. It is therefore normal to ascribe to them an aspiration to a situation where this relation can flourish perfectly.

In the second subdivision (11-12), the expression used about Sara is surprising, because meaning literally «received power for spurt of seed (*sperma*)», it would normally apply to a man. It has therefore been thought that the text was corrupt and that it should read: «Sara being sterile, Abraham none the less received strength…». This solution is not obvious, because the text may mean «received strength for the foundation of a progeny». Another surprising feature of the text is that the author does not hesitate to ascribe an attitude of faith to Sara, whereas the account in Genesis ascribes a sceptical laugh to her (Gen 18,12-14). It is true that, according to this account, Sara later pulled herself together and denied her laughter (Gen 18,15).

The next sentence (12) does not speak of Sara but of Abraham, because it is Abraham, and not Sara, who received the promise of an innumerable progeny (Gen 15,5; 22,17). Once cured of her sterility, Sara was no longer an obstacle to the fulfilment of this promise.

The parallel subdivision (17-19) shows that this fulfilment seemed endangered by an order of God himself, to whom Abraham showed himself generously docile. God ordered him: «Take your son, your only son, Isaac [...] you shall offer him in holocaust» (Gen 22,2). Abraham got ready to obey: «He bound his son Isaac and put him on the altar», but the angel of the Lord stopped him immolating his son telling him: «Do nothing to him, for now I know that you fear God» (Gen 22,9-12). The preacher says, however, that Abraham «offered Isaac», giving the verb «to offer» a meaning of readiness and not of actual immolation. He first puts the Greek verb in the perfect, which expresses the durable effect of a completed action: Abraham is henceforth «he who offered God his son». Then the preacher puts the verb in the imperfect, «he was offering», which sets before our eyes the spectacle of Abraham offering his son. Instead of saying, with Gen 22,12, that Abraham thus showed his fear of God, the preacher highlights the faith of Abraham. The fear of God is actually an attitude of deep faith. The test also strengthened the faith of the patriarch: not doubting God's fidelity to his promises, he understood that the immolation of Isaac itself would not place any obstacle to their fulfilment, because «even from among the dead, God is capable of arousing». In reality, Isaac did not have to be aroused from death, because he is not really dead. Still, the fact that he came out alive from what was to have been his sacrifice constitutes a prefiguration of the paschal mystery of Christ, his death offered and his resurrection.

This long paragraph ends dynamically at a quick pace (20-22). It shows the propagation, throughout the successive generations, of the blessing coming from God. The blessing bestowed «by faith» concerns «things to come» (20; see Gen 27,29-40), which unites hope to faith. Concerning the «dying Jacob» (21), «blessing each of the sons of Joseph» (see Gen 48,13-20), the preacher adds a detail taken from the Septuagint (Gen 47,31), different from the Hebrew: Jacob «bends over the top of his staff». This detail is still enigmatic. The only other place where there is a question of the staff of Jacob is Gen 32,11 where Jacob declares: «With my staff I passed over the Jordan». This expression may recall the staff of Moses, which served to open a passage through the Red Sea (Exod 14,16). Does the preacher see here the prefiguration of another «staff», the cross of Christ, which opened quite another passage? There are no clues to help decide the matter.

The mention of the «departure» from Egypt (*exodos*) taken by «Joseph at life's end» and the «orders he gave about his bones» (22) clearly show his faith in the word of God and his hope of getting to the promised land (see Gen 5,24-25; Exod 13,19; Josh 24,32).

3

The faith of Moses

23 By faith, Moses, after his birth,
was hidden for three months by his parents,
for they saw that the little child was beautiful
and they did not fear the king's edict.
24 By faith, Moses, having grown up,
gave up being called son of the daughter of Pharaoh,
25 preferring to be ill-treated with the people of God,
rather than for a time having enjoyment of sin,
26 reckoning greater riches
than the treasures of Egypt
the opprobrium of Christ;
for he had his eyes fixed on the reward.
27 By faith, he left Egypt,
not fearing the anger of the king,
for, as seeing [the one who is] the Invisible
he held on.
28 By faith, he kept the Passover and the application of the blood,
in order that the exterminator of the first-born
may not touch them.
29 By faith, they crossed the Red Sea,
as through dry land,
but in attempting it
the Egyptians were drowned.
30 By faith, the ramparts of Jericho fell,
having been surrounded for seven days.
31 By faith, Rahab, the prostitute,
did not perish with the indocile,
having peacefully brought in the scouts.

A. *COMPOSITION*

Like the previous ones, this long paragraph is marked out regularly by the anaphoric repetition of the word *pistei*, «by faith». The pace slackens in the second example (24-26), which offers a profound reflection on the relation between Moses and Christ. In this long section, the mystery of Christ appears more than once in filigree form, but this passage is the only one where the name of Christ is overtly pronounced.

A very clear-cut parallelism is noticeable between the first two examples (23-24) with chronological progression: «Moses after his birth» (23), «Moses grew up» (24). The name of Moses does not appear in what follows. The verbs in it are without any subject expressed (27, four times; 28a). The subject is not expressed in verse 29 either, where it goes into the plural, «they crossed», the liseners have to supply it, which they do easily, since it is a matter of crossing the Red Sea. This omission of the subjects makes the style quicker and the argument more pressing.

Brevity already marks the first example (23). The logical connections in it are only understood if one knows the story and, in particular, the undisclosed content of the «king's edict», ordering the murder of the male children of the Hebrews (Exod 1,22).

The second example, on the contrary (24-26), gives many explanations. An antithetic parallelism in it contrasts the ill-treatment «with the people of God» with «the enjoyment of sin» at the court of Pharaoh. Then a corresponding antithesis contrasts the «opprobrium of Christ» with the «treasures of Egypt».

In the third example (27), there is antithesis between the vision of him who is «*the Invisible*» and «the anger of the *king*». The vision of the Invisible gives strength not to fear the anger of the king. «He held on», affirmative, is in parallel (synonymous by the idea, antithetic by the form) with «not having feared», negative.

The style of the fourth example (28) is very concise. Once again, we have to know the biblical account to understand what is meant by the *pros-chysis* of the blood, not «shedding», which is called *ek-chysis*, but «application» of the blood to the stiles and lintel of the front doors of all the houses where the Israelites were living.

It is the same for the fifth example (29), in which the preacher does not say exactly who those were who «crossed the Red Sea» dryshod and whose destiny was the opposite of that of the Egyptians, who «were drowned». Here there is an antithetic parallelism, arranged in chiastic form.

The sixth example (30), is extremely brief. The seventh (31) rapidly suggests, in two antitheses, a double subject of astonishment. It is, in fact, astonishing that a «prostitute» should not be allotted the same fate as «the indocile». Besides, it is astonishing that this prostitute should have performed, at her own risk in face of the danger, a generous action in favour of strangers. But it is precisely this second subject of astonishment that provides the explanation of the first.

B. *BIBLICAL CONTEXT AND INTERPRETATION*

«By faith, Moses» (23): this beginning puts Moses immediately in relation with faith; it is, in reality, a question of the faith of his parents, but it can be said that this faith was aroused by the sight of their little child: «they saw that the little child was beautiful» (23; see Exod 2,2). The sentence suggests that in the child's physical beauty, its parents perceived, «by faith», the sign of a project of God, which gave them the courage to infringe «the king's edict», as the midwives had infringed it earlier out of profound respect for God (see Exod 1,17), an attitude of faith, as we have said.

In the second subdivision (24-26), the preacher is not so dependent on the story in Exodus. The expression «grew up» (24) comes from Exod 2,11, but there introduces an episode which the preacher does not mention, the murder by Moses of an Egyptian who was hitting a Hebrew (Exod 2,11-12). The story in Exodus does not say that Moses denied his adoption by the daughter of Pharaoh, an adoption recorded in Exod 2,10, but it suggests it, because it shows that Moses did not stay attached to his foster-mother, who is not mentioned any more, but concerned himself with the fate of «his brothers» by race, the Hebrews, «and he saw what their forced labour was» (Exod 2,11). The preacher then recalls the story of the calling of Moses, in which God says: «I have seen that my people is ill-treated in Egypt» (Exod 3,7). Moses «preferred to be ill-treated with the people of God rather than having [at the court of Pharaoh] enjoyment of sin» (25), the court of Pharaoh being idolatrous (see Wis 19,13).

This choice by Moses was based on a conviction of faith. In the light of faith, «the opprobrium of Christ» is recognized as being of greater worth than «the treasures of Egypt». How could Moses have any idea of what «the opprobrium of Christ» is? The context shows that it was a very harsh and humiliating fate, accepted in complete solidarity with the persons who have to be saved. To become «the pioneer of their salvation», Christ had to be «made perfect through sufferings» (Heb 2,10). Moses experienced that, he understood that opprobrium taken on to ensure the salvation of the people of God has infinitely more value than the material treasures of Egypt, which lead to spiritual perdition.

Let us note in passing that when considering the story of Moses in the light of Christ, the preacher is led to depart considerably from the account in Exodus, which never expresses contempt for the riches of the Egyptians, but, on the contrary, tells how God called upon the Israelites to ask the Egyptians for «items of silver and gold» (Exod 3,21-22). «Thus they plundered the Egyptians» (Exod 12,36).

The third subdivision (27) gives rise to difficulties. If the statement: «he left Egypt», is interpreted to refer to the first departure of Moses (Exod 2,15), the text that follows it directly contradicts the Old Testament account, because it says that Moses «did not fear the anger of the king», whereas the account states that «Moses took fright [...], he fled» (Exod 2,14-15). It must therefore be understood that the preacher wishes to speak of the departure for the Exodus. In the preparation for the Exodus, Moses was not afraid to face Pharaoh on several occasions (Exod 5,1; 7,10; 8,4-8), and to answer him boldly (Exod 10,24-29). This boldness was obviously based on faith. God is not visible, but faith makes it as if he were seen, for it is «a means of knowing realities that are not seen» (Heb 11,1). «As if seeing the Invisible, Moses held on».

The rest of the text (28-31) then rapidly, in 4 sentences, recalls the story of the Exodus. It does not recount everything, but only two episodes at the beginning (the celebration of the Passover and the crossing of the Red Sea) and two episodes at the end (the fall of Jericho and the salvation obtained by Rahab). Nothing is said of the march in the desert. It came up in the parallel section (II A; in 3,7-4,11), but in the negative perspective of the incredulity of the people, a perspective contrary to the one in this section. Hence the preacher does not speak of it here.

Of Moses, the preacher says very soberly that «by faith he kept the Passover and the application of the blood». The Book of Exodus does not say that, but it allows it to be said. In Exod 12,2-20 the Lord gives Moses and Aaron long instructions on the Passover; in Exod 12,21-24 Moses passes on to the elders of Israel a summary of these divine instructions; in Exod 12,28 it is said that «the sons of Israel [...] did exactly what the Lord had commanded Moses and Aaron». It can therefore be said that Moses, by the faith in the word of God, «has done» all of this, that is to say he had it done.

The application of the blood of the slaughtered beast is prescribed in Exod 12,7.22. Its efficacy in preserving from «the exterminator» is affirmed in Exod 12,13.23. The listeners to the sermon may then think of the efficacy of the blood of Christ, which the preacher has affirmed and explained in Heb 9,14.

On the passage of the Red Sea (29) the account of the Exodus shows in Exod 14,1-4 that Moses and the sons of Israel believed in the word of God and conformed to it. The passage itself is recounted in Exod 14,24-31; the conclusion declares that at the sight of this prodigy, «the people had the fear of the Lord; it had faith in the Lord and in Moses, his servant» (Exod 14,31). The people thus passed, like the royal officer in the gospel (John 4,50.53), from an initial faith to a deeper faith. In a vigorous antithesis, the preacher expresses the complete contrast between the fate of believers and that of idolaters. For believers, the Sea is transformed into dry land, while the idolaters are «drowned» in it (this verb is taken from the Canticle of Moses, Exod 15,4 LXX). The Book of Wisdom observes that God uses the same elements, «changing their properties» (Wis 19,18), on the one hand to punish the wicked, and on the other, on the contrary, to save «those who trust in him» (Wis 16,24).

From the passage of the Red Sea, the preacher suddenly jumps to the capture of Jericho (30; Josh 6), without mentioning the long crossing of the desert or the crossing of the Jordan. He expresses himself very elliptically: «By faith, the ramparts fell»! It has to be understood obviously that the faith of the Israelites showed itself in their docility to the instructions given by God in Josh 6,2-5, and that it achieved the collapse of the ramparts (Josh 6,20). God had ordered going round the ramparts for a period of seven days (Josh 6,3-4).

To the capture of Jericho is linked the fact that Rahab and her family had their lives saved (31), while all the other inhabitants of the city were massacred (Josh 6,21). Even before the taking of the city, Joshua had ordered that Rahab and her family be spared (Josh 6,17). This order was executed (Josh 6,23.25). The reason given for this exception is that Rahab «had hidden the messengers sent by Joshua to spy out Jericho» (Josh 6,17.25). The preacher expresses a deeper reason, the faith of Rahab, which had inspired her with this action. This faith manifests itself effectively in the words the prostitute addresses to the messengers: «I know that LORD has given you the country» (Josh 2,9), «LORD, your God, is God up there in the heavens and down here on earth» (Josh 2,11). Like the episode of the passage of the Red Sea, the one of the salvation of Rahab shows a contrast of situation. The religious motive, this time, is more clearly indicated, because instead of saying «the inhabitants of Jericho», as he said «the Egyptians» (29), the preacher chose to say here «the indocile» (31), thus suggesting that by closing the doors of their city to the Israelites, the inhabitants of Jericho were lacking in docility and faith and therefore deserved to perish.

4
Successes and trials of faith (32-40)

32 And what more can I say?
I shall indeed be short of time, if I speak in detail
of Gideon, Barak, Samson, Jephthah,
of David as well of Samuel and the prophets,
33 they who, BY MEANS OF FAITH,
subjected kingdoms, administered justice,
obtained [the fulfilment of] promises, muzzled lions' mouths,
34 extinguished the power of fire, escaped from the edges of the sword,
recovered from sickness, became valiant in war,
repulsed armies of foreigners;
35 women recuperated by *resurrection*
their dead.
But others were tortured,
not accepting deliverance,
in order to obtain a better *resurrection.*
36 Still others, of derision and of whips underwent the trial,
and of bonds and prison;
37 they were stoned, they were sawn in two;
by the blade of the sword, they died;
they went around in sheepskins, in goatskins,
deprived [of everything], oppressed, ill-treated,
38 they of whom the world was not worthy,
in deserts [they were] wandering, and mountains and caves
and holes in the ground.
39 And all those, having had good testimony BY MEANS OF FAITH,
did not obtain [the fulfilment of] the promise,
40 God having provided us with something better:
that apart from us they would not be made perfect.

A. *COMPOSITION*

The preacher ends this section with a great oratorical flight. He begins with an oratorical formula of «preterition», that is to say he names a whole series of personages, saying that he does not have time to speak of them in detail (32). An inclusion then starts with the expression «BY MEANS OF FAITH»; it goes on until verse 39. This expression is found only in these two passages of the speech. Moreover, the word «faith» is absent from all the rest of this long paragraph, which gives it a very different look from the other paragraphs, in which the word «faith» is constantly repeated.

The whole text outlined in this way (33-39) is structured according to a great antithetic parallelism. First of all there are the successes obtained «by means of faith» (33-35b); contrasted with them then are the trials undergone by the believers (35c-38). The transition is provided by two contrasted uses of the word «resurrection» (35a and 35e). The first use expresses the greatest earthly success of faith: raising the dead. The other use expresses the hope which backed up the heroism of persecuted believers: hope of a «better resurrection», which gives access to eternal life; it gave them the courage «not to accept deliverance».

The part on the successes of the faith (33-34) has a regular structure, which produces a powerful cumulative effect: 8 times we have, in parallel, the order verb + complement; the subject, expressed at the beginning by a relative pronoun in the plural, is always the same. A closer parallelism between the «mouths of lions» and the «edges of sword» is noticeable, and another between «war» and «armies».

The part on the trials of faith (33c-38) is much more animated. The 1st example is accompanied by an explanation (the hope of a better resurrection), which enlightens everything that follows. The examples that follow are arranged in diverse ways. Another subject introduces them: «Still others». Pairs of words are often found: «derision and whips», «bonds and prison», «they were stoned, they were sawn in half», «in sheepskins, in goatskins»; next there is a group of 3 participles: «deprived, oppressed, ill-treated», followed, in powerful contrast, by an antithetic remark: «they of whom the world was not worthy»; the contrast is taken up immediately, with the final remark about the very uncomfortable places of refuge of these heroes of the faith. This ending, in Greek, has a very harmonious rhythm, well suited to its function. The translation has tried to be faithful to it.

The conclusion comes next (39-40). It comprises 4 members. The first two are in antithetic parallelism: to a positive observation, on the good testimony received by the elders, is opposed unexpectedly a negative observation, the non-fulfilment of the promise. The two other members give the explanation of this paradoxical fact, by design of God which favours Christians. By their grammatical form, these two members appear antithetic: an affirmation is succeeded by a denial. But by content, they are in synonymous parallelism: to a «for us» («God provided for us») there corresponds a «not without us» («that it be *not without us* that they be made perfect». As last word, the author chose a very significant verb: *teleioun*, «to make perfect».

B. *BIBLICAL CONTEXT AND INTERPRETATION*

After the formula of preterition (32), the author lists some personages of the Old Testament, but without following chronological order. 3 pairs of names are observable in which that order is reversed: «Gideon, Barak», for Barak (Judg 4-5) and Gideon (Judg 6-8); «Samson, Jephthah», for Jephthah (Judg 11-12) and Samson (13-16); «David as well as Samuel», for Samuel (1Sam 1-16) and David (1Sam 16,11-1Kgs 2,10).

These changes in order intend to produce an accumulative effect difficult to control and thus prepare the rest of the text. The latter does not contain any quotation from the Old Testament, but only more or less clear allusions to episodes in the history of the Israelites.

The first statement, «they subjected kingdoms» (33) finds good support in the story of Gideon who triumphed over the Madianites (Judg 7), for the biblical account shows that Gideon's victory was not obtained by human means, but thanks to faith-inspired docility to God (see Judg 7,2.4.7). One can also quote the case of Barak, who triumphed over the king of Hazor (Judg 4,14-16), that of Jephthah who vanquished the Ammonites (Judg 11,29-33) and the victories of king David over the Philistines (2Kgs 5,17-25): «David acted as the Lord had ordered him and he beat the Philistines» (v.25).

The second expression, literally: «they carried out justice», is a Hebraism, with several possible meanings. It can be an allusion to good works: in Matt 6,1 almsgiving, prayer, fasting. But here, it is more a question of action taken to have justice prevail, like that of David, who «administered equity and justice to all his people» (2Sam 8,15).

In the third expression, literally: «they obtained promises», the word «promises» means obviously «the things promised», as in 6,12 or 9,15. The absence of the article is to be noted; it shows that it is not about «the» promise of the eternal inheritance, but of temporal promises, like that of God to Gideon: «I will deliver Madian into your hands» (Judg 7,7), a promise that was fulfilled (7,22). There is therefore no contradiction between this affirmative sentence and the negative sentence in verse 39, where the word «promise» is in the singular and where it is preceded by the article: «they did not obtain the promise,» the one about entry into God's rest.

The actions described next (33) have a less general bearing. «They muzzled lions' mouths» alludes to Samson (Judg 14,6) and David (1Sam 17,34). «They extinguished the power of fire» (34) recalls the story of the three youths in the furnace (Dan 7); these youths intrepidly express their faith, see Dan 3,17. In «they escaped from the edges of the sword», the expression «edge of the sword» is a Hebraism, generally used in the singular (Gen 34,26; Josh 8,24). The author uses the plural to obtain a parallelism with the «mouths of lions». David escaped from Goliath's sword (1Sam 17), Elijah escaped from a threat of death (1Kgs 19,2-3); he even escaped from those who came to arrest him (2Kgs 1,9-12). Elisha likewise (2Kgs 6,31).

For «they recovered from sickness», one can quote the case of the healing of Hezekiah, a case in which the prophet Isaiah acted (Isa 38) and that of the healing of Naaman by the prophet Elisha (2Kgs 5); these are cures obtained by prophets, but not for themselves.

The next allusions, to military exploits, may be illustrated by many episodes in the historical books, in particular in the story of the Maccabees. The faith of Judas Maccabeus is clearly expressed in more than one circumstance. Before a battle, this hero of faith declares: «victory in combat does not depend on the size of the army, but on the strength that comes from heaven» (1Macc 3,19). Before another combat against greater numbers and better armed enemies, «Judas tells his men: «Do not fear this multitude [...] let us cry to Heaven [...] it will crush this army before us today and all the nations will know that He who redeems and saves Israel exists» (1Macc 4,8-11). And «the nations were crushed» (4,14).

In 11,35, the grammatical break is not without significance: a new subject appears: «women»! The author could have kept the same masculine subject and said: «they raised dead people», because he is alluding here to the miracle of the prophet Elijah (1Kgs 17,17-24) and to that of Elisha (2Kgs 4,18-37), but the power of faith appears better if these two miracles are placed in relation with «women», terribly afflicted by the death of their child. The faith of the woman comes out especially in the second miracle (2Kgs 4,20-22.30). Thus ends, with two victories over death, the list of the triumphs of faith.

Immediately in contrast with this comes the beginning of the list of the ordeals of faith: «But others were tortured» (35). These ordeals are in reality the occasion of even more heroic and fruitful victories, because it takes more courage to refuse deliverance than to run into battle; more fruitful, because this resistance obtains «a better resurrection», not just a temporary return to life on earth, but entry into eternal life.

The preacher here alludes to the Israelite martyrs of the persecution under Antiochus Epiphanes. They declared themselves «ready to die rather than transgress the laws of [their] fathers» (2Macc 7,2). Their courage was upheld by great faith in the resurrection of the dead. Under torture, one of them proclaimed: «The king of the world, after we have undergone death for his laws, will make us rise up for an eternal revivification of life» (2Macc 7,9; see also 7,11.14).

The description of the ordeals of faith is in obvious contrast with that of the earthly triumphs of faith. It contains allusions to biblical episodes. Jeremiah, for example, was arrested and imprisoned (Jer 37/44.5); the prophet Elijah had to flee into the desert to save his life (1Kgs 19,3); as clothing, he had a «sheepskin» (in Greek *mēlōtē;* in the Septuagint, this word is only found in connection with Elijah: 3Kgs 19,13.19; 4Kgs 2,8.13.14). «By blade of the sword, they died» is an allusion to the word addressed by Elijah to God: «They have killed your prophets with the sword» (1Kgs 19,10.14). «They were sawn in half» corresponds to a tradition about the martyrdom of the prophet Isaiah, reported in The Ascension of Isaiah (5,1-14) and other apocryphal works.

In this context of painful and humiliating ordeals, the remark inserted by the author —«those of whom the world was not worthy»— is like a flash suddenly illuminating the darkness. It expresses the paradox of the situation by stressing the extraordinary dignity of the heroes of faith and it suggests understanding that this situation corresponds to a mysterious design of God.

The conclusion (39-40) is unexpected. After the impressive list of ordeals courageously undergone by the heroes of faith, one would expect a positive conclusion, which would be a proclamation of the reward they gained. One is therefore astonished to hear the preacher expressing a negative conclusion: «they did not obtain [the fulfilment of] the promise». The last verse gives us to understand that this conclusion is inspired by the faith of the author in the decisive role of Christ. To be able to enter into God's rest, the just of the Old Testament had to wait for Christ to mark out the way to it with his paschal mystery and to «make [them] perfect with his unique sacrifice» (10,14). He is the «forerunner» (6,20). No one could enter before him into the heavenly sanctuary. In his humanity «made perfect» by his sacrifice, he is himself the «new and living way» (10,20). It follows that Christians have a better destiny than that of the early heroes of faith. The latter could not be «made perfect» before the Christians and without them; they could not have had, before them and without them, «full freedom to enter into the sanctuary», because that «full freedom» was obtained by «the blood of Jesus» (10,19). In this conclusion, the author shows full awareness of the privileged situation of Christians.

Chapter 16

The necessary endurance (12,1-13)

The transition between the two sections of this fourth part is got ready at the end of the first section with the introduction of the personal pronoun «we» in two expressions: «for us» and «not without us» (11,40). This pronoun had never been used before in this very long section, which speaks of the faith of the elders and therefore expressed itself in the third person. The pronoun «we» comes back immediately after, at the beginning of the second section: «That is why *we* also…» (12,1) and it is repeated a second time a little further on; the sentence is exhortative: «*let us run* the trial set before *us*» (1). The preacher then takes on a more direct tone, in the second person plural, from verse 3 to verse 13, except for a return to the first person in verse 9.

The link with the first section is reinforced by the reference to the «crowd of witnesses», that is to say of all the heroes of the faith listed in the section that has just finished. Before becoming witnesses, the latter «obtained good testimony thanks to their faith» 11,39). A last use of the word «faith» (12,2) reinforces the transition even more.

. *COMPOSITION*

A first subdivision (1-3) puts Jesus forward as a model of endurance. Then the preacher quotes an exhortation from the Book of Proverbs (3,11-12), which introduces the theme of «correction», and he comments on it (4-11). The link between the two themes is provided by verse 7, which declares: «It is for the sake of *correction* that you endure». A double final sentence a) concludes the section (12) and b) announces the next part (13).

An approximative inclusion between «let us run (*trechōmen*)» (1) and «straight paths (*trochias*)» (13) marks the boundaries of the section.

1. Enduring as Jesus did (1-3)

1 That is why we also,
    having around us so great a cloud of witnesses,
    [and] having cast off every burden and the sin that besieges us,
with *endurance* LET US RUN *(TRECHOMEN)* the ordeal set before us,
2 looking at the initiator and the perfecter of faith, Jesus,
    who, instead of the joy that was set before him,
        endured a cross, disregarding the shame,
        and sat at the right of the throne of God.
3 Consider, indeed, him who *endured* on the part of the sinners towards him
        such a contradiction,
    so that you may not weaken in your souls, discouraged.

The two first participles are in antithetic parallelism; the first, «having», introduces what we have; the second, «having rejected», introduces what we have rejected. We have the stimulating presence of the «witnesses», that is to say of the spectators at the competition. Everything that can slow the race down has been rejected. The main clause highlights the word «endurance» (1d), which is then backed up by two uses of the verb «to endure» (2c.3a). This clause is completed by a call to look at Jesus. These two stichs (1d and 2a) occupy the centre of a small unit, the first part of which (1abc) concerns Christians and the last part (2bcd) concerns Jesus. This last part is composed of three stichs of which the first and the last speak of joy (2b) and honour (2d) while the central stich (2c) speaks, in antithesis, of torment and of shame.

The final sentence also is in antithetic parallelism: with the endurance of Jesus (3ab) is contrasted the possibility of a lapse by Christians through discouragement (3c). But the consideration of the endurance of Jesus must be an obstacle to that possibility, which weakens the antithesis.

2. Accepting paternal correction from God (4-11)

4 You have not yet resisted until blood
    in fighting against sin
5 and you have forgotten the exhortation
    addressed to you as to sons:
    my SON, do not make light of the correction of Lord
        and do not be discouraged when you are reproved by him,
6 for he whom he loves, Lord corrects,
        he beats every SON he receives.

In the Greek text, the word translated here «in fighting» (4b) is a derivative of the word *agōn*, used in 1d in its sense of «sporting contest»; it also has the sense of «combat». Thus there is an initial parallelism between this passage and the previous one.

The introduction to the quotation from the Book of Proverbs is composed of two clauses (4ab and 5ab) the content of which offers a certain degree of parallelism: insufficient resistance to sin (4ab), insufficient attention to the text in Proverbs (5ab).

The text in Proverbs is in synonymous parallelism in each verse. In the first distich (5cd), the parallel elements follow each other in the same order: to «do not make light», a negative attitude, there corresponds «do not be discouraged», and to «correction of Lord» there corresponds «reproved by him».

In the second distich, the order is in chiastic form: to the first element, «he whom he loves» corresponds the last, «every son he receives»; and to the second, «he corrects», the third corresponds immediately, «he beats». The unity of the whole is provided by the parallelism between «correction of Lord» (5c) and «Lord corrects» (6a), expressions arranged in chiastic form. The word «son» also serves as an inclusion. «Lord» is without any article; this word is treated as a proper name; it translates YHWH, the proper name of God in Hebrew.

7 It is with a view to correction that you endure [that],
it is as towards sons that God behaves;
who, indeed, is the son whom the father does not correct?
8 Now, if you are without any correction,
in which all share,
you are therefore illegitimate, and not sons.
9 Moreover, the fathers of our flesh, we had them as educators,
and we respected [them],
are we not going to submit much more to the father of the spirits,
and we shall live?
10 These, in fact, [it is] for a few days [and] according to what seemed good to them
[that] they corrected us,
but He, [it is] according to what is useful,
in order that we may receive share of his holiness.
11 All correction, for the moment, does not seem to be [a reason] for joy,
but of sadness,
later, however, [it is] a peaceful fruit [that] it brings to those who
are exercised by it, [a fruit] of justice.

The first stich (7a), as we have said, makes the link between the theme of endurance, developed in the first verses (1-3), and the theme of correction, which has just been introduced by means of the quotation from the Book of Proverbs (5-6). The theme of endurance is then dropped.

The two first stichs (7ab) take up the two most important words of the text quoted: «correction» and «son». The name of «Lord» is not taken up, it is replaced by the name of «God». The preacher applies the statement from Proverbs to his listeners: correction is God's way of acting towards his sons. Between the second stich and the first, no verbal contact can be discerned, but they are none the less in complementary parallelism, because of their relation to the text quoted. By basing itself on this text, the second stich (7b) notes that the «correction» is given by God and corresponds to a relation of filiation. The third stich (7c) comes to bear this out; the themes of correction (7a) and of filiation (7b) come together there and their connection is made closer: the rhetorical question suggests that there is no filiation without correction.

The next verse (8) applies this idea to the listeners and once again takes up the terms «correction» (8a) and «son» (8c), but in two different stichs. An antithetic term, «illegitimate», is added.

Verse 9 presents an antithetic parallelism between «the fathers of our flesh» and «the Father of the Spirits» and at the same time some *a fortiori* reasoning, «much more», for «the Spirits» are obviously superior to «the flesh».

Verse 10 continues the antithesis and the *a fortiori* argument, as indicated by the initial *gar* («in fact»). As in verse 9, the verb «to correct» is expressed only in the first member of the parallelism; it is implied in the second member. The two critical remarks in the first member («for a few days» and «according to what seemed good to them») are contrasted with the two positive estimates in the second member («according to what is useful» and «in order that we may share in holiness»); the second positive estimate makes the immense significance of the first explicit; both are in contrast with «according to what seemed good to them». The expression «for a few days» does not have a clearly expressed antithetic parallel, but implicitly it does: «to share the holiness of God» is in contrast with it, because God's holiness is eternal.

Verse 11 puts what correction produces «for the moment», «the sadness», and what it produces «later», in antithetic parallelism with «a peaceful fruit of justice». The first member also contains an inner antithesis between the «joy», not obtained then, and the «sadness» which, on the contrary, is caused.

3. Conclusion (12-13)

12 That is why, your drooping hands
and your weak knees,
straighten [them]

13 and make straight PATHS *(TROCHIAS)* for your feet,
in order that what is lame may not be crippled,
but rather healed.

A «that is why» introduces the double conclusion which starts with two parallel expressions: «your drooping hands and your weak knees». Their parallelism is closer in Greek than in the translation, because the Greek text twice has the prefix *para*, «beside» with the participles; this expresses the idea of negligence.

The liaison between the first sentence and the second is supplied by the idea of uprightness contained in «straighten», *an-orthōsate*, and resumed in «straight paths», *orthas.* Then again, after «hands» and «knees», it goes down to the «feet». The aim of the exhortation is expressed in a final clause that contains an antithesis between one thing to be avoided, «crippled», and one thing to be obtained, healing.

BIBLICAL CONTEXT AND INTERPRETATION

Enduring as Jesus did (1-3)

After describing the promises accomplished by the heroes of faith and the ordeals they overcame, the preacher switches to an exhortation tone. The passage from one to the other takes place without difficulty, because the description was a eulogy; it therefore implicitly contained an appeal for imitation. The preacher, however, has a surprise in store for us: instead of presenting the heroes of faith as models to be imitated, he presents them as «witnesses» at a sporting competition in which the listeners to the sermon are involved. Such witnesses are, of course, very qualified to assess the performance. Their presence in great numbers —they form «a cloud»!— is therefore particularly stimulating.

The model set up to be looked at is «Jesus». He is not set forth as a model of faith, but of endurance: «he endured the cross», «he endured contradiction»; the listeners are therefore called upon to «run with endurance». The transition is thus made to the second theme of this part Four; it was announced before the other one in 10,36.

To take part in the competition, the athletes had to have «cast off every burden». In 1Cor 9,25 Saint Paul expresses a similar idea: «Every athlete deprives himself of everything». The translation «having cast off» is not perfectly exact. The Greek verb used by the author means more precisely «to lay aside». This verb played an important part in primitive catechesis. There it expressed the first requirement of Christian conversion and baptism: «laying aside all malice» (1Pet 2,1), «all uncleanness» (Jas 1,21), laying aside the old and dirty clothes one had as a sinner (see Rom 13,12; Eph 4,22.25; Col 3,8), the other requirement being adherence to Christ by faith. The idea of «leaving aside» one's clothes corresponds completely to the sporting metaphor, because athletes undressed completely.

From metaphor, the author passes to reality by adding that there is also need to have lain aside «the sin besieging us» (literally: «easily circumventing»). The author comes back immediately after to the metaphor when speaking of «running a race» in sport. As in other passages (2,1.3; 4,1-2.14-16; 6,18-20), the author takes care to include himself fraternally in his exhortation. He does not say: «with endurance *run*», but «...*let us run*».

The aim of the race is to reach Jesus where he arrived «as forerunner» (6,20). It is on him that our eyes must be fixed from afar (*aph-orōntes*), remembering the way he followed to get to God. As often before (3,1; 4,14; 6,20; 7,22), the name of Jesus is preceded by titles describing him. The titles we find here are not easy to translate or interpret. The translation offered tries to give at least some aspect of the expression.

The first title, *archēgos*, is in relation with the word *archē*, which means «beginning» and «to be able»; the ending —*ēgos* adds the idea of «leading». The title can mean «initiator», «founder», «chief», «cause». I have translated it «initiator», to keep the idea of beginning.

The second title, *teleiōtēs*, is in relation with the word *telos*, «end», with the adjective *teleios*, «finished», «perfect», and with the corresponding verb, *teleioun*. It is a noun of action, non-existent in Greek before this sole use in the Bible. It designates «the one who finishes», «the one who makes perfect». I translate it «finisher», to keep the idea of finishing.

It is clear that the author wants to state that Jesus is at the beginning (*archē*) and at the end (*telos*) of faith. He opened up the way of faith and he brought it to its perfection. But how are we to understand these statements more precisely? Is it by being himself a believer that Jesus founded the faith and that he became its «finisher»? Some exegetes —and not the least among them: Westcott, Delling, Grässer— say so. Others, on the contrary, exclude this interpretation (Teodorico, Spicq). For a doctrinal reason, Saint Thomas Aquinas was categorical: «Granted that, as from the first instant of his conception, Christ fully saw God *per essentiam*, faith could in no way have been present in him» (*Summa Th.* III[a], qu. 7, art. 3).

From the exegetical point of view, the problem is not easy. Let us first of all note that the expression in Heb 12,2 certainly does not allow us to consider Jesus as a simple believer, because the two titles it contains attribute a unique position as regards faith to him, an active role, in both arousing it and in making it perfect.

It should also be remarked that the relation of Christ with God is never expressed in the New Testament by means of the Greek verb *pisteuein*, «to believe», whereas this verb has very many occurrences in it (241). The New Testament never says: «Jesus believed in God». This fact is certainly significant; it suggests that the more deep relation of Christ with God was of another order and that also emerges from the words of Jesus, when he declares: «No one knows the Son but the father and no one knows father but the Son and anyone to whom the Son wishes to reveal him» (Matt 11,27). From his unique filial relation with God Jesus had direct, immediate awareness, and not knowledge by faith, based on a revelation coming from without, as is the case for the adoptive children that we are. At the deepest level of his human conscience, there was therefore in Jesus, no room for a theological faith relation with God.

But a human conscience exists on many other levels and there is reason for thinking that at these other levels Jesus was in a similar situation to that of simple believers, because he was not in the situation of Son of God; he was «in everything like his brothers» (2,17; 4,15), which means: «in the condition of a slave» (Phil 2,7) and not of a Son; still worse: «in the likeness of sinful flesh» (Rom 8,3). At those levels, therefore, he could feel and experience everything that simple believers feel and experience. When he «offered pleas and supplications to Him who could save him from death» (Heb 5,7), he was in a situation of darkness and anguish. The gospels show that he did not know whether it was possible or not that «this chalice pass far» from him; his awareness as Son still continued to assert itself, for he said: «Father [...], not as I will, but as you will!» (Matt 26,39). His trust in his father was total, like his docility, full of «religious respect» (*eulabeia*: Heb 5,7). His fidelity was maintained without faltering, in spite of terrible ordeals; he was «tested on all points like us, but without *sinning*» (4,15). Trust in God, docility, religious respect, fidelity: all these attitudes have a very close connection with faith. Jesus was the perfect example of it. In this sense he was «the initiator and finisher of faith» (12,2).

However, it is mainly by the mystery of his passion and resurrection that he fully earned that title, because, by that mystery, he made the «fullness of faith» possible for all his disciples(10,22), which leads them straight into intimacy with God (10,19-21).

The preacher immediately mentions this mystery by speaking of the «*cross*» endured by Jesus and of his being seated «on the right of the *throne* of God». To obtain a more expressive antithesis, the preacher inserts the word «throne» into the usual expression, which says simply «on the right of God» (Rom 8,34; Col 3,1; Heb 10,12; 1Pet 3,22) taking its inspiration from Ps 109(110),1. Contrasted with the «cross» is «the throne», but their relation is not simply one of contrast, because it is by enduring the «shame» of the «cross» that Jesus obtained the «glory» of sitting on «the throne of God». Right at the beginning of his homily, the preacher clearly expressed this connection by saying that it is «*because* of the death he suffered» that Jesus was «crowned with glory and honour» (2,9). Here, as in 2,9, the author insists on the stability of this glory by using the verb «to sit down» in the perfect, as, in 2,9, the participle «crowned». In the earlier uses (1,3; 8,1; 10,12), the verb «to sit down» was always in the aorist: «he sat down», to stress the action of taking a seat, rather than the position adopted.

Before speaking of «the cross» of Jesus, the author mentions «the joy that was offered him» (12,2). His sentence is not clear. Because of the ambiguity of the preposition *anti*, it can be understood in two ways, not only different, but opposed. It can be understood as meaning that Jesus renounced the joy to which he had a right; «instead of» this joy, he chose the cross. It can be understood to mean, on the contrary, that to obtain the joy, he suffered the cross: «in exchange for» the joy of his glorification he agreed to face his passion.

The fathers of the Church understood the text in the first sense, which better expresses the self-denial of Christ. This sense corresponds to what the author says in 11,24-25 about the self-denial of Moses, who «gave up being called son of the daughter of Pharaoh and chose rather to be ill-treated with the people of God». The Christological hymn in the letter to the Philippians offers a similar perspective (Phil 2,6-8): Christ gave up the right he had to be treated as equal to God and suffered the cross.

The other interpretation can call upon several arguments. In 12,16 the sense of *anti* is «in exchange for»: Esau «in exchange for one dish», that is to say in order to get one dish, «sold his birthright». In the case of Moses, this second perspective is expressed after the first, in 11,26: Moses «had his eyes fixed on the reward». And it is this concern with reward, present implicitly in 11,6 as well, that is suggested to Christians in 10,35, just before the appeal for endurance: «Do not lose your confidence, which has a great reward. Of endurance, in fact, you have need...». It is therefore possible to hesitate between the two interpretations.

In his reflection on the cross of Christ, the author does not insist on the physical sufferings that torment caused, but on the «shame» resulting from it. To be sure, it was above all about a degrading torment, designed to produce a strong dissuasive effect. The author then stresses another aspect of Christ's passion, along the same lines, but also containing mention of the adversaries: from them Jesus endured a radical «contradiction». It is in this light that, in Luke's gospel, the passion of Christ is foretold by the aged Simeon: the son of Mary was destined to be «a *contradicted* sign» (Luke 2,34; Rom 10,21). For anyone entrusted with proclaiming to all an important message, there is nothing worse than being contradicted.

The adversaries of Jesus are called «the sinners», which corresponds to the word pronounced by Jesus in Mark 14,41, just before his arrest: «The hour has come, behold, the Son of man is being delivered into the hands of sinners» (see also Matt 26,46; Luke 24,7). Here, this mention of sinners shows that the contradiction Jesus faced was completely unjust. His attitude of patience constitutes an example to that extent more eloquent.

The contemplation of this example is set before the listeners as a remedy for temptations to spiritual discouragement and falling away (3). The author continues to follow up the metaphor of the race in sport: he uses two verbs, «to fall away» and «to be discouraged», used by Aristotle concerning runners (*Rhet.* III,9: 1409b,1), but he is careful to state that he wants to speak of the falling away of «souls» and not of physical exhaustion.

2. Accepting paternal correction given by God (4-11)

The next sentence (4) continues in the same sense by pointing out that the combat of Christians is not a competition in sport; it is a spiritual combat «against sin», and it must possibly go «as far as blood», until the sacrifice of life, until martyrdom. The listeners are engaged in combat, but they have not yet gone that far. They must continue with courage. The mention of blood calls to mind the passion of Jesus, who shed his blood and «by his own blood entered once and for all into the sanctuary, having found eternal redemption» (9,12). The contradiction he endured on the part of sinners led him to this sacrifice and to this glory. He thus traced out a way to be followed, a very demanding way but sure to succeed.

The preacher then addresses a reproach to his listeners: «you have forgotten», which is rather a way of attracting their attention to the text he is going to quote to them. It is an «exhortation»; he makes it personal by saying that it is addressed to them «as to sons». This exhortation is therefore paternal and at the same time brings consolation and comfort. The Greek word used, *paraklēsis*, also expresses these two other nuances.

The text quoted (Prov 3,11-12) actually begins with the title of «son» and it ends likewise. But a change is to be noted: at the beginning, «my son» expresses a relation of master to pupil. The master says «my son» to his pupil, or simply «son», of very frequent occurrence in the Book of Proverbs (Prov 1,8.10.15; etc.); but at the end of the citation, it is a question of a filial relation with God himself.

This text expresses very profoundly the value of tribulation. This value was recognized earlier in Greek literature: the trials of life teach people wisdom. Concerning Heb 5,8 we have already noted that the Old Testament sees in them God's educative action as well and therefore a way of being placed in relation with God. In Ps 118(119), for example, the psalmist says to God:

> Before being afflicted, I was going astray,
> now, I observe your promise. (v. 67)
> A good thing for me to be afflicted,
> in order to learn your wills. (v. 71)

This theme finds better expression in the texts that call to mind a filial relation with God. Concerning the tribulations undergone in the course of crossing the desert, Deuteronomy declares: «Understand therefore that the Lord your God corrected you as a father corrects his child» (Deut 8,5). The Book of Wisdom says likewise, addressing God: «You tested them as a father who warns» (Wis 11,10).

The most beautiful text is the one the author quotes, because the parallelism between «whom he loves» and «every son he receives» shows that the filial relation established by God is a relation of love. The same outlook is found in the «Psalms of Solomon»; they say that God «will warn a just person like a son with an act of love; his correction is as for a first-born» (Ps Sol 13,9; see also 18,3-4).

On the translation of the word *paideia* as «correction», it is good to note that in classical Greek, *paideia*, derived from the word *pais*, «child», has the sense of «education» and not of «correction», but in the Septuagint, it most often has the sense of «correction» and this is the case in the text from Proverbs, as witnessed by the parallelism between *paideuei* and *mastigoi*. This second verb means «he beats»; the first must therefore be translated as «he corrects». The biblical tradition conceives education in an energetic way: «Do not spare the infant correction, if you strike him with the stick, he will not die from it» (Prov 23,13; see also 13,24; 22,15); «Lashes with the whip and correction, that is wisdom at any time» (Sir 22,6; see also 30,1).

When suffering comes, one is spontaneously tempted «not to think much of it», that is to say not to see any use in it, no positive aspect, and therefore to get discouraged or even rebel. The Book of Proverbs opposes this temptation by pointing out that through suffering and trials, God performs a very positive action of «correction» which manifests his eternal love and reinforces the filial relation with him. Therein is powerful comfort. Instead of letting oneself be overcome, there is reason, on the contrary, to feel intimate satisfaction with this manifestation of fatherly love on the part of God, and even to be proud of it, it is at the same time the fulfilment of a fatherly ambition, motivated by love.

When commenting on the text, the preacher highlights its content well. He starts by stressing the fact that the ordeal endured is not a matter of senseless suffering, but that it has educative value and corresponds to the normal relation between a father and his son. He therefore says to the Christians: «God is treating you like sons», a great motive for profound satisfaction and pride! The author is skilful enough to reverse completely the spontaneous outlook, according to which the ordeal arouses worry and concern; he shows, on the contrary, that the absence of trials ought to be worrying; it would mean the absence of the filial relation.

After showing the need for correction, the author makes a comparison between the education given by human persons and the one given by God (9-10). The latter, obviously, is of far greater value. A rhetorical question, based on *a fortiori* reasoning, is a call to draw consequences from it.

To obtain an antithesis with «Father of the spirits», the author speaks of the «fathers of our flesh», which is obviously one-sided, the relation between fathers and their sons not being limited to the flesh. The sentence actually shows it immediately, because it mentions their role as «educators», entrusted with correcting their children.

Hesitation is possible about the meaning of the verb expressing the result of the paternal correction. If this verb is given a complement, the fathers, it means «to respect», as in Matt 21,27. If, on the contrary, it is thought that it is used without any complement, it means «to retire within oneself» or «to be abashed» as in 2Thess 3,14; Tit 2,8. In the first case, the expression «and we respected them» has immediately a correspondent in «we will be subject»; the end «and we will live» is then a grand finale with no correspondent in what precedes it. In the second case, on the contrary, «and we retired within ourselves» has its parallel in «and we will live», a much better thing, obviously.

The author calls God «the father of the spirits», a unique expression in the Bible, yet provided for, in a way, by the one in the Book of Numbers that says «the God» —and not the father— «of the spirits of all flesh» (Num 16,22; 27,16). Curiously, the Septuagint inserted an «and» before «of all flesh»; it says: «the God of the spirits *and* of all flesh», which makes the antithesis expressed by our author between «the fathers of our flesh» and «the father of the spirits» impossible. The author therefore was careful not to copy the Septuagint in this case.

The word «spirit» can be understood in different ways: «the spirit of man that is in him» and «knows the secrets of man» (1Cor 2,11), or the principle of the spiritual life, life distinct from simply psychic life (1Cor 2,14-15), because it is sharing in the Holy Spirit (see 1Cor 2,12). The verb «to live» can be interpreted in two corresponding ways. The author does not say so, but the relation established in his sentence between submission to the Father of the spirits and the life that is passed on suggests that he wishes to speak of the spiritual life and of its principle.

The heavenly father gives the spiritual life; the correction he administers aims at ensuring the right growth of that life. This correction must therefore be accepted with greater docility than that shown to the «fathers of the flesh», and with greater trust in its efficacy.

The next verse (10) makes the difference between divine education and human education more explicit. Human education has a short temporal span, «for a few days», and its criteria are uncertain: it is based on «what seems good». Divine education, on the contrary, has certain criteria. The author does not only say that it is done «for our good» or «for our advantage», for that intention would not differentiate it from human education; he says more precisely that it is given «according to what is useful», a measure that God knows and which is not uncertain, like «what seems good».

The purpose God has in mind is then admirably defined, which reveals God's extraordinary generosity and the extent of his paternal ambition for those whom he receives as his sons and daughters. He wants «us to receive a share in his holiness», that is to say he wants to give us a share in his holiness, which is the greatest gift he can give, because his holiness is what defines him best in himself. The biblical notion of the holiness of God is very rich and very profound. It includes a negative aspect of separation. God is the wholly other. There is absolutely nothing profane in him and he strikes fear in everything that is profane. Contact with the very holy God reveals man's impurity to him. «Woe is me, cries the prophet Isaiah, I am lost, for I am a man with impure lips…» (Isa 6,5). But this holiness is also unutterably and inexhaustibly rich.

God wishes to communicate his holiness to us because he loves us and because he wishes to bring us into full communion with him. This project of love can take shape only through a divine action that radically cleanses and transforms us. This action is necessarily achieved through trials.

After underlining the great difference there is between divine correction and correction administered by humans, the author adds a consideration which applies to «all correction» and concerns the contrast between the effect produced by correction at the moment itself and its further result. The idea is not new. Aristotle expressed it earlier saying: «Correction has bitter roots, but its fruits taste good» (remark quoted by Diogenes Laertius, 5,18). Like the Stagirite, our author speaks of «fruit», but he makes the thought more explicit. He distinguishes «the moment» of the correction and what comes «later». He expresses two different nuances in this matter: at the time of the correction, the effect produced is only an impression one has; it is what «seems», but does not correspond to the profound reality. «Later», the true result is revealed: the correction «bears fruit». Implicitly, the preacher calls upon his listeners not to give way to the feeling of sadness. In that he agrees with the letter of James, which explicitly expresses this call by saying: «Esteem it a great joy when you fall into all sorts of trials, knowing that the testing of your faith produces endurance» (Jas 1,2-3; see also 1Pet 1,6-7).

The «fruit» of correction is first called «peaceful» and then fruit «of justice»; this last word is separated from the first two and kept for the end, which underlines its importance. The statement: «it bears peaceful fruit of justice» can be understood at two levels, the level of education in general and the more specific one of the spiritual life. In general, good education produces a pacifying result. It leads to human equilibrium, in which the various faculties and tendencies find their rightful place. It makes the person capable of harmonious relations with others. This «peaceful fruit» is a fruit «of justice», understood in the biblical sense of what makes a person a «just person», because education represses bad tendencies, corrects faults and teaches the right way of thinking and behaving.

Applied to the spiritual life, the same statement takes on a deeper meaning, it is about the education that God gives through the trials of life. God wants to give us the peace and justice of his kingdom. Peace and justice are Messianic good things. They were obtained for us through the passion of Christ, but we can only receive them if we agree to share in that passion. «It is certain, this saying: if we are dead with him, with him we shall live; if we endure, with him we shall reign» (2Tim 2,11-12). «We are co-heirs of Christ, if, that is, we suffer with him to be, with him also, glorified» (Rom 8,16-17). According to Jas 3,15-18, the «fruit of justice», which «is sown in peace», is in connection with «the wisdom from on high», quite different from human wisdom. Saint Paul, on his part, wishing the Philippians to be «full of fruit of justice», added: «that comes through Jesus Christ for the glory and the praise of God» (Phil 1,11).

Divine education is therefore much more demanding than human education, but it is much more fruitful.

3. Conclusion and transition (12-13)

The conclusion is related to the metaphor from sport used at the beginning. Athletes must not have «drooping hands», nor «weak knees» and, on the other hand, a race calls for «straight paths for your feet». The application to the Christian life is transparent. It requires firmness, courage, perseverance and perfect rectitude in conformity with the will of God.

The author takes his inspiration from two texts of the Old Testament, without quoting them explicitly. The first is taken from an utterance of the prophet Isaiah announcing a liberating action by God and says: «Make tired hands strong and weak knees firm, say to the faint-hearted: Courage, fear not…» (Isa 35,3-4). To keep to the metaphor from sport, the author omitted mentioning «faint-hearted». He again remembered the same utterance in the next verse when speaking of «what is lame»; Isaiah actually announces that «then the lame will leap like a stag» (Isa 33,6).But the main idea in verse 13 comes from the Book of Proverbs, which says: «My son, […] make straight the paths for your feet» (Prov 4,26).

The text in Isaiah is perfectly suitable when concluding an exhortation to endurance, the more so because it is taken from a very beautiful oracle of eschatological promise: «Behold, it is your God […] it is he who is coming to save you» (Isa 35,4). The prophet announces that «those freed by the Lord will return […] an eternal happiness will transfigure their face» (Isa 35,10). Nothing supports endurance better than a great hope (see Heb 10,36).

The text of Prov 4,26 is not itself any longer in relation with the theme of endurance, but, as we have already said, it introduces another theme, that of Christian action, which will be the theme of the Fifth and last part of the homily (12,14-13,18).

The link between the two sentences of this conclusion is perfect, because the first speaks of «hands» and «knees» and the second speaks of «feet»; we stay in the same metaphorical register. But we move on from the idea of valiantly putting up with trials to that of steering activity in the right direction. The same transition from one theme to the other is found in the letter of James who, after speaking of trials and endurance, adds: «But let endurance be accompanied by a perfect work» (Jas 1,4).

The context of Prov 4,26 clearly shows that the metaphor applies to people's conduct, because he orders: «Do not swerve to right or left, turn your foot *from evil*» (4,27).

To strengthen his exhortation, the author expresses its double purpose, one negative, avoiding twisting one's foot; the other positive, getting a cure. Taking up a term from Isa 33,6, «the lame», the author changes its gender, making it go from masculine, which designates a person, to neuter, which designates a part of the body. The sense of the exhortation thus becomes more general: instead of applying to one or other member of the community, to the exclusion of the others, the exhortation applies to both of them. Every person must act in such a way that «what is lame» in it may not limp but, on the contrary, «be healed». It is with this positive outlook that this section and the whole part end.

Part Five

Call for the right conduct in the search for holiness and peace (12,14-13,18)

Chapter 17

Seeking sanctification (12,14-29)

n the form it takes in the last verse of Part Four of the homily (12,13), the announcement of the theme of part Five lacks precision. The form used is obviously metaphorical: «Make straight paths for your feet». In what could these «straight paths» consist? The beginning of the Fifth part specifies this immediately, saying: «Pursue peace with all and sanctification, without which no one will see the Lord» (12,14). The «straight paths» must therefore lead to having good relations, on the one hand, with one's neighbour, «peace with all», and on the other, with «the Lord», thanks to «sanctification». In this double orientation, it is not difficult to recognize the double dimension of charity: «You will love the Lord your God ... You will love your neighbour...» (Matt 22,37.39 and parallels). The author reverses the order in his announcement, but respects it in the development. In his announcements, as we have mentioned, he puts in the last place what he wants to develop first.

After speaking of the faith of the elders and of endurance, which is in connection with hope, the author prepares to speak of charity. The three theological virtues, as will be recalled, were mentioned in the conclusion to the central part (in 10,22-24) and related to the sacrifice and the priesthood of Christ (10,19-21).

COMPOSITION

A general inclusion marks the boundaries of this part. To its beginning: «Pursue peace» (12,14), corresponds the final sentence: «May the God of peace...» (13,20). This inclusion is strengthened by the repetition of «the Lord» in 12,14 and 13,21 (literally, 13,21 says: «the Lord of us»).

A partial inclusion can be perceived between the expression in 12,15: «not to withdraw from the grace of God» and the one in 12,28, which, literally, calls for «having grace». After a short paragraph of exhortation in detail (13,1-6), another partial inclusion marks out a fuller paragraph (13,7-17). To: «Remember your leaders» (7) corresponds: «Obey your leaders» (17), and to «their conduct» (7) corresponds «wishing to lead us» (18).

This part is therefore composed of three paragraphs, to which is added a solemn closing wish (13,20-21). Two fuller paragraphs (of 16 and 12 verses) frame a shorter paragraph (6 verses). This disposition corresponds exactly, in reverse, to that of the first part (1,5-2,18), it, too, divided into three paragraphs, two longer ones (10 and 14 verses) and a shorter one (5 verses), which are preceded by an exordium (1,1-4). The composition of the First Part is more evident because of a change of genre: the longer paragraphs are doctrinal exposé; they are separated from each other by a short paragraph of exhortation. The Fifth par does not have any change of genre; it is entirely exhortation. But the differen paragraphs are shown by an abrupt change of rhythm and an absence of grammatical liaison. The first paragraph has a sustained rhythm. The intermediat paragraph begins, on the contrary, with a very short injunction (three words, in Greek), followed by another (four words). The third paragraph starts with a fully rounded and complex sentence (13,7).

The abrupt change of rhythm between 12,29 and 13,1 puts many commentators off and gives rise to all sorts of hypotheses and conjectures. Several think that the homily ends with chapter 12 and that chapter 13 is an appendix, a different literary unit, the work of another author. These are mistaken positions, due to a wrong assessment of the author's stylistic skill. The end of ch.12, «for our God is a consuming fire» (12,29), certainly does not come as the conclusion of all the homily. The solemn sentence in 13,20-21 is, on the contrary, a perfect conclusion, for it summarizes both the doctrinal exposés (20) and the exhortations (21) and ends with a short doxology and an «amen». Nothing is missing!

1. Announcement of the two themes (12,14)

14 Pursue peace with all and sanctification,
without which no one will see the Lord,

2. First paragraph: sanctification (12,15-29)

15 seeing to it that no one [remains] without the GRACE of God,
lest any root of bitterness, in growing, cause
trouble and lest thereby many be defiled,
16 lest anyone [be] a debauched or Godless person,
like Esau who for one dish, sold his own birthright.
17 You know, of course, that, wishing later to inherit the blessing,
he was disqualified; he did not, in fact, find any way of obtaining a
change of idea, although he sought it with tears.

18 *You have not approached*, in fact,
a [reality] that can be touched and which was burnt by fire,
and darkness and gloom and tempest,
19 and a trumpet blast and a voice that spoke;
Those who heard it objected to it,
asking that not one word be added to it.
20 They did not bear with the injunction:
Even if it is a beast that touches the mountain, it will be stoned,
21 and so terrible was what appeared,
Moses said: I am afraid and trembling.

22 But *you have approached*
Mount Sion and a city of the living God, heavenly Jerusalem,
and thousands of angels in festive gathering
23 and an assembly of first-born enrolled in the heavens
and God, judge of all,
and spirits of the just, made perfect
24 and mediator of a new covenant, Jesus,
and a blood of sprinkling that speaks louder than [the blood of] Abel.
25 See that you do not reject the one speaking.
For if they did not escape, having rejected the one who warned on earth,
how much more we, who turn away from him who [speaks] [from the height] of the heavens,
26 he whose voice shook the earth then,
now makes a proclamation, saying:
Once more, I will shake
not only the earth, but also heaven.
27 Now, the words «once more» indicate
the destitution of things that are shaken because made,
so that those may remain that are not shaken.
28 That is why, receiving an unshakeable kingdom,
having gratitude (lit. «having GRACE»),
with it let us worship in a way acceptable to God
with profound respect and fear,
29 for our God [is] a consuming fire.

A. *COMPOSITION*

After the initial sentence (14) which states the double theme of the part, it is naturally, as in 3,1 or in 11,1, the second theme that immediately holds the attention, the one about the relation with «the Lord» (14). «God» is immediately named, in a warning against indocility towards his «grace» (15); the next proposition contains an allusion to a passage from Deuteronomy that stigmatizes idolatry (Deut 29,17); then a reference to the profanation committed by Esau and to it being impossible for him «to inherit the blessing» continues in the same vein.

The long sentence in 12,15-16 offers a triple parallelism. After the participle «seeing», three times in Greek we have the phrase «lest any…». The style swells gradually. The first time, the phrase is followed by one clause, which is elliptical; literally: «seeing to it that no one [remain] without the grace of God» (15). The second time, there are two co-ordinate clauses: «seeing to it […] that no root of bitterness in growing cause trouble and that through it many be defiled» (15). The third time, a first, elliptical, proposition is completed by a subordinate proposition: «seeing to it […] that no one [be] a debauched or godless person, like Esau who, for one dish, sold his birthright» (16). This last case later becomes the subject of a dissuasive commentary (17).

Then comes a long passage (18-24), built on two antithetic sequences. The first sequence begins with «You have not approached ...». The second contrasts with it saying: «But you have approached...». It is about two religious experiences; the first, depressing; the second, on the contrary, uplifting.

The first sequence follows a tortuous path. Its beginning is obscure and has caused attempts at correction. It says literally: «For you have not approached [something] that is touched and was burnt with fire»; it could also be taken as: «... and a fire that was consumed». Then comes a series of three parallel terms: «and darkness and gloom and tempest»: and then two parallel expressions in chiastic arrangement: «and blast of trumpet, and a voice of words». The second expression unleashes a whole set of tumultuous observations (10-21), which ends with a confession by Moses: «Afraid am I, and trembling» (21).

The second sequence, on the contrary, presents a very regular grammatical construction. After the verb «you have approached», we have a long series of nine complements in the dative, accompanied by one detail or another, which none the less gives the sentence a certain variety. None of the nouns has the article, which accentuates the cumulative effect. The first three complements are in synonymous parallelism: «Mount Sion and city of living God, heavenly Jerusalem» (22). The next two are also in parallelism: to «thousands of angels» corresponds «assembly of first-born [...] in the heavens» (22-23). A certain relation is then perceptible between «God judges» and the «just» (23). The relation is more evident between the two final expressions, because the «blood of sprinkling» is the blood of «Jesus», the blood of «new covenant» (24).

After this long passage (18-24) which, without being itself directly exhortative, none the less supports the exhortation, the author comes back to a warning. We therefore have the arrangement A (15-17) —B (18-24)— A (25-29). The transition is provided by a link-word, «that speaks» (24-25). The expression «that speaks louder» anticipates the *a fortiori* argument in the warning, but the basis of this argument is the antithesis between «on earth» and «from the height of the heavens» (25). The verb «to object» links the sentence with the event recalled in verse 19, in which «those who heard objected...», an allusion to Deut 4,25-27 and 18,16. The antithesis in verse 25 between «earth» and «heavens» returns in verse 26, but is left standing, because God foretells that he will reserve the same fate for the earth and heaven: they will both be shaken and moved. The place is therefore taken by another antithesis, which contrasts things which are shaken, because they belong to the first creation (see Heb 1,10-12), with those that are not shaken, because they belong to the new creation.

A conclusion (28-29) is thus introduced, which is no more one of warning, like the beginning (25) of this passage, but has, on the contrary, a positive ring to it. Christians are now receiving an «unshakeable kingdom», the «kingdom of God», which is «justice, peace and joy in the Holy Spirit» (Rom 14,17). They are therefore called to an attitude of thanksgiving, which is the basis of worship acceptable to God. This attitude is impregnated with «profound respect» and of «fear» of God, for one must not forget the greatness and holiness of God.

BIBLICAL CONTEXT AND INTERPRETATION

Introduction (12,14)

At the beginning of this last part, the preacher calls upon his listeners to «pursue», that is to say to seek actively «peace with all and sanctification». The call «seek peace and pursue it» is already there in the Old Testament; a psalm expresses it: Ps 33(34),5; it is quoted in 1Pet 3,11. This call is taken up more than once in the New Testament (Rom 14,19; 2Tim 2,22), which states that peace must be sought, as far as possible, «with all persons» (Rom 12,18). The author immediately makes the same point. He adds nothing more, because he wants to develop this theme further on. Actually, he will only partly develop it, in 13,1-4.16-17, without insisting on the universal dimension.

«Sanctification», however, will hold his attention immediately. In the mentality of the ancient world, this term did not express a striving for moral perfection, but a search for a relation with the divine world. Holiness, as we said apropos of 12,10, is what defines the very being of God. Contact with the holiness of God is dangerous for whoever does not have the indispensable preparation, that is to say sanctification.

The latter can be conceived in several ways, very different from each other. The natural way of understanding it was the sanctification obtained by means of rites of separation from the profane world. The author admitted the existence of this sanctification by ritual separation, when he declared that «the blood of goats and of bulls and the ashes of a heifer sanctify those who are defiled» (9,13), but he immediately stressed the inadequacy of this sanctification by stating that it only procured «purity of the flesh», that is to say outward purification, required for taking part in the former sacrificial worship, which was itself outward. It is therefore not of this kind of sanctification that he wants to speak

«due»: «For one who works, the salary is not given like a favour, but as something due» (Rom 4,4). The basis of the Christian life is the gracious favour of God, the gift of salvation through the sacrifice of Christ. God «loved us first» (1John 4,19). But this free gift must be accepted in life by every person. All are called to «approach with assurance the throne of grace to receive mercy and find grace» (4,16). The grace of God has an aspect of dynamism, the dynamism of generous love that has to be accepted actively. To hold back by preventing this dynamism from transforming the whole of life is a serious fault which offends the love of God and places people in a state of perdition.

The second warning (15bc) is expressed in metaphorical terms, of which the interpretation is far from being evident. What is this «root of bitterness» of which the growth must be prevented, because it would produce trouble and defilement? John Chrysostom observes that the author does not say «bitter root» but «root of bitterness», because a bitter root can produce fruit full of sweetness (as we have seen, that is precisely what Aristotle says about «correction»), whereas the author wants to speak of a root that produces bitter fruit.

The meaning of the text becomes clear when its relation to the passage in Deuteronomy is seen; the author borrows several expressions from it: Deut 29,17-18. This passage warns the Israelites against the temptation of «turning away from the Lord our God by going off to serve the gods of the pagans» (Deut 29,17). It is therefore about a warning against apostasy, as in Heb 10,29. The text used by the author is the one in Deut 29,18 according to a variant in the Septuagint which, due to a scribal error, departs from the Hebrew text. The correct Greek translation speaks of a root growing «in gall and bitterness». Instead of saying «in gall», in *cholē*, the variant changes the order of two Greek letters and puts the verb *ochlē:* «it causes trouble». This variant introduces a new idea into the text, that of harm caused to others. The author exploits this idea by saying: «and lest by it many be defiled». He thus shows himself attentive to the consequences that the fault of a Christian can have for the community.

The third warning (16) gives precision to the thought by using the bad example of Esau, recounted in Gen 25: «Esau sold the birthright to Jacob» (Gen 25,33). The author states: «*his own birthright*» and «*for one dish*», underlining the scandalous contrast. The account in Genesis concludes by saying: «Esau despised the birthright» (Gen 25,34). Our author therefore brands Esau as a profaner. The birthright was actually held as sacred. To despise it to the extent of selling it at a derisory price constituted a profanation. The author thus stays within the perspective of worship. It will later be understood, in the third paragraph, why he is especially interested in the case of Esau; he will then speak again actually about questions of food (13,9-11).

The other qualification, «a debauchee», seems less suitable for the personage of Esau, but it must be noted that the rabbinic tradition, commenting on Gen 26,34, ascribes sexual disorders to Esau. It must be remembered, on the other hand, that the Old Testament closely associates idolatry with sexual impurity. The infidelity of Israel to its God is accused of adultery and prostitution (see Hos 1,2; 2,4; Ezek 16 and 23). Sexual impurity excludes from the worship of the true God. The link between impurity and profanation is expressed especially concerning Jewish priests in Lev 21,7-14: «They shall not take as wife a prostitute or a defiled woman» (21,7); «If the daughter of a priest profanes herself by being a prostitute, she profanes her father and must be burnt with fire» (21,9).

In the New Testament, the Apocalypse enthusiastically adopts the Old Testament outlook when it speaks of the great «Prostitute», with whom «the kings of the earth have fornicated» (Rev 17,1-2) and who «was drunk with the blood of the saints» (17,6). On the other hand, the apostle Paul establishes a special relation between sanctification and sexual purity, and therefore an opposition between sanctification and impurity: «God has not called us to impurity, but to sanctification» (1Thess 4,7). «The body is not for fornication, it is for the Lord» (1Cor 6,13).

To strengthen his warning, the author is careful to recall that Esau's failing is not without consequences (17). This is what the Book of Genesis shows at length (Gen 27). The author summarizes the account by saying that Esau wanted «to inherit the promise». The choice of the verb «to inherit» establishes a link with Christians, for they are «the heirs of the promise» (Heb 6,17), «those who will inherit salvation» (1,14; 6,12; 9,15). Between «blessing» and «promise», the link is close. The blessing guarantees the fulfilment of the promise.

At the bedside of the dying Isaac, Esau was «disqualified», excluded. He could not obtain «*the* blessing», the one reserved for the first-born and which is related to the history of salvation. He asked for it with cries (Gen 27,34) and tears (27,38), but Isaac remained inflexible. The author says literally that Esau «found no chance to repent (*metanoia*)»; the expression is surprising; it would lead one to think of a conversion of Esau that had become impossible after his fault, like that of Christians fallen back into sin in spite of their baptism (Heb 6,4-6). But the story in Gen 27 obliges us to take the word *metanoia* in its more general sense of «changing one's mind» and to understand that Esau failed to get his father to change his mind and decision. Speaking of Jacob, Isaac declared: «I have blessed him and he will stay blessed» (Gen 27,33) and he did not bless Esau. A sound lesson for Christians who would be tempted to abandon their position as first-born (see Heb 12,23) and to come to terms with the Jewish or the pagan world!

Let us note, in finishing, a contradiction that the author let slip into his text: here, in 12,17, he says that Esau could not «inherit the blessing», but in 11,27 he declared that Isaac «blessed Jacob and *Esau*». In Gen 27, it is never said that Isaac blessed Esau. At the end, however, moved by the tears of Esau, Isaac pronounces some predictions concerning him (27,39-40), very different, as regards form and content, from the solemn blessing given before to Jacob. It is possible, none the less, to call these predictions a blessing, —and that is what the author does in 11,27— because they come in answer, but not immediately, to the insistent request from Esau: «Bless me also, my father» (27,38). But it is still very clear that this imitation blessing is of the second degree. It is not «*the* blessing» (Heb 12,17) which guarantees the accomplishment of God's great plan. There is therefore really no contradiction between the sentence at 12,17 and the one at 11,27.

To back up the three warnings in 12,15-17, the preacher reminds his listeners that they are in a special religious situation, and therefore a particularly demanding one. A conjunction *gar*, «in fact», expresses this logical connection, but the latter cannot be grasped very well, because the preacher starts by describing the situation in which his listeners *are not* and immediately after, by way of contrast, their privileges.

Between the two parts of the text (18-21 and 22-24), the contrast is complete. On the one hand there is an oppressive atmosphere of darkness and of phenomena that cause fear. These phenomena are expressed in an impersonal way, which makes them more impressive. A «voice» is heard, but it is not identified and therefore calls forth a negative reaction of rejection. A pitiless «injunction» is expressed against a beast. At the beginning, no particulars are given about the place and time of these events. It is only right at the end (21) that the name of Moses, who is mentioned, reveals that the author is speaking of the theophany on Sinai. What is most remarkable in his description of this theophany is that God is never named in it and that it is not even presented as a religious experience, but simply as a fearful event that frightens Moses himself. What terrible iconoclastic boldness on the part of the author! It leaves us aghast. And what certitude about the superiority of the Christian religious experience over what was considered the peak of the revelation of the Old Testament! We should recognize, though, that the author is not expressing explicitly a negative judgement on the Sinai experience. He limits himself to saying that this is not the Christian experience and he refrains from naming Sinai.

But it is very clear that he is speaking of Sinai. «The mountain» quoted in «the injunction» (20) is «the mountain of Sinai» (Exod 19,11); it is because «the Lord will come down there» that it is then forbidden «to touch» it, under pain of stoning, even for a beast (Exod 19,12-13). On the other hand, many terms in the description are taken from Deut 4,11-12 (in Greek): «You have approached... the mountain was burnt by fire... darkness, gloom, tempest,... you heard a voice speaking...»; the «blast of trumpet» comes from another text (Exod 19,16) as does the reaction of «those who had heard», expressed in Exod 20,18-19; Deut 5,23-26. This last passage specifies several times that it was «the voice of *God*» that the Israelites had heard (5,24.25.26) and that they asked not to hear any more, frightened as they were. Our author was careful to omit that too positive detail. A significant omission!

The other half of the text (22-24) has a completely different ring to it. Instead of an oppressive, impersonal and numbing atmosphere, we find a calm situation, very rich in interpersonal relations and very stimulating. God is named twice, Jesus once as well as the angels, the first-born, the just; the new covenant is mentioned.

The verb «you have approached» (in Greek, a perfect) expresses the present result of a past action. What action? Christian conversion, obviously; their adherence to Christ by faith and baptism (see 10,22) have placed Christians in relation with a whole spiritual world. This world is in close relation with the history of Israel: the author calls it mount Sion and city of Jerusalem. At first a Canaanite name for the fortified acropolis of Jerusalem (2Sam 5,7), «Sion» had become the name of the hill on which the Temple was built (see 1Macc 4,36-38) and, by metonymy, the name of the Temple itself. But what the author wants to speak about is not a material building, it is about a spiritual reality, the perfect accomplishment of the idea of the Temple. This change of level becomes manifest when the author declares that the «city of the living God» is the «heavenly Jerusalem», and not the Jerusalem here below (see also Gal 4,25-26; Rev 3,12; 21,2.10). Of the «city of the living God» the author has already spoken, firstly apropos of Abraham who, in his nomadic existence living in the tent, «was waiting for the city that has foundations and the architect and the builder of which is God» (11,10), then apropos of all the patriarchs, who yearned for a «heavenly homeland»; God «prepared a city for them» (11,14-16). It is obviously in the mystery of Christ that this city was prepared (see John 14,2) to receive all the believers into heaven.

In the heavenly city, the «living God» spreads life in profusion, and joy. The author speaks «of thousands of angels in festal gathering». He takes his inspiration in that from descriptions of the heavenly court, like the one in Daniel, who, speaking of «the Ancient one», that is to say of God, declares: «A thousand thousand served him, and ten thousand times ten thousand, standing before him» (Dan 7,10). In the first part of his homily, the author spoke of angels in a rather negative way, depicting them as inferior to Christ (1,4-14). It can now be seen that he does not despise them at all, but recognizes, on the contrary, their dignity as spiritual beings. Being near the angels means sharing in an intense spiritual life, in the contemplation, adoration and praise of God (see Ps 137(138),1).

The next expression is in a relation of synonymous parallelism with the mention of angels, for it speaks of the heavens by mentioning an «assembly (in Greek: *ekklēsia*) of first-born enrolled in the heavens» (23). But is there synonymy in the strict sense here? Some exegetes think so and say that this expression designates a category of angels. Other exegetes reckon, on the contrary, that it is synonymy in the broad sense, as is often the case in biblical parallelisms. This second interpretation is preferable. Actually, to say of these «first-born» that their names are enrolled in the registers of heaven is implicitly equivalent to saying that they themselves are not yet in heaven—they are therefore not angels—but that a place is reserved for each one of them there. It is to his disciples, and not to angels, that Jesus said: «Rejoice at your names being written in the heavens» (Luke 10,20). The «assembly» in question is therefore the Church, which bears in Greek the name of «*ekklēsia*», used here by the author, as in the sentence at 2,12 where he designates the assembly of the «brothers» of Christ, namely the Christians, «holy brothers, who have a heavenly calling» (3,1).

They are called «first-born». This title belongs chiefly to Christ; it was applied to him in 1,6 as a Messianic title based on Ps 88(89),28. But from Christ, it spread to the Christians, for they are «sharers in Christ» (3,14), they have a share in his dignity and his privileges, in particular in his rights as first-born. Here we understand why the author was earlier interested, in 12,16, in the question of Esau's birthright. Christians have a birthright; they must be careful not to sell it!

In Israel, the first-born belonged in principle to God (Exod 34,19-20) and ought to have consecrated themselves to his service, but, at God's command, they were replaced, in that service, by the Levites (Num 3,40-45). Now, thanks to the blood of Christ, the first-born, all Christians are in a position to «pay worship to the living God» (9,14; see 10,18-24). There is therefore no reason to try to identify, as some exegetes do, a special category of Christians to whom the title of «first-born» would be reserved. All Christians are first-born, who, by the new birth of baptism, have been made worthy to serve God.

God is then named (23b). Christians have not only approached a city built by God; they have approached God himself. That is, obviously, the most impressive point about their situation. In the text, it occupies a central position. The author makes it even more impressive by qualifying God as «judge of all». This title is unexpected here. It jars after the previous remarks, all very positive and stirring. But it is significant: it shows that the author is not forgetting the overall outlook of this paragraph (12,15-29), which is one of warning. This title calls to mind the menacing words in 10,30-31: «The Lord will judge his people. It is fearful to fall into the hands of the living God». He thus anticipates the return to the perspective of warning, which he will make two verses further on (25).

But the author comes back first to the positive outlook. In parallel with «judge of all», he does not place sinners, who would deserve to be condemned, but the «just who are made perfect» who have deserved a favourable sentence. More precisely, the author speaks of «spirits of the just» a bit like the Book of Wisdom, which mentions the blessed destiny of the «souls of the just» (Wis 3,1-8). «Spirit» and «soul» are terms that are often equivalent (Wis 15,11; 16,14), but a distinction is possible, as shown by texts like 1Thess 5,23 and Heb 4,12: the soul is the principle of physical life; the spirit, the principle of the spiritual life, which is of another order. After the loss of physical life, the spirit remains, and is judged by God.

The title «the just» is traditional among the Jews. It is found both in the New Testament as well as in the Old. It designates the people who behave correctly in their relations with God and with their neighbour.

Here, it is about «the just who have been made perfect» At the end of ch. 11, the author declared that God did not wish that the just of the Old Testament «be made perfect» before the Christians. This affirmation gives us to understand that the perfection in question is in dependence on the mystery of Christ. The latter was «made perfect» by his sufferings (2,10; 5,8-9) and, at the same time, «by a unique oblation he made perfect those who receive sanctification» (10,14). The perfection he gives is a priestly perfection, which makes it possible to enter «into the sanctuary», the heavenly one, already, in a certain way, in this life (10,19), but in a complete way after death. The condition, actually, for receiving it effectively, is that of sharing personally in the mystery of Christ, by learning, like him, «through suffering, obedience» (5,8), by resisting, like him, «until blood» that is, until death, «in the fight against sin» (12,4) and in thus receiving, like him and with him (see John 17,19), communication with «the holiness» of God (12,10). In that way «the spirits of the just» —whether of the Old Testament or the New— were «made perfect» and have been received, after their death, into God's presence.

In Greek, the idea of perfection is tied to that of finality and is therefore easily associated with that of death (see Wis 4,7.14). Speaking of a martyr, an author says that «the very certain seal of death made him perfect» (4Macc 7,15). The letter to the Hebrews greatly enriches the theme, in the light of the mystery of Christ.

After naming, in the presence of God, «the spirits of the just», the author speaks of «Jesus» (24). This order in the text may seem strange. In the presence of God, should not Jesus, «the Son of God» (4,14; 10,29) be named immediately? The order the author chose is explained by the intention of speaking at the end of the blood of Jesus, «blood that speaks», and of thus preparing the final exhortation, which asks «not to refuse him who speaks» (25). If the author had ended by talking of the «just people made perfect» his text would have had a triumphal ring and would not at all have made way for the return to a severe warning. Speaking, on the contrary, of Jesus as mediator of a covenant, as well as of his blood, which is «the blood of the covenant» and must not «be held as profane», as he said in 10,29, the author has woken up his listeners to the sense of their responsibility. The mention of «God, judge of all,» (23) was already going in that direction.

This responsibility results from their special situation. From him who has received much, much is required. Having Jesus as covenant mediator is an unheard of privilege. In the negative part of this passage (18-21), the author did not mention the Sinai covenant, which would have constituted a positive element in the picture, imperfect as it was. He now names the covenant of which Jesus is the «mediator» (9,15). He gives it an unusual description. Before, he took up the description given it in the oracle in Jeremiah: «new» (Jer 31,31), in Greek *kainē*, which means «of a new kind», different from the Sinai covenant. He now calls it «fresh», in Greek *nea*, feminine of *neos*, an adjective which expresses the freshness of youth (*neotēs* means «youth»). The covenant founded by Jesus is not only of a new kind; it is at the same time radiant with youth, springing up like a source of fresh water.

From Jesus, covenant mediator, the author passes quite naturally to his blood, which he used generously to found the covenant. He calls this blood «blood of sprinkling», which is another way of expressing his relation with the covenant, for it is an allusion to the rite of foundation of the Sinai covenant: with «the blood of the covenant», Moses «sprinkled the Book itself and all the people» as well as «the tent and all the objects of worship» (9,19-21).

Of this «blood of sprinkling», the author says that it «speaks louder than Abel», that is, «than the blood of Abel», because it is through his blood that Abel, «being dead, still speaks» (11,4; Gen 4,10). In what sense does the blood of Jesus speak «louder» than the blood of Abel? To this question Saint Gregory the Great, commenting on the Vulgate which translates the Greek adverb *kreitton* with «*melius*», «better», says in answer that, instead of crying out for vengeance like the blood of Abel, the blood of Jesus obtains mercy. This interpretation is attractive, unfortunately, it does not fit the immediate context, which does not speak of mercy, but of authority and severity. The adverb *kreitton* does not express the idea of goodness, but of strength (*kratos*) or of value.

This last expression paves the way therefore for the return to the warning exhortation (25-29). The author is still attentive to the double aspect of the spiritual situation of Christians and he makes his listeners attentive to this double aspect: more marvellous graces of God, but also great responsibility (see 1Pet 1,17-19).

Like several previous exhortations (2,1-4; 10,28-19; 12,9-10), the warning in 12,25-26 is based on a comparison between the Christian situation and that of the Israelites in the Old Testament. Here, the comparison bears on the position of «the one speaking»: he is «on earth» for the Israelites; he speaks «from the height of heaven», in the case of Christians; it is therefore more serious «to reject» him.

At first sight, it would seem that the pronoun «those» designates the Israelites at Sinai, who «objected to» (19) the voice they heard. But this identification comes up against two great difficulties: the first is that at Sinai God spoke «from the height of heaven» (Exod 20,22; Deut 4,36); the second is that the refusal to listen to God directly was not considered a fault, nor did it meet with any punishment, but, on the contrary, was approved by God himself, who says to Moses: «I have heard the words of this people. Everything they have told you is right» (Deut 5,28). «They have spoken well. I will raise up to them, from among their brethren, a prophet...» (Deut 18,17-18). It must therefore be concluded that in saying «he who warned on earth», the author does not mean God, but Moses, the human mediator of the word of God, and is alluding to the frequent episodes of arguments he had with the Israelites. He mentioned one of these episodes in the long warning in Heb 3,12-4,11, the episode of the revolt of the Israelites against Moses and Aaron (Num 14,2), the result of which was that none of them could «escape» punishment (Num 14,22-23.29).

The preacher does not draw any reassuring conclusions from the superior nature of the Christian revelation. Quite the opposite, he draws from it «all the more so» a threat of severe punishment in the case of indocility. He places this threat in an eschatological perspective of universal upheaval, using for that purpose an oracle given by the prophet Haggai (Hag 2,6.21), in which the Lord announces the shaking of earth and heaven.

The interpretation of this passage of the homily presents more than one difficulty. The previous context is coherent only if the author is contrasting the voice of Moses with the voice of the glorified Christ. Seated at the right hand of God «in the heavens» (8,1), it is «from the height of the heavens» that he henceforth speaks. But in verse 26, it seems that it is a question of the voice of God. Is it not that voice which «then», that is to say on Sinai, «shook the earth»? And is it not that voice that expresses itself in the oracle in Haggai? Let us start with this second question. In the Hebrew text of the prophet, the affirmative answer is explicit: «Thus says YHWH Sabaoth». But the translation of the Septuagint leaves open the possibility of a different answer, because instead of YHWH, it has *Kyrios*, «Lord», and in the New Testament, the title of «Lord» is not reserved exclusively to God; it is also ascribed to the glorified Christ, and in a divine sense (John 20,28; 1Cor 12,3; Phil 2,11). It is to the glorified Christ that the author ascribed, at the beginning of his homily, the final upheaval of earth and the heavens: «Like a garment you will roll them up» (Heb 1,12). Creator of heaven and earth as Son of God (1,10), the glorified Christ will be the eschatological judge of «the universe» (Acts 17,31).

This recourse to the text in Heb 1,10-12 gives us therefore the answer to the second question. According to the author, the voice of Christ now accomplishes he oracle of Haggai. An answer to the first question is suggested to us at the same ime: if the author is attributing the whole of creation to Christ as Son of God, nothing prevents ascribing to him the divine voice which, on Sinai, «shook the earth» (12,26).

To speak of the eschatological upheaval and give an account of it, the author uses an original expression: «the destitution of the things that are shaken because made». The «because made» is an allusion to creation. The Septuagint says: «In the beginning, God *made* heaven and earth» (Gen 1,1) and a psalm repeats that the Lord «*made* heaven and earth» (Ps 120(121),2). In his paschal mystery, Christ inaugurated a new creation, which is of another order, «incorruptible» (1Pet 1,4; 1Cor 15,42.50); he has thus shown the first creation is provisional and will be «removed», leaving room for realities «that are not shaken» and are destined, on the contrary, to «remain» (27c) (see 1,11-12).

The eschatological upheaval therefore has a positive purpose. In expressing this purpose, the author goes from a warning speech to a positive exhortation, based on anticipated sharing in the hoped for happiness. Christians, actually, now receive in faith the «unshakeable kingdom», for this kingdom exists already; Christ founded it.

In consequence, the first duty of Christians is to have gratitude to God, literally «to have grace», as in Luke 17,9; 1Tim 1,12 and 2Tim 1,3. «Through it» above all, through gratitude, worship acceptable to God is paid. Going back to the Old Testament, a psalm says so with insistence. There God rejects the immolation of victims and says: «Whoever offers thanksgiving gives me glory» (Ps 49(50),13-14.23). In the New Testament, the apostle Paul calls for thanksgiving «in every circumstance» (1Thess 5,18), «at all times, for everything» (Eph 5,20), and he himself gives an example of it, regularly beginning his letters with thanksgiving.

To thanksgiving, the author calls for adding, in the worship paid to God, «profound respect» and even «fear», thereby imitating Jesus, who prayed with «profound respect» (5,7). The extreme goodness of God towards us —he gives us «an unshakeable kingdom»— must not make us overlook his greatness and his holiness. To forget it would be to lose contact with him. The author takes care to guarantee the authenticity of this contact by quoting a burning sentence in Deuteronomy: «The Lord your God is a consuming fire» (Deut 4,24; 9,3); he adapts this sentence to his audience by saying: «our God ...». This quotation has at the same time the effect of bringing the end of the paragraph into harmony with the warnings that characterize it.

Chapter 18

Peace with all (13,1-6)

After the long paragraph which is connected with the theme of the relation with God by means of «sanctification», the preacher passes on to the theme of relations with others, announced when speaking of «peace with all» (12,14).

1 Let brotherly love remain!
2 Of hospitality, be not forgetful,
for through it, without knowing it, some have had angels as guests.
3 Remember prisoners, as being linked with them,
the sick, as being yourselves also in a body.

4 Let marriage be honoured in every respect,
and the marriage bed be undefiled!
for the debauched and the adulterers, God will judge [them].

5 Without love of money, the conduct,
you being content with present [possessions],
for he said:
no, I shall not leave you
and no, I shall not abandon you,
6 *so that*, full of confidence, we [can] say:
Lord for me [is] a help,
and I shall not fear.
What will a man do to me?

COMPOSITION

The beginning of ch. 13 is, quite obviously, the beginning of a new paragraph. As we have already noted, an abrupt change of rhythm is observable in it. Some exegetes think they also detect a change of style and therefore of author in it. One of them writes: «The transition from noble imagery and sustained reasoning to this formless jumble of rather commonplace admonitions is so abrupt as to be painful» (C. C. Torrey, *J.B.L.* 30, 1911, p. 149). Does a close examination of the text confirm this opinion? Not at all! It completely contradicts it. The rhythm changes, but the style is just as elegant as in the preceding chapters.

The general disposition is harmonious. Its plan is as follows:

1-2a two precepts of charity, parallel,
2b- one reason («for») backs up the second; it speaks of angels,
3 two precepts of charity, parallel.

4a two precepts of chastity, parallel,
4b- one reason («for») backs it up; it speaks of God.

5a two precepts on the spirit of poverty, parallel,
5b- one reason («for») backs it up, it quotes the word of God,
6- one consequence is drawn from it, it quotes Scripture.

The harmony of this composition is undeniable. Two somewhat longer passages frame a somewhat shorter passage in it. Let us remember in passing that a similar arrangement is to be found in the first part (1,5-14; 2,1-4; 2,5-18) and in this Fifth Part itself (12,14-29; 13,1-6; 13,7-21). The author is a great artist!

Three times we find the sequence: two precepts, a reason. The first reason speaks of angels; the second speaks of God; the third quotes an utterance by God contained in Scripture and it is followed by a parallel conclusion that quotes another saying from Scripture.

The same sense of harmony comes again in the detail. The author is following the canons of biblical parallelism. He uses the various kinds of parallelism, of content (synonymous and antithetic) and of form (identical arrangement and arrangement in chiastic form) with skilful variations, avoiding monotony.

In the first pair of precepts (1-2a), the parallelism in Greek is very close between *phil-adelphia*, «love of brothers», and *philo-xenia*, «love of guests», but the first word is in the nominative, the subject of a positive verb, «let it remain», whereas the second is in the genitive and depends on a verb preceded by a negative, «do not forget».

The reason (2b) is in connection with the love of guests .

The second pair of precepts (3) begins with a positive verb, «Remember», which takes up the idea expressed at the end of the first pair, in the negative, by «do not forget», an excellent way of making the transition. In this second pair, there is only one verb; it introduces two complements; each of them is followed by a detail introduced by the conjunction «as», which dispenses the author from adding a sentence with «for».

In the third pair (4a) there is no verb. The precepts are expressed by nominal sentences. These are arranged in chiastic form: adjective-noun then noun-adjective. The first adjective has a positive form and content; the other adjective expresses a positive situation, but with a negative word: «not-defiled».

The reason (4b) corresponds to the two precepts, but by antithesis and in chiastic order: «debauched» is opposed to «not-defiled»; «adulterers» is opposed to «marriage».

The first word of the fourth pair of precepts (5a) corresponds in form (*a-philargyros*, «without love of money») to the last word of the preceding pair (*a-miantos*, «without blemish»). The second member of the pair expresses the precept with a simple participle, «contenting yourselves», a way of acting often found in Paul (Rom 12,9 *bis*.10.11 *bis*.12 *ter*, etc.; Col 3,16 *ter*.17) and in Peter (1Pet 2,18; 3,1.7 *bis*.9 *bis*), probably under the influence of Semitic rhetoric.

The reason (5b) is based on a quotation from Scripture. The author chose a text built up on a particularly sound synonymous parallelism, with two double negations.

In the conclusion (6), the text quoted presents an antithetic parallelism between the first stich and the third. It is arranged in chiastic form: to the first word of one, «Lord», is opposed the last word of the other, «a man»; to the last words of one, «for me a help», are opposed the first words of the other, «what will do to me?».

The central element is isolated, but the author draws it out of its isolation by putting, in the introductory sentence, a word, *tharrountas*, «full of confidence», which is parallel to it. It corresponds, actually, in affirmative mode, to the negative expression, «I shall have no fear».

The result is that the whole is structured according to the a b a' b' plan:

a) full of confidence we can say:
    b) Lord [is] for me a help,
a') I shall have no fear
    b') What will a man do to me?

Between a and a' the parallelism is synonymous, with opposition of positive form (a) and negative (a').

Between b and b', on the contrary, the parallelism is antithetic and is arranged in chiastic form, as I have just shown.

The composition of this small paragraph is therefore in perfect harmony with that of preceding chapters. The abrupt change of rhythm is not at all a change of style. It should rather be recognized that, far from being neglected, the style is here particularly elegant, as is the structure. Both correspond to the usages of biblical rhetoric in a way that leaves nothing to be desired.

B. *BIBLICAL CONTEXT AND INTERPRETATION*

The first impression that this paragraph gives is of being very sharply distinguished from the end of the previous paragraph, and even of the complete absence of any relations. The author has just said: «let us pay worship to God»; he says now: «Let brotherly love remain» (13,1). Where is the relation? In reality, this very abrupt transition is certainly intended, not only to mark the literary division between the two paragraphs, but also to suggest a profound doctrine about the true way of understanding the worship to be paid to God. Do you want to pay God a worship acceptable to him? Love your brothers! Suggested here by the succession of the two themes, this unexpected connection is expressed very explicitly a little later: «Beneficence and solidarity, do not forget them, *for those are the sacrifices that God accepts*» (13,16). This outlook corresponds perfectly to the teaching of the gospels, according to which to the commandment of the love of God is closely linked that of love of neighbour (Matt 22,37-40; 1John 4,21). It corresponds even more to the renewal of the idea of sacrifice in the letter to the Hebrews: the sacrifice of Christ did not consist of a ceremony of ritual separation performed in a holy place, but in an act of complete solidarity with his brothers (2,17; 4,15), according to the design of God which is a design of love. The author has already expressed, in 6,10, a very close link between the love of God and the service of the brothers: it is by «putting themselves at the service of the saints» —that is to say of Christians— that the listeners have shown love for the name of God.

«Brotherly love», is taught in the Old Testament right from its beginning by stigmatizing the crime of Cain (Gen 4). It gives this love a wide field, because by «brothers» it means «the children of your people» (see Lev 19,17-18). The New Testament radically renews its understanding by revealing that by faith in Christ and baptism, all believers, whatever people they belong to, become «sons of God» (Gal 3,26-28) and therefore «brothers» (Acts 15,23). In consequence, they must be full of «brotherly love» and «love each other intensely» (1Pet 1,22). God himself teaches «brotherly love» and his teaching is so effective that they do not need anyone to write to them about this matter (see 1Thess 4,9-10).

The preacher is aware of the existence of that brotherly love among his listeners. He recalled several manifestations of it (10,33-34). That is why he does not call upon them to have it, but only asks that this love «remain», that it be kept up (13,1).

On «hospitality» (2), the preacher makes an allusion to models present in the Old Testament. The most perfect model is certainly Abraham «at the oak of Mamre», «running» to welcome three guests (Gen 18,2) and «running» again to get an excellent meal ready for them (18,7-8). The story reveals that in this way he welcomed the Lord himself (18,13). Gideon likewise got a meal ready for «the angel of the Lord» (Judg 6,19) and Manoah, the father of Samson, offered to prepare one (Judg 13,15). It was only later that «Manoah understood that it was the angel of the Lord» (13,21). Of Tobit, also, it is said that «he did not know» that Raphael «was an angel of God» (Tob 5,4), but this episode does not speak of hospitality.

In the New Testament, the apostle Peter recommends Christians to be «hospitable without grumbling» (1Pet 4,9); Paul, for his part, calls upon them to «pursue» hospitality, that is to say to practise it diligently. The pastoral epistles ask that the «overseer», in particular, be «hospitable» (1Tim 3,2: Titus 1,8).

The preacher next calls for solidarity towards «prisoners», without further specification, but he is certainly thinking, in first place, of the apostles and Christians in prison because of faith., The listeners have already practised this solidarity «at an earlier period» (10,34). The preacher is aware of this; he uses a present imperative that could be translated: «Keep thinking about the prisoners» and he suggests very close solidarity, as if they were sharing their fate.

On the subject of the «sick», the same conjunction, *hōs*, «as», has a different sense. It does not mean «as if», but «in so far as»; it introduces a real fact, of which the listeners are asked to become aware, and not a possible, but non-existent situation that they would be called upon to imagine. They, too, are actually «in a body».

On the respect due to marriage (4), the preacher has a peremptory expression, as also against sexual faults. The prohibition of adultery being one of the ten commandments, it is clear that «God will judge» transgressors (and will punish them…!).

Against the love of money, the Old Testament remarked that «whoever loves money hardly escapes from sin» (Sir 31,5). «Many have sinned for love of gain» (Sir 27,1). «Better give alms than store up gold» (Tob 12,8). The gospel is much more radical. It teaches contempt for money, «mamon of iniquity» (Luke 16,9.11), and the beatitude of poverty (Matt 5,3; Luke 6,20). «The love of money is the root of all evils» (1Tim 6,10).

Trust must be placed in the Lord and not in material riches; they give only an illusion of security. To stir up trust in the Lord, the author quotes one of his promises, several times repeated. It is addressed by God himself to Joshua after the death of Moses (Josh 1,5), but Moses, before his death, had already passed it on to all Israel (Deut 31,6), then to Joshua (31,8) in view of his important mission.

The trust thus aroused is then expressed by a passage from Ps 117 in Greek, verse 6. This psalm is part of the Hallel, which the Jews recited at the paschal meal (see Matt 26,30). It is often quoted in the New Testament. It expresses magnificently gratitude for the victory given by God and entire trust in him.

Chapter 19

What it takes to be a Christian (13,7-18)

7 Remember your LEADERS
who announced the word of God to you;
considering the outcome of their CONDUCT,
imitate their faith.

8 Jesus Christ yesterday and today, the same,
and for ever.
9 By diverse and strange doctrines
do not be led astray.
For it is well for the heart to be fortified by grace,
not by regulations about food,
that were of no avail to those who regulated their lives on them[1].
10 We have an altar from which have no right to eat
those who pay worship at the tent,
11 for the animals of which the blood is carried for sin
into the sanctuary by the high priest,
have their bodies burnt outside the camp.
12 That is precisely why Jesus,
to sanctify the people with his own blood,
suffered outside the gate.
13 Let us therefore go out [to go] to him, outside the camp
bearing his opprobrium.
14 For we have here no lasting city,
but we are in search of the [city] to come.

15 Through him let us offer at all [times] to God a sacrifice of praise,
that is to say a fruit of lips that confess his name,
16 and beneficence and solidarity, do not forget them,
for they are sacrifices that God accepts.

17 Obey YOUR LEADERS and be subject to them
—for they watch over your souls, as having to give an account of them—
so that they may do so with joy and not with sighing,
for that [would be] harmful to you.
18 Pray for us, for we are sure that we have a conscience in order,
wishing in all things to have correct CONDUCT.
19 (I urge you all the more to do this, so that I may be restored to you sooner.)

A. *COMPOSITION*

This last great paragraph, which precedes the solemn conclusion to the homily (13,20-21), expresses, in the form of exhortations backed up by doctrinal considerations, some important requirements of the Christian situation.

It is framed within a double inclusion: «YOUR LEADERS» (7a) form an inclusion with (17a) and «CONDUCT» (7c) with «CONDUCT» (18b).

At the beginning of the inclusion, it is about the first leaders of the community (7a) and of their conduct (7c). At the end, it is about the leaders then in office (17a) and of the conduct of the preacher himself (18b).

1 Literally: «those who in them walked».

After the beginning of the inclusion, a concise expression, without any verb (8), sets the general tone: «Jesus Christ» is always «the same». The next sentence (9a) corresponds to it, in antithetic form, by ordering people *not* to accept «diverse» and «manifold», (*poikilos*) doctrines.

Then a discussion on one of these doctrines is introduced, the one concerning «food» (9d); an antithesis contrasts it with «grace» (9c).

The discussion draws an argument from a rite prescribed for sacrifices of expiation and performed «outside the camp» (11); it places the passion of Jesus in parallel: «he suffered outside the gate» (12).

Starting out from this circumstance, which is decisive for the question of food, the author then passes unexpectedly to another theme: going out, to go to Jesus, «outside the camp».

He then calls for two forms of offering of sacrifices, which he places in parallel (15-16). Then comes the end of the inclusion, about obedience to the leaders (17), as well as a request for prayers, with an allusion by the preacher to his own conduct (18).

Verse 19 is not part of the homily. Written in another style (with «I» instead of with «we») and implying a situation of separation, it was added to the homily when it was sent to a distant community.

B. *BIBLICAL CONTEXT AND INTERPRETATION*

This paragraph is in relation to the two themes announced in 12,14: to the theme of «peace», by the attention given to church relations (7 and 17) as well as by the appeal for «solidarity» (16), to the theme of «sanctification», by the mention of «grace» (9) and of sacrificial worship (10-12; 15-16) and by the appeal to «go out from the camp» to go to Jesus, who suffered «to sanctify the people» (12-13).

The preacher shows himself concerned about the cohesion of the community, in faith and in discipline. To strengthen this cohesion, he encloses his text within two exhortations which are about relations with the «leaders». The community must preserve the memory of its first leaders and imitate their faith (7); it must be docile to its present leaders and facilitate their ministry (17).

Frequent in the Septuagint, the title of *hēgoumenoi*, «leaders», is only given here (7.17.24), in the New Testament, to the authorities of a Christian community, normally called *presbyteroi*, «elders», or *episkopoi*, «inspectors». *Hēgoumenoi* was kept in the Greek Church. In a more general sense; it is found in the gospel of

Luke, where Jesus says, literally: «Let the leader be like the servant» (Luke 22,26), «let the one who leads be like the one who serves».

The first function of leaders was to announce the word of God (7b), a priority in terms of time, because, without this announcement, faith cannot be aroused (Rom 10,14), the Christian community cannot be set up. This is a priority that remained afterwards as a continual requirement in the ministry.

The next expression (7c) contains an allusion that was clear to the listeners, but is obscure to us. What does the author mean when he speaks of «the *outcome* of their conduct»? The word «outcome» (*ekbasis*) is very rare in the New Testament. The only other occurrence is in 1Cor 10,13; along with the trial God gives an «outcome», a way out. In the Old Testament, the word is used only in the Book of Wisdom (Wis 2,17; 8,8; 11,14). The first of these texts is perhaps enlightening in our problem, for it speaks of «the outcome» of the life of the persecuted just person. «In the eyes of the foolish», this outcome was death (Wis 3,2), but in reality, it was very positive: «They are in peace» (3,3), rewarded by God (3,5).

The «outcome» of which the author speaks was obviously very positive also: it was a victory of their faith. Was it the victory of martyrdom? Did they go «as far as blood» (12,4) in their victorious combat? This hypothesis is not improbable, but the text is not explicit enough for the matter to be decided. The vagueness of the expression is perhaps due to the fact that the itinerant preacher intended to give his homily in several Christian communities, whose first leaders had not all had the same «outcome of their conduct». They had, in any case, all shown themselves «models of the flock» (1Pet 5,3). Christians are therefore summoned to «imitate their faith» (7d); the latter was not simply mental adherence to a doctrine, but was faith lived out, a new way of life.

Christian faith is above all an adherence to a person, the person of «Jesus Christ». The author names him (8) in an incisive sentence that cuts short any hesitation, a nominal sentence, without any verb. This sentence proclaims the perfect stability of Christ, who is therefore the strongest support for faith one could wish for.

It is obviously of the glorified Christ that the author speaks, because, during his mortal life, Jesus was subject to change, like other people. He was «made perfect» (5,9; 7,28). In his human nature he acquired a perfection he did not have at the first moment. But this perfection is henceforth eternal. He has «become high priest for ever» (6,20; 7,16-17).

What Christ was «yesterday», that is to say at the time of the Christian conversion of the listeners, he still is «today», at the moment when they hear the homily, and he will stay so «for ever». He is «the same».

With this oneness of Christ throughout the ages, the author contrasts the multiplicity of doctrines propagated at that time, which was liable to get Christians to lose the rectitude and stability communicated by faith in Christ. In the New Testament, many are the texts that express concern over this. The apostle Paul had to struggle against «another gospel» (Gal 1,6; 2Cor 11,4), «another Spirit» (2Cor 11,4), against «the prescriptions and doctrines of men» (Col 2,22). The pastoral epistles warn against «doctrines of demons» (1Tim 4,1). The second letter of Peter excludes «false prophets» (2Pet 2,1). Saint John also struggles against «false prophets» (1John 4,1-6), against «many seducers» (2John 7), and exhorts people to «remain in the doctrine of Christ» (2John 9-10).

The preacher then passes to a particular doctrine which is in relation with «food» (9cd). The expression «strengthens the heart» can have a physiological meaning. The psalmist declares that «bread strengthens the heart of man» (Ps 103(104),15); it stops him from «falling weak». But in speaking of «strengthening the heart *through grace*», the preacher immediately gives us to understand that he does not wish to speak of the life of the body, but of the spiritual life. And in saying «food», he is really talking about alimentary observances. He thus makes the task easier for himself by obtaining a more expressive antithesis, between spiritual grace and material food.

The author has already spoken of «food» in the sense of alimentary observances in the middle of the central section, in 9,10. He put these observances in close relation with the former sacrificial worship, «incapable of making perfect in his conscience the one paying worship» (9,9). He called them «rites of *flesh*» and contrasted them with the sacrifice of Christ, «who by *eternal Spirit* offered himself to God». Being an offering of love, the sacrifice of Christ moves people from a religion of observances, which is the spontaneous way of conceiving religion, to a religion of self-giving in love.

The problem of alimentary observances was at that time perceived very vividly. In general, insistence was placed on its negative aspect: one had to abstain completely from impure food. The declaration by Peter in Acts 10,14 is significant: «Oh no, Lord! I have never eaten anything defiled or impure». Saint Paul deals with this question in several of his letters, because it created great problems in Christian communities (Gal 2,11-14; 1Cor 8,1-13; 10,14-31; Rom 14;

Col 2,16-23; 1Tim 4,3-5). They are precepts of abstinence that most often hold his attention, but he also pronounces upon the aspect of positive obligation when saying: «It is not food that will recommend us to God, [...] if we eat it, we are no better off» (1Cor 8,8). It is that aspect also that the author criticizes, denying that «food» can spiritually «strengthen» «the heart» of a person. What kinds of food is he thinking of? Contact with the sentence at 9,10 suggests that he is thinking of alimentary precepts in the Old Testament and similar practices.

Some exegetes think they can see an attack on the eucharist here, but that is quite wrong, because the author speaks here of food for the body and the eucharist is not food for the body, but a sacrament for the «heart» (see John 6,63). Saint Paul shows this well when he tells the Corinthians first to take their meal at home, «in the house» (1Cor11,34), before coming to share the Supper of the Lord.

The author then has a strange expression for denying the spiritual use of this food. He says literally: «not with food in which those who walked were not benefited». The verb «to walk» in Hebrew expresses the way of behaving. In Greek, it is very often used in this sense by Paul. The author therefore means that those who, for religious reasons, practised alimentary observances, did not find any spiritual profit in them. Material food cannot be of any spiritual use. Correct in itself, this position of the author can yet be criticized by pointing out that practising alimentary observances out of docility to God provides the person with spiritual benefit. But the author could reply that this spiritual benefit does not come from the food; it comes from the attitude of docility. The discussion could go on.

The next sentence (10) is surprising and has caused much discussion. It is surprising because, coming after a criticism of alimentary observances, it itself expresses an alimentary prohibition, imposed on «those who pay worship at the tent» and does not hold for «us», that is to say for Christians. The truth is that the author does not explicitly say that this prohibition does not hold for «us», but his sentence says it implicitly, because it says that «*we have* an altar» and points out that we ourselves have the right to eat from that altar. To eat from an altar means obviously to eat the flesh of victims offered on that altar. In the first letter to the Corinthians, after speaking of «communion in the blood of Christ» and «in the body of Christ» (1Cor 10,16), Saint Paul, asks the following question about «Israel according to the flesh»: «Are not those who eat the sacrifices in communion with the altar?» (1Cor 10,18).

What is «the altar» that «we have»? Because there is a question of «eating» from this altar, some think that this altar represents the eucharist, but the answer to them is that at the Last Supper there was no altar, there was only a «table» (Luke 22,21) and, in sacrificial worship, it is correct to distinguish altar and table properly. In the first Letter to the Corinthians, after speaking of being «in communion with the altar», by «eating the sacrifices» (1Cor 10,18), Saint Paul speaks quite naturally of the «table» on which it is eaten (10,21), because it was not eaten on the altar, it was eaten at a table (see 1Cor 8,10). It seems preferable therefore to identify the altar with the cross of Jesus, the place where he offered his sacrifice, while recognizing that the verb «to eat» then alludes to the eucharistic table where Jesus says: «Take, eat, this is my body» (Matt 26,26), the breaking of bread showing that this gift of communion comes from the altar of the cross, for it is the sign of his generous death.

The author affirms that there is incompatibility between Christian worship and the alimentary observances of the Old Testament. He declared before that Christ «abolished the first worship to establish the second» (10,9). He shows here that Christ abolished in particular an alimentary observance tied to the former worship, the one that forbade «eating the flesh of victims offered for sin of which the blood was taken [...] into the sanctuary» (Lev 6,23). Now Jesus was «offered to take away sins» (9,28) and «by his own blood he entered into the sanctuary» (9,12). In saying to his disciples: «Take, eat, this is my body», Jesus abolished for them the former prohibition. But «those who pay worship at the tent», reject this abolition. They therefore do not have the right to share in the Christian eucharist, whereas Christians are obliged to, for Jesus said: «If you do not eat the flesh of the Son of man [...], you do not have life in you» (6,53).

Several exegetes have maintained, however, that, on the contrary, the expression: «those who pay worship at the tent», applies here to Christians and that the sentence forbids them therefore from sharing in the eucharist by receiving communion. This interpretation is inadmissible. In itself, it is true, the expression could apply to Christians, because it could be said that they pay worship at a tent, «the greater and more perfect tent», through which Christ «entered into the sanctuary» (9,11-12). But in the sentence at 13,10, this interpretation is impossible because this sentence expresses a clear distinction, and even opposition, between Christians and «those who pay worship at the tent». To speak of Christians, the author uses the 1st person plural: «we have», as in 6,19; 8,1; 13,14; whereas for others he uses the third person and says: «they do not have». Besides, when the author says «the tent», without any other qualification, he means the tent that served as sanctuary during the Exodus (8,5; 9,21), described at length in 9,2-8. Lastly, the expression in 13,10 is similar to the one in 8,5, which speaks of those who «pay worship to a figure and sketch of heavenly realities»; everything goes to show that the two expressions are synonyms and contain the same pejorative suggestion of criticism of a worship that lacks authenticity. It therefore has absolutely nothing to do with Christians, who, for their part, «pay worship to God» (9,14; 12,28).

The ritual of Kippur specifies that the victims of the sacrifices on that day shall be taken away «outside the camp» and «burnt» (Lev 16,27). The sacrifice of Christ was at once similar to those of Kippur and very different (see 9,7-14.24-26). It was similar, because the blood fulfilled an essential function at it and because Christ entered into a sanctuary. It was very different, because the blood was not the blood of animals and the sacrifice was not offered in the temple in Jerusalem, but in a profane place. Moreover, after the sacrifice, the body of Jesus was not burnt. The author therefore refrains from expressing too close a parallelism; instead of speaking of burning, in the case of Jesus, he speaks of passion: «Jesus [...] suffered» (let us note that this passion was not, in this case, a rite coming after the sacrifice, it was an integral part of the sacrifice); when mentioning Jesus, the author does not speak of «taking the blood into the sanctuary», but expresses, in new terms, the positive purpose of his passion: «to sanctify the people with his own blood», and he highlights a detail that enables him to show a parallelism between the passion of Jesus and the former rite. It was «outside the camp» (Lev 16,27) that the victims sacrificed at Kippur had to be «burnt»; «For this reason», that is to say in order that there may be correspondence with this prescription of Scripture and that it thus be made manifest that the death of Jesus was a sacrifice of expiation for sins —«for this reason», it is «outside the gate» of the city that Jesus «suffered». This detail suffices for the author to establish a connection and to suggest a conclusion: since Jesus died in a situation that corresponds to the prohibition in Leviticus (Lev 6,23; 16,27), «those who pay worship at the tent do not have the right» to «eat from this altar», that is, they do not have the right to take part in the sacrificial meal associated with the cross, the «altar» of the sacrifice of Christ. Attachment to former observances in worship is incompatible with sharing in the «Supper of the Lord» (1Cor 11,20).

The author clearly suggests this conclusion, but he does not express it explicitly. He leaves his audience the pleasure of discovering it themselves. That will be easy for them, because this conclusion corresponds exactly to the position he expressed in verse 10.

He himself passes abruptly, at the risk of disconcerting his listeners, to a consequence for Christian life (13). For if the passion of Jesus, suffered «outside the gate», has a consequence for «those who pay worship at the tent», it also has one for the conduct of Christians.

But before considering this consequence, let us complete the commentary on the previous verse by going back to the positive purpose of the passion of Jesus: «to sanctify the people with his own blood» (12). It can be said of this expression, actually, that it brings about the synthesis of four important affirmations by the author. In speaking of the «*people*», it is connected with the sentence at 2,17, which expresses the purpose of the priesthood of Christ: he had to «become high priest [...] to blot out the sins of the people». In speaking «*of the very blood*» of Christ, it is connected with the sentence at 9,12 which declares that «*by his own blood*» Christ entered once and for all into the sanctuary, having found an eternal redemption». In speaking of the efficacy of the blood of Christ, it is connected with the sentence at 9,14 which expresses this efficacy by saying: «the blood of Christ [...] *will purify our* conscience from dead works to pay worship to the living God». Finally, in speaking of «*sanctify* with his own blood», it corresponds, but in a complementary way, to the sentence at 10,10 which states: «in this will [of God], *we have been sanctified* by the oblation of the body of Jesus Christ once for all». The correspondence with the expression at 10,29 is more exact; this speaks of the «*blood* of the covenant [...] in which [a Christian] had been *sanctified*».

As can be seen, the expression in verse 12 is admirably chosen for recalling and completing, in this final paragraph, the teaching of the author on the sacrifice and the priesthood of Christ.

Christians must associate themselves with Christ's sacrifice in real life. To exhort his listeners to do this, the preacher starts with the detail he has just mentioned, a detail not found in the gospel accounts of the passion, but which was evident to all: a person condemned to death was not executed within the Holy City, but in a profane place, «outside the city» (Acts 7,58). In a parable of which the meaning is transparent, speaking of the «son», Jesus says: «They cast him out of the vineyard and killed him (Matt 21,39).

It is therefore «outside the gate» of the city that Jesus suffered. In consequence, Christians must «go out to go to him»; the author then does not take up the expression «outside the gate», but reverts to the expression it is based on: «outside the camp» (Lev 16,27), about which «outside the gate» indicated the accomplishment. To clarify the meaning of his exhortation, the author adds: «bearing his opprobrium» (13). For Jesus, actually, being excluded from the Holy City and dying like a condemned person was an extreme humiliation; in this connection, the author spoke of «shame» (12,2).

For Christians, what does «going out, to go to him, outside the camp» mean in practice? Let us note first of all that the author does not say, as do some translations: «Let us go out to meet him». He does not speak of «meeting», but only of going «to him». To speak of «meeting» puts things in a different perspective from that of the gospels, which call upon people rather to «follow» Jesus (Matt 4,20.22; 8,22; 9,9; etc.), each one carrying their own cross «behind» them (Matt 10,38; 16,24). The author was faithful to this gospel outlook when he presented Jesus as our «forerunner» (6,20), who «inaugurated a new and living way for us» (10,20). So it is to follow him that we must «go out of the camp». In reality, «to go out of the camp» is in fact to follow him, he who went out of the city «bearing his cross» (John 19,17).

But what does «going out of the camp» mean? In the context, this expression applies firstly to the question of «food» (9), that is to alimentary observances. These effectively constitute a kind of «camp»; they set up a protective sociological barrier. Those who conform to them separate themselves from others. This is well seen in the episode at Antioch, where we see Cephas «drawing back and separating himself» (Gal 2,12) from Christians of pagan origin. Christians no longer have the right to accept this kind of segregation, for Christ «of the two has made a unit and has removed the barrier that separated them» (Eph 2,14). He communicates his universal charity to us, which impels us to «pursue peace with all» (Heb 12,14).

The expression «to go out of the camp» is not limited to this aspect. Christians must also refuse to stay enclosed in pagan society. They must free themselves of all the ways of thinking, judging and behaving that are in conflict with faith in Christ and with his love. There is a liberation there, but it is not easy to keep, because it inevitably causes painful tensions. Christians must face the contempt of the society they live in. They are criticized, rejected and even persecuted. They must know that they are thus bearing «the opprobrium» of Christ. Far from being overcome by this, they can, on the contrary, experience great joy in it (see Matt 5,11-12; Acts 5,40-42; 1Pet 4,13-14).

The need to break away, «go out of the camp», is placed by the author in relation to the eschatological outlook of Christians, who do not have on this earth «a city that lasts», but are in search of the city «to come» (14). The author makes his Greek sentence more suggestive by means of an alliteration: to *menousan*, «that lasts», he opposes *mellousan*, «which is to come».

The situation Christians are in is similar to that of the patriarchs, described in 11,13-16 with the same verb, which means «to look for». In this passage, there is a contrast of place between «on earth» (11,13) and «heavenly» (16). The patriarchs realized they were «strangers passing through on the earth» (11,13) and they aspired to a «better, that is to say heavenly» homeland (11,16). In our text, 13,14, the contrast expressed is in part one of place («not here»), in part one of time («to come»), but in reality, it is not temporal, but qualitative. «To come», in fact, is not to be taken in the sense of a reality that does not yet exist, but of an eschatological reality that exists already, because it was created by the paschal mystery of Christ. Of the city «to come» the author has said that «God has prepared it» (11,16). It is the «city of the living God, heavenly Jerusalem» It exists already. Christians have «approached» it (12,22). For them, however, it still has a future look about it, because they have not yet fully entered it finally. They have, so to speak, already put a foot in, by «faith» (4,3) and «hope» (6,18-20). They have already «tasted the powers of the age to come» (6,5). They do not therefore stay bogged down in the material realities of the earthly world which are transitory. They go out from the camp.

But this is not to lead a leisurely and as it were unreal life. They are called, on the contrary, to live a generous life, characterized by two kinds of «sacrifices» (15-16). The outlook is thus completed in a very positive way.

These two verses are extremely interesting and important, because they define Christian worship in its twofold dimension, vertical (praise of God) and horizontal (service of the brothers). These two dimensions cannot be separated. Praise of God is offered in communion with the brothers; this is shown by the verb in the plural: «let us offer» as well as by the church-centred setting of the paragraph (7 and 17). Reciprocally, service of the brothers is done in a spirit of offering to God.

It is really a matter of Christian worship, because the first thing the author says is that this worship passes «through him» that is to say through «Jesus», named at the beginning of verse 12 and still present in the thought of the author, who refers to «him» twice in verse 13.

Christ's priestly mediation is a fundamental requirement in Christian worship. The author demonstrated this well in the central part of his homily. All human attempts at mediation were radically powerless. Christ then offered himself to God and through the generous offering of his life, in perfect filial docility towards God and in perfect fraternal solidarity with us, he became the perfect «mediator» (8,6; 9,15; 12,24). Christians are «those who *through him* approach God» (7,25).

According to the sentence at 10,19-20, to enter into intimacy with God, Christians have at their disposal «the blood of Jesus» and «his flesh», which suggests his mediation in the form of sacramental action. Our context goes along the same lines (see 13,10). The text in 13,15, however, does not limit the perspective to sacramental celebrations, because it is a call to offer the sacrifice of praise «at all times», and not only in moments of liturgical celebration. It corresponds, from that point of view, to the exhortations of the apostle Paul, who calls for «thanksgiving in all circumstances» (1Thess 5,18), «at all times for everything» (Eph 5,20). It corresponds to them more closely than it seems, because «to offer a sacrifice of praise» here means in reality «to give thanks»

In the Old Testament, the «sacrifice of praise» really was a sacrifice, with immolation of a victim. Concretely, it was a sacrifice of thanksgiving. This is seen clearly in Psalm 106(107), which calls upon the faithful to offer «sacrifices of praise», because they «cried to the Lord in distress» and «from their anguish he delivered them» (Ps 106,19.22). Another psalm asks the question: «How shall I repay the Lord for all the good he has done to me?» and, a little later, he answers it saying: «I will offer the sacrifice of praise» (Ps 115,3.18 LXX).

But our author is not alluding to those texts. He is not summoning Christians to offer God immolated animals. He has radically criticized this kind of offering (in 9,9; 10,1.4.11) and recalled that God does not want any of them (10,6.8). He has alluded, in his criticism, to another psalm in which God declares that he has no need of «the flesh of bulls» nor of the «blood of goats» (Ps 49(50),13; see Heb 9,12; 10,4). The expression «sacrifice of praise» used by the author has to be understood with this psalm as background, that is to say it must be understood in opposition to the immolations of animals. In this psalm, in fact, after asking ironically: «Am I going to eat the flesh of bulls? The blood of goats, am I going to drink it?», God expresses his desire through these words of the psalmist: «Offer God a sacrifice of praise», that is to say, according to the context, a prayer of thanksgiving and not immolation of animals.

In its primitive context, the psalm was open to a less radical interpretation which would be content with relativizing the importance of the immolation of animals, without excluding it. But in the light of the mystery of Christ, the radical interpretation becomes necessary and that is the one the author adopts. Christ suppressed the former worship (10,9); he replaced it with the perfect offering of himself, made «once for all» (7,27; 9,12; 10,10).

Here, in 13,15-16, the author completes the perspective by showing what the faithfuls' part in the new worship is. This part consists in uniting their own lives to Christ's sacrifice to send them up to God. That is done in two ways, both of them necessary, corresponding to the two dimensions of the offering of Christ. With his sacrifice, Christ glorified God and saved his brothers; in his life, the Christian must thank God and serve his brothers.

To fill out the meaning of «sacrifice of praise», the author states that it is about «a fruit of lips that confess his name», the name of God. The expression «fruit of lips» comes from Hos 14,3 in the LXX, while the Hebrew text, instead of «fruit», has the word «bulls». The «fruit of lips» could actually, in other contexts, mean a promise to offer sacrificed animals to God, as in Psalm 65(66),13-15. But here, this interpretation is excluded; it is a question of «lips that confess the name» of God, that is to say which proclaim, in thanksgiving, that «the Lord is good, eternal is his love» (Ps 117(118),1.29; 135(136),1.26; 137(138),2-3). The basic thrust of Christian prayer is thanksgiving for the love God has given us and which he gives us in Christ. This thanksgiving has its chief expression in the eucharist, where it is united to the thanksgiving of Christ himself, but it also expresses itself «at all times», not only in thought and in words, but also in deeds performed with thankful love (Col 3,17).

The other dimension of Christian worship consists in practising «beneficence and solidarity» (16). The preacher recommends «not forgetting them», because it could easily be forgotten that this activity of charity is an integral part of Christian worship. The latter simply cannot be confined to prayer and religious ceremonies. It is only authentically Christian if it includes at the same time the practice of fraternal charity through «beneficence» towards the needy and the unfortunate, and through «solidarity» with all. The author stresses that this generous practice really is part of Christian worship; in this connection he goes back to the word «sacrifice» which he used in the previous sentence and he again expresses the relation with God: «those are *sacrifices* that God accepts». The Old Testament expressed this idea earlier. It is found, for example, in Sirach, who declares:

> To show oneself charitable means making an offering of pure flour,
> to give alms is to offer a sacrifice of praise (Sir 35,2).

The mystery of Christ gave this outlook the strongest confirmation.

Let us note here that the insistence of the author on the «unique» character (10,12.14) of the sacrifice of Christ, offered «once for all» (7,27; 9,12; 10,10), putting an end to the multiplicity of former sacrifices (10,9), this insistence does not prevent him from admitting a plurality of Christian sacrifices, offered through the mediation of Christ. The priesthood of Christ, in fact very different in that from the former priesthood, can be shared in. The unique sacrifice of Christ communicates to Christians the ability to offer, in union with him, other sacrifices which are like it, that is to say that these are not rites of sanctification by separation, but, on the contrary, vital, real-life offerings, all in the interest of communion with God and communion between human persons.

The solidarity of Christians is church-centred solidarity. The author makes this understood immediately by calling upon his listeners to show docility towards their «leaders» (17). To the present authorities of the community the same title is given as the one given to its founders (7). Thus is manifested the continuity of the ministry. But two other aspects of it are expressed. The first leaders «announced the word of God» (7), which was in connection with the first priestly description of Christ, «trustworthy high priest» (3,1-6). This first description also includes the idea of authority «over his house» (3,6). The leaders share in this and that is why we have to «obey» them and «be subject» to them (17a). They also share in the other priestly quality of Christ, «merciful high priest» (2,17; 4,15-16): «they watch over your souls», says the preacher, that is to say «they deprive themselves of sleep» (verb *agrypnein*, and not the simple *blepein*, as in 3,12 and 12,25) «for the good of your souls» (with the preposition *hyper*, and not *epi* as in Luke 2,8). Here (7 and 17) we see that the «leaders» of the Church have a special share in the priesthood of Christ. This pastoral ministry is a responsibility of which the leaders *will have to* (in Greek, the verb is in the future) «give an account» to the Lord. In saying that, the preacher makes the listeners more open to obedience to their leaders, because he thereby arouses in them a certain sympathy for them: having to give an account to the Lord is a fearsome obligation! The listeners are therefore called upon to facilitate the task of the leaders (17c). With consummate psychology, the preacher points out to them at the end that it is in their own interest (17d).

He then adds a request for prayer for himself (18). He backs up this request with a reason that may seem strange. He does not say: «Pray for us, because we really need your prayers for our itinerant ministry» (see Rom 15,30-32 and Eph

20 And may the God of PEACE,
who brought up from the dead the great shepherd of the sheep,
in a blood of eternal covenant,
our LORD Jesus,
21 equip you with every kind of good thing,
to do his will,
doing in us what is acceptable in his eyes
through Jesus Christ,
to whom glory for ever and ever!
Amen.

A. *COMPOSITION*

First let us recall that an inclusion attaches this final good wish to the last part of the sermon by taking up the words «PEACE» and «LORD» from the beginning of that part (12,14).

The sentence is united, moreover, to the immediate context by a conjunction of co-ordination, «And» (in Greek: *de*).

This final good wish is expressed in one sentence, which has only one verb in a personal tense, an optative, literally: «may he equip you!». Our translation has added another, because it had to translate with a relative clause («*who* brought up»: 20b) a Greek participle preceded by the article (literally: «the having brought up»).

The sentence is divided into two clearly distinct but complementary parts. The first part (29) is constituted by the grammatical subject, «God», and all its appendages, and they are numerous. They summarize, in original terms, the doctrinal content of the homily. The second part (21) contains the verb and its complements, to which is added a short doxology. Without being directly exhortative, it corresponds to the exhortations of the homily.

Each part ends in naming Jesus and in giving him a title: «our Lord» first, «Christ» next. In the second part, a parallelism between «doing his will» and «doing in us what is acceptable in his eyes» is noticeable; but the subject of the action is different: these are the listeners in the first case, God himself in the second.

The style is full and solemn, comparable to the one in the exordium. As in the case of the exordium, the fulness of style is not obtained by means of a learned structure of several subordinate clauses, but with the help of very simple procedures; in the present case: two participles, an infinitive, various complements, including a relative pronoun which introduces a very short expression of doxology in the form of a nominal clause.

B. *BIBLICAL CONTEXT*

The literary genre of this sentence is not that of a prayer, because the preacher is not addressing God in it. It is the genre of a wish for divine blessing, comparable to a certain extent, to the formula of sacerdotal blessing in Num 6,24-26 or to those in Ps 19(20), 2-6. In the New Testament, this kind of wish is found, in 1Thess 3,12-13, for example, and in 5,23 (with: «may the God of peace...») or Rom 15,13 (with: «may the God of hope...»), but no wish for a blessing has the same function as that in Hebrews, which summarizes a doctrine and recalls exhortations. The case of Heb 13,20-21 is unique; it shows the preacher's great talent.

The expression «The God of peace ...» is also found in Rom 15,33, but with a very short wish, without any verb expressed: «with you all. Amen». In 2Thess 3,16 we have: «may the Lord of peace give you peace ...». In short sentences, which are not wishes, but statements in the future, there is «The God of peace...» in Rom 16,20; 2 Cor 13,11 and Phil 4,9. It can therefore be said that it is a Pauline expression taken over by the author of the letter to the Hebrews.

C. *INTERPRETATION*

For the first time in this long homily, instead of speaking of Christ sitting «at the right hand of God» (1,3; 8,1; 10,12; 12,2), or of his entry «into heaven itself» (9,24), the preacher speaks of his resurrection «from the dead» (20b), but he speaks of it in an original way, without using the usual verbs, «to rise up» (Mark 8,31; etc.), or «to awake» (Matt 16,21; etc.). He uses, on the contrary, the verb «to make to rise again» which he finds in a text in Isaiah (Isa 63,11) concerning Moses. The author attributes the resurrection of Jesus to an action by God, as do many texts in the New Testament (Acts 3,15; 4,10; etc.; Rom 4,24; 8,11 etc.). The text from Isaiah recalls that God «made the shepherd of the sheep rise up», Moses, «from the sea». The author implicitly presents Jesus as the new Moses. In saying «the *great* shepherd of the sheep», he expresses the superiority of Jesus over Moses, which he has already affirmed in 3,3. This superiority manifests itself in the difference between «to make to rise again *from the dead*» and simply to make «rise again out of *the sea*». This way of expressing the resurrection of Jesus does not present it as an individual glorification that would only concern Jesus himself, but as a decisive event for the destiny of the whole flock of which Jesus is «the great shepherd». The author thereby alludes to his doctrine on the priesthood of Christ. To say «the great shepherd» is another way of designating Christ as «high priest». However, let us point out that the relation is not so close in Greek as in English, because, instead of the adjective «high» the Greek title has the prefix «archi-». Its literal translation would be «archpriest». Still, the author has created a close relation, because in 4,14 he called Christ, literally, «high archpriest». Christ, the «great shepherd», went before the flock as «forerunner» (6,20); he «inaugurated» for the flock «a new and living way» (10,20).

The author confirms this perspective by adding that the resurrection was achieved «in a blood of eternal covenant». The relation thus made between the resurrection of Christ and his blood corresponds to biblical anthropology, for which «the *nepeš*», the vital breath (see Gen 2,7), «is in the blood» (Lev 17,11). But in the blood of Christ, there is more than just vital breath. The author has shown that the sacrifice of Christ had as result the establishment of a relation between his blood and the Holy Spirit, who inspired him to shed his blood, according to God's plan, for the salvation of his brothers; this perfect docility, so to speak, impregnated his blood with Holy Spirit and thus made it able, not only «to purify our conscience with a view to the worship of the living God» (9,14), but able also, and first of all, to raise up his body. The resurrection of Christ, as we know, is not a simple reanimation, a return to earthly life; it is a complete transformation of the human nature of Jesus which made his body a «spiritual body» (1Cor 15,44). This transformation is the work of the Holy Spirit, who took the blood of Christ as instrument.

The author says more precisely «a covenant blood». Indeed, it is because Jesus, through his sacrifice, made his blood «a covenant blood» that his blood became the instrument of his resurrection. In other words: the death of Jesus was a death that triumphed over death and produced the resurrection, because it was a death transformed, by the power of love, into a means of establishing the covenant, with God and among mankind.

The covenant is here described as «eternal», which is very well suited to a conclusion. The expression is not found elsewhere in the New Testament, but it is frequent in the Old, starting with the Book of Genesis (Gen 9,16; 17,13.19) and it comes back persistently in the prophetic oracles concerning the end of time (Isa 55,3; 61,8; Jer 32,40; Bar 2,35; Ezek 16,60; 37,26). Once a promise, it has become full reality thanks to the blood of Christ.

Having thus recalled the marvellous divine work achieved in a recent past, the preacher formulates a wish for the present and the future (21). He does so first for his listeners (may God «equip *you*...»), but then includes himself in it saying «*us*», as he often does in his exhortations.

The author is not exhorting his listeners here, but he takes up a theme he has dealt with in his exhortations, «to do the will of God» (10,36) and he completes it by situating it in a perspective of deep faith, which makes everything depend on the generous intervention of God. «To do the will of God», in fact, is not an enterprise that a human person could accomplish with their own strength. The relation between God and the faithful is not like the relation between superior and inferior, in which the superior gives orders and the inferior carries them out. It is not enough to know the will of God to be able to fulfil it. The experience of Israel and of the old Law was revealing in this matter! It is indispensable that God himself should act. That is why the author expresses the desire that God «equip» the faithful «with every kind of good thing» (21a); much more! He expresses the wish that God himself «may do in them what is acceptable in his eyes».

That really is the «new covenant», in which God does not limit himself to making his Law known outwardly by carving it on stone, but he writes it «on hearts» (Jer 31,33; Heb 8,10; 10,16) and accomplishes it himself through his action. The author here aligns himself with the teaching of Saint Paul, who writes to the Philippians: «It is God who, through his action in you, gives you to will and to do» (Phil 2,13). All that, obviously, «through Jesus Christ», for it is through him that God carried out his plan of salvation and continues to carry it out.

The author then ends with an acclamation of praise, a doxology: «to whom glory for all ages!» The verb not being expressed, one can hesitate between an affirmative sense: «to him belongs the glory ...» or an optative sense: «may to him glory be given...», but it is not necessary to chose; the chances are that the author wanted to suggest both.

Another hesitation is possible: to whom is this acclamation addressed? Is it «Jesus Christ» or is it «the God of peace»? The translation given here inclines towards «Jesus Christ», named just before, whereas «the God of peace» is named only at the beginning of this long sentence. But the situation is different in the Greek text, where the name of God is recalled twice by a pronoun. The Greek, in fact, says, literally: «to do the will of *him*... what is acceptable in the eyes of *him*...». Besides, God is quite obviously the principal personage in this concluding wish. To him the resurrection of Christ is attributed, he is the grammatical subject of the main verb («may he equip you») and of the two participles («having brought up» at the beginning of the sentence and «doing in us» at its end). Normally, a doxology has the principal personage as addressee[2]. It is therefore preferable to recognize that the doxology has «the God of peace» as addressee and that the solemn conclusion of the homily thus ends as it began by giving God the first place and Jesus Christ the place of mediator.

2 There is the same kind of situation in Rom 16,27, where the doxology immediately follows, as here, the expression «through Jesus Christ», but clearly refers «to God who alone is wise». Another example is the sentence in 1Pet 4,11. A doxology is addressed in 2 Pet 3,18 to Jesus Christ, but it is in a sentence in which God is not named. The situation is different in the Apocalypse, which does not hesitate to address a doxology to Jesus Christ after naming God (Rev 1,6-7) and which addresses other doxologies at the same time «to him who sits on the throne» and «to the lamb» (Rev 5,13; 7,10).

Chapter 21

Dispatch note (13,22-25)

In the text we have, the final «amen» of the homily is followed by a short dispatch note, in a very different style. It is not necessarily by the same author as the homily.

22 I beseech you, brothers, bear with the words of exhortation; in fact,
with few [words] I send [it] to you.
23 Know that our brother Timothy has been released;
with him, if he comes quickly enough, I shall see you.
24 Greet all your leaders and all the saints. Those in Italy greet you.
25 Grace with you all.

Let us remember firstly that this note is preceded by a sentence in the same style, inserted between the end of the paragraph 7-18 and the conclusion 20-21.

19 More urgently I ask you to do that [that is to say: «pray» (18)], that I quite quickly may be restored to you.

This sentence, which uses the 1st person singular, is quite distinct from the previous one which has the 1st person plural. It is closely linked with the dispatch note: two words are identical («I ask» and «quite quickly») and there is a similar situation («being restored» and «being released»). Let us note, besides, that «more abundantly» is a very frequent expression in Paul (10 occurrences).

We know absolutely nothing about what the hope of «being restored», expressed by the one who inserted this sentence, refers to. Nor do we know anything about an arrest of Timothy, who was later «released».

The dispatch note actually speaks of sending a letter: «I am sending to you», or «I am dispatching to you» (verb *epistellō*, whence comes «epistle», different from *apostellō*, whence comes «apostle», a verb used for sending people on a mission). The author uses the epistolary aorist, as in Gal 6,11 and Phlm 19 and 21, literally: «I dispatched to you». Somewhat strangely, he calls upon his correspondents to «*bear with* the words of exhortation», which leads one to suppose that this speech was not specially written for them and that certain passages, of reproach in particular, as in 5,11-13, do not correspond to their situation.

Taking the expression «words of exhortation» literally, some exegetes think that the homily is primarily exhortation and they play down the importance of its doctrinal content. This mistakes the meaning of the expression used and lacks objectivity. The expression «words of exhortation» appears only one other time in the New Testament, in Acts 13,15, and it does not there designate a simply exhortative speech, but a long sermon by the apostle Paul which first includes a long exposé of the history of salvation and a proclamation of the Christian faith (13,16-39). The exhortation that follows only occupies two verses. The case of the letter to the Hebrews is similar. Its main content is doctrinal right from the exordium and from the first part (1,5-2,18), which comprises only a short exhortation of 4 verses as opposed to 27 verses of doctrinal exposé, but especially in the central part, in which there is a doctrinal exposé extending over 87 verses without the slightest trace of exhortation. The exhortations themselves underline the importance of the exposés by appealing for a consolidation of the faith. The main contribution of the letter to the Hebrews is, quite clearly, a consolidation of the Christian faith and not a series of exhortations, but, as a good preacher, the author is always careful to appeal to his listeners not to be content with a theoretical faith, but always to carry it over into the reality of their lives.

After calling on them «to bear with» the sermon, the author of the note passes on an item of news concerning Timothy. The only personage of this name in the New Testament is the disciple and «collaborator» (Rom 16,21) of Paul. He is mentioned 6 times in the Acts of the Apostles and 17 times in the Pauline letters. Paul several times calls him «the brother» (2Cor 1,1; Col 1,1; Phlm 1), but never «our brother», as in this note, according to the critical edition (which chooses the text of the better manuscripts, as against the majority of the others, which have simply «the brother»).

«Released», Timothy still has not got back to the author of the note. The latter announces that, if Timothy «comes quickly enough», he will take him as companion on a visit to the addressees of the note. In several of his letters, Paul expresses the intention of coming «to see» his correspondents (Rom 15,23-24; 1Cor 16,5-7; Phil 2,24). Our text (Heb 13,19.23) offers some resemblances with that of Phil 2,19.23-24, in which Paul, the prisoner, expresses the intention of sending Timothy «quickly» to Philippi and the hope of arriving there «quickly» himself also.

Then come the greetings to be passed on and the greetings passed on, items found regularly at the end of letters, those of Paul, but also those of Peter (1Pet 5,13-14) and of John (2John 13; 3John 15). The title «your leaders» is taken up from the preceding context (13,7.17). The expression «all the saints», which denotes Christians (see 3,1 and 6,10), comes in the greetings in Rom 16,15; 2Cor 3,12; Phil 4,22.

The designation «*those of Italy* greet you» is surprising with its lack of precision. It can be compared with the salutation sent by Paul to the Corinthians coming «from the Churches of Asia» (1Cor 16,19); instead of naming the city of Ephesus, where he was at the time, Paul names the whole Roman province of Asia, of which Ephesus was the capital. Is the author of the note in Italy? Or is he sending the letter to Italy to a Christian community to which he is passing on the good wishes of a group coming originally from Italy? It is impossible to know.

The wish that grace may be received at the end is typically Pauline. It is found, in various forms, at the end of all the Pauline letters and no other, but only, in addition, at the end of the Apocalypse (Rev 22,21). The form it takes here is identical with the one it has at the end of the letter to Titus: «Grace with you all» (Titus 3,15). It is still shorter at the end of the Letter to the Colossians, which says simply: «Grace with you» (Col 4,18).

This final wish takes the place, in the Pauline letters, of the usual wish for good health, found in Acts 15,29 and 23,30. For Christians, grace is much more important than health!

A question arising about this dispatch note is that of its author. Was it written by the author of the homily or someone else and if so, by whom? The difference of literary genre, which is evident, is not decisive in the matter, because the same author can compose a sermon with the greatest care and then jot down on paper some lines of a letter in a familiar style. What gives rise to the problem in the case of the Letter to the Hebrews is the very firm conviction, in the oriental Church, of the Pauline origin of this document. The tradition affirmed that this letter came from Paul. It was therefore spontaneously reckoned that it was entirely the work of Paul. But a Clement of Alexandria, an Origen realized that its style was very different from that of the apostle. «Who wrote it?», exclaims Origen, «God knows!» There is therefore reason for declining to affirm the Pauline authenticity of the homily and speaking only of Pauline origin. But what does Pauline origin mean?

A plausible explanation, suggested by Estius as early as the 16th century, consists in saying that the apostle Paul, correctly assessing the worth of the homily, the work of one of his collaborators, guaranteed it with his authority by writing the dispatch note in his handwriting. At the end of his own letters, which he dictated to a secretary («Tertius» for the Letter to the Romans: Rom 16,22), Paul wrote out some lines, to authenticate his letters; he says this explicitly in 1Cor 16,21; Col 4,18 and 2Thess 3,17. This hypothesis can call for support on the presence, in the note, of several Pauline traits: the «I beseech you, brothers» (Rom 15,30; 16,17; 1Cor 1,10; 16,15; see also Rom 12,1; 1Cor 4,16; 1Thess 4,10; 5,14), the mention of «Timothy, our brother» and the final wish for «grace». These clues are not without consistency.

This hypothesis has the great advantage of corresponding perfectly to the literary data and of furnishing a satisfactory explanation of an important fact: the great solidity of the tradition of the Eastern Church, which affirms the Pauline origin of the Letter to the Hebrews.

Conclusion

The methodical examination of the text of the Letter to the Hebrews leads to the conclusion, without a shadow of doubt, that here we have —a unique case in the New Testament— the complete text of a Christian sermon, followed by a very short dispatch note. Being a Christian sermon, this work does not fit into any of the three categories recognized by Graeco-Latin rhetoric. It is neither a lawyer's plea before a tribunal, nor a politician's speech seeking to convince an assembly, nor a set speech on some solemn occasion. Christian preaching corresponds to none of these three kinds. It has its own originality. It proclaims faith in Christ and commits the listeners to conform their life to this faith.

The Letter to the Hebrews is above all a thorough investigation into faith in Christ. It is a serious mistake to see mainly an exhortation in it. Of course, it is also an exhortation, but in dependence on the exposé on the faith. The author has made a discovery that no one, it seems, had made before him. He discovered that the second oracle in Psalm 109(110) applies, like the first, to the glorification of Christ and adds something very important to the first. The first oracle, applied to Christ right from the beginning of Christian preaching (Acts 2,34), shows him seated at God's right hand. The second, more solemn than the first because it is guaranteed by an oath from God, states that this glorification is a priestly glorification. Jesus, who could not be a priest according to the Law of Moses, became a priest through his paschal mystery and was proclaimed by God «priest for ever», and even «high priest», because he was «priest according to the order of *Melchisedek*», a person who was priest and king.

Having made that discovery, the author was not content to publish it by proclaiming, according to Scripture, Christ became «high priest for ever»; he did much more: in the light of the priestly oracle, he went into the whole mystery of Christ and grasped all the new aspects of his priesthood and of his sacrifice, new aspects which are the perfect accomplishment of the Old Testament, that is to say that they have a threefold relation with the Old Testament: 1) a fundamental relation of continuity; 2) as well as a relation of difference on the points that left certain things to be desired; and 3) a relation of definite improvement.

The author then proceeded with order and method. First he began, in an early part, by helping his listeners to pass from a traditional Christology to a priestly Christology. Traditional Christology proclaims that Christ was glorified as son of God, after suffering his Passion in solidarity with mankind. The author shows that Christ thus reached a position of mediator between God and mankind, in other words: a position of «high priest» (2,17).

Having said that, the author exposes his priestly Christology at length. He expounds it in two clearly distinct, but complementary stages. Many commentators do not see these two stages; they see just a great exposé of priestly Christology, which goes, according to them, from the end of chapter 4 until the middle of chapter 10. That is a serious mistake; it prevents one from understanding the author's doctrine properly. It cuts off, in fact, the priesthood of Christ from its relation to the proclamation of the word of God, which is an essential dimension to it, expressed in 3,1-6.

Moreover, these commentators do not see that the author, at an early stage, expresses the relation of continuity with the Old Testament. Christ the high priest «is trustworthy *like* Moses» (3,1-2); he was named high priest by God «*like* Aaron» (5,4-5). He fully possesses the two priestly qualities: «trustworthy for relations with God» (2,17) and «merciful» (2,17) for relations with mankind. Overlooking this continuity stage seriously upsets the balance in the author's theology.

The second stage stresses, on the other hand, the differences and demonstrates the superiority of the priesthood of Christ, which is not «according to the order of Aaron» (7,11), and that of his sacrifice, for which he did not use «the blood of goats and of calves but his own blood» (9,12) and thanks to which he did not enter «into a work-of-hands sanctuary, but into heaven itself» (9,24).

In his homily, the author does not place a watertight barrier between a doctrinal part and a moral part, but, as an excellent preacher, he is concerned always to insert doctrine into life. As from the middle of the first part, he takes care to summon people not to «neglect salvation» (2,3). In the second part, after a short exposé on Christ the «trustworthy high priest» (3,1-6), he has a long exhortation against «incredulity» (3,12.19) and «indocility» (4,6.11). The central part is enclosed in two important exhortations, which are parallel (5,11-6,20 and 10,19-39). The second, especially, is important because it provides the liaison between the great doctrinal exposé (7,1-10,18) and all the rest of the homily, which is predominantly exhortation.

All this takes us very far from Graeco-Latin rhetoric. Let us remember, in particular, that the latter prescribed placing the most important elements in a speech at the beginning and at the end and the less important ones in the centre. Our author did exactly the contrary: he put the most important points of his doctrine in the middle, underlining their importance with a very vigorous call for attention (5,11-12).

This way of composing corresponds to Semitic rhetoric, which attracts attention to the central part of the development. The whole of the Letter to the Hebrews is a magnificent concentric composition, the central part of which is also concentric, with, at its centre, a section arranged according to the plan A B A - A' B' B'. In the centre, the name of «Christ» (9,11) shines out over all.

This way of composing is related to mental habits quite different from our western habits, which lead us to compose mainly in a linear and not circular fashion. The biblical authors are less concerned with establishing a logical connection between one sentence and the next than they are with bringing out a multiplicity of relations between the various elements in the text. They thus stir up a different mental activity, which can be thought more productive because to understand properly it is important to know how to compare.

What has just been said about the composition as a whole is also true for the details of the text. The latter continually uses biblical parallelism, in its most diverse forms, the principal ones of which are synonymous parallelisms and antithetic parallelisms; their arrangement can go in the same direction, A B A' B', or in reverse direction A B B' A', in chiastic form. Here again, mental activity is stimulated to make continual comparisons which reveal nuances that a linear text is unable to express.

It seems to me highly desirable that exegetes let themselves be educated more and more by the biblical texts themselves, instead of trying, as often happens, to impose inadequate categories coming from elsewhere on them.

Bibliography

ATTRIDGE, Harold W., *The Epistle to the Hebrews*, Philadelphia, Fortress Press, Hermeneia, 1989.

BONSIRVEN, Joseph, *Saint Paul, épître aux Hébreux*, Paris, Beauchesne, Verbum Salutis, 1943.

BRAUN, Herbert, *An die Hebräer*, Tübingen, Mohr, HNT 14, 1984.

BRUCE, Frederick Fyvie, *Commentary on the Epistle to the Hebrews*, London, Marshall, The New London Commentary on the N.T., 1964.

BUCHANAN, George Wesley, *To the Hebrews*, Anchor Bible 36, Doubleday, New York, 1972.

CASALINI, Nello, *Agli Ebrei.* Discorso di esortazione, Jerusalem, Franciscan Printing Press, SBF Analecta 34, 1992.

CHRYSOSTOM, John, in *Epistolam Pauli ad Hebraeos*, Migne P.G. 63, 9-236.

ELLINGWORTH, Paul, *The Epistle to the Hebrews : a Commentary on the Greek Text*, Grand Rapids, Eerdmans, The New International Greek Testament Commentary, 1992.

ESTIUS, Gulielmus, *In epistolam B. Pauli apostoli ad Hebraeos*, Cologne 1631; Mainz, 1844.

GRÄSSER, Erich, *An die Hebräer*, Zurich, Benziger/Neukirchener, EKK XVII, three volumes, 1990, 1993, 1997.

HÉRING, Jean, *L'Épître aux Hebreux*, Neuchâtel and Paris, Delachaux and Niestlé, CNT, 1954.

JAVET, Jean-Samuel, *Dieu nous parle. Commentaire sur l'épître aux Hébreux*, Neuchâtel and Paris, Delachaux and Niestlé, L'actualité protestante, 1945.

KOESTER, Craig R., *Hebrews*, New York, Doubleday, Anchor Bible 36, 2001.

KUSS, Otto, *Der Brief an die Hebräer*, Regensburg, Pustet, Regensburg N.T. 8, 1966.

LANE, William L., *Hebrews 1-8, Hebrews 9-13*, Dallas, Word Books, Word Biblical Commentary 47A, 47B, 1991.

MICHEL, Otto, *Der Brief an die Hebräer*, Göttingen, Meyer Komm. 13, [6]1966.

MOFFATT, James, *The Epistle to the Hebrews*, Edinburgh, Clark, International Critical Commentary, 1924, [2]1948.

SPICQ, Ceslas, *L'Épître aux Hébreux*, Gabalda, Paris, Études Bibliques, 2 vol., 1952-53.

THOMAS AQUINAS, *Super Epistolam ad Hebraeos lectura*, in *Super Epistolas S. Pauli lectura*, ed. R. Cai, Torino, Marietti, 1953, vol. II, pp. 335-506.

WESTCOTT, Brooke Foss, *The Epistle to the Hebrews*, London, MacMillan, 1889, [3]1914.

Index of Authors

P

Q

R

S

T

U

W

A new perspective to study the Gospels of Mark, Matthew and Luke

Meynet offers an entirely new perspective on the study of the Synoptic Gospels, adding further insights within the growing body of modern research into the meanings of the Gospels of Maththew, Mark and Luke. Utilizing the rhetorical method of analysis, of wich he is leading proponent, Meynet studies the composition of the Gospels and makes it possible to understand them in systematic and until now unexpected ways.

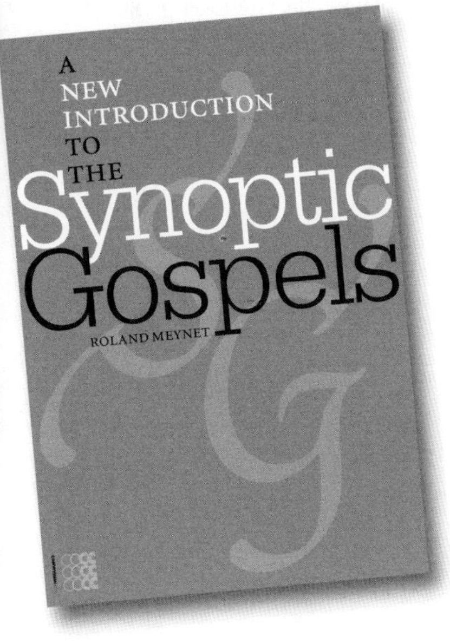

Roland Meynet S.J. is presently professor of Biblical theology at the Pontifical Gregorian University in Rome and was the former director of its Department of Biblical Theology. He is a founding member and currently the secretary of the International Society for the Studies of Biblical and Semitic Rhetoric.

BUY IT AT:

www.conviviumpress.com

A New Introduction to the Synoptic Gospels
ROLAND MEYNET
ISBN: 978-1-934996-11-9
440 Pages
Rhetorica Semitica

A Different Priest
The Letter to the Hebrews

This book was printed on *thin opaque smooth white Bible paper,* using the *Minion* and *Type Embellishments One* font families.
This edition was printed in D'VINNI, S.A., in Bogotá, Colombia, during the last weeks of the first month of year two thousand eleven.

Ad publicam lucem datus mense ianuari in Epiphania Domini